FRIENDSHIP & BETRAYAL

By the same author

Burying Caesar
The History of *The Times:* The Murdoch Years

FRIENDSHIP & BETRAYAL

Ambition and the Limits of Loyalty

GRAHAM STEWART

*

'If you want a friend in Washington, buy a dog'
— PRESIDENT HARRY S. TRUMAN

Weidenfeld & Nicolson
LONDON

First published in Great Britain in 2007
by Weidenfeld & Nicolson

1 3 5 7 9 10 8 6 4 2

© Graham Stewart 2007

A CIP catalogue record for this book
is available from the British Library.

ISBN 978 0 297 64661 7

Typeset by Input Data Services Ltd, Frome

Printed in Great Britain by Butler and Tanner Ltd, Frome and London

Weidenfeld & Nicolson

The Orion Publishing Group Ltd
Orion House
5 Upper Saint Martin's Lane
London, WC2H 9EA

The Orion Publishing Group's policy is to use papers that are
natural, renewable and recyclable products and made from wood grown
in sustainable forests. The logging and manufacturing processes are
expected to conform to the environmental regulations
of the country of origin.

www.orionbooks.co.uk

To The Revd Stanley Newton
who told his grandson stirring tales
of Wolfe and the Heights of Abraham

CONTENTS

ILLUSTRATIONS

ACKNOWLEDGEMENTS

Historians are usually expected to take 'the long view' but I would like to thank my agent, Georgina Capel, and my editor, Ion Trewin, for adopting this patient and measured approach with me. Six years appear to have elapsed since we first agreed on the subject matter for this book and they have been constant in their support throughout. During this lengthy period, Jane Clark's kindness has been especially remarkable; no writer could wish for a better place to labour than among the groves of Saltwood. I am also most grateful to Lucy Standring, the châtelaine of Linver. Many valuable improvements to the text have been suggested by Jean-Marc Ciancimino, Tristram Hunt, Alexandra Ranson, Bunny Smedley, Eleanor Thorp and my excellent copy-editor, Linden Lawson. The longest view of all continues to be taken by my mother and father. For their love and support I shall always be grateful.

Graham Stewart
Saltwood,
Kent

27 June 2006

INTRODUCTION

Ambition and the Limits of Loyalty

'It is painful to consider,' admitted Samuel Johnson about friendship, 'that there is no human possession of which the duration is less certain.' Shared experiences, common assumptions and the pleasure derived from another's company are all vulnerable to the revisions of changing circumstances. If private individuals discover that their bonds can be untied by time and chance then it is hardly surprising that the pressures of public life make enduring friendship a rare commodity in politics. It is not always true, as David Lloyd George claimed, that 'there is no friendship at the top'. But, the closer to the summit of power ambitious individuals climb, the more hazardous they find the conflicts between personal attachments and their interpretation of the 'common good'.

Even when there have been complex and even honourable reasons for one friend's decision to deny another, the victim usually interprets the deed in the most singular and selfish terms. So easy to pronounce and so familiar to all who hear it, the cry of 'Judas' has lost none of its resonance down the centuries. For this reason, a definitive world history of friendship and betrayal would demand an historian untroubled by repetition and readers with formidable powers of endurance. This book draws on examples from across centuries and nations, but it highlights three stories that epitomise the problems that friends must confront when they enter the political arena together. Part One, 'Courtiers', tells the story of Queen Anne and Sarah, Duchess of Marlborough and looks at how widening differences of rank and authority can be managed – or mismanaged – and the way in which the introduction of a new 'favourite' can ensure a powerfully jealous reaction from the long-standing friend she displaces. Part Two, 'Revolutionaries', relates the tale of one of the United States' greatest Founding Fathers, Benjamin Franklin, and his relationship with his longest-serving political partner, Joseph Galloway. They were two ambitious men who were brought together in one common cause only to find themselves bitterly divided by the onset of another, greater, campaign – the American War of Independence. Part Three, 'Liberals', concerns Herbert Henry Asquith and his best friend, Richard Burdon Haldane. It is the account of two men who entered British politics together in the 1880s with a shared outlook and a desire to do everything in their powers to help one another reach their respective ambitions of Prime Minister and Lord Chancellor. But having achieved these offices, harsh political necessities intervened and only one of them was marked out to pay the sacrifice.

In these and so many other tales of political ambition, single-mindedness, indeed selfishness, appears a necessary quality in the scramble for preferment. Yet, as this book seeks to demonstrate, it is not simply the struggle to succeed that ruptures bonds of mutual confidence. Reaching the summit can also preclude normal friendly associations, since it isolates those at the peak from colleagues with whom they had previously been on terms of greater equality. That monarchs, prime ministers and presidents are often accompanied most closely by their suspicions is hardly surprising. It is not just that they fear being let down, for they even learn to fear being served too well. The successful subordinate who bolsters the leader's hold on power may – through the very display of competence and the influence and flattery that follow – even drift unintentionally across the indistinct boundary into rivalry. These considerations are hardly conducive to lasting friendship, ensuring that commitments of reciprocal loyalty are subverted to relationships of temporary mutual convenience. Regardless of the multitude of friends surrounding them at the commencement of their political ascent, ultimately, great leaders usually find that when they reach the summit, they are alone.

This is not a predicament peculiar to politicians. In business, sport, science, showbusiness and the arts there are countless examples of friendships that turned sour because 'a life-long friend' severed a bond in the single-minded pursuit of a personal goal. However, in such areas of accomplishment a relationship's breakdown is primarily a personal tragedy which only rarely has implications beyond affecting those immediately involved. At worst, retribution for the rebuff might result in the creation of a rival company or the search for a new patron. The falling-out could lead to a rush of negativity (public denunciation; vituperative literary criticism) or even provide a positive spur to fresh effort and creativity in the hope of outshining the former friend. Regardless of how bitter the reaction to a broken relationship may prove, there are usually alternative opportunities to rebuild a career with the help of others.

In politics, the options are more limited. There may be plurality of debate and party, but not of power. By its nature, an effective government is a monopoly. Those on the outside can hope to influence it or some day to replace it, but, in the meantime, they cannot rival it. Having been kicked off the ladder, the means of getting back on to the higher rungs are limited. To do so may even be impossible if the only way back involves making a wholly implausible ideological compromise with an alternative faction in the party or an opposition group. Thus the stakes being played for are all or nothing and there is usually a co-dependence between a relatively small number of colleagues or supporters for advancement. In this respect, personal chemistry is the science of politics.

An analysis of political partnerships needs to distinguish the friend from the acolyte. The latter tend to outnumber the former. Indeed, it was only through defeat and failure that some lost leaders learnt to distinguish their acolytes from their genuine friends. This book concerns relationships that were initially held together by authentic fidelity rather than pure cynicism. Its focus is not the familiar path trodden by aspiring dictators who attach themselves to an emerging leader, become that leader's protégé and then use the preferment shown them as the means to seize power themselves. Repetitive behaviour of this kind quickly poisons trust between the ambitious, creating endemic suspicion and a neurosis for which wielding and holding on to absolute power presents itself as the only remedy. As so much of Latin America's twentieth-century history demonstrates, such duplicity has a tendency to rebound. Even Alfredo Stroessner – who managed to rule Paraguay continuously for thirty-five years after ousting his former patron Federico Chávez in 1954 – was finally deposed by his own sometime protégé General Andrés Rodriguez. What goes around has a habit of coming around, eventually.

Not all acolytes are so cynical. Charismatic leaders have always attracted followers whose devotion is genuine. Such relationships may facilitate generosity and protectiveness. Yet, they cannot be egalitarian in nature. The difference between respect and reverence, loyalty and worship, was unquestionably apparent in predemocratic Europe, where the head of state was not just first among men but held up as anointed by God. The principle of 'divine right' had the desired effect of creating a distance between kings and commoners that genuine friendship struggled to bridge. In Britain in 1610, James I referred to the high company he believed he kept when explaining that, 'Kings are not only God's lieutenants upon earth and sit upon God's throne, but even by God himself they are called gods.' Such attitudes create bars to easy familiarity.

By the time James I's great-granddaughter, Anne, ascended the throne, the doctrine of 'divine right' had taken a fatal knock. Yet, even kings before then depended upon their subjects not just for advice and information but also for company. James fell for such a favourite himself in George Villiers, whom he created Duke of Buckingham. He sought to reassure his Privy

Counsellors that he loved Buckingham 'more than any other man' and that this was not inappropriate since 'Jesus had done the same as he was doing ... for Christ had his John and he had his George'.[1] His audience was not impressed by this analogy. They thoroughly disliked their King's closeness – perhaps dependence – on his friend's political counsel. To their horror, Buckingham proved equally masterful in retaining the confidence of James's son and successor, Charles I. There was widespread relief when his enduring hold on royal favour was ended by an assassin's dagger through the left breast. It was also through violence that Edward II's court separated him from Piers Gaveston, the companion with whom he had supposedly become overly intimate.

Part One of this book explores how, despite the complications involved between those of different social status, friendship is possible even in a palace. Indeed, the experiences of James I and Edward II point to how intense such relationships could become. Given the potential for stirring jealousy, the sentiment of the poet Rudyard Kipling comes to mind – 'If all men count with you, but none too much.' Had this been the approach adopted, Piers Gaveston and the Duke of Buckingham might have met more peaceful ends. The record suggests that sincere friendships between royals and non-royals have a better chance of longevity if developed in childhood and before the cares of kingship come between monarch and subject. Two obvious seventeenth-century examples of this are to be found in the Dutch court where William, Prince of Orange and Hans Wilhelm Bentinck became firm friends and in the Palace of Whitehall in London when Princess Anne sought to spend all her spare moments with Sarah Jenyns. It is hard to imagine that Anne would have formed so intense a bond with Sarah if they had first met after Anne became Queen. It may also be suggested that princesses who are not expected to ascend the throne find it easier to make early friendships. To female royals, ladies-in-waiting can be a comforting and protective sorority against an adult and male-oriented environment. Likewise, because queen consorts do not wield the power of kings, they have fewer professional impediments to keeping their friendships in good repair. Yet, as such, they are hardly politicians in the usual sense of the term. There is also, of course, the matter of love affairs between royalty and members of the opposite sex, but these tend to fall outside the strict category of friendship.

For royalty it may be that the more easily sustainable friendships are with those who remain uncontaminated by the cares of political decision-making. In this respect, friends are a relaxation from the harder aspects of governing and are not want-to-be players in the drama themselves. The story of the relationship between Queen Anne and Sarah Jenyns, later Duchess of

Marlborough, is a salutary lesson in what can happen when politics comes between a crowned head and her closest companion. But in Part Two of this book, a different aspect of friendship at the top is examined. It concerns friends who are brought together through – rather than despite – politics. Away from the mannered formalities of court culture, the eighteenth century saw a flowering of challenging ideas, propagated in journals and newspapers, learned institutions, taverns, coffee shops and clubs. Beside the traditional allegiances to throne and altar came fresh affiliations delineated by the new philosophies for society's improvement. Concomitant to this, parliamentary debate was increasingly determined by the weight of parties, or, at least, organised factions. Here was an environment conducive to friendships being made by shared ideals and common political aspirations.

In the British Parliament of the 1760s and 1770s, Whig opponents of over-assertive royal authority like Charles James Fox and Edmund Burke became allies. From this state they developed into friends even though in temperament and private conduct, Fox, as the worldly and dissolute gambler son of Lord Holland was markedly different to Burke, the clean-living philosopher whose father was a Dublin solicitor. Fox had gone to Eton; Burke's early education had been entrusted first to Catholics in the open air of Ballyduff and then to Quakers in Co. Kildare. Burke was Fox's senior by twenty years. But it seemed not to matter. The parameters of public life and a common cause given impetus by challenging authority, making speeches, developing and testing arguments drew Fox and Burke inexorably together. Something similar could be said during the same years of the relationship at the core of Part Two between the two leaders of the Anti-proprietary Party in Philadelphian politics. Benjamin Franklin and Joseph Galloway came from different backgrounds but found themselves fighting the same corner in the Pennsylvania Assembly. Common attitudes provided the basis for personal attachment and an interdependence which entwined not just Franklin and Galloway but also Galloway with Franklin's son, William.

But what happens when allies in a great cause begin to respond differently to the political realities that continue to confront them? Navigating these hazards is especially frustrating for ideologically driven radicals and revolutionaries. Otto von Bismarck described politics as the 'art of the possible'. The craft is in getting a strategic advantage from a tactical compromise. High ideals may have to be unpicked or contaminated by sops to other entrenched interest groups. This is usually the process that frays fraternity between politicians who had shared common visions when together in opposition but who, given the chance to govern, find law-making less easy than phrase-making. Uniting to remove the iniquities imposed by a mutual enemy is one matter; agreeing on what should replace the old order becomes more difficult when the aftermath of reform or revolution falls short of expectations and demands adjustment to circumstances.

The response to insurrection in America cast Franklin and Galloway on different sides, the threat to civil order turning Galloway into a counter-revolutionary and transforming Franklin into his sworn enemy. The French Revolution caused exactly the same divergence between Fox and Burke. On hearing that the Bastille had fallen, Fox rejoiced that a bastion of absolutism had been brought crashing down. Burke, however, focused on the frenzy of its breakers, the mob, and foresaw anarchy. The ensuing revolution forced the two men to decide whether their friendship was worth fudging their principles. With his easy temperament, Fox believed they could agree to disagree on the greatest question of the age, disparaging one another publicly while remaining on cordial terms privately. Burke did not see how this was intellectually possible or morally laudable. After all, for all his generous-hearted sentiments, Fox had become an apologist for revolutionaries who would soon be sending the French equivalents of Burke to the guillotine. In May 1791, with MPs transfixed by the unfolding drama, Burke stood on the floor of the House of Commons and announced his friendship with Fox was at an end. Fox rose to reply but was so overcome with emotion that it was some moments before he could collect himself. With tears trickling down his face (and Burke's too) he recalled their twenty-five-year friendship and expressed the hope that their current disagreement should not interrupt the old intimacy. But he would not retract his condemnation of Burke's new-found conservatism. As far as Burke was concerned, this settled it. When, six years later, Burke lay dying, Fox asked if he might come and see him, to effect a reconciliation before it was too late. Burke's wife wrote back, thanking Fox for his concern, but making clear:

> it has cost Mr Burke the most heartfelt pain to obey the stern voice of duty in rending asunder a long friendship, but that he deemed this sacrifice necessary; that his principles remained the same; and that in whatever of life yet remained to him, he conceives that he must live for others and not himself. Mr Burke is convinced that the principles which he has endeavoured to maintain are necessary to the welfare and dignity of his country, and that these principles can be enforced only by the general persuasion of his sincerity.[2]

Consequently, Fox's offer was politely declined.

In Galloway and Franklin, Burke and Fox, we see examples of friendships that went in diametrically opposed philosophical directions in response to revolution. But even revolutionaries who stick together for the duration of the struggle rarely agree once it has delivered them the power to shape the future. Pierre Vergniaud's observation that 'the revolution, like Saturn, devours its own children' is well worn, principally because it has frequently proved so apt. It is true that the French Jacobins, Maximilien Robespierre and Louis de Saint-Just, worked together in a partnership of remorseless self-certainty but it is difficult to imagine that the enveloping chaos would not have rent asunder their alliance too had their own downfall and execution not first intervened. Saint-Just 'held his head like a Holy Sacrament'. This was surely ominous for those whose thoughts he found wanting. By contrast, the achievement of the United States' Founding Fathers was not that they were all fond of each other or shared a common vision of the republic they were creating, but rather that they managed to contain their enmities sufficiently to see their fledgling project through a difficult infancy when its future seemed in doubt. In this way, the American Revolution did not repeat the course of its British predecessor, the English Civil War, whose winners were only able to establish a short-lived republic. Nor did it end up like its successor, the French Revolution, whose leaders reacted to the resulting crisis and disorder by guillotining each other, before succumbing to the power of a new Caesar. This is what made the interaction of America's revolutionaries distinct not only in their own time, but also from so many failed imitations.

Political cultures purged of the fever of permanent revolution settle into a more orderly state and this facilitates the creation of a less polarised environment where disagreement can be tolerated without the assumption that it may lead to violent conflict. After the United States had been established and stabilised, only the continuance of slavery – dodged for the sake of unity by the Founding Fathers – proved a domestic dispute beyond peaceful settlement. In the last two hundred years of British history, only Ireland's status within the United Kingdom periodically looked as if it might be a domestic issue decided by bullets. Two centuries of relative stability cannot but have an effect on the institutions of government and the temper of those who hope to inhabit them. The suggestion that the Houses of Parliament is 'the best gentlemen's club in London' emphasised the extent to which, for some of its less vexed members, politics – a profession that demands no professional qualification – can be a cosy berth in which to make friends, gossip and occasionally gloat at the downfall of less agreeable members of the fraternity.

For a significant proportion of their inhabitants, Capitol Hill or Westminster provides not only a splendid location to make acquaintances but also a place to sustain those links that have been formed either at school or at 'Ivy League' universities like Harvard and Yale or their British equivalents. Regardless of whether they were Liberal or Conservative, Queen Victoria's Cabinets were largely populated by those who had been contemporaries at Eton or Harrow, Oxford or Cambridge. The twentieth century made little difference, for although it broadened the intake of schools attended, many of the ambitious thinkers of the Left transpired to be graduates not of 'the university of life' but of the institutions on the Cam or Isis as well. In particular, the two universities' undergraduate debating societies, the Oxford Union and the Cambridge Union, proved political nurseries for successive generations to meet and bond in an untroubled student atmosphere, before moving upwards into the more serious adult version. Passing through the Cambridge Union in the late 1950s and early 1960s were no less than eight future Cabinet ministers in Margaret Thatcher's government – including two who served her successor, John Major, as Chancellor of the Exchequer and one who would later lead the Conservative Party.* They had mostly come from a variety of grammar schools, but the opportunity to meet similarly motivated individuals at a formative period in their lives doubtless encouraged them to take themselves seriously and to believe that spending evenings arguing propositions across dispatch boxes while dressed in black tie was a perfectly normal way to make the transition to adulthood. They may have disagreed on issues and caballed on rival 'slates' to advance up the student ladder, but the shared experience gave them a common platform which made familiarity and the possibility of friendship natural.

Undergraduate life at Balliol College and the Oxford Union certainly gave Herbert Henry Asquith, the politician central to Part Three, the impression that he was the equal of anyone in his generation and the self-confidence to aim for the top. This was especially important to one who had come from an undistinguished social background. But it was taken seriously too by those born with greater advantages. The thirty-year friendship between two of Asquith's near-contemporaries, the Tory politicians St John Brodrick and George Curzon, began at Eton. In 1878 Curzon followed him up to Balliol, to fill, as Brodrick prophesied, 'that brief interval which must intervene between Eton and the Cabinet'. Both were elected Presidents of the Oxford Union, although Brodrick topped off his student days with a First Class degree while Curzon went down – to his chagrin – with a Second. It was not just similar political ambitions that kept them in touch. 'The Brodder'

---

* Leon Brittan, Kenneth Clarke, Norman Fowler, John Gummer, Michael Howard, David Howell, John Nott and Norman Lamont.

became Curzon's confidant over his complicated love life and, as such, a keeper of secrets. Brodrick entered Parliament in 1880 aged twenty-four. Curzon followed in 1886, aged twenty-six. A mere twelve years later the precocious Curzon was appointed Viceroy of India. Brodrick wrote to him that it had been 'one of the brightest elements in my life, to work with you and see you gaily flying the fences which I have laboriously climbed'.[3]

If he was honest with himself, it was also somewhat galling. Despite an unsuccessful spell as Secretary of State for War, Brodrick hoped to succeed Curzon as Viceroy. But in 1903 he was sent not to Government House, the Viceroy's palace in Calcutta, but to the India Office in Whitehall. With Curzon's tenure not yet complete, this made Brodrick Curzon's senior in London. The new Secretary of State for India's expressions of friendship had always bordered on the sycophantic. As Curzon's biographer has put it, Brodrick 'was also jealous of Curzon's superior talents, and ... resented the Viceroy's failure to take his views more seriously. Placed suddenly and unexpectedly as his former hero's superior, he took advantage of the position to enforce the missing deference.' What followed was a series of acts of denigration, designed to put the Viceroy in his place. Differences over Tibetan affairs caused a breach that was never healed. Brodrick proceeded to override Curzon on policy and personnel and when, in 1905, Curzon was goaded into resignation, his by now ex-friend even secretly petitioned the King not to give the returning Viceroy the customary high-ranking peerage. Three years later, Brodrick – elevated to the title Viscount Midleton – attempted to renew the friendship. He asked Curzon if their differences justified 'life passing away in bitterness and neglect after thirty years of unstinted friendship'. Curzon preferred to leave matters as they were 'and not rake up the past. Too much is involved in it that touches the innermost springs of my being. I have been too deeply scarred to wish to reopen the wounds.'[4] Truly, it is not just high principles that can come between friends bound by early ties. Slow-working but deep-seated envy and small-mindedness can be just as pernicious.

What most of the protagonists in *Friendship and Betrayal* have in common is a motivation to prove themselves, if necessary, at the cost of others whom they would ordinarily hold in high regard. It is easy to be censorious of such behaviour. After all, the depiction of politics as a process of clashing personalities rather than principles is natural to those who believe that the fading demarcation of ideological division since the end of the Cold War is evidence of an effective 'end of history'. Dominated by values and beliefs that are shared rather than challenged, politics in the western world – although not in lands beyond – is reduced to a conflict about the personal merits of those seeking to be chief managers of the consensus. We are asked to believe that what was once the stock of epic drama has been reduced to the bland sauce of soap opera. Few storylines were as long-running in British politics in the first years of the twenty-first century than the ill-concealed feud between the Prime Minister, Tony Blair and the Chancellor of the Exchequer, Gordon Brown. Sometime colleagues who had shared not only the same parliamentary office but also the same prescription for reforming the Labour Party, their personal antipathy surfaced at the prospect of leading it to victory. And in the years that followed, much of their disagreement appeared to be less about policy divisions than about their different inter-pretations of what the deal they had struck for the leadership actually involved. At the same time, similar allegations of a breached promise lay at the heart of testiness between Australia's Prime Minister John Howard and his increasingly impatient deputy leader and Treasurer in the government, Peter Costello. Despite the excitement these grudges caused among those closest to the action, to much of the electorate such simmering feuds had little real resonance.

Yet, the evidence that history is nearing its end is difficult to sustain in the dust of Ground Zero and the alleyways of Fallujah. We are not yet in a position to evaluate the full effects of decisions taken by the likes of Blair and Howard, let alone whether they would have been differently enacted by a Brown or a Costello. The age of consequence-free, or at any rate, con-sequence-light, politics is yet to emerge and it certainly does not apply to the cultures in which the individuals in this book lived and thought. Although their desire for power was a product of egoism, or an attempt to overcome insecurity by exorcising their own innermost insecurities, the central characters in this work had – or convinced themselves they had – moral obligations to a wider community. Ambition for self was not neces-sarily in conflict with ambition for a cause or belief. Their intention to aid what they believed to be the common good involved them in choices that were far more difficult than those that would have confronted a simple Nietzschean *Übermensch*, freed from ties to others. We are familiar with allegations about politicians who, once elevated to power, betray their prin-ciples. But what, then, do we have to say about those who sever personal ties in order to stay true to their principles? In recognition of this difficulty, the narratives of friendship in this book are placed within a deeper and more detailed context: the political controversies that so excited the individuals concerned. For without the politics, bonds of fidelity might never have been broken.

Each study is a self-contained story that presents a different facet of the common theme. Each is a tale of human strengths and weaknesses and how the vagaries of personal relationships can determine the course of a reign (Queen Anne and Sarah, Duchess of Marlborough), build a great republic (Benjamin Franklin and Joseph Galloway) or destroy a long-established political party (Herbert Henry Asquith and Richard Burdon Haldane). In each of these stories, we see how friendship can be shattered not only through nakedly selfish motives but also through the belief that obligations to friends can be legitimately put aside if they conflict with other considerations such as the obligation to 'the country' or the preservation of ideals that the continuation of the friendship appears to threaten. Ultimately the reader will judge the worthiness of the actions of the characters caught up in these dilemmas. What the book demonstrates is that exercising authority makes it extremely difficult to sustain the closest personal relations. True friendship, like love, involves a commitment of exclusivity between those who enter into it. The quest for power and the demands of other groups and considerations on those who wield it, threaten that exclusive bond. Friendship involves mutual recognition. Power delineates a chain of subordination. How the ambitious cope with this dichotomy is the theme unifying the stories in this book.

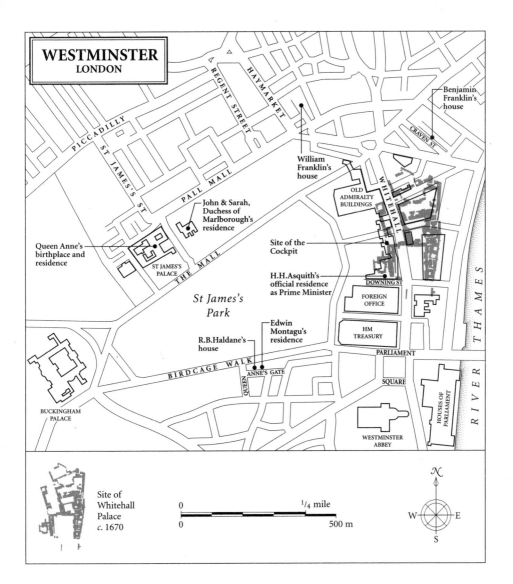

WESTMINSTER
LONDON

Benjamin
Franklin's
house

CRAVEN ST

HAYMARKET

REGENT STREET

PICCADILLY

ST JAMES'S ST

PALL MALL

William
Franklin's
house

OLD
ADMIRALTY
BUILDINGS

WHITEHALL

John & Sarah,
Duchess of
Marlborough's
residence

Site of the
Cockpit

Queen Anne's
birthplace and
residence

ST JAMES'S
PALACE

THE MALL

H.H.Asquith's
official residence
as Prime Minister

DOWNING ST

FOREIGN
OFFICE

St James's
Park

HM
TREASURY

RIVER THAMES

Edwin
Montagu's
residence

PARLIAMENT

R.B.Haldane's
house

BIRDCAGE WALK

QUEEN ANNE'S GATE

SQUARE

HOUSES OF
PARLIAMENT

BUCKINGHAM
PALACE

WESTMINSTER
ABBEY

Site of
Whitehall
Palace
c. 1670

0   ¼ mile

0   500 m

N

W   E

S

PART ONE

COURTIERS
Queen Anne and Sarah, Duchess of Marlborough

*'Intrigues, jealousies, heart-burnings, lies, dissimulation
thrive in [courts] as mushrooms in a hot-bed. Nevertheless,
they are necessary evils, and they afford a great school
both for the heart and head.'*

LADY CHARLOTTE BURY,
FORMER LADY-IN-WAITING TO QUEEN CAROLINE, 1838

ONE

Girlfriends

It was an unsuitable part for a princess. The dramatist conceded that 'to write a clean, decent, and inoffensive Play, on the Story of a Rape' was 'a difficulty greater than the invention of the Philosophers Stone'. But what tempted him 'into so great a Labyrinth, was the fair and beautiful Image that stood at the Portall, I mean the exact and perfect Character of Chastity, in the person of Calisto'.[1]

John Crowne had worked ceaselessly since receiving the commission to write a masque for King Charles II in which the monarch's nieces would perform leading roles. It was a tall order and in late 1674, as autumn contracted before winter, preparations were not going well. Plays were a regular feature at the royal court of Whitehall Palace, but this production was supposed to outshine them, harking back in quality to the elaborate masques that the King had recalled from his youth when Ben Jonson and Inigo Jones had collaborated on displays of the highest expense and artistic contrivance. With only three incompetent tragedies to his name, it was not clear that Crowne was Jonson's worthy successor. Indeed, he owed his appointment less to his own suitability than to the meddling of the rakish Earl of Rochester, who, in the furtherance of an artistic spat, was determined to prevent the more obvious candidate, the Poet Laureate, John Dryden, from receiving the commission. This was scarcely Crowne's concern. Failure would not only reflect badly on him, it would ridicule the twelve- and ten-year-old girls who were to take centre stage and on whom the throne might ultimately depend: Princess Mary and her sister, Princess Anne.

Acting the part was an important preoccupation for a family seeking to rebuild its right to rule, having escaped its enemy's grasp by the camouflage of an oak tree. The beheading of King Charles I and the indignities that his sons and heirs, Charles II and James, Duke of York, had suffered dodging first the soldiers of the English Republic and then the slights of refugee status among the splendours of Europe's *anciens régimes* inevitably encouraged them in their desire to reburnish the dazzle of monarchy upon its restoration at home. Thus masques, with their combination of play-acting, music and dance, signalled the royal house of Stuart's desire to shake off the taint of being *le Roi Soleil's* poor relation.

There could be no more appropriate location for this royal theatricality than the Palace of Whitehall, the sprawling 1,400-room labyrinth occupying a twenty-three-acre site beside the River Thames in London. The palace was – until it was engulfed in flames in 1697 – the Stuart dynasty's principal residence. Navigated through a profusion of tradesmen's entrances and narrow alleyways leading on to concealed back stairs and obscure, dimly lit passageways, it was a breeding ground for the politics of intrigue and deceit. Along its ratlines, doubtful characters could pass in and out with a minimum of advertisement – a considerable benefit for scheming courtiers and opportunist courtesans. Tudor window frames, wooden gantries and rickety, jutting balconies afforded views of the palatial village, obscured only by the unplanned profusion of pitched roofs and uneven heights. Artifice was all around. New façades concealed the functional and, at times, shambolic workmanship behind. Buildings resembled stage sets in which temporary structures were, with a quick shifting of props and heaving of pulleys, transformed according to taste and fashion. This was a court of constant adaptation where offices assigned to the King's ministers – haphazardly tacked on to the adjoining royal apartments – looked as temporary as their occupants' claim upon them.

Amid this clutter, a number of buildings made a more forceful impact. The most splendid – and the only one still standing three hundred years later – was the magnificent Banqueting House that Inigo Jones had designed for King James I. Its ceiling had been richly decorated by Rubens with the allegories of Minerva spearing Lust, Bounty trampling on Avarice, Hercules clubbing Envy, and Government trampling on Rebellion. Beneath these suddenly inappropriate images Charles I had passed before stepping out from a first-floor window on to the execution scaffold on a cold January afternoon in 1649. Behind the Banqueting House was a much older structure, the Hall. This was where the main theatre in the palace complex was located. Sir Christopher Wren was charged with overseeing improvements to its auditorium and throughout the winter of 1674–5 it became the scene of frantic activity as rehearsals for the great masque competed with the banging and wrenching noises emanating from a team of carpenters hard at work extending the stage.

Perhaps this was not the acting debut of the two little princesses, Mary and Anne, for they may have performed previously in a comedy put on at their father's home – St James's Palace, across the park from Whitehall.[2] But the masque now proposed was the first time they would take the stage in front of a sizeable gathering of the royal court. Having received tuition, Mary's dancing skills were highly regarded and Anne had already shown an interest in drama. The script Crowne was writing for them was therefore designed as a showcase for their talents. They had spent much of their childhood upriver at the royal nursery – their father, James, Duke of York, who was the King's younger brother and heir presumptive to the throne, having taken the view that Richmond, then separated from the smells and conspiracies of London by several miles of green fields and pasture, was a better environment for royal children than the fetid atmosphere of Whitehall. Now they were considered to be of an age when they could assume a more public profile. But whether either girl would one day ascend the throne, remained to be seen. Charles II might yet produce a legitimate heir who would take precedence over James in the order of succession. Even if this proved impossible, James might be delivered of the healthy son he so desperately wanted, thereby displacing his two daughters' chances. But until either eventuality transpired, the House of Stuart's future hopes continued to rest with the two little princesses, who were now expected to tread the boards of the Court theatre in costumes 'all covered with jewels',[3] delivering the lines written for them in voices retrained by professionals to project beyond their natural childish reach.

They could have been forgiven for feeling overawed. A huge red, white and blue curtain masked the stage, which was framed with classical columns. In their pit, the musicians tuned up. They were dressed as Indians, in taffeta cherry, blue and yellow gowns. Candles flickered in their sconces and in high candlesticks around the elevated royal dais where the King sat under a regal canopy of crimson velvet trimmed with gold and silver, 'quite as much a part of the show as the people on the stage'.[4] He sat there joyfully oblivious to the fact that the lavishness of this contrivance obscured the view of those seated to his rear. Behind the stage, sixty actors awaited their cue, surrounded by a retinue of 180 wardrobe assistants and assorted scenery shifters who had to be ready to raise and lower backdrops that ranged from the prospect of the Thames to a celestial temple in the clouds. It was not just the bejewelled princesses whose appearance needed fussing over. The costume of the 'Emperor of America' was covered with six thousand multicoloured swans' feathers.

Set out in five acts, interspersed with music and dancing and taking at least four hours to perform, the masque would undoubtedly test the acting skills and endurance of the two princesses, to say nothing of the patience of the audience. Its title was *Calisto, or The Chaste Nymph*. Mary played the lead, Calisto, one of the goddess Diana's nymphs. Anne had a supporting role as Calisto's sibling, Nyphe. Waiting in the wings was a *dramatis personae* of the Stuart court. Listening for his cue to dance onstage was the Duke of Monmouth, the most handsome and dashing of the King's illegitimate children – and the most headstrong. He was not the only such offspring that Charles II watched on the court stage that night. Lady Anne Fitzroy, his daughter by Lady Castlemaine, now the thirteen-year-old bride of the Earl of Sussex, was also in the cast as were at least two professional actresses with intimate knowledge of the monarch's bedside manner, Mrs Mary Knight and Moll Davis. The goddess Diana was played by the rather more virtuous Margaret Blagge who was about to marry Sidney Godolphin, later to be among the most important politicians of his age. But, in retrospect, it was perhaps a wilful fourteen-year-old maid of honour dressed up as Mercury who would give the most telling performance. Her name was Sarah Jenyns. In *Calisto* her character had a pivotal role, bringing about much of the trouble in order to impress her lover, the envious nymph Psecas. In real life, it was her co-star the young princess Anne whom she would hypnotise.

Disguise and sexual role reversal were the staples of *Calisto*. Old Father Thames became female in order not to stretch the comely Moll Davis's acting talents beyond credulity. The damsel normally astride the bull, Europa, also changed sexes so that the professional actor, Charles Hart, could assume the position. Such was the Duke of Monmouth's favour with his royal father, it was not considered fitting that he should be seen dancing on the stage with a girl of lesser rank. So he performed his minuet accompanied by six male courtiers instead. Off the stage, no such conventions applied: he was about to commence a torrid and ultimately tragic affair with Lady Henrietta Wentworth, the fourteen-year-old girl playing the role of Jupiter. In the masque, she was involved in a scene where, disguised as the goddess Diana, she attempted to rape Mary's character, Calisto. Thus, while it was not thought seemly to stage a production in which one of the King's bastards was seen dancing with a lady-in-waiting, it was considered acceptable entertainment to watch a young girl (pretending to be a god disguised as a goddess) hoping to rape the heir to the throne's daughter. James watched with the rest of the admiring court as Lady Henrietta, her lecherous advances resisted by the virtuous royal nymph, delivered her despairing rebuke: 'Your killing beauty is one great offence; But your chief sin is too much innocence.'

From this low, the plot diverted on to a happier course. Foiled in the attempt to seduce Calisto, Jupiter proceeded to become her protector while Sarah Jenyns's character, the troublemaker Mercury, also managed to make amends. The bizarre proceedings drew to a close with a troupe of French performers dancing around the stage dressed up as tribal Africans. They rediscovered their lost beauty in the cheeks of the two young princesses for whom Jupiter offers 'the small dominion of a star' – only to rescind the offer so that they may first serve Great Britain. Having descended from the heavens, Jupiter proposed a toast to Mary and Anne in an epilogue addressed to their uncle, the King:

> *Two glorious nymphs of your godlike line,*
> *Whose morning rays like noontide strike and shine,*
> *Whom you to suppliant monarchs shall dispose*
> *To bind your friends and to disarm your foes.*[5]

Whatever its artistic merits, it was certainly a spectacle. Did James gain a momentary inkling of trouble to come when the character played by the Duke of Monmouth was lauded on stage as a hero by Roman soldiers and 'Crown'd with a Mural Crown'? As events were to transpire, the Mercurial Sarah Jenyns could not have been better cast than as the manipulative orchestrator of so much of the plot's mischief. And, amid the sexual role reversals and devotions of love between the female leads, there remained the small figure of the ten-year-old princess Anne, delivering her lines with a strong and clear voice. When, at the end, she took her bow, the curtain fell on what proved to be the most lavish court theatrical of the Restoration period.[6] Had they but realised it at the time, the audience had also been treated to strange premonitions for the future of the realm.

When *Calisto* was first performed, Princess Anne and Sarah Jenyns had already known each other for about four or five years. Sarah was Anne's senior by five years and if her later assertion that 'in all [Anne's] parties for amusement, I was sure, by her choice, to be one'[7] was an exaggeration the two were nonetheless well acquainted by the time they were dressing up together in court theatricals.

Sarah Jenyns (Jennings, in modern spelling) had grown up in the genteel poverty of a once prosperous gentry family whose nominal wealth in property had been outstripped by the pressing demands of mounting debt. Her grandfather had not helped matters by siring twenty-two children. Her father, an MP in the Parliament that requested Charles II's restoration to the throne, had been faced with little option but to sell off chunks of his inheritance to meet more immediate commitments. These financial pressures contributed to an acrimonious home life and Sarah's parents separated. Sarah was eight when her father died, leaving the various family members to fight over what was left of the estate. It was hardly surprising that Sarah wanted to escape. But doing so was not easy. The brief Elizabethan fashion for tutoring the daughters of the well-to-do had fallen casualty to the following half-century's disruptions and although Sarah could read and (somewhat idiosyncratically) write, she had received no formal education. The principal opportunity for girls in Sarah's situation at the time was a propitious marriage. However, her family's depleted wealth made a good match less likely. One option might have been a career on the stage, where women were at last allowed to tread the boards that had previously been the preserve of male actors. From early on, Sarah developed the looks, manner and temperament of a great actress. Instead she decided upon entering the only other profession in which women in seventeenth-century Britain could make their name. Her elder sister Frances had gained a place at the royal court in 1664 and Sarah decided to follow her sibling's example, throwing herself into the ritual theatricality of life and opportunity in the royal bearpit.

It was not exceptional for a girl from a non-titled family to mix with a Stuart princess. For all his duplicity and cunning, Charles II's air could be one of surprising informality. Despite attempts, by the extravagance of theatrical display, to give the impression that nothing had changed, the period in exile had disrupted the more rigid routine of the pre-Civil War court and there was not quite the same fixation with immutable degrees of social ranking that so excited Saint-Simon and the courtiers who waited upon Louis XIV at Versailles. Consequently, among those who filed into the Palace of Whitehall were scions of relatively impoverished but respectable families who had rendered the royalist cause some service during the Civil War and having lost their burnish during the eleven-year Republic hoped to regain some of it with the King's return.

The young Princess Anne certainly had no reason to look down on those of relatively undistinguished families – for on her maternal side she came from such origins herself. Her mother, Anne Hyde, was the daughter of the self-made lawyer Edward Hyde, who had risen from obscurity to serve as Charles's adviser during his exile and subsequently became the principal minister in the first years after the Restoration. Hyde had been horrified to discover that his daughter – who was a maid of honour in the exiled Stuart court – had taken social ascension to a yet higher summit by getting pregnant and engaged (seemingly in that order) to the heir to the throne, Charles's brother, James, Duke of York. The Stuarts mixed with their social inferiors, but marrying them was different. No commoner had married so highly since Catherine Parr had become Henry VIII's sixth wife more than a century before and the subsequent commotion revealed the mixed social mores of the royal circle: Edward Hyde suggested his daughter be confined to the Tower of London; James tried to wriggle out of marrying the girl and several of his companions came forward to testify in unseemly detail how they too had been recipients of the twenty-three-year-old's easy virtue.

This was not the end of the indignity. When Charles insisted that the marriage went ahead (it was contracted in a rushed hole-in-the-wall ceremony by a chaplain and two witnesses) James's French mother, Queen Henrietta Maria, made a fool of herself by at first refusing to receive her new daughter-in-law, only subsequently to climb down at the King's insistence and go through the motions of welcoming the girl into the royal family. Nobody, however, managed to prevent the Bishop of Winchester from prying closely at the birth of the first child and troubling the labouring mother to answer impertinent questions in between her grunts as to whether she could be sure the little head emerging was a royal one.

Of the eight children Anne Hyde bore James only the two daughters – Mary, born in 1662 and Anne, in 1665 – survived. James coped with this disappointment by redirecting his attentions back to other women, including one of his wife's more attractive maids of honour. This was Sarah Jenyns's elder sister Frances, immortalised for her beauty by the Comte de Grammont's epithet 'La Belle Jenyns'. But however much Frances liked to flirt with the King's brother, she refused to sleep with him. Exasperated, James transferred his attention to a new mistress who shared his animalistic impulses: Arabella Churchill. None foresaw that Sarah Jenyns and John Churchill, siblings of these two of James's mistresses, would eventually unite in one of the most famous married political partnerships of British history. At the time, the major casualty of James's philanderings was his wife. Anne Hyde was witty and well educated and according to Samuel Pepys (who worked with James at his office in the Admiralty) she led her husband 'by the nose' in 'all things but his codpiece'. She was painted by the court portraitist, Peter Lely, sensually cloaked in loose-fitting fabrics, while behind her a stormy sky symbolised her scarcely repressed passion. The distress at her husband's antics took its toll, manifesting itself in comfort eating on such a scale that while James 'exhausted himself by his inconstancy and was gradually wasting away,' she became 'one of the highest feeders in England'.[8] She died (probably of breast cancer) in 1671, crying out to James warnings of the terrible agonies death involved. The diarist John Evelyn noted that 'None remembered her after one week, none sorry for her; she was tossed and flung about and everyone did what they would with the stately carcass.'[9]

From their father's philandering, as from their mother's funeral, the two surviving daughters were shielded. Although she grew up with few distinct memories of her late mother, the young princess Anne had inherited not only her Christian name but also the chubby physical characteristics of her Hyde forebears. But there was, too, the unsettling reflection that while other Hyde relations pushed themselves forward, the first of her meritocratic gentry antecedents had suffered the fate of Icarus serving his royal in-laws. In 1667, when Anne was only two years old, her grandfather, Edward Hyde, having been the principal architect of the Restoration Settlement, Lord Chancellor of England and ennobled as Earl of Clarendon, became the scapegoat for leaner times. Impeached and banished, he ended his days in exile. This was a cruel fate given the circumstances in which he had provided such service to the King, back in the days when it was royal fortunes that had been driven out of the realm.

Not that the young princess was much exposed to the harsher political realities awaiting her in the future. Apart from a largely unsuccessful trip across the English Channel to have an eye trouble treated, most of Anne's early years had been spent not with her father at Whitehall, or St James's Palace, but upriver in the royal nursery at Richmond. Once the great palace of the Tudor dynasty's founder, Henry VII, the building had been ravaged by time, neglect and part-demolition during Cromwell's Republic. By the Restoration, its grandeur and size had been much reduced, but as the location for the royal nursery it was perfect. A square tiled open gallery led out to an orchard parade ground where 223 trees stood guard, presenting an array of fruits. There, among the lodging turtle doves, Anne and her elder sister Mary were free from the restricted and stultifying environment of court. Richmond was an ideal child-sized principality where the Stuart girls could wander the grounds, play hide and seek in the woods and admire the dash of the royal hunt as it galloped past.

This sense of escapism continued in Anne's education, which fitted her better for a life in domestic service than for ruling Great Britain. Sewing and embroidery were on the curriculum, formal schooling in the constitutional duties of monarchy was not. However, music was encouraged and Anne was said to be a proficient guitarist and to possess a beautiful singing voice. Gibson, the three-foot-six former court dwarf and his equally minute wife provided instruction in drawing. But a renaissance education, such as that which Elizabeth I had been given as a princess – or for that matter which Anne Hyde had received as the daughter of an ambitious lawyer – was not on offer. Neither Anne nor her sister Mary were, it seems, expected to engage in learned discourse with some latter-day Erasmus. That French language teaching was given priority was an indication perhaps that their expected fate was to be determined by the exigencies of international diplomacy. At twelve, Mary was already approaching the age at which her marriage into one of the rival European dynasties was becoming a fitting matter for discussion.

Their father was certainly thinking about the future of the realm and, having concluded that he needed a new young wife to bear him a male heir, James diverted Mary Beatrice d'Este, the fifteen-year-old sister of the Duke of Modena, from a calling to the convent. In Westminster, anxious parliamentarians wrung their hands in anguish at the intrusion of an Italian Catholic into the royal family. Petitions were raised trying to prevent the union or, yet more ludicrously, permitting it only so long as it was not consummated. Ironically, these were petitions to which the girl in question would gladly have added her name. She was horrified at the news that she was to be married to the forty-year-old heir to the throne of Britain – a country of which she had not, until that moment, heard. However, her rushed attempts to become a nun were frustrated by the Pope, who assured her that she had a yet higher calling: to breed Catholic heirs for a Protestant throne. The marriage went ahead. To his daughters, James announced Mary Beatrice's arrival with the news that he was providing them with a 'play-fellow'[10] and the bewildered young Italian princess soon found herself passing time with her new stepdaughters in games of blind man's bluff and hide and seek. In the winter she got a particular thrill from toboggan rides and pelting her austere husband with snowballs.[11]

James's former object of desire, Frances Jenyns, had been one of the maids of honour to his first wife and, at the age of thirteen, Sarah Jenyns was appointed to fulfil the same role for his second wife. The position of maid of honour was poorly paid and the requirement to be at the royal beck and call often irksome. But it was also a stepping stone for a young girl to meet and marry someone of rank and wealth – as Anne Hyde had most spectacularly demonstrated when, as a maid of honour to the Princess of Orange, she had attracted James's leering gaze. It also provided a Crown-funded marriage dowry. Given the precarious finances of the Jenyns family, the opportunity to make a suitable match was of enormous importance to Frances and Sarah. Yet, while tripping into the arms of the monarch or the heir to the throne might bring earthly rewards, maids of honour found themselves vulnerable to lesser courtiers of yet more nugatory chivalrous intent, and of these there were a seemingly limitless number in the Restoration court. It was, as later recalled from the rectitudinous safety zone of old age, 'a Court where Vice and folly had all those marks of honour and approbation as might dazell the eyes of young persones'.[12] It said much for

Sarah's character, or at the very least her savviness, that despite ever-ripening healthy looks, she ended up as the only one of Mary Beatrice's maids of honour not to fall from grace – either at the hands of James or one of his courtiers.

This was not a court at which to leave young princesses unattended. Perhaps the central feature of Anne's girlhood was the extent to which she and her sister were protected from the attentions of young men. This, of course, was not a peculiarity of the Stuart court. More than two hundred and fifty years later, ponies were the playmates deemed safe for the future Queen Elizabeth II. Those males Anne was entrusted with were either elderly clerics overseeing her moral development or, sadly, baby brothers who died before they could talk. Only one brother survived long enough to see his third birthday – but not quite his fourth. Consequently, Anne grew up with an almost entirely feminine peer group. In the nursery at Richmond, besides her sister, Anne's most immediate friends were the six sprightly daughters of her governess, Lady Frances Villiers. This extended sisterhood provided a world of confidences and jealousies, governed by the poker-faced expressions necessary for unceasing rounds of card games and the private devotions delivered in tightly sealed and furtively exchanged *billets-doux*. On occasion, boundaries may have been crossed. According to gossip, Miss Hobart, the eldest of Mary Beatrice's maids of honour, did not conceal her passion for another of the maids, Miss Stuart. As well as her friendship with Sarah Jenyns, Anne formed an attachment to Mary Cornwallis until the latter was asked to leave court. According to Sarah, Mistress Cornwallis's departure came shortly after her correspondence with Anne, expressing the depth of her feelings, had been intercepted.[13]

In the 1670s, Sarah was not yet the principal girl in Anne's life. Mary Cornwallis's removal coincided with the Princess's growing attachment to Frances Apsley. Unfortunately, Anne had a rival for Frances's affection in her sister Mary. The beautiful daughter of Sir Alleyn Apsley, James's Receiver General and the Treasurer of Charles II's Household, Frances was adored by Mary who deeply resented her sister's attempts to muscle in on the friendship. 'There is no true love without jealousy,' Mary proclaimed grandly in a letter to Frances, whose play-acting with Anne increasingly became too much for her to bear. Feeling left out, Mary sat reading the dialogue in a play by Nathaniel Lee in which Sophonisba speaks to Massinissa on the subject of unrequited love. The scene, Mary wrote to Frances, made her want to cry, 'but before my hapy rival I wode not show my wekn[ess]'.[14]

The exaggerated language of Restoration theatre was to these young girls the natural manner to express what were doubtless mere adolescent crushes.

Nonetheless, Mary was by this time eighteen years old. In the context of the period, she was an adult. The ongoing absence of male peers encouraged her to extemporise. She began to refer to Frances as her 'husband'. Indeed, the possibility that Frances might actually end up properly married and thereby separated from her 'wife' was enough to send Mary into gushes of wild protestation, unrestrained by the cold barriers of punctuation:

> I love you with more zeal then any lover can I love you with a love that ner was known by man I have for you excess of friandship more of love then any woman can for woman & mor love ever the constanest lover had for his mistress. You are loved more then can be exprest by your ever obedient wife, vere affectionate friend, humbel sarvent to kis the ground where once you go to be your dog in a string your fish in a net your bird in a cage your humble trout.[15]

In case she had not made herself clear, she tried again:

> I am more and more in love with you every time I see you & love you so wel that I cannot express it no way but by saying I am your louse in bosom.

And again:

> I have now no thing to doe but to wish you did love me half so wel as I love you my dear dearest dearest dearest dearest dear Aurelia oh I am in extasie to think what hapynes I am now arrived at here I wil stay – here I wil set up my stage for ever if you wil give me leave and always be your ever afectionatt frind – obedient wife and loveing – I don't know what to say my hapines is so great.[16]

This may have been language borrowed from the romantic novel, but it was hardly that of the haughty princess, over-conscious of her royal station, condescending to the daughter of a court functionary. The extent to which Mary and Anne passed through adolescence in emotional thrall to girls who were well connected but scarcely their social equal was most telling. Indeed, they both seemed almost oblivious to any distinction between their own rank and that of the gentry class who comprised their peer group – the class, of course, from where their maternal Hyde antecedents had sprung. In Mary and Anne's rivalry for Frances Apsley's attention, Sarah Jenyns was often used as the go-between, covertly passing letters between them in order that their devotional contents might escape the prying eyes of the royal governess, who, having discovered one of the letters and upon reading it, considered it her duty to put a stop to the correspondence. For her part, Sarah had become tired of the strictures from her own mother. Mrs Jenyns believed that the constant threat posed by court life to her daughter's chastity necessitated unceasing maternal vigilance. When Sir Alleyn Apsley asked Mrs Jenyns to vacate the grace and favour apartment she had been given in St James's Palace as a refuge from her creditors, she at first refused to leave without taking her sixteen-year-old daughter with her. Sarah had no intention of retiring to a life of obscurity with her mother in St Albans and was relieved to be left behind when Mrs Jenyns was eventually persuaded to vacate her apartment.

The Restoration had re-established not only the monarchy but also the supremacy of the Church of England. Protestant Dissenters, like Roman Catholics, were penalised for their refusal to accept the Communion of the state Church. Despite the Catholicism of their French mother, both Charles and James had been brought up in the High Anglican tradition; and, in Anne Hyde, James had first married the daughter of the politician who became principally associated with restoring the Anglican settlement. Yet, in the latter part of the 1660s, both James and his first wife had covertly started following Roman rites. The Catholic faith naturally appealed to James's conservative political views about order and authority. It led him to question the legitimacy of a Reformation that contradicted the instruction in the Gospel of St Matthew that 'Thou art Peter and upon this rock I shall build my church'. However, given the political risks involved in converting to Rome, he had initially resolved to keep his new faith secret. When the Pope insisted that James could not publicly continue to take Anglican Communion, Charles ordered his brother to ignore the papal stricture and keep the pretence going. It was not until 1676 that he completely abandoned taking the Church of England Sacrament. By then, his conversion had long since passed from state secret to national concern.

Wedged between the age of Faith and the age of Reason, Charles II offered the adhesion of cynicism. Those who were taken in by the monarch's easy familiarity ran the risk, as the Whig historian and future Bishop of Salisbury, Gilbert Burnet, put it, of finding out 'how little they could depend on good looks, kind words and fair promises, in which he was liberal to excess because he intended nothing by them'.[17] On religion he developed a policy that was both deceitful towards his ministers and hypocritical to his brother. He had concluded in 1670 a treaty with Louis XIV in which Britain would assist the

French in crushing the Dutch, Britain's great rivals in the struggle for maritime trade. But without Parliament's knowledge, the Merry Monarch had also accepted the Sun King's money and the promise of French troops to help repress possible rebellion in return for promising to convert to Roman Catholicism at the first politically auspicious moment. Outside Ireland, the British realm was firmly Protestant and Charles recognised that while it was financially useful to string the French King along on the basis of a vague promise of future intent, it was necessary to tread carefully for the present. Similarly, while the King could not prevent his brother's heartfelt conversion, he could impress upon him the need to avoid demonstrating the fact in public. Over his brother's children he felt able to exert his regal powers with yet greater authority. In order to calm public apprehension, Charles insisted that Mary and Anne must be brought up Anglican. Furthermore, when the time came, they must marry Protestants.

The King's insistence was not to be easily defied and although James deeply resented the fact that his own daughters were being instructed in a faith that now directly contradicted his own, he nonetheless felt obliged to concede to his brother's demand, in line with the will of Parliament. In old age, James recalled that he had told the girls' tutor how much 'it was against his will that his Daughters went to Church & were bred Protestants; and that the reason why he had not endeavour'd to have them instructed in his own Religion, was because he knew if he should have attempted it, they would have immediately been quite taken from him'.[18] He could not have found a less receptive listener to these pleas than Henry Compton, the future Bishop of London, who provided Anne and her elder sister with daily religious instruction and was one of the most stalwart defenders of the Anglican tradition. James grew to hate Compton, whose unshakeable belief in the primacy of the Church of England made a particular impression upon Anne. Given the limited scope of the secular education offered to her, this rigorous instruction in devotion to the Anglican Church developed into her central intellectual preoccupation. As her faith deepened, so her distance from her Catholic father grew. In time, it would become the force that determined almost all her actions, even if it meant hacking off the bonds of kith and kin that had supported her throughout the early years of her life.

But it was an act of *realpolitik* as well as that of religious conviction that separated Anne's sister from the rest of the family. James might have hoped that Mary would marry the French Dauphin, thereby helping to bring about the twin goals of deepening alliance with France and securing her conversion to Catholicism, but King Charles and politicians in Westminster – who were fearful of Louis XIV's growing dominance – determined otherwise. Mary was given just a fortnight's warning that she was to be married to William, Prince of Orange, stadholder of the Dutch United Provinces where she would be expected to spend the rest of her married life. William of Orange was Charles's sole nephew, and as such was next in line to the British throne after Mary and Anne. Crucially, he was Protestant – a political reality that made James feel obliged to write to the Pope to apologise for the marital union. Even more perturbed was Mary herself. Pretty even by the fine standards of Stuart women, her opinion of her intended husband did not improve on first acquaintance. William was twelve years older than she and four inches shorter. Sombre and long in the face, he was a diminutive asthmatic with a bent back. He looked less a noble statesman than an apprentice Shakespearean actor auditioning for the part of Richard III. Against her will, Mary was married to him on 4 November 1677, King Charles misjudging the temper of the occasion with a succession of off-colour jokes.

Anne was not there to say goodbye and good luck. Whitehall had been struck by an outbreak of smallpox. The royal governess, Lady Frances Villiers, died of the disease. Anne herself lay stricken and, seemingly, fighting for her life. Her moral guardian, Henry Compton, was alarmed, lest her weakness might provide the opportunity for an enforced bedside conversion to the Church of Rome. For his part, James was more concerned about keeping from her any news that might cause her distress. Consequently, it was only after Anne had recovered that she learned that her sister had already left for a new life in Holland. The regular inquiries into Anne's health that she had been receiving from Mary throughout the period of danger had been faked in order to keep up the pretence that Mary was still in the palace, anxiously awaiting her recovery in another room. It was December before Anne was at last considered to have made a full recovery and allowed to visit her Catholic stepmother. It was a fatal error. She passed on the virus to her infant stepbrother, Charles, Duke of Cambridge: the male heir that Mary Beatrice had at last produced while Anne had been ill. 'I do easily believe the trouble you had for the loss of my son,' James wrote to his new Dutch son-in-law, 'I wish you may never have the like cause of trouble, nor know what it is to lose a son.'[19] Anne regained her rank in the succession.

It was still too early for Anne's marriage to be considered seriously but Sarah Jenyns, five years older and with at least some latitude in marital matters, had blossomed into a confident, open-faced girl with flowing hair. Like her elder sister Frances, she was liable to turn heads. Dispensing with the frizzy ringlets that had long been the fashion, she swept her hair back and down in a new, less mannered and more carefree style. Godfrey Kneller painted her with her head nonchalantly tilted to one side but with blue eyes fixing the viewer with a determined cocksure glare. There was nothing demure about her aspect. It was not the sort of face that retreated behind a fluttering fan. Rather it was the look that attracted the attention of one of James's most dashing pages.

John Churchill was ten years Sarah's senior but his path had already crossed that of the Jenyns family. His father, Sir Winston Churchill, was the cousin of an up-and-coming lawyer who had purchased land that the Jenyns had been forced to sell back in 1652. The estate, near Bristol, was already known as Churchill, a coincidence that may have attracted the purchaser's curiosity in the first place. This was not all. There were the contrasting responses of the coquettish Frances Jenyns and the brazen Arabella Churchill in their affairs with the heir to the throne. In the case of Arabella Churchill – whose physical attractions became clear to most courtiers when, upon her falling from a horse, they caught sight of her shapely thigh – this resulted in her bearing James two sons and two daughters. The small brood included a son given the name James FitzJames, who was created Duke of Berwick. Born on the wrong side of the royal bed, Berwick would grow up to fight for the other side of the English Channel, ultimately leading the French army into battle against the forces of his stepsister Anne, commanded by his uncle, John Churchill.

It is unlikely that Sarah would have so quickly risen to prominence at court if her elder sister had not already caught James's eye. Similarly, John Churchill made the most of his sister Arabella's hold over James although with a suitably cavalier approach he also sought a leg-up by bedding down with one of King Charles's more superannuated mistresses, Barbara Palmer, Duchess of Cleveland. As John Churchill's famous twentieth-century descendant put it, 'the charms of thirty-two are rarely more effective than when exerted on the impressionable personality of twenty-three'.[20] Inevitably this high-risk strategy ended in exposure, perhaps literally (rumour had it that Churchill had been forced to leap naked out of the Duchess's bedroom window when the King came knocking) and the dashing young roué was dispatched to seek death or glory in command of a British regiment in the service of Louis XIV. Possibly Charles was less concerned than the court might have imagined, for by the time of her three-year affair with John Churchill, the Duchess was a waning star in the royal planetarium of mistresses. But at any rate, young Churchill came off the richer for the escapade, for the Duchess had been so generous in funding his attempts to establish himself socially that by the time he was permitted to return to St James's Palace, she had retired to Paris with both a child and considerable debts as

consequences of her indulgence of him. She proceeded to mark her retirement from royal service by having an affair with a celebrated rope-dancer.
For his part, Churchill had his eye on a more suitable companion with whom
to realise his ambitions.

Sarah Jenyns presented a challenge for John Churchill. Despite her
mother's concerns, she was not easily compromised and certainly not by a
precocious chancer with a reputation for seduction. When he started del-
uging her with praise she responded by playing so hard to get that he
complained that she was treating him 'like a footman'.[21] Her subtext was
clear: if he wanted to sleep with her, he had to marry her. However, his
parents, unimpressed by the Jenyns's diminished wealth, took the view that
it was Sarah who was rather 'below stairs' and tried to persuade their son to
marry the richer Katherine Sedley instead. This proposal foundered when
Katherine Sedley succeeded Arabella Churchill as the heir to the throne's
lover. Undaunted, John Churchill pursued his own choice of prey with such
tenacity that he eventually succeeded in gaining Sarah's hand. They were
married in private shortly after Princess Mary's departure to the Netherlands,
keeping the fact secret for several months as was often then the custom in
court circles. Sarah even stayed on as one of Mary Beatrice's maids of honour
until the following year.

John Churchill was fast becoming one of James's most indispensable
companions. Thus by her marriage, the newly styled Sarah Churchill entered
into an association with the heir to the throne and his circle that was much
more acutely political than anything she had known as a friend of his
daughter or a maid of honour to his wife. With King Charles's failure to sire
a legitimate heir, there was now no doubt that the succession would pass on
his death to James. This caused a crisis. The prospect of a Roman Catholic –
particularly one with such an austere manner and dogmatic views as James –
becoming head of state and Supreme Governor of the Church of England
so terrified Whig politicians that they threatened to mobilise Parliament and
the country to force his exclusion from the succession. So strident were the
calls – fortified by a hysterical witch-hunt manufactured by Titus Oates's
wild allegations of a 'Popish Plot' – that a blanket refusal to countenance a
breach in hereditary rights risked a fresh civil war. When a general election
strengthened the pro-Exclusion Whigs' parliamentary muscle at the expense
of James's Tory sympathisers, Charles felt he had no choice but to request
that his brother exile himself from the realm until such time as the issue
could be settled favourably.

However reluctantly, James was obliged to comply and on 3 March 1679,
with Mary Beatrice at his side, he set sail for the Spanish Netherlands, unsure

how long he would be kept away. At the very last moment, Charles had prevented Anne from boarding the ship with her father. James was grieved by this parting and petitioned his brother to relent, which, in August, he eventually did – on the condition that Anne would be safely returned within a couple of months. The royal exile had cause to be fearful that history was about to repeat itself as he and his retinue settled down in Brussels, the same city in which he had been forced to kill so much time during Cromwell's Republic. With him was John Churchill, whom he entrusted to undertake a confidential mission to Paris to plead with Louis XIV for money so that Charles could run the country without recourse to Parliament. Churchill was also chosen to accompany James on a single fleeting and secret trip back to England when rumours of the King's faltering health suggested the wisdom of being in the kingdom in case he were to die. To avoid his identity being discovered, James made the journey dressed as Churchill's manservant.

For her part, Anne, put up at the Prince de Ligne's palace, did not enjoy being left in Brussels. Despite the 'limonade cinemont water and chocolate sweet meats all very good', she lamented to Frances Apsley that, 'I have a good heart thank God, or els it would have been down long ago'.[22] Her retinue included her Anglican tutors, ready to protect her from the Catholic influences of the capital of the Spanish Netherlands. Forbidden from entering Catholic churches, she was left to note the display of graven images in shop windows, writing to Frances that 'the more I see of those foolerys & the more I heare of that Religeon the more I dislike it'.[23] But she was not to be given long to muse on the ways of the idolatrous Continentals. On his covert mission back to see his brother – whose illness abated – James had gained permission to spend the remainder of his political quarantine in Scotland, a country whose narrow political class could be expected to remain loyal to his claim to the Scottish throne, even if their English counterparts sought to deny him the English crown. With the decision to move on from Brussels, a brief stop was made at The Hague which provided Anne with her first opportunity to see her sister since Mary's marriage to William of Orange. Then it was back to London from where Anne would again be separated from her father as he turned to face his next posting in Edinburgh. That his political future had not been resolved during the Brussels sojourn was evident by the ambiguous nature of the reception he received on the progress north.

With about thirty thousand inhabitants living cheek by jowl on a congested site, the Scottish capital was the second largest city in the British Isles. James had set up court in Holyroodhouse, the palace of his Scottish ancestors, where in 1566 Protestant nobles had dragged forth the Catholic David Rizzio from before the eyes of his presumed lover, Mary Queen of Scots, and stabbed him to death. The palace now had newly enhanced francophile castellations and fresh detailing but it still had a hemmed-in feel, sitting on a narrow plane at the foot of Arthur's Seat – an extinct volcano fancifully imagined to have been where the ancient king of the Britons made his last stand. The hill brooded over the palace like a lightly sleeping lion. Nor was there much of an avenue of escape at the palace's west entrance. A long, straight processional street, the Royal Mile, lined on either side by pre-cariously constructed medieval high-rises, led directly up to the ramparts of Edinburgh Castle. Atop its volcanic outcrop, the fortress was another dead end, perched on the edge of a precipice.

By the time Anne was eventually allowed to join her father in Scotland, the political situation had improved in London. But in Edinburgh, James was demonstrating a darker side of his character. He made the most of the fact that while torture was illegal under English law, it was not definitely proscribed under Scottish jurisdiction. He used the country's supine par-liament, housed half-forgotten midway up the Royal Mile, to support his will. The resulting persecution of the more extreme Presbyterian Scots was stepped up on the orders of a prince who kept under his clothes, next to his chest, a chipping of wood supposedly belonging to the cross on which Christ was crucified.

James's capacity for cruelty – at a time when he was supposed to be on political probation – was a telling foretaste of how he regarded disobedience. How much of this was recognised by Anne at the time is impossible to assess. Sarah Churchill, who was with her at Holyrood, later claimed that her own attendance at some of the Presbyterians' trials gave her a lifelong insight into the fallibility of royalty in the exercise of its authority. Whether at the time she really 'cried at some of these Trials, to see the Cruelty that was done to these Men only for their choosing to die rather than tell a Lye'[24] cannot be vouchsafed. At any rate, Anne seems to have been primarily diverted by the entertainments on offer in and around Holyrood. If the story is to be believed, she and her girlfriends were responsible for introducing Scottish ladies to the pleasures of tea-drinking. The palace's indoor tennis court was turned into a playhouse and there a performance of Nathaniel Lee's *Mithri-date* was put on with Anne in the starring role. The staged theatricals of heroes and goddesses continued to provide a safer surrogate for the darker drama unfolding beyond the Holyrood stableyard.

The resolution of the Exclusion Crisis in England curtailed the enforced Scottish vacation. The Whigs may have been united in their opposition to James's succession but they were divided between those who wanted the crown to pass directly to his Protestant daughters, and the more extreme

Whigs, assembled around the Earl of Shaftesbury, who were angling for the radical solution of passing the throne on to Charles's illegitimate son, the Duke of Monmouth. When, in March 1681, the radical Whig faction rejected the King's proposal for Mary and her husband William to act as regents during James's reign, Charles seized his opportunity to pull rank and show up their extremism. The King dissolved Parliament, and believing their arrest to be round the corner, Shaftesbury and his confederates went from hunters to hunted. The charters of the Corporations were appropriately gerry-mandered to ensure the arch-Whigs' power base was swept away.

In February 1682, James received his brother's permission to return south with his position much strengthened. But there was to be one further unsettling incident. Three months later, accompanied by John Churchill, he set sail for Scotland in order to bring back Anne and his wife Mary Beatrice. His vessel, the *Gloucester,* foundered off the Norfolk coast. Other boats were not far away and an immediate order to abandon ship might have saved a crew of over one hundred souls. Instead James opted to stay on board well after it should have been obvious that the ship was going down. This may have been an intentional display of the calm disposition expected of his station, but it was an act of obstinacy that ensured that none of the rest of the crew could escape. Only when it was far too late did he board the lifeboat with his various pets and a few select companions. One account spoke of the doomed sailors, raising a last cheer for their royal master as he was rowed away to safety while they resigned themselves to a watery grave. Another suggests that the crewmen were so desperate in their attempts to clamber on to James's lifeboat that he had to hand Churchill his sword to fend them off – in panic in case they capsized his one means of escape. Whatever the exact nature of events, it was an unsavoury episode and when he was eventually reunited with Sarah, Churchill certainly gave her to understand that he was unimpressed by James's handling of the incident – even though, in allowing him to share the royal rescue craft, James had saved Churchill's life.[25]

In fact, it was not surprising that Churchill was one of the select few that James saved from drowning. Both in Brussels and in Edinburgh, he had become a trusted and indispensable aide. James conceded that 'I would not willingly have Churchill from me.'[26] On 21 December 1682 he was granted a Scottish title, Lord Churchill of Eymouth, and with Sarah – now Lady Churchill – given rooms in St James's Palace. Slowly but surely, James was elevating John and Sarah, just at the time they were beginning to harbour doubts about his suitability to become king.

Anne was now seventeen. As far as her uncle and father were concerned, the longer the question of whom she was going to marry was deferred and the more independent she felt herself becoming as time passed, the greater the risk that her own preferences might come to obstruct a successful resolution of the issue. Specifically, there was the danger from scandal and gossip about an unsuitable man in whose company she was said to be spending too much time. Such talk even reached The Hague, prompting her sister Mary (who was increasingly adopting the priggish tone of her husband) to fear for Anne's reputation, 'for I think nothing more prejudicciell to a young woman then ill company'.[27] The predator in question was Lord Mulgrave. He was a thirty-four-year-old bachelor noted for being a brave soldier with an interest in poetry – a combination likely to appeal to a naive girl and to alarm a vigilant father. Consequently and notwithstanding his hardly respectable excuse that he was 'only ogling' the princess,[28] Mulgrave found himself assigned to take part in an expedition to Tangier aboard a ship with a leak.

The Mulgrave affair highlighted the need to see Anne safely married before another court rake did her honour greater irrepair. There had already been a half-hearted attempt to make something out of a visit to England by Anne's German cousin, Prince George of Hanover. But nothing came of it, probably because the union did not coincide with Charles's and James's political objectives of the moment. However, in May 1683 Charles hatched a plan for Anne to marry the thirty-year-old Prince George of Denmark. Blond and agreeable-looking, this George had distinguished himself by saving the life of his brother, the Danish King, in battle. Politically the match was also acceptable because – unlike Mary's betrothal into the Dutch House of Orange – a union between the British and Danish royal families did not threaten Whitehall's rekindled appeasement of Louis XIV. Thus the deal was struck even before either Anne or George had set eyes on one another.

Unlike her sister, Anne was not expected to go away to live in her husband's country. Although she would assume the title Princess of Denmark, married life would be conducted on the home turf and arrangements were made to bring her intended husband over to England. It was a match that suited the increasingly omnipresent Churchills as well. Sarah's brother-in-law had been in attendance at the Danish court, rising to become Prince George's gentleman of the Bedchamber. Perhaps because of this, John was chosen to escort George to Britain for his marriage. Happily, and unlike her sister's experience, Anne liked what she eventually saw. The wedding took place on 28 July 1683 at the chapel in St James's Palace, the ceremony taken by her vigilant tutor, Henry Compton, Bishop of London. Married to an essentially decent husband, with the possibility of children, the deepening friendship of John and Sarah Churchill and no more than a remote prospect of ever having to assume the throne, Anne had every reason to look forward to a contented life.

TWO

Mrs Morley and Mrs Freeman

When Anne had been married for a year the King presented her with the Cockpit, a block of royal apartments in Whitehall Palace. They surrounded an oddly shaped structure whose original sporting purpose had given the adjacent apartments their insalubrious name. The rooms were poky and, from the outside, the central octagonal-shaped building resembled an eccentric early observatory, with a tall cupola in place of a large glass telescope protruding from its pitched roof. Whitehall Palace was dissected by a central vertebra, unimaginatively entitled 'The Street' and the Cockpit (its site was close to where Downing Street now runs) was located on the west side of this thoroughfare amid arcades of courtly pleasure. A Tudor bowling alley and a galleried tennis court were its immediate neighbours. The rooms looked out over the open expanse of St James's Park where King James I had once created a small royal zoo, complete with a couple of crocodiles. More recently the grounds had been remodelled, an ornamental canal dug and four long avenues of trees planted. Open to the public, the park was the strolling domain of courtiers and the exercise ground of those eternally hoping for a socially advantageous introduction.

The substantial part of the palace complex, however, was contained around a series of courtyards on the eastern side of The Street and was connected to the Cockpit side by a couple of gatehouses. The more elaborate of these was the Holbein Gate, which also contained part of the residence of the grandest of Charles II's mistresses, the French-born Louise de Kéroualle, Duchess of Portsmouth. In all, she was allotted no less than twenty-four rooms and sixteen garrets – which according to John Evelyn were decorated with 'ten times the richness and the glory' of those assigned to Charles's Portuguese wife, Queen Catherine of Braganza. The King's private apartments, on the east side of The Street, backed on to the River Thames with stone steps and wooden jetties protruding into the water. Exiled from the mannered elegance of the French court, the Comte de Grammont considered Whitehall a 'vast and unmagnificent Palace' whose 'skirts' were washed by the Thames – upon which royal barges filled with court beauties glided between the heavier craft of tradesmen, transporting goods and trading insults with loafing ferrymen.

Unrealised plans existed to turn Whitehall into a marble-hearted palace like the Tuileries or the Escorial. Inigo Jones's Banqueting House was the only fragment of what might have been achieved if sufficient funds and determination had been available. Instead an air of unreality presided over the miniature town, as if it was one of the show villages on the banks of the River Volga that Prince Potemkin's enemies falsely alleged he had constructed to impress Catherine the Great. The stench of London in summer sent Charles II upriver to Hampton Court, or a little further still, to Windsor Castle, with its magnificent chapel and round tower in the shape of a drum. A new palace was earmarked for a site in Winchester and Charles's love of the turf made Newmarket another royal stamping ground. There, even in 1684, at the age of fifty-four, the King jockeyed his own horse first across the finishing line. Anne shared this zest for outdoor sports, her own particular enthusiasm being as a huntswoman. But at Whitehall, her great diversion was more indolent. Gambling had become the accepted pastime of society ladies. Even as a child, Anne had enjoyed card games, and her religious sensibilities never intruded upon playing on a Sunday. Marriage failed to divert her from rounds of crimp or basset. Her stepmother, Mary Beatrice (Mary of Modena as she was popularly known) sometimes joined her, as did the two leading women in the King's life, his wife the Queen and the Duchess of Portsmouth. It was around this card table that Sarah, Lady Churchill, was increasingly often to be found shuffling the pack.

Anne's affection for Sarah had grown in intensity as her feelings for her childhood confidante, Frances Apsley, had waned. Frances had married Sir Benjamin Bathurst, who was appointed Comptroller of Anne's and George's Household. Years later, Anne discovered that Sir Benjamin had been profiteering from this post by selling positions there – an action she considered unworthy, and she contrasted it with Sarah's sense of efficiency and probity.[1] But long before that, Sarah had come to be seen as the Princess's boon companion. Upon getting married, Anne had wanted Sarah to serve as her principal lady of the Bedchamber and Groom of the Stole. Instead, James had insisted upon Anne's aunt, Lady Clarendon, who in Sarah's tart phrase 'looked like a mad-woman, and talked like a scholar'.[2] Upset, Anne had written to console Sarah and to assure her that 'you have not a faithfuller friend on earth that loves you better then I do. My eyes are full, I cannot say a word more ...'.[3] But although Sarah had to be content with the post of junior lady of the Bedchamber, events soon conspired to make amends when Lady Clarendon quit her position in order to join her husband in Dublin where he had been appointed Lord Lieutenant of Ireland. This time, Anne was not to be dissuaded. Sarah received the honour that formally recognised what in reality she had already become – the woman at Anne's side.

For a relationship that in every other respect gathered such intensity, exclusivity and ultimately jealousy – emotions that cut through whatever was laid in their path – it did remarkably little to subvert the two womens' respective marriages. Temperamentally, Anne and Sarah represented the attraction of opposites as surely as their marriages represented that of equals. Sarah had met her match in John Churchill in a passionate bond of two strong-willed characters. While in her old age she was unforgiving about many things, she always believed the gift of 'a very kind husband' to be 'the greatest comfort of this life'.[4] He was dashing, quick, peculiarly talented and ambitious to succeed. He was a man who believed, in the later rhetoric of Lord Birkenhead, that the world continued to offer glittering prizes to those with stout hearts and sharp swords.

For all their shared background in the art of soldiering, there were few obvious similarities between Lord Churchill of Eymouth and Prince George of Denmark. Anne's husband was heavily built, good-natured, indolent and slow. It was considered a point in his favour that he did not seek to meddle actively in British politics. But instead it meant that he lived a largely unfulfilling existence in which heavy drinking became a reason for getting up rather than going to bed. 'I have tried him drunk and I have tried him sober,' Charles II was supposed to have concluded early on about his new nephew, 'but there is nothing in him.'[5] When he was sober he had a passion for the miniature, and his podgy hands were often kept busy assembling delicate models of sailing ships. Behind his back his father-in-law, James, mocked him with the nickname that had become his incredulous catch-phrase: 'Monsieur Est-il Possible'. Writing home to Denmark, George sketched his life at the Stuart court: 'we talk here of going to tea, of going to Winchester, and everything else except sitting still all summer which was the height of my ambition. God send me a quiet life somewhere for I shall not be long able to bear this perpetual motion.' It is not difficult to see why the court's smart crowd thought him an amiable buffoon.

Anne was impervious to such sneers, finding in her Danish husband a dependable companion. Built upon this strong if semi-submerged rock, the marriage prospered in every respect but the one that was supposed be the sign of its success. As royal stud to the house of Stuart, Prince George's main purpose was to perform the role usually given to the female consorts of the British royal family – to secure its survival. In this, apparent success soon gave way to failure and disappointment. He was to be married to Anne for almost a quarter of a century during which time the two of them grew old and ill together: George expanding his girth through the pleasures of over-indulgence, Anne suffering pain and growing stout from constant pregnancy. After coming to England, George achieved nothing of lasting significance either through his own endeavours or as a patron of others. But the tragedy of his quiet love for his wife was that it produced no surviving heir.

Anne's relationship with Sarah was built upon different foundations. Physically, it was Sarah, who was the more imposing. She had a good figure and kept her strawberry blonde hair lustrous by daily washes in honey-water. Everything about her deportment spoke of confidence. In contrast to her sister Mary, Anne was not especially attractive. Even in youth, she had a tendency toward dumpiness. Her bout of smallpox had left its mark on her skin. But she had long and strong chestnut hair, delicate, pretty hands and another considerable attraction no portrait painter could convey: a full and pleasing voice.

The royal Princess looked up to her commoner-born lady-in-waiting like a younger, slower schoolgirl admiring the self-confident head girl in her dormitory. Sarah provided Anne with what she lacked in herself and failed to get from her husband: spark, cunning and – a rare commodity in those who move among royalty – unbounded candour. As Sarah put it in later years, she gained Anne's affection 'without the assistance of flattery; a charm, which in truth her inclination for me, together with my unwearied application to serve and amuse her, rendered needless'.[6]

The burgeoning and increasingly affectionate correspondence between Anne and Sarah in these years has provided later generations with the testament of the two young women's deepening friendship. Anne obeyed Sarah's instruction to destroy her letters after reading them. 'I kissed your dear kind letter over & over', Anne once assured Sarah, 'and burnt it much against my will.'[7] Sarah, however, did not burn all of the correspondence she received from the Princess. One consequence of this has been that while there remains ample evidence of Anne's feelings for Sarah, Sarah's responding endearments have not survived to tell the other half of the story. Historians have thus explained the rationale for their relationship primarily from Anne's perspective, concentrating on her regard for Sarah's unflinching honesty and more worldly-wise insights into life.

What was it that so attracted Sarah to Anne? There was, of course, the prospect of gaining power and influence from a member of the royal family. But Sarah had that anyway: after all, James, poised to be the next king, was an enthusiastic benefactor of her husband and this favour was far more likely to yield the couple political advancement. There was also the influence of Sarah's elder sister, Frances, who had now married another member of James's intimate circle, Lord Tyrconnel, and had converted to his Catholic religion.

So even without the blandishments of Anne – a princess who would probably never ascend the throne – the Churchills were a more than sufficiently well connected couple in the nexus of royal patronage.

Anne became the godmother to Sarah's third daughter in February 1684. The girl was named Anne in her honour. The two women shared together the joys and pains of pregnancy and in the early years of her life with Prince George, Anne was naturally eager to learn from Sarah's experiences of marriage and motherhood. She was also keen to share the anxieties of the political world that surrounded them. Sarah was genuinely interested in affairs of state and it was natural, rather than merely self-seeking, that she should want to spend time with someone who was, albeit involuntarily, a part of that world. Sarah became the tutor in politics and constitutional studies that Anne's father had omitted to provide for her in the royal nursery. No doubt being treated as the font of wisdom was a pleasurable experience for one with Sarah's naturally bossy temperament but there was more to it than that. Her regard is evident from the references to it in Anne's return correspondence. After expressing her sadness at having to follow the instruction to burn Sarah's letters, Anne told her that 'I do assure you you need never be in pain about your letters for I take such care of them 'tis not possible any accident can happen that they should be seen by any body'.[8]

While she may have lacked Sarah's sparkle, Anne's personal qualities could not be denied, as Sarah – even after they had fallen out – conceded when she favourably contrasted Anne's open and unassuming character with the more typical attitude of royal personages who 'for the most part, imagine they have a dignity peculiar to their birth and situation, which ought to raise them above all connexion of friendship with an inferior'.[9] Ultimately, it was Sarah, not Anne, who showed the greater degree of personal hurt when the relationship turned sour. When, eventually, Anne transferred her affections to another woman, Sarah's hysterical reaction went far beyond what might be explained by a sense of losing political influence or displaying wounded pride, for it resembled not so much sadness at the passing of a friendship, as a feeling of betrayal at the termination of a mutually binding partnership.

Closeted together in the Cockpit, neither woman could have imagined that such recriminations would lie ahead. In her years as the Princess's premier lady-in-waiting, Sarah also enjoyed spending time with her other friends in and around Whitehall Palace. She was particularly drawn to an emerging ally of her husband. This was Sidney Godolphin, the Cornishman Charles II had appointed to a post in the Treasury. Others Sarah enjoyed being with included Anne's nursery playmate, Barbara Villiers, who had married Colonel John Berkeley, and the transparently ambitious politician

Robert Spencer, Earl of Sunderland and his wife. Anne tolerated them for Sarah's sake while harbouring reservations about their character. Such friendships played on her sense of insecurity, for the problem was that Anne was a princess with an inferiority complex – a disability that was if anything made more acute by her exposure to Sarah's sparkle and chutzpah. 'I hope that next to Lord Churchill I may claime the first place in your heart', Anne begged Sarah, for 'I know I have a great many Rivalls which makes me sometimes feare loosing what I so much value.'[10]

To get away from the world of the Cockpit, Whitehall and Westminster, Sarah usually retired to Holywell, the family home in St Albans where her children were being brought up. During these trips and Anne's own visits to England's spa resorts to take their healthy waters, the Princess became almost obsessive, writing to Sarah every day. 'I cannot live without you' she protested in one letter, and passed the time gazing at the portrait of Sarah she kept at her side, musing that it was 'a pleasing thing to look upon when I can't see the original'.[11] James described his daughter's fixation with Sarah as 'une passion démesurée'.

For his part, the ageing King Charles continued to stave off the loneliness of power through the comfort of lovers. The Duchess of Portsmouth had come to outstrip the others in the influence she sought to exert, promoting the political interests of the Earl of Sunderland and James's exercise of authority. When, in 1684, she appeared to be dying, Charles raced to be by her side and both he and James started crying when their beloved 'Fubbs' gasped out that nothing should come between the two of them as brothers. When she proceeded to recover, the gaiety of the Whitehall Babylon returned. The diarist John Evelyn famously recorded Charles, in his fifty-fifth year, 'sitting & toying with his Concubines, Portsmouth, Cleveland & Mazarin: & c. A French boy singing love songs, in that glorious gallery, whilst about 20 of the greate Courtiers & other dissolute persons were at Basset round a large table, a bank of at least 2000 in Gold before them ... it being a sceane of utmost vanity; and surely as they thought would never have an End: six days after was all in the dust.'[12]

The final hours of Charles II became the subject of much controversy. Having heard that his brother had been incapacitated by a stroke, James went to his bedside. The entourage of onlookers was swelling by the moment. With the King refusing the offer of the Anglican Sacrament, James leant close to him and a whispered exchange took place. This completed, James shooed nearly all of the onlookers out of the room. The doors were shut firm. Up the back stairs came the ancient figure of Father Huddleston, the priest who had aided the royal fugitive when he was on the run from

Cromwell's Roundheads in 1651. The last rites of the Roman Catholic Church were administered and on 6 February 1685, his niece Anne's twentieth birthday, the King's life drew peacefully to its close.

King James II had none of his brother's easy charm. Even his seduction technique was heavy-handed. The Comte de Grammont once observed him closing in on Elizabeth Hamilton: 'He entertained her with what he had in his head; telling her miracles of the cunning of foxes and the mettle of horses; giving her account of broken legs and arms, dislocated shoulders, and other curious and entertaining adventures; after which his eyes told her the rest.'[13] Yet, despite his own record as an adulterer, he hated the open licentiousness that had been the hallmark of Charles II's court and made clear that he expected higher morals now that he was master of the house. In his own case, this meant entertaining his mistresses more discreetly than before – a small private apartment in Whitehall sufficing for hurried assignations. As for the wits who had kept the late King amused, James simply did not find them funny.

The new monarch liked to have every meat dish he ate accompanied by the same 'universal sauce' – an unappetising recipe of dry toast beaten in a mortar, parsley, vinegar, salt and a little pepper.[14] He had a political outlook to match. His room for manoeuvre was circumscribed not only by the temper of Parliament but by the limits of his own imagination. He lacked Charles's intelligence and cynicism and without the second of these attributes it was impossible to assess the quality of advice offered from ministers like Sunderland, who – seeking to ingratiate himself for personal gain – told the King what it was thought he wanted to hear rather than what was sound counsel. Indeed, in the judgement of the Crown's political operator in Scotland, the Duke of Lauderdale, James even compared unfavourably with King Charles I, for he 'has all the weakness of his father without his strength'. Like Charles I, James believed in divine right. The lessons that he drew from a childhood scarred by the execution of his father and his own time in exile were unfortunate ones: that his father had been too weak and that his subjects were too strong. When, in 1687, James had the fortification of the Portsmouth naval base stepped up, it was to construct defences on the landward side.

Catholic emancipation was James's goal and on the second Sunday of his reign he attended a public Mass in the royal chapel in Whitehall. But, in seeking to re-establish Catholicism beyond the palace walls, James was constrained by three considerations. First, there was his promise not to destroy the Protestant established Church of England. Second, there was the difficulty of convincing Parliament to repeal the Test Acts which restricted the holding of political office to those prepared to take the Anglican Communion. Third, there was the possibility that if his second wife, Mary of Modena, failed to produce an heir, the throne would revert on his death to his Protestant daughters. With a sympathetic Parliament, they could be expected to repeal their father's more overtly pro-Catholic measures as surely as Mary Tudor's regime had been undone by the succession of her Protestant half-sister, Queen Elizabeth I.

Thus, establishing a Catholic settlement by force was never a sustainable policy. Bringing it about by stealth, however, was another matter. Unlike France's Louis XIV, James was not an absolute monarch: he could seek to bribe, cajole and suspend Parliament but he could not tax or legislate without its say-so. But there were other means of trying to subvert it, and getting a friendly judiciary to find legal loopholes was one method. James believed that if the Test Acts could be undermined there would soon be a natural and spontaneous reassertion of the Catholic faith throughout the kingdom and this would be the cornerstone of a settlement for Catholics that would outlive his own reign.

The early challenge to his authority came not from Parliament, but from a blood relation. The Exclusion Crisis that appeared to have been so well buried proved capable of one last after-tremor, for on 11 June 1685 Charles II's illegitimate son, the Duke of Monmouth, claimed to be the rightful sovereign and accused James of having murdered the late King. Militarily and politically misconceived from start to finish, Monmouth's rebellion was an amateur affair, playing on the credulity of the peasants of the West Country and attracting almost no aristocratic following. James turned to John Churchill to assist the Earl of Feversham in quelling the revolt and Monmouth's ragbag force was scattered after attempting to attack the royal army near Sedgemoor in Somerset. Three days later the man who would be king was captured dressed as a shepherd. It was Monmouth's last and least convincing performance. He pleaded to James to show mercy. This loss of dignity went in vain and on 15 July he was beheaded, the executioner repeatedly botching his swipes at the neck and having finally to terminate the ordeal with a knife.

James was determined to make the most of his victory. Judge Jeffreys was dispatched to undertake his 'bloody assizes' of West Country opposition: around eight hundred rebels were sent off as slaves to the plantations of the West Indies and perhaps a further four hundred were executed, their corpses left swinging in the breeze by the principal roadsides as a warning against dissension like Spartacus's men strung up along the Appian Way. James had used the crisis to argue the need for a standing army and – in breach of the Test Acts – appointed almost a hundred Catholic officers into the armed forces as an emergency measure. When the politicians subsequently objected, he prorogued Parliament. In any case, his lawyers found a way of giving him what the Tory politicians had refused him and, never a man for half-measures, James soon set about promoting Catholics into key positions out of all proportion to their numbers in the country and far beyond the specific scope of the Law Court's judgment.

Civil as well as military office was affected. A council of leading Catholics increasingly became the King's sounding board for ideas while one by one James sacked the principal ministers of his government except for Sunderland, who became the Church of Rome's least convincing convert of 1687. The Churchills' papist brother-in-law, Lord Tyrconnel, was put in charge of Ireland and – ominously to Protestants – given command of the army there. He proceeded to staff it with his co-religionists. Other key positions were also reassigned to Catholics, including command of the Fleet, governorship of the Tower of London and the Lord Privy Seal. Throughout the country, potentially troublesome JPs were dismissed and replaced by Catholics. Corporations like the Inns of Court and college fellowships at Oxford and Cambridge also became targets for James's positive discrimination policies. Royal interference in these institutions was not new, but the manner in which James systematically replaced those of one religion by another left little room for doubting that a full-scale purge was under way. He also hoped to dispense with the Habeas Corpus Act, the law that, in preventing arbitrary arrest without trial, provided a degree of protection to otherwise law-abiding political opponents that did not exist in absolutist Continental Europe. James could not have picked a more disastrous time to pursue these policies, however. They coincided with Louis XIV's revocation of the Edict of Nantes which ended the last shreds of toleration afforded France's Protestant minority. To those nurtured on tales of the St Bartholomew's Day Massacre and the persecution of English Protestants under 'Bloody Mary', events in France appeared to foreshadow James's intentions for his own people. His failure to condemn Louis' actions naturally heightened suspicions – and these darkened with the flesh-creeping tales carried by the boatloads of Huguenots arriving in Britain in search of asylum.

During these shouts and alarms, Anne had been closeted with her husband and friends at the Cockpit. With no public role assigned her, she whiled away time cutting the cards with her girlfriends, while slowly but surely the old guard changed around her father's throne. 'I am sorry you have so ill luck at dice' Anne consoled Sarah on 12 August 1686, 'yesterday I won three hundred pounds but have lost almost half of it again this morning.'[15] To support such a lifestyle, Anne's £30,000 annuity from her father – supplemented by the income from her husband's Danish estate – was insufficient. Aware that she was sliding increasingly into debts she could not honour, she appealed to her father. The go-between in the ensuing negotiation was Sarah's friend, Sidney Godolphin. He succeeded in persuading James to give his daughter a one-off sum to clear her commitments.

But getting out of debt was less important to Anne than establishing a more permanent legacy. Her first pregnancy ended unhappily in April 1684 with a stillborn daughter. However upsetting, the loss of a child in this way was not unusual for the time, and in the early years of her marriage she had no reason to believe that it should prejudice the prospect of a healthy brood in the future. Sarah had also lost her first baby, Hariote, in infancy, and seemingly healthy children had followed. In Anne's case there was an added pressure because the failure of either her elder sister or her father to produce an heir meant that it was possible her own offspring might one day sit on the throne – ensuring that Britain would be once again a Protestant state. It was a relief, therefore, when she successfully gave birth in successive years to two daughters whom she named Mary and Anne Sophia, for the latter of whom she asked Sarah to stand as godmother.

The period of maternal happiness did not last long. In early 1687, just as Anne recovered from a miscarriage, smallpox claimed the lives of both her babies, Mary and Anne Sophia, within six days of one another. As if this was not a crushing enough blow, Prince George also went down with the disease and doctors feared the worst. Anne, however, refused to give up and despite being distraught at the loss of her two baby daughters, she did everything possible to tend to her husband while he fought for his life. Slowly he turned the corner and Lady Russell reported that she never saw anything 'more moving' than the sad sight of the two bereaved parents together: 'Sometimes they wept, sometimes they mourned; in a word, they sat silent, hand in hand; he sick in bed, and she the carefullest nurse to him that can be imagined.'[16]

Every personal twist of fortune in the house of Stuart had become skewered by its political implications. Prince George's smallpox attack and worsening asthma gave Catholic courtiers hope that Anne would soon be a widow who could be remarried to a more suitable – by which was meant Catholic – husband. Anne had come to detest her stepmother, the Queen. Mary of Modena's religious zeal had already caused great irritation in Whitehall and Anne kept her sister in The Hague briefed about how their stepmother 'pretends to have a great deal of kindness to me' but that the sickly sweet smile concealed the venomous fangs of 'a very great bigot' who 'hates all Protestants'.[17] A *raison d'état* had forced the two sisters to be separated by Princess Mary's marriage to William of Orange. Now it was the force of politics that brought them back together with a series of coded messages coming and going between The Hague and the Cockpit. When Anne asked her father for permission to travel to The Hague to visit Mary – whom she had not seen for nearly eight years – James forbade her. His advisers assured him that he could not risk his two Protestant daughters caballing together, doubtless encouraged in patricidal talk by William. As the historian J.P. Kenyon has put it, 'the Whitehall of the Stuarts was like the court of some Visconti or della Scala princeling, with the ruler's closest relations his most hated and suspected enemies'.[18]

It might appear that this state of affairs put the Churchills in an impossible position. Sarah was Anne's confidante. Of James's remaining Anglican court-iers, John was one of the closest to the King. Outsiders certainly had cause to wonder where the Churchills' allegiances really lay. After all, Sarah's brother-in-law was the arch-Catholic, Lord Tyrconnel. John's sister Arabella was the mother of James's illegitimate son, the Duke of Berwick, whom some of the more desperate Catholics hoped James might one day legitimise and create heir ahead of his Protestant daughters. But while many opportunists suddenly rediscovered the faith of their ancestors, Lord and Lady Churchill made no move to follow suit. With her sister Mary in Holland, Anne was the only Protestant member of the royal family in Britain, and her actions – almost ostentatiously attending Anglican services – were increasingly assum-ing a character of defiance. On 17 May 1687, Sarah's husband dispatched a secret communication directly to William to assure him that Anne 'was resolved, by the assistance of God, to suffer all extremities, even to death itself, rather than be brought to change her religion'.[19] So there it was, they had all decided – come the worst – which way to jump.

In April 1687 James issued his Declaration of Indulgence, conferring religious liberty on all subjects. For once, Jesuit priests and Quaker preachers found themselves united in thanksgiving. But if Anglican hands were clasped in prayer, it was not in praise. Parliament would be recalled to ratify the Declaration, but only after a new House of Commons had been elected from a choice of candidates that the King had rigged to the advantage of the Catholics and Dissenters. In the meantime, his attempt to force the reading of a second Declaration of Indulgence from the pulpit of every church was met with a petition from seven bishops – including the Archbishop of Canterbury – asking him to rescind this order on the grounds that they believed his dispensing authority was illegal. Rather than bow to his senior clergy, James decided to confront them. The seven bishops were duly arrested on charges of publishing a seditious libel and dispatched to the Tower of London. As they went in their carriages to their incarceration, they blessed the passing crowds that assembled to salute them on the route through the City of London. If a Protestant people were anxious to know what to expect from an unbridled Catholic monarch, then the locking-up of their foremost clergymen could hardly have sent a worse message. On 10 June 1688, two days after the bishops' arrest, came the news that the Queen had given birth to a son, James Francis Edward. Normal (Protestant) service would not be resumed on the King's death. Instead, the Stuart succession, it seemed, had been guaranteed as a Catholic one after all. What James most dearly wanted had at last been granted him.

As the new Prince issued forth his first cries, none felt a deeper sickness in the pit of the stomach than his half-sister Anne. Her own attempts to become a mother had so far ended only in tragedy. That the stepmother she loathed had succeeded where she had failed was too much to bear. It was an assault on her faith, an assault on her place in the succession, an assault on her womanhood. So hard to take did she find the news that she created a false reality of denial. Three months prior to the birth Anne had started sowing the seeds of doubt, writing to her sister Mary in Holland that the Queen's 'great belly is a little suspicious' and that 'her being so positive it will be a son, and the principles of that religion being such that they will stick at nothing, be it never so wicked, if it will promote their interest, give some cause to fear there may be foul play intended. I will do all I can to find it out if it be so.'[20] The following week she wrote that 'whenever one talks of her being with child she looks as if she were afraid one should touch her. And whenever I happen to be in the room as she has been undressing, she has always gone into the next room to put on her smock. When she is brought to bed, nobody will be convinced it is her child, except if it prove a daughter.'[21] When a boy was indeed born, not even the presence of the Lord Chancellor, most of the Privy Council and a small army of midwives and hangers-on could convince Anne (who was away taking the waters in Bath at the time) that the child had not been smuggled into the bed in a warming pan. 'It may be it is our brother', she sighed in a commiseratory letter to Mary, 'but God only knows . . .'.[22]

On 30 June, the trial of the bishops ended with a sensational verdict of not guilty. The law courts had made a mockery of the King's will. The jubilation –

which manifested itself in street parties across the capital and beyond – was matched by fear about how James might react. That night Anne's former tutor, Henry Compton, Bishop of London, together with a group of senior peers of the realm (soon to be celebrated as the 'Immortal Seven') wrote to William of Orange, asking him to save the country. Any reason for William to flinch at striking his father-in-law had gone – for he knew James was quite prepared to let Louis XIV crush the Dutch Republic.

James's first reaction was to have two of the judges who had presided over the bishops' trial dismissed from the bench; he then foolishly attempted to prosecute all those who had lit bonfires to celebrate the clerics' release. Only when the evidence became irrefutable that his Dutch son-in-law was assembling an invasion armada did he suddenly backtrack, putting his policies in reverse. These measures appeared the result of panic under pressure and did nothing to shore up the King's fading status. On 3 November 1688, crowds on the coast watched the most extraordinary sight as 'the Protestant wind' blew two hundred troop transport ships guarded by forty-nine warships through the Straits of Dover and west down the English Channel, foiling an attempt by the Royal Navy to intercept them off Beachy Head. On 5 November, the anniversary of the Gunpowder Plot, William of Orange landed at Torbay. With him were nearly 15,000 Dutch, Scottish, English, Swedish, German, Swiss and Huguenot troops. Peers of the realm slowly but steadily began to pledge themselves to William's cause. The 'Glorious Revolution' was under way.

Whitehall was in turmoil. Upon whom could James rely? The Catholic courtiers, of course, were loyal, but few of those had the necessary talent to save his kingdom. Lord Churchill had proved himself at Sedgemoor when dispatched to defeat Monmouth's rebellion and although James was certainly suspicious of Sarah's influence upon Anne it would be a remarkable feat of disloyalty if her husband bit the hand that had for so long fed him. On 16 November, as he prepared to go out to confront the invasion, James drew up his will, leaving his estate to his wife and – in place of his daughters – his baby son and heir. He instructed the Bishop of Ely that if he should be killed, the news should be broken gently to Anne, now pregnant for the seventh time. He did not want anything to happen that might cause her another miscarriage. The following day, James rode out from London at the head of his army with Anne's and Sarah's husbands at his side. He did not know that they had already both decided to betray him.

Royal families might be imagined to regard blood as thicker than water. But the clues that this bond was about to be cast aside should have been apparent. Anne's absence from her half-brother's birth had been convenient, as had been Churchill's failure to honour a request that he should join the throng of observers for the Queen's delivery. The moment her father left his capital, Anne had a note to William smuggled out of Whitehall. It assured him of her support 'in this so just an undertaking'.[23] But until they knew for certain that their husbands had deserted to the rebels, Anne and Sarah had to continue to give the impression that they were praying hourly for the deliverance of their King from his enemies. This meant putting on a performance far more convincing than any of the theatricals of their childhood. Watched closely by Whitehall's Catholic community, Anne and Sarah tried to give off an air of calm and even normality; continuing to roll the dice and reorder their hand of cards, trading Jacks and Kings, as their husbands prepared to do the same.

At Salisbury, James's forces halted. Intelligence suggested that William's army was somewhere near Exeter. Ironically, if James had taken Churchill's advice and struck quickly, momentum might still have been on his side. Instead he chose to listen to the majority opinion of his officers who wanted to fall back in order to block the road to London. This proved to be the decisive moment for Churchill. On the evening of 23 November he ate supper with his King. By the morning he had betrayed him, having slipped out of the camp in the night and deserted to William's forces.

Bishop Burnet, adviser to William and chronicler of the age, reported that Churchill, 'a very smooth man, made for a court' was 'much censured' for his actions:

> for as he had risen in the king's service through several degrees up to be a favourite, so a kindness which had begun upon the king's commerce with his sister [Arabella] was now so well fixed, that no man had more of personal favour and had found greater effects of it than he had. His coming into this design had the appearance of treachery and ingratitude, which has brought him under much reproach.[24]

In view of the opportunities he had given Churchill, it was hardly surprising that James was furious to discover his flight. It was while James was trying to attend to his morning prayers the following day that he was interrupted with the news that Prince George had also slipped his leash and gone over to the other side. In later life James channelled the contempt he felt for his son-in-law's action by describing the defection as less unfortunate than the loss of a single lowly trooper.

Sarah and Anne were still waiting anxiously together in the Cockpit when the news of their husbands' defection reached them. For their own security, time was of the essence. Sarah rushed to a safe house in Suffolk Street, just north of Whitehall Palace, where she knew the Bishop of London was hiding. There she finalised plans for her escape to safety with Anne. This was all carried out in the nick of time, for within hours an attempt was made to seize Churchill's assets and to put Sarah under house arrest. An order to place Anne under armed guard was clearly imminent. James was returning to Whitehall, where he intended to await William's advance on London. Sarah recalled that Anne's very words to her were that 'rather than see her father she would jump out a window'.[25] Finding a way of slipping out of the Whitehall Palace now became the immediate priority.

Anne and Sarah could not walk out of the Cockpit building because there were guards posted outside Sarah's door. Fortuitously, though, Anne had recently had a private staircase built linking her private rooms to those of Sarah. On the night of 25/26 November, taking with them only a servant and Barbara Berkeley (née Villiers), Sarah and Anne made their escape along the connecting staircase and out of the rear of the building. There, according to plan, a carriage was waiting to take them to the Bishop of London's City residence in Aldersgate Street. Disguised, they left London. Reaching William's forces – which were now proceeding towards Oxford – would be difficult because the road was blocked by James's army. Instead the girls struck out north to Nottingham where support for the rebellion was mounting. Once they were out of harm's way, they could relax and let their disguise slip. Wherever they went, crowds came out to cheer them.

They had got out just in time. When soldiers arrived to place Anne under house arrest, they found the Cockpit in turmoil. Sir Benjamin Bathurst, Frances Apsley's husband, had been awoken at eight o' clock by the alarm of women's voices and on getting up found Anne's nurse, Mrs Danvers, fretting excitably that someone had abducted the princess leaving 'the bed cold with all her yesterday's cloaths even to her stokings & shoes left behind'.[26] In her rush to get away, Anne, like Cinderella, had left a single shoe in the mud. In the evening, James arrived back in London and was told of his daughter's flight. 'God help me!' he mourned, 'Even my children have forsaken me!' He started to cry.[27] He would never see either of his daughters again. In a letter to the Queen, Anne attempted to justify her actions by claiming that she was 'so divided between duty and affection to a father and a husband', before proceeding to lay the blame on those Catholics whose meddling had endangered James's rule. 'The Prince of Orange,' asserted Anne optimistically, 'designs the King's safety and preservation.'[28]

It was true that William had stated upon landing that he sought not to usurp his father-in-law's throne but merely to see the sources of discontent redressed by the calling of a Parliament that would not be stuffed by the King to do his own bidding. But if James hoped he could call William's bluff with general assurances to this effect, he was mistaken. With momentum on his side, William had no intention of calling off his military advance on the capital and letting James off the hook. With William's army closing in, James feared that he would only be allowed to retain the crown on terms that would be intolerable to his dignity. He was thinking not only about himself but also of his infant son. The desire of so many of James's enemies (and for that matter his daughters) to believe the fiction that the Prince of Wales was indeed a warming pan impostor made the prospect of a fresh Exclusion Crisis over the son's right to succeed to the throne highly probable.

Confronting this dismal prospect, James clung to the comforts of his faith and the experience of history – particularly his own. He and his brother Charles had been forced to flee into exile when their father lost the English Civil War. Yet, the unpopularity of the usurping republican regime meant that little more than a decade later they had returned to rule in triumph. Might not Providence repeat itself, ensuring that James and his infant son would sooner or later be welcomed back – and on their own terms rather than under the dismal constraints with which staying on appeared to saddle them?

James's negotiations with William now became stalling tactics while he arranged for his wife and baby son to be evacuated safely to France. Had Anne not escaped, she might have found herself bundled into exile as well. On 21 December James sneaked out of Whitehall Palace taking leave of his subjects with as little advertisement as his daughter had given his sentries the previous month. Getting into a boat, he was rowed across the Thames, pausing only to drop the symbol of royal authority, the Great Seal of England, into the murky river's consuming depths. His first attempt to get on a boat for France was dashed when he was apprehended by Kentish fishermen, but it was not in William's interests for him to be detained and he was allowed to slip away a second time. He landed at Ambleteuse on Christmas Day, his conversation full of loathing for the double-dealing of John, Lord Churchill, the courtier-soldier he had raised from nothing.[29]

Like King Lear – blinded by his own foolish pride to the cold-hearted scheming of Regan and Goneril – James could only have felt betrayed by the connivance of his two daughters in his downfall. Whatever he had been as a King, he had not been a cruel father. Indeed, despite his earnest prayers that they would become Catholics and the lectures from the Pope to translate words into deeds on this matter, he had made no more than the most half-hearted attempts to convert them. The morning after his daughter Mary returned to Whitehall Palace as its new Queen, she was spotted in her nightclothes bouncing up and down on the beds and opening and closing the closets of what had been her father's home.[30] Anne initially displayed no outward doubts about the course she had taken in the defence of a Protestant realm. Ostentatiously sporting the orange colours of the victor, she was back with her friends in Whitehall when news arrived that James's second attempt to flee his kingdom had been successful. In all likelihood this meant that Anne would never see her father again. According to Lord Clarendon, she reacted to the news cheerfully and called for a game of cards.[31]

If anything, it was Sarah who came to recognise the unsettling aspect of the *coup d'état*'s success. 'King James, who would have been a very good King, if it had not been for Popery,' she later reflected, 'was drove out of England without shutting up a shop, tho' he had many Friends.'[32] From this, a lesson was clear. What had appeared to be the certainty of absolute power could, in reality, be removed in an instant.

Neither Anne, Sarah, their husbands, nor most of the native-born politicians who had connived in the uprising against James's increasingly arbitrary style of statecraft could have foreseen the extent of the revolution they had set in motion. Later generations, fashioned in their perspective by propagandists of the Whig cause, came to celebrate the upheaval of 1688–9 as a 'glorious' settlement, in which the monarch was bound by and committed to uphold a Bill of Rights which forever banished the spectre of absolutism from the British shore. From that date on, Britain appeared set upon a shining path of parliamentary supremacy and individual liberty – at least for the great Protestant majority. At the time, it was less clear what was happening. That William would himself take the throne in partnership with his wife was not what most of the prominent figures who had joined the revolution had intended. But James's flight had created a power vacuum which William, at the head of the only functioning army, was best suited to fill. In any case, Mary had made matters awkward by refusing to accept her father's vacant throne unless William sat there with her. The next few years were to be uncomfortable ones even for many of those who had thrown in their lot with the insurrection. William transpired to be a charmless man with a casual attitude to his new realm. Many of those who felt passed over came to find his bias for his Dutch friends every bit as distasteful as James's former favouritism for Catholics. As the snubs accumulated, and the uncertainty over the new King's longevity mounted, many began to reopen lines of communication with their old master, the King over the water.

At first John and Sarah Churchill – as taken aback by the pace of change as everyone else appeared to do well out of the new dispensation. William raised John to the earldom of Marlborough. Furthermore, he confirmed him in command of the English regiments of his forces for the wars that would now commence against Louis XIV and gave him the task of remodelling the army, an office according him much personal financial gain selling commissions. This appearance was deceptive. Although William had bene-fited from his new Earl of Marlborough's desertion from James's camp, it was not an act he admired. A man who could betray one master was capable of doing the same to his successor and William had no intention of elevating his glamorous General into the role of a latter-day Warwick the Kingmaker. He found him 'very assuming'[33] and Mary went further, describing him as someone who should 'never deserve either trust or esteem'.[34]

Thus the first vestiges of a personal frostiness between William and Mary and Anne's friends became manifest. Common sense suggested that the Marlboroughs should keep quiet and bide their time – for they had not exactly done badly out of the new regime and they could be sure that Anne would shower them with whatever they wished for on succeeding to the throne. But would that day ever come? Neither William nor Mary were noted for good health – it certainly seemed that Mary would die childless – but they still could outlive Anne, who was only five years William's junior. This was an alarming prospect, for while the new co-rulers had their doubts about the Earl of Marlborough then they had none about his Countess – they detested her. An absence of personal chemistry was part of the problem, but it was what they saw as her pernicious influence upon Anne that particularly galled them. Mary had become her husband's dutiful wife and she expected Anne to be her dutiful sister. If the two of them had spent the last few years closeted together in the Cockpit they might have recognised one another on these terms, but the enforced separation had instead seen Anne turning to Sarah for a lead and an inspiration.

Foolishly, Sarah lost no time in marking her card when she intervened in the debate over how much money should be settled upon Anne from the Civil List. This was none of her business. Amid unseemly haggling, Sarah did her utmost to impress upon her mistress the need to talk tough in negotiating the grant, which she felt should be £70,000 a year. It might have been a demonstration of Sarah's zeal in fighting for Anne's interests, but this unrealistic demand only acted to increase the resentment between Anne, her sister and brother-in-law, and Parliament. Mary claimed she might have been tempted to repair her fast-tarnishing relationship with her sister 'but I saw plainly, she was so absolutely governed by Lady Marlborough that it was to no purpose'.[35] In the end, Parliament voted Anne an annual grant of £50,000. In turn, Anne gave Sarah £1,000 a year to supplement her £400 salary as first lady of her Bedchamber. 'I beg you would only look upon it as an earnest of my goodwill, but never mention anything of it to me,' Anne wrote of the gratuity to Sarah, 'for I shall be ashamed to have any notice taken of such a thing from one that deserves more than I shall be ever able to return.'[36]

It soon became clear that the fallout between the sisters' camps was not limited to William and Mary's dislike of Sarah's bossy presumptuousness. First and foremost, William was preoccupied with drawing the wealth and arms of his new kingdom into the European struggle against France, rather than with wasting time humouring his relations in London – it was not, after all, as if his Stuart in-laws were famed for their notion of family unity. Although Prince George had leapt at the opportunity to accompany William on the Irish campaign against James's supporters, he was denied the rank he believed his title and connection demanded. He felt humiliated when William would not even let him share his coach. Such pettiness did nothing to endear the King to Princess Anne. His ill-disguised indifference towards her manifested itself in his determination to prevent her from gaining any worthwhile experience of affairs of state. In letters to Sarah, Anne did not hide her dismay at the attitude of her regal brother-in-law, or, as she called him, 'the Dutch abortive'.[37]

Happily for Anne, William chose to spend as much time as possible with his army on the far side of the English Channel. During these absences, Mary ruled as chairwoman of an executive 'Council of Nine'. By common consent, she was the most attractive of the Stuart women but her childhood sense of mischief had been tempered by her years as the stadholder's wife. At court she became a great patron of the art of needlework, which 'took ladies off from that idleness which not only wasted their time but exposed them to many temptations'.[38] Yet, even she occasionally found this composure stifling and was wont to miss a stitch when her husband's hunched back was turned. One nocturnal escape in search of her capital's earthly pleasures included a furtive visit to the *Folly* on the Thames, London's premier floating parlour of sin.[39] On another occasion – while William was away wresting the Irish realm from her father on the banks of the Boyne – she slipped out to shop, visit a fortune teller and go to the theatre. To her embarrassment, she discovered that Dryden's plot concerned a queen who had usurped the throne from her father. Eyes in the audience darted up to where she was sitting. Indeed her shopping spree was no better considered, for it involved consorting with women who were actually prostitutes. When William returned to London, he was furious to learn of his wife's escapades and suggested that the next time she visited a brothel she might like to invite him too. In fact, Mary's private life was certainly less complicated than her husband's (who, aside from persistent allegations of homosexuality, conducted a long-term affair with his wife's one-time nursery friend, Betty Villiers) and it was her sister she regarded as the wayward one. Perhaps like King Lear's scheming daughters, the curse of deserting a father was mutual jealousy and suspicion. But most of all it was the intensity of Anne's affection for Sarah that Mary made it her mission to destroy.

The nature of the bond between Anne and her first lady of the Bedchamber has never ceased to be the source of speculation. At the time of the Glorious Revolution Bishop Burnet wrote that Sarah 'is indeed become the mistress of her [Anne's] thoughts and affections and does with her, both in her court and in her affairs, what she pleases'.[40] Many years later, when they had irrevocably parted company and Sarah had few kind words to say about Anne, she nonetheless still wanted it to be known how close they had previously been. 'It is certain', boasted Sarah, that Anne 'at length distinguished me by so high a place in her favour, as perhaps no person ever arrived at a higher with queen or princess.'[41] Writing in the third person, Sarah recalled the intensity of Anne's crush:

This favour quickly became a passion; and a passion which possessed the heart of the Princess too much to be hid. They were shut up together for many hours daily. Every moment of absence she counted a sort of tedious lifeless state. To see the Duchess [i.e. Sarah] was a constant joy; and to part with her for never so short a time, a constant uneasiness, as the Princess's own frequent expressions were. This worked even to the jealousy of a lover. She used to say *she desired to possess her wholly*, and could hardly bear that she should ever escape from this confinement into other company.[42]

There is much in Sarah's subsequent retelling of events that does not survive closer scrutiny, but on this substantive point there remains ample evidence to support her claim. 'The Princess's own frequent expressions' testify that the relationship was far more involved than merely the debt of gratitude a member of the royal family might feel for a faithful servant. Anne simply did not seem to acknowledge the truth that there was any inequality between herself, as heir presumptive to the throne, and her first lady of the Bedchamber. Sarah recalled how:

She grew uneasy to be treated by me with the form and ceremony due to her rank; nor could she bear from me the sound of words which implied in them distance and superiority. It was this turn of mind, which made her one day propose to me, that whenever I should happen to be absent from her, we might in all our letters write ourselves by feigned names, such as would import nothing of distinction in rank between us.[43]

Sarah chose as her pen-name Mrs Freeman, which she thought reflected 'my frank, open temper', leaving Anne with Mrs Morley; 'and from this time', recalled Sarah, 'Mrs Morley and Mrs Freeman began to converse as equals, made so by affection and friendship'.[44] Such was the familiarity and attachment of the two that at one stage the ladies Freeman and Morley were writing to each other every day. Given the subsequent destruction of Sarah's letters, the survival of only Anne's side of the correspondence could have given the impression that the intensity of the affection was all Anne's, but this assumption was directly contradicted by Anne herself, with her insistence that Sarah 'wrote to me as [I] us'd to do to her'.[45] Certainly, Mrs Morley's missives are proof enough of a possessive and demanding love which bordered on an unhealthy obsession. Even Sarah's self-improving autodidactism could be scolded if it got in the way, with Anne contrasting Sarah's readiness to find 'spare minutes to look on Seneca' while, on occasion, being supposedly too busy to reply instantly to her letters.[46]

Anne's jealousy of Sarah's other female friends intensified. When she learned that Sarah had quarrelled with Lady Fitzharding (the former Barbara Villiers) she egged Sarah on to turn what was really only a brief disagreement into an irrevocable parting. Anne had long since fallen out with the gold-digging Villiers sisters with whom she had shared her Richmond nursery. About Barbara she felt 'sure she hates your faithfull Mrs Morley & remember none of her famely weare ever good for any thing'. The fact that Barbara had also taken the risk of assisting in Anne's escape from the Cockpit in 1688 clearly counted for naught. Upset when Sarah and Barbara proceeded to patch up their differences, Anne wrote to deplore Sarah's sweet susceptibility, chiding that, once again, 'you weare made up till at last you weare as much bewitched by her as ever'.[47] Periods of separation from Sarah aggravated Anne's over-possessiveness. On one occasion she went so far as to swoon, 'I cannot live without you, and thou I wish you and Mr Freeman [the Earl of Marlborough] everything your own harts can desire, you must not think, nor nobody els I am sure can, if it is reasonable for you to live out of ye world as long as I am in it.'[48]

Clearly Anne was in love with Sarah. This is not the same as asserting that she was her lover, for it is easy to be misled by the theatrical language in which she steeped herself or the level of physical intimacy that was at that time considered normal. As we shall see later on, Sarah muddied the waters by claiming that Anne did have lesbian tendencies but that they were played out not with her, but with Anne's eager-to-please and far more socially inferior maid, Abigail Masham. There was no code governing how royalty conducted its private life, merely precedent. It was common practice for kings and princes to have mistresses and even to father children by them without serious political ramifications. In this respect, the Duke of Monmouth's attempt to seize the throne was an exception – and based upon his doubtful claim to be the legitimate heir. The implications when queens and princesses behaved in the same way with the opposite sex were rather greater. Elizabeth I had perhaps come the closest to risking scandal, and many felt her close friendships with politically ambitious men like the Earl of Leicester were unwise, as she herself eventually came to accept. Her rival across the northern border, Mary Queen of Scots, had gone further – and contributed to her own undoing as a consequence. Neither these political problems nor the embarrassment of becoming pregnant existed in Anne's seeking companionship with a woman rather than a man. Unfortunately, in fixing upon Sarah as her confidante, Anne had fallen for a woman whose husband clearly did harbour high political ambitions which – in the eyes of his enemies – he planned to realise through his wife's hold over the heir to the throne. The success of Anne's and Sarah's relationship thus depended upon whether love and power could be prevented from cross-contamination.

The modern reader interprets a considerable amount into Anne's and Sarah's letters but the sapphic endearments that pepper the surviving correspondence mask the extent to which the two women continued to be tied by their mutual experiences and expectations as wives and mothers. Besides Henrietta (born in 1681) and Anne (in 1683), Sarah gave birth to one child a year between 1687 and 1690: Jack, Elizabeth, Mary and finally Charles (who died aged only two). For her part, Anne's almost perpetual state of pregnancy made her reliant upon Sarah's support. Inevitably these attempts to produce an heir for England took their toll on her health and added pounds onto her weight.

Between 1696 and 1700, Anne suffered a further five miscarriages. But at least by then she was a mother – for in July 1689 (nine days after Sarah's daughter Mary was born) Anne was delivered of a son: William, Duke of Gloucester. This birth caused much pleasure. And then, ominously, the first outpouring of joy started to give way to concern. Anne could not get him to breast-feed, and only after a long search in which applicants were given 5 guineas each for their troubles, was a woman discovered who could provide milk for the boy on whom the ultimate future of the house of Stuart's Protestant succession appeared to depend. It did not seem to matter that the wet-nurse in question, a Mrs Pack, was even by the unexacting standards of the time a woman of poor personal hygiene who was considered by one of the royal doctors to be more suitable for suckling duties in a pigsty than for a future king. Be that as it may, Mrs Pack played her part and, however weakly and feebly, the little boy clung on to life.

Despite naming her son William, Anne's production of an heir did nothing to bring her closer to her childless sister, Mary. The extent of their rift found expression in a sense of grief that Anne belatedly felt for their exiled father. Gone was the seemingly cavalier attitude with which she had abandoned him. Surrounded by his shadow court of equally washed-up exiles at the palace of St Germain, James had become a pathetic curiosity for visiting French aristocrats, some of whom doubtless concurred with the judgement of Madame de Lafayette that 'as one listens to him, one realises why he is here'.[49] In December 1691, Anne at last plucked up the courage to write to him. In her letter she expressed concern 'for the misfortune of your condition' and asked for forgiveness:

> as to what you may think I have contributed to it, if wishes could recall what is past, I had long since redeemed my fault. I am sensible it would have been a great relief to me if I could have found means to acquaint you earlier with my repentant thoughts, but I hope they may find the advantage of coming late, of being less suspected of insincerity than perhaps they would have been at any time before.[50]

What had brought about this change of heart? First and foremost, it was the slights Anne was enduring from her sister and brother-in-law. But the influence of her best friend and her husband was also at work – indeed she had written to her father at Marlborough's prompting for he was now wholly disillusioned with the new regime. William was treating him with the same contempt he meted out to the wheezing Prince George. Despite Marlborough's obvious abilities in the field, he had been brought into William's 1689 Irish campaign against James only after the land campaign had been largely won at the Boyne – although his subsequent work securing the Irish ports helped ensure there would be no Jacobite counter-attack. He had also served with William in the Low Countries offensives against Louis XIV, yet he felt cold-shouldered. He was one of many infuriated by the King's favouritism for his Dutch cronies over his English advisers, helping to organise a parliamentary petition against the employment of non-Britons in offices of state. This announced publicly Marlborough's opposition to the style of William's rule. In private he was going further and, via his family relations in attendance at the exiled Stuart court at St Germain, he signalled his desire to make amends to James for betraying him. James's illegitimate son, the Duke of Berwick, as Marlborough's nephew was one of these conduits of information while another was Sarah's Catholic sister, Frances, the lady of the Bedchamber to Mary of Modena. Despite Sarah's obvious aversion to popish ways, the fact that both she and her husband had such close relations in the enemy camp provided William and Mary with ammunition to attempt to rid Anne of Sarah's supposedly pernicious influence.

In 1692, Marlborough was stripped of his command and all his offices. Furious that Anne was giving Sarah £1,000 a year, Mary wrote to her, advising her to dispose of Sarah's services, not least because to fail to do so would keep Marlborough 'being where he ought not'.[51] Anne refused to listen to her sister's admonitions, protesting that she could not be separated from the woman she loved. This plea was met by an order from the Lord Chamberlain for Sarah's removal from the Cockpit. But if William thought that this one strike would cut the Churchills back down to size, he had not counted upon Anne's stubborn determination to stand by her friends. This took as public a form as Anne could muster. She deliberately showed her defiance by entering the Queen's presence at Kensington Palace with Sarah at her side, a direct breach of etiquette given that Sarah's husband was in disgrace.[52] Angrily, Mary wrote to Anne to assure her that the display had infuriated her and that 'I know what is due to me and expect to have it from you'.[53] She demanded that she drop Sarah immediately. Anne responded, 'you must needs be sensible enough of the kindness I have for my Lady Marlborough to know that a command from you to part with her must be the greatest mortification in the world to me, and indeed of such a nature as I might well have hoped your kindness to me would have always prevented'.[54]

Despite these brave words from her protector, Sarah reluctantly packed her trunks and departed the court, leaving Anne promising to seek her rehabilitation. She was staunch and unstinting in this cause, writing to assure Sarah that she would 'go to the utmost verge of the earth rather than live with such monsters'.[55] Sarah nevertheless felt she had no option but to offer her resignation as the Princess's lady of the Bedchamber. Anne would not hear of this and – according to Sarah – 'fell into the greatest passion of tenderness and weeping that is possible to imagine'. Such was her sense of loss that Anne's letters to Sarah at this time took on a hysterical air. In one, the Princess wrote that she 'had rathere live in a cottage with you then reinge

Empresse of the world without you'.[56] In the same vein, she also made plain that 'if you should ever do so cruel a thing as to leave me from that moment I shall never enjoy one quiet hour. And should you do it without asking my consent (which if I ever give you may I never see the face of heaven) I will shut myself up and never see the world more.'[57] William responded to the visible unhappiness of his sister-in-law with typical acts of pettiness, removing her guards from her and making sure she received no special favours. Even the printed text of the sermon was specifically omitted from her pew when she turned up to attend services in the Chapel at St James's Palace. Amid the lofty splendour of her family's palace, Anne was being made to feel the draught.

She had fled her father's Whitehall once in the dead of night; now she found herself taking her leave from her sister and brother-in-law. Her destination was not exactly a cottage but rather Syon House, not far from the Richmond nursery where her earliest childhood allegiances had been formed. There she was reunited with Sarah, the other orphan of court. At Syon on 17 April 1692 Anne gave birth. No sooner was the delivery complete than the baby – a boy – was pronounced dead. Within hours Mary was standing before a sister struggling to come to terms with the disappointment of losing a child and the discomforts of seventeenth-century gynaecology. But the Queen's opening command was not an inquiry into Anne's health or a heartfelt expression of sympathy. Instead, she had come to demand Sarah's expulsion: 'I have made the first step, by coming to you, and I now expect you should make the next by removing my Lady Marlborough.'[58] Anne said she would not sacrifice her companion, so Mary turned around and left. The two sisters would never meet again.

Arriving back in her palace, the Queen instructed all members of her court that they were on no account to visit the sick Princess. If they did, they would no longer be received at court. But Mary had a further card up her sleeve. At the time, William was away with his troops in the Low Countries and there was no let-up in his unpopularity at home. A Jacobite invasion force was gathering on the far side of the English Channel, poised to strike. James was planning on coming over with it, determined to oust his usurpative family from his throne. Goaded by her council of advisers, Mary's insecurities were played on and talk of a Jacobite revival was everywhere. On 4 May she sanctioned Marlborough's arrest at his London town house in Jermyn Street. Charged on suspicion of high treason, he was carted off to the dank incarceration of the Tower of London. Evidence of his further intriguing with James had been produced. Produced was the operative word, for it had been fabricated by a fraudster and placed in a flowerpot in the Bishop of

Rochester's palace (the initial failure to find the document did not prevent Marlborough's arrest, even before the supporting evidence had been located).

Marlborough's arrest put Anne in a desperately tight spot. Given the gravity of the charges, she could not possibly continue sheltering with the wife of a man detained on suspicion of treason. But nor would she forsake her friend, assuring Sarah, 'let them do what they please, nothing shall ever vex me, so I can have the satisfaction of seeing dear Mrs Freeman; and I swear I would live on bread and water, between four walls with her, without repining; for as long as you continue kind, nothing can ever be a real mortification to your faithful Mrs Morley, who wishes she may never enjoy a moment's happiness, in this world or the next, if ever she proves false to you'.[59] Anne was particularly distraught at the thought that Sarah might decide it was in her mistress's best interests for them to part: 'I hope in Christ you will never think more of leaving me, for I would be sacrificed to do you the least service, and nothing but death can ever make me part from you. For if it be possible, I am every day more and more yours.'[60]

As if the predicament of having a husband detained in the Tower facing the possible fate of a traitor was not enough, Sarah also had to cope with the sudden death of her youngest son, Charles. But this blow was followed by relief: the evidence against her husband was proved to be a forgery. 'Lord Marlborough had friends, who would bail him,' Sarah proclaimed, 'but that one of his best friends was a paper that lay upon the table, which I had often kissed, The Act of Habeas Corpus.'[61] As the Earl could not be held any longer in the absence of formal charges being made against him, he was released on 15 June and immediately went to join Sarah at Holywell.

Although the French invasion fleet's defeat at La Hogue reduced the state of national alarm, there was no sign of any court rehabilitation being offered to the Earl and Countess of Marlborough. For Sarah, exclusion from the vipers' nest of Whitehall had its compensations, as did the fact that she could now spend time with a husband whose soldiering career had until now so frequently carried him into harm's way. At last the two could be together and Marlborough kept himself busy supervising the transformation of the grounds around Holywell into formal gardens. In later years, when he was once again far away fighting in Europe, Marlborough found consolation in remembering these hours devoted to wife and garden, times when, away from the stresses and strains of war and intrigue, he would stand with Sarah at the perimeter of Holywell's grounds listening to the nightingales singing in the fields beyond.[62]

Anne, too, frequently made the journey up to St Albans, happy to enjoy the relaxed atmosphere of Holywell and excited to be able to spend time with Sarah. Putting the friendship before family, before indeed Crown and country, Anne remained as much *persona non grata* at court as did the Marlboroughs. Consequently she lived in reduced circumstances, lodging in a house off London's Piccadilly. Sarah also went to visit her there, and it was on one of these occasions that she received the news that her mother, old Mrs Jenyns, had suffered a stroke in her home up the road from Holywell. Sarah immediately raced back and Anne sent her doctors in pursuit. Hopeful the physicians might bring about a recovery, Anne kept up a daily dispatch of anxious letters, repeating her regular expression of self-abasement before her favourite: 'I hope in Christ your Mother will do well & am sorry with all my Soul I have this occasion to serve you. I have nothing more to say but beg my dear Mrs Freeman would always be so just as to beleeve I would go round ye world upon my baire knees to do her or hers ye least service & she may be assured ye least command from her shall be obeyed with all ye hast emaginable by your faithfull Morley.'[63] 'Serve you', 'obeyed', 'faithfull' – an unwitting interloper would not have realised that 'Morley' was the princess and 'Freeman' the lady-in-waiting. But not even royal physicians could save Sarah's mother. Worried that the stress could not be doing Sarah any good, Anne even offered to have the milk from an ass she kept in St James's Park sent up regularly to Holywell in the belief that Sarah would benefit from its supposed qualities. When all was over for Mrs Jenyns, Anne wrote in sympathy: 'I cannot see that you have any just cause to reproach your self for any thing. I am confident you never omitted ye least title of your duty to your Mother while she was living & in her sickness you have shown your self ye best & tenderest daughter that ever was.'[64]

Barred from court, not on speaking terms with her sister, rebuffed by her brother-in-law, her father mouldering away in embittered exile, her own mother long since in the grave, her movements monitored by the King's spies and with a well intentioned but largely invisible husband – was it any wonder that Anne threw herself into caring for Sarah and her family and that being with her, writing to her and awaiting her replies was the great comfort of her life? Sarah was not only a friend but a virtual lifeline in these times of otherwise deep unhappiness for Anne. Indeed, the tense stand-off with her own family might have continued indefinitely but for a sudden thunder clap that in December 1694 broke the stifling atmosphere: Mary was struck down with a sudden attack of smallpox. Anne's request to visit her sister's bedside was refused on medical grounds. On 28 December Mary died, aged thirty-two, leaving William to reign alone. He had not been the most constant husband, but the loss of his wife affected him deeply and, for a while, he was disconsolate. Certainly Anne grieved too – both for the loss of her sister and for the fact that there had been no formal reconciliation before the end. But Anne soon came to recognise that her sister's death presented an opportunity to try and patch up relations with her dismissive brother-in-law. The attempt met with a positive response and Anne was invited back to court and allowed to make the place of her birth, St James's Palace across the park from Whitehall, her home. In March 1695, William even received Marlborough for the first time since his arrest and before the year was out Sarah and John had been given rooms in the palace, on the south side overlooking St James's Park. The veil of suspicion had been lifted; if not in full favour, the Marlboroughs were at least tolerated back at court.

The King was gambling in deciding to give Marlborough a second chance. William was aware that during this time many of the most senior men in his adopted country were still paying into a political insurance fund by keeping in touch with James's exiled court at St Germain. While Marlborough was innocent of the trumped-up charges that had been brought against him in May 1692, he nonetheless shared the belief that the risk of continuing to correspond with his former master was less than the risk of not doing so. Propagandists and historians subsequently made much of this, suggesting that his supplying the Jacobite court with (already well known) information of a pending attack on the French naval base at Brest was tantamount to treason. If it was treason, James and his circle did not recognise it as such, for it seems St Germain did not think Marlborough's protestations of secret devotion amounted to much in practice. He was not entrusted with any of the plans to foment a Jacobite rising and when the Duke of Berwick made a secret trip to England in late 1695 to test the lie of the land, he made no effort to communicate with his nephew.

Marlborough's true position could probably best be described as one of constructive ambiguity. As far as William was concerned, the principal reason for re-engaging his talents was pure political expediency. Dutch commanders whom he had put in charge of Marlborough's soldiers had not proved up to the task. After years of mixed fortunes in which campaigning had been repeatedly bogged down in protracted sieges, peace was reached in 1697. But it was not a peace that was thought likely to endure. Marlborough was certainly the commander best able to prosecute the struggle when it resumed and, much as William did not care for Sarah's hold over Anne, the friendship of the next Queen with the wife of such a man could prove crucial. After all, the alternative to Marlborough playing an ascendant role after William's death was the possibility that Anne's uncle, Laurence Hyde, Earl of Rochester, would do so – and he was no supporter of the Continental commitment.

Thus it was so that, after all their mutual resentments and suspicions, the childless King William III finally found in John Churchill, Earl of Marlborough the surrogate for the son he had always been denied and the warrior who would continue his struggle against French domination in Europe.

While this brief moment of peace was used to prepare for the next war, the social life of the court continued to deteriorate. In 1697 one of William's Dutch chambermaids dried her laundry too close to a fire and accidentally caused Whitehall Palace to go up in flames. The fire quickly took hold of the medieval timbers that propped up so much of the artifice and when the smoke eventually cleared it was to reveal the charred ruins of the anterooms and painted galleries where generations of courtiers had fawned and frolicked. William seemed unmoved by the loss, for he had never much cared for the place and preferred Kensington Palace and Hampton Court where the air was better for his asthma. Whitehall's magnificent baroque Banqueting House had survived along with a number of the less impressive buildings, but William showed no interest in restoring the rest. Slowly but surely, the old court world drifted, diminished, elsewhere.

For all its *bijou* charm, Kensington Palace's lack of facilities provided William with an excuse to avoid the sort of large-scale plays and balls he so clearly hated. Even those events he could not escape depressed him and it was for these occasions that the widower King increasingly relied upon Anne to accompany him as a royal hostess. The rapprochement was not easy and suffered a number of setbacks: when in 1701 Anne learned the news from St Germain of her father's death she immediately put her household into mourning, only to have the order countermanded by William.[65] But, in other respects, William was unmistakably making the effort to build bridges with the successor he hoped would employ Marlborough to renew the struggle against France.

It was doubtless to ensure that the next generation continued to persevere with this obsession that William also chose to take an interest in the development of Anne's lone surviving child, the infant William, Duke of Gloucester. The King had made his mistress's sister, Barbara Lady Fitzharding, the boy's governess and, in June 1698 when the child was nine years old, he made Marlborough his governor. This was a notable honour, made more so by the King's expressed hope that the boy would learn much from his governor's character. But the little Prince's health was a cause for concern. His forehead bulged despite the efforts of doctors to lance what appears to have been water on the brain by sticking pins into his head to let the liquid ooze out. This did not enhance his looks and even his otherwise doting mother had to concede sadly that 'thou I love him very well, I cant bragg of his beauty'.[66] Because he seemed to have such difficulty getting back up whenever he fell down, there was a tendency to carry him everywhere. To Anne's consternation, Prince George seemed to be under the misapprehension that on these occasions slapping his son would help.

Desperately, Anne did everything she could for her weak child, taking him away over to Kensington in the hope that he would benefit from the better air. In her letters to Sarah, Anne would, with ominous frequency, refer to her son as 'my poor boy'. Doses of the prescribed quinine were making him queasy: 'My poor boy has vomited this afternoon' Anne confided to Sarah, 'whether it will prove anything or no God knows. However tis impossible to help being alarmed at every little thing'.[67] Bishop Burnet endeavoured to spend his three hours a day with the boy explaining 'to him the forms of government in every country' and acquainting him 'with all the great revolutions that had been in the world' on top of 'a copious account of the Greek & Roman histories & of Plutarch's Lives' before moving on to the intricacies of 'the Gothic constitution & the beneficiary & feudal laws'.[68] This apart, everything possible seems to have been done to give him a happy childhood. He was driven around in a child-sized coach drawn by miniature ponies. He also had a small gang of playmates, one of whom was Sarah's son, Jack, who was promoted to 'Lieutenant-General' of the nursery-yard army. Even the naturally undemonstrative King William was moved by the royal child's sweet nature; given his own trials with ill health, he perhaps warmed to a sickly little boy who enjoyed dressing up as a soldier to swap salutes with genuine guardsmen. But none of these enchantments of youth could keep smallpox from striking at the moment of its choosing. In July 1700, having just celebrated his eleventh birthday, the boy was taken seriously ill. For four days Anne kept a vigil at his bedside while he tossed and turned in a state of semi-delirious agony. On 30 July, just as Marlborough was rushing back to be with him, he died.

Anne was beside herself with grief. Shutting herself away, she refused to see any of her confidantes – with, of course, the sole exception of Sarah. When the Duke of Gloucester had been born in July 1689 he had been Anne's seventh attempt at producing an heir and she had proceeded to become pregnant another ten times. In the end, all seventeen increasingly fraught attempts at becoming a mother had ended only in desolation and despair. Amid the cares of a public life in turbulent times, this was the greatest grief to afflict Anne, a mother forced to endure the ordeal of outliving every single one of her children. It was a personal tragedy of immense proportions and if it intensified her more obvious characteristics – her stubbornness of will as well as the sustenance she gained from her devotion to the Church – then it was hardly surprising. Perhaps, as one of her biographers has suggested, the losses ensured that 'when she finally acceded to the throne, it was with the superior will of an invalid who has endured a full measure of suffering'.[69]

But was this how she herself viewed such trials? Anne was an intensely devout woman burdened by a guilty conscience. As the years had passed she had come to question her own role in ousting James from his anointed throne. Was her failure to produce an heir divine retribution for deserting her father? She had left him to the fate of the sad and lonely exile, betrayed by his own daughters, condemned to waste his last years as a seasonal attraction for carriage-loads of French aristocrats. The only action Anne could perform by way of recompense was to allow the throne to pass on her death to James's Catholic son and heir, James Francis Edward. But this threatened to reintroduce all the problems she wanted the country to leave behind: the Church of England 'in danger', unsuitable alliances abroad, perhaps an unrelenting attempt to reconvert the realm to its old religion. These she could never bring herself to allow.

While Anne attempted to come to terms with her grief for her lost son – for there could now be no prospect of any further children – the politicians weighed up what this meant for the long-term future of the succession. Anne's sorrows excited Jacobite hopes and in order to kill off such hopes forever, Parliament passed the 1701 Act of Settlement: after Anne's death, the throne would bypass the claims of James II's Catholic children in favour of the nearest Protestant relations to the house of Stuart. Anne, it seemed, would thus be succeeded by another woman, the Electress Sophia of Hanover, who was King James I's granddaughter. This was now the law, but what happened in practice would be anyone's guess.

The new century brought with it a crisis that would re-embroil Britain and most of Europe in war, for it was not just at home that the succession was the subject of alarm. The last Spanish Habsburg ruler had died and Louis XIV of France made evident his support for the claims of his own grandson to the Spanish throne and all the imperial riches in the Americas that came with it. This awesome prospect of French global predominance was sufficient to ensure that the great European coalition to prevent it was inexorably drawn back together. The War of the Spanish Succession was ready to begin. The British Army had been transformed by the experiences of the last decade into an increasingly effective fighting force and William entrusted Marlborough with the baton of command as well as making him ambassador-extraordinary to the Netherlands.

But William himself was not to live to see any more action. On 20 February 1702, with Europe back on the brink of war, he was badly thrown from his horse and his injury proved too much for his frail and exhausted body. When he died on 8 March – at fifty-one, the same age as the Earl of Marlborough – his kingdom passed to the woman he had until so late in the day disregarded. Anne had no direct experience in affairs of state and was physically weakened by her persistent attempts to become a mother, but she was forced to put realities behind her. As the heralds and town criers announced the succession of a new queen in all market places of England, Wales, Scotland and Ireland, Anne braced herself for a test far greater than any that she had faced as a princess. She knew upon whom she could lean for support.

THREE

Keeping the Key

Anne came to the throne ninety-nine years after England's Gloriana, Elizabeth I, had departed it. The intervening century had been one of conflict and division in which the house of Stuart had lurched from crisis to catastrophe and back. With her all-English tastes, Anne now had the chance of becoming a unifying figure: to be, and to be seen to be, the new Gloriana.

Three days after William's death, Anne stood before her Parliament. Time's passage – having chipped away at her health and vigour – had done nothing to dull her qualities as an actress. Most of all, she had retained the gift of a strong, clear, projecting voice. The assembled politicians were equally impressed with the content of her performance, not least her assurance that she would do all in her power to forward the country – 'As I know my heart to be entirely English'.[1] This was interpreted as a conscious snub to the memory of her late Dutch brother-in-law. No doubt it was, but it also echoed Elizabeth I's celebrated speech to her troops at Tilbury when she inspired them to resist the Spanish Armada with the assurance that she had 'the heart and stomach of a king, and of a king of England too'. Anne was crowned Queen on 23 April 1702 – St George's Day – magnificently made up like a bride arriving at the parish porch to celebrate her wedlock to the nation. Her hair, bouffanted-out with a wig 'of locks and puffs', glittered with inlaid diamonds which 'at the least motion brill'd and flamed'.[2] The weight of jewellery and make-up concealed the truth that the thirty-seven-year-old underneath it all was neither young nor fit. Nevertheless, having been carried through the streets to Westminster Abbey on a chair, she raised herself and stood upon reaching the great west door. She then proceeded at a stately pace, a small tidal wave of synchronised bowing from those on either side accompanying each step of her long walk up the aisle to her throne. The ceremony lasted five hours.

It was this ability to rise to the occasion that the childless Anne Stuart shared with the Virgin Queen. The comparison with the last, greatest ruler of the house of Tudor was explicitly made: Anne even appropriated for herself Elizabeth I's motto, *Semper Eadem*. She also readopted the old practice of a royal procession to Bath. On her first excursion there as Queen she approached the city in her carriage, accompanied on either side by a troupe of dancers, and on arrival was greeted by a welcoming party that comprised not only 'a fine Company of the Citizens, all clad like Grenadiers' but also 'about 200 Virgins richly attired, many of them like Amazons, with Bows and Arrows, and others with gilt Sceptres'.[3]

Vainly searching for the pleasures that once existed in the now ruined Whitehall Palace, the courtly cynics and self-seekers grumbled that court life no longer offered the low delights of Charles II's nights. In marked contrast, what Anne was trying to do was to bring the spectacle of monarchy to the plain-dealing people who stood up for her English prejudices and knelt with her Anglican devotions. Although she revoked the notion of divine right, she revived the tradition of attempting to heal sufferers from scrofula – the King's Evil – by allowing them to touch her. She told Sarah that she wanted 'to touch as many poor people as I can' and towards this objective she worked tirelessly. Such were the crowds of her lowest subjects pressing forward for her healing caress that it has been calculated that during the court season she often touched between two and four thousand people a week – one of whom was the boy who would later be famous to the world as Dr Samuel Johnson.[4] By way of overcoming her own failures to start a family, Anne projected herself as the mother of her people.

It was not that Anne saw her role as merely ceremonial: to comfort the lame, the halt and sick. No amount of family dysfunctionality could obviate the fact that she was a Stuart, and one whose mother was a member of the intensely political Hyde family. Indeed, when she was well enough to do so, she proved to be more diligent in the execution of her constitutional responsibilities as head of state and Supreme Governor of the Church of England than any of the Stuarts. An average day would start with morning chapel and would include a succession of meetings with government ministers and ambassadors as well as reading and signing numerous official documents. She attended Cabinet meetings twice a week (an attendance rate unmatched by any other British monarch, before or after) and also turned up at the House of Lords to listen when the subjects of debate interested her.[5]

The diplomacy of Elizabeth I had been a constant balancing act in which the Queen by evading her own betrothal to any of the Continent's imperial suitors had sought to prevent her realm becoming a pawn of the great European powers. While Anne was determined to continue William's life work of preventing French domination abroad, her primary task of statecraft was to avoid becoming the prisoner of either Whig or Tory faction at home. Lacking the formal rigidity that would later come to mark the party system, the factional tags were loose designations that embraced many shades of opinion and opportunism. Generally though, the two issues that meant most to Anne – the maintenance of the Anglican Church's rights and the prosecution of the war on the European continent – were those that marked the differences between Whig and Tory. The Tories were determined to uphold the Anglican supremacy while the Whigs were more enthusiastic backers of Marlborough's military campaigns on the Continent. Finding a balance of ministers, rather than being at the mercy of either party, was thus in the Queen's own interests. In his post as Lord Treasurer, Sidney Godolphin was the nearest to what would later be thought of as a prime minister. Like his friend and ally Marlborough, Godolphin hoped to avoid being categorised as belonging to either parliamentary faction and regarded his service to the Queen as predicated upon this state.

As far as Anne was concerned, Godolphin was the ideal choice. He and Marlborough became the driving forces in the new administration, the other portfolios being distributed between what Anne hoped would be a politically shrewd balance of Whigs and Tories. Always more partisan in her admiration for the Whigs, Sarah harboured doubts about this search for equipoise. Lacking Anne's belief that a strong Tory presence was necessary to shore up the security of the Church of England, she did not see the need to give them a foot in the door of government. But it was one of the seemingly more moderate Tories, Robert Harley, the Speaker of the House of Commons, who harboured yet greater political ambitions and whose machinations Sarah needed to watch particularly closely.

When Anne was not dealing with her male politicians – deciphering their true intentions, making use of their talents and their ability to deliver parliamentary majorities, trying to get them to overcome their mutual suspicions of one another – she spent her time with her ladies-in-waiting. Wherever possible this meant being with the one she elevated above all others, the woman whose husband would carry the weight of Britain's arms in the struggle for mastery of Europe. The freshly anointed Queen generously bestowed her gifts upon Sarah. As Groom of the Stole and Mistress of the Robes, Sarah held the two most senior offices of the Bedchamber. Her daughters, Henrietta and Anne, were made ladies of the Bedchamber. Sarah was also appointed Keeper of the Privy Purse, a position that allowed her to oversee the Queen's personal finances. Knowing how much Sarah liked the place, Anne even made her Ranger of Windsor Park, since 'anything that is of soe much satisfaction as this poor place seems to be to you, I would give my deare Mrs Freeman for all her days, which I pray God may be many and as truly happy as this world can make you'.[6] Sarah adored the house in

Windsor Great Park with which the sinecure came – an elegant lodge that until then had been the refuge of the late King William's favourite, Hans Bentinck, Earl of Portland.

Indeed, financially, both John and Sarah Churchill were now doing rather well out of their friendship with the new Queen. Along with the Order of the Garter, Anne had appointed Marlborough Captain-General of her forces and bestowed upon him the lucrative post of Master-General of the Ordnance. He was now in a position to draw a £60,000 income from his various offices.[7] Sarah's court offices brought in a sum approaching £6,000 a year. These salaries fructified in her own accounts, which she maintained entirely separately from those of her husband. Sarah also gained her own page boy, whom she selected solely because (as she later admitted) he was 'the handsomest Boy that ever I saw in my Life'.[8]

But Anne was bestowing upon Sarah more than the trinketry of wealth and titles. The symbol of the Groom of the Stole's office was a large gold key. On formal occasions, Sarah wore this emblem of her influence at her waist. It opened the door to the privy gardens, the galleries and state rooms of the palace. It opened the door to the Queen's bedchamber.[9] It meant not only that Sarah had unrestricted access to Anne but also that she was her gatekeeper, guarding admittance to others who wanted her ear. This had obvious political ramifications, especially when Anne was too tired or unwell to hold her normal round of state meetings. At times like these, the Queen remained cocooned in her private apartments with Sarah and a select few allowed to join her. It was little wonder this arrangement infuriated those politicians, and in particular those Tories, who had reason to fear what Sarah might be saying about them.

On the surface it seemed that both Anne and Sarah were locked in a partnership of power made impregnable because it suited them both so well. Yet, they needed to have a care, for although there was no shortage of precedents for friendships between monarchs and those of lower birth, the history of royal 'favourites' (as Sarah was perceived to be) meddling in high politics had few happy endings. In the fourteenth century King Edward III had greatly elevated the presence of women at the English court and even took one of his Queen's ladies, Alice Perrers, as his mistress. When his mental grasp had begun to falter, so the wily Alice's influence had tightened. She began to accrue estates and great wealth while using her position to browbeat the judiciary into disallowing legal challenges to her rapacious avarice. But even medieval England had a Parliament worthy of the name and in 1376 King Edward had been forced to banish her or lose a vote of revenue. The decision was subsequently reversed, but Alice's return to favour was brief.

Realising Parliament remained hostile to her and was awaiting its moment to strike again, Alice knew she was not safe without the King as protector. As he lay dying, she allegedly wrenched the rings from her royal lover's fingers and was already out of the palace grounds and heading out of the gaze of history by the time he breathed his last.

She was not the only royal favourite to generate intense resentment. Elizabeth I's relationships with ambitious men like the Earls of Leicester and Essex eventually went sour and in Essex's case ended on the scaffold. Charles II was always thought to be overly infatuated with his mistresses – and the foremost of these, the Duchess of Portsmouth, was certainly not averse to establishing her own font of political patronage, to the scarcely repressed fury of those outside it.

These, of course, were relationships with the opposite sex – relationships not just of friendship but of physical attraction – and in the case of mistresses, of consummated passion. Yet, those monarchs who, like Anne, sought companionship with their own sex fared no better. In some cases, this too strayed beyond friendship and into disaster, as did the doomed love between Edward II and Piers Gaveston. James I's favourite, the widely despised Duke of Buckingham, was murdered when his mismanagement of national affairs continued into the reign of Charles I. For his part, Charles I valued loyalty, but not of the mutually binding sort of which true friendship is made. Thus, when he felt it politically expedient to appease his most vociferous opponents, he allowed his right-hand man and Lord Lieutenant of Ireland, the Earl of Strafford, to be sent to the block. Strafford went, observing ruefully the folly of placing one's trust in the word of princes.

But the most compelling example was also the most recent: the extraordinarily close bond that had existed between the late King William and Hans Willem Bentinck. They had met in Holland in 1664 when the then Prince of Orange was fifteen and Bentinck, who was from a Dutch noble family, fourteen. William soon secured court positions for him and they quickly became virtually inseparable. Such was the strength of the bond that when William was struck down by smallpox and at death's door, Bentinck bravely chose to stay at his bedside for sixteen days and nights so that he too might contract the disease, hoping thereby to draw the potency of the fever away from William. It was certainly a selfless act and eventually Bentinck and William both recovered. When he became King in Britain, William granted Bentinck the earldom of Portland, showering him with gifts and properties with such extravagance that he became a subject of envy and loathing from the native-born Britons over whom he was elevated. Injudiciously, Bentinck made no attempt to conceal his general dislike of his adopted countrymen and Marlborough was at the forefront of the very public campaign to have him booted back to Holland: an intervention that further prejudiced the King's view of his most talented soldier. Marlborough's campaign singularly failed to poison the relationship: more than two hundred letters survive from William to Bentinck in which the depth of the King's feelings for him is transparent. Inevitably, Jacobites and others with an axe to grind quickly concluded that these intense feelings for the strikingly handsome Bentinck smacked of homosexuality. But in the end it was not the schemes and suppositions of outsiders and ill-wishers that brought about the rupture. Rather it was Bentinck's over-possessive and envious nature. He became insanely jealous when William began paying more attention to the amiable Arnold van Keppel, whom he ennobled as Earl of Albermarle. Incensed, Bentinck resigned his court offices and flounced off to Paris pursued by letters from William assuring him that he loved him no less just because he also cared for Keppel. Ultimately it was time that proved the great physician. As William lay dying he called for his old favourite to be with him. In the end, the two were together – as they had been in their youth facing united the onslaught of smallpox. The King's last act was to reach out for Bentinck's hand, placing it upon his heart where it remained as the beat gradually faded to nothing.

For Anne, the lessons of William's relationship with Bentinck should have been obvious. Whoever was the monarch's favourite inevitably would attract the odium of those who felt excluded. As Sarah put it, 'there were but few Women that would not have poysond me for the Happynesse they thought I enjoyed'. The excessive favour William had shown Bentinck had been hugely resented and it was ironic that it had been none other than Lord Marlborough who led the campaign to put a stop to it. Now it was Marlborough's power base that was being attributed to his wife's undue influence over the new Queen. This was the most obvious but by no means the only aspect of the William/Bentinck relationship which Anne and Sarah should have heeded. The intensity and longevity of Bentinck's devotion had been such that he proved unable to come to terms with the introduction of fresh competition. Might Sarah feel equally snubbed if Anne's attention began to wander towards another woman, especially one with rival political allegiances?

Indeed, if the fallout was spectacular enough, it could trigger a series of events that might lead not only to the resignation of Marlborough from his command but to Godolphin stepping down as Lord Treasurer, thus removing the bulwarks that prevented the Queen from becoming the prisoner of either Whig or Tory faction of politicians. After all, the Marlboroughs had established a deep and sincere friendship with Sidney Godolphin, who regarded himself as much Sarah's friend as he did her husband's, and when erroneous rumours spread that the two were rather more than friends, Sarah made it clear that she was the possession of no man and was quite capable of being alone with one without 'doing whatever can been thought infamous'.[10] Godolphin so trusted Sarah and valued her judgement that he used to let her read his official correspondence. That an eighteenth-century monarch's first minister entrusted his state business to the eyes of a non-royal woman – let alone one who was not even his wife – was in itself an extraordinary tribute to Sarah's abilities and *élan*. Anne very much approved of this government of friends and in her letters to Sarah she began to add touching comments about 'Mr Montgomery' – her pet name for the faithful Godolphin. 'Every day makes me more & more sensible of the great Blessing God Almighty has given me in three such Friends as your dear self, Mr Freeman & Mr Montgomery', Anne told Sarah, rejoicing that it was 'a happiness I believe no body in my sphere ever enjoy'd before'.[11] While the four stuck together, all would surely be well. But could a house of cards so constructed withstand the removal of any one element?

In 1702 such fears seemed needless, for the Churchills' fortunes had never looked more promising. Anne raised their titles from Earl and Countess to Duke and Duchess of Marlborough. A dukedom was the highest rank in the peerage, an extraordinary advance for a man who had been born in respectable obscurity. Sarah had also been busy dynasty-building. The Godolphin and Churchill families had already been formally brought together in 1698 when Sarah helped to arrange the marriage of her daughter Henrietta to Godolphin's son Francis. Anne gave the newlyweds a personal gift of £5,000. In 1700 the second of Sarah's four surviving daughters, Anne (who had, of course, been named in honour of her mother's friend and patron) had married another apparently up-and-coming politician of the age, Charles Spencer, soon to be 3rd Earl of Sunderland. Thus Althorp, the Spencers' estate, was added to the growing list of political salons that Sarah patronised.

In 1703 Sarah succeeded in determining the marriage of her then fifteen-year-old daughter, Elizabeth, to the future Duke of Bridgewater. Anne gave the couple £10,000. Two years later Sarah brought about another coup by marrying off her seventeen-year-old daughter, Mary, to the wealthy future Duke of Montagu. Despite Marlborough's hesitancy at arranging such a match (Sarah had first entered into negotiations for Mary's betrothal when the girl was only thirteen years old and her intended husband almost a year younger), Sarah believed she was sensibly ensuring her daughters' financial security. She was also securing the Churchills' political fortunes firmly among the great Whig families. Whatever her husband – who wanted to be the prisoner of no party – desired, his far more partisan wife was resolute in her belief that the Whigs were the only sure guardians of the nation's freedom and the defenders of the true interests of herself, her husband and family and – if only she knew what was good for her – the Queen as well.

Using her daughters as pawns in these arranged marriages contrasted with Sarah's more liberated views when it came to her own rights. She jealously guarded her financial independence from her husband and began to invest in high-risk schemes in which Godolphin often acted as her adviser and stockbroker. To Sarah, accumulating a fortune was almost as great a passion as her interest in government. She was even at first wary of accepting Anne's generous offer of raising Marlborough to a dukedom. Sarah felt that sustaining the obligations and lifestyle that such an exalted title demanded would require a huge income from the sort of landed estate that the family lacked and that this would eventually create an unsustainable burden for their descendants. It was these fears that led Sarah to press for the accompanying £5,000 pension to be continued for the Duke's heirs in perpetuity. Parliament thought otherwise. Anne tried to compensate for this blow by offering Sarah an additional £2,000 a year for the rest of her life out of her own funds. Anne wrote to Sarah with the offer 'for no body need know', hoping that Sarah would 'only comply with the desires of your poor unfortunate, faithful Morley, that loves you most tenderly and is with the sincerest passion imaginable yours'.[12] Sarah turned down her patron's kindness – only nine years later to reclaim the sum, plus interest. The motivation for Sarah's clumsy handling of the Queen's generosity also lay behind her intention to see her daughters married to those who could afford to keep them in the style to which they had become accustomed. Sarah was nothing if not worldly, and this gave her an abiding insecurity because of the transitory flicker of fame and fortune. She did not want her own children to suffer the embarrassing fate of her cousins, the Hills, whose hard times she helped to alleviate by feeding and clothing them and finding junior positions in the Queen's service so that they might avoid what would otherwise have been the path of destitution. Little did Sarah know that it was this act of charity towards distant relations, far more than her acts of avarice and ambition for her own children, that would, in time, come to rebound against her so spectacularly.

If, having lost all seventeen of her own children, Anne was jealous of Sarah's family, then she certainly avoided demonstrating the fact. Her possessiveness towards Sarah was designed to rid her of other women's affections, not as a means of keeping Sarah from her husband. For large parts of the next decade

Marlborough would be marching and bivouacking across the European continent. He corresponded with Sarah as regularly as eighteenth-century communications across a war-torn Europe allowed. It was more than apparent to them both that a stray musket ball could at any moment sever what the years had wrought together. When on 20 May 1702 Marlborough set sail from Margate for the Continent and the uncertain fate of warfare, Sarah stood on shore, watching the craft conveying him further and further out to sea. On board the ship, her fifty-two-year-old husband kept his telescope fixed on the lone figure standing on the cliffs, until the spot became a speck and the speck shrank beyond the reckoning of the strongest optics. These departures cut away at their married life together, but when reunited the emotions of deep passion immediately surfaced. The story of Marlborough returning from the wars to pleasure Sarah with his riding boots still on has outlived its provenance but there is little doubt that they enjoyed a stormy but passionate relationship. Once, in the midst of a blazing row, he tried to calm her by complimenting her on her tresses as she sat trying to brush her hair. Overwrought, Sarah picked up a pair of scissors, sheared off the tresses and flung them at him. Silently he picked them up from the floor and walked out of the room, leaving her to reflect upon her self-mutilated image in the mirror of her dressing table. Many years after his death, the aged Sarah opened a cabinet. Inside, her late husband had stored all the effects that meant most to him. There, most carefully laid out, was the severed tress of hair.

When tragedy struck at the heart of the Marlboroughs' family life, it was not via a messenger from a foreign battlefield but much closer to home. In February 1703, while a student at Cambridge University, their only son, Jack, caught smallpox. Alarmed, Sarah made haste to his bedside and Anne sent up her doctor to tend the boy. It was all in vain. Sarah was distraught. Temporarily back from the Continent, Marlborough was there to comfort her, and Godolphin, Jack's godfather, also came to share in the grief. Sarah was too overwrought to accept visits from others, including an offer from Anne. By common consent, Jack had been a charming young man and this is certainly an impression borne out by his surviving letters. Godolphin had high hopes for him and Jack once so touched Anne with a minuet he danced that she wrote to Sarah a line of congratulation: 'I realy do beleeve in time he will make a very fine dancer, therefore I hope you will encourage him in it'.[13] Instead he had been planning to accompany his father on his next military campaign when the fever had struck. Sarah wanted to be alone with her grief in Holywell and it took continual pleading from Anne to entice her to return to St James's Palace. Even then she did not feel up to making public appearances. The only sightings of her came from the boys of Westminster School, who could see her draped in black, wandering listlessly around the cloisters of the abbey, sharing it with the vagrants and vagabonds who took refuge there. Sarah's prolonged grief, at the age of forty-three, manifested itself in a series of phantom pregnancies. To Anne's alarm, Sarah was so unhappy that she even considered retiring from her position at court. Marlborough too, distracted by the tragedy and tired of continual Dutch interference with his war plans, was showing signs of wanting to resign his command. Depression and disillusion now threatened what had until so recently seemed to be an all-consuming ardour for power. With Godolphin also considering his future, Anne pleaded that she could not carry on without them. It was a letter of spirited eloquence from a Queen who realised how dependent she was on her friends:

> It is no wonder at all that people in your posts should be weary of the world, who are so continually troubled with all the hurry and impertinences of it; but give me leave to say you should a little consider your faithful friends and poor country, which must be ruined if ever you put your melancholy thoughts in execution. As for your poor, unfortunate, faithful Morley, she could not bear it; for if ever you should forsake me, I would have nothing more to do with the world, but make another abdication [a reference to her father's flight]; for what is a crown, when the support of it is gone? I never will forsake your dear self, Mr Freeman nor Mr Montgomery [Godolphin], but always be your constant and faithful friend, and we four must never part till death mows us down with his impartial hand.[14]

Anne had been looking out from a window seat in the gallery of Windsor Castle when she noticed the dust-covered horseman galloping at full tilt towards her. For eight days he had ridden across Europe to bring the news of deliverance on the battlefield of Blenheim. The message, hastily scribbled on the back of a bill from a tavern, was in the Duke of Marlborough's hand and carried the instruction to be given to the Queen to 'let her know her army has had a glorious victory. Monsr Tallard [the French commander] and two other generals are in my coach and I am following the rest.'[15] Anne burst into tears of relief and gratitude. It was the nation's first truly decisive victory on European soil since Henry V's archers had decimated the French knights at Agincourt almost two hundred and ninety years previously. In London, the bells pealed and Sarah was given the honour of accompanying Anne alone in the state coach to the service of thanksgiving in St Paul's Cathedral. For the last thirty years, the great baroque temple had been rising to Sir Christopher Wren's designs and as its completion – crowned with a mighty and controversial dome – drew near, its gigantic power conveyed national as much as spiritual potency. The captured French flags (128 ensigns and 34 standards) were processed through the streets of the City on their way to Westminster Hall. Meanwhile, at Versailles the atmosphere could not have been more different. So humbled by Marlborough's army was Louis XIV that he issued an edict banning all news of the battle. This was a very different Sun King to the one who had two years previously greeted Anne's declaration of war with the contemptuous quip that it meant he was 'growing old when ladies declare war on me'.

The victory could not have come at a better time. Marlborough had appreciated that with the French armies – supplemented by those of the Elector of Bavaria – threatening Vienna, the theatre of war had moved away from the Low Countries. It had been through an extraordinary feat of logistics that Marlborough had marched down into Bavaria, joined up with the Austrian army of Prince Eugene, and smashed the French forces on the Danube at Blenheim on 13 August 1704. It was a huge gamble, for his foray into the heart of Europe had been treated with the greatest scepticism by those Tories at Westminster whose enthusiasm for the venture knew very definite bounds. They had been preparing to mount a challenge in the expectation of his humiliation. What prices might they have extracted: relieving Marlborough of his command; forcing Anne to part with Sarah? The victory at Blenheim dispelled all that at a stroke, apparently vindicating the policy of Continental engagement in the War of the Spanish Succession, and giving the Queen fresh heart in placing her trust in the soldier Duke and her favourite Duchess.

In December Marlborough returned home. Already sharing with his wife title, riches and influence, the question of how he might be further rewarded for his services presented itself. The Holy Roman Emperor had given him the Bavarian principality of Mindelheim as a present for the victory at Blenheim. For Sarah, the thrill of becoming the new Princess of Mindelheim was marred by her failure to locate the pinprick on the map. Yet, however small the principality, it marked yet further elevation for England's most socially escalating couple. Anne felt that the crown estate near Woodstock in Oxfordshire was the very least she could bestow. It was where King Henry II had wooed the fair Rosamund, concealed from his watchful Queen in a hidden closet within a maze. It was also where the future Elizabeth I, at that stage the flame-haired princess of Protestant hopes, had been imprisoned on suspicion of intriguing against her Catholic elder sister.

The Churchills' palace – for it was to be a palace, not just a large house – would be built at the Queen's expense. It would be named after the Duke's great victory as a gift from a grateful nation. Fatally, no price was fixed, a fact that encouraged the architect, Sir John Vanbrugh, to indulge his theatrical taste in architectural monumentalism far beyond what Sarah had in mind. The estimate reached £100,000 before work had even started in earnest and as the years went by Sarah so fell out with Vanbrugh that it was his assistant, the no less capable Nicholas Hawksmoor, who ended up finishing much of the work. Yet, whatever bickering the building work caused, there could be no greater example of the fruits of a royal friendship set in stone. Blenheim Palace was a gigantic assertion of bombastic baroque, far removed from the feminine domestic style associated with the name 'Queen Anne'. Its ostentatious magnificence contrasted with the reduced circumstances that Anne accepted as her own lot: making do in London with the simpler royal residences at St James's and Kensington and refusing to rebuild the half-destroyed Whitehall Palace because of the expense it would involve. It was little wonder that so many of Westminster's parliamentarians were finding the Queen's infatuation with her favourite couple painful to behold.

For his part, dealing with battlefield realities had made Marlborough contemptuous of the posturing of Westminster's gentlemen politicians. The battle of Blenheim may have put an end to French hopes of outright victory but it did not settle the question of the Spanish succession and consequently it seemed certain the war would drag on, possibly for years. In November 1704 John wrote to Sarah expressing how little he shared her enthusiasm for entrusting his fate to the Whigs alone and affirming his determination to continue in command in order 'to leave a good name behind mee, in countrys that have heardly any blessing but that of not knowing the detested nams of Wigg and Torry'.[16]

The Tories had exploited their gains in the 1702 general election to push through the House of Commons a Bill ending Occasional Conformity – the practice whereby nonconformist Protestants could hold office by dint of the most infrequent of nods to the Anglican rites. Ever the Anglican fundamentalist, Anne even cajoled her husband (who as a Lutheran might be thought to have reason to support the conveniences of Occasional Conformity) to shuffle off to the House of Lords to vote to end the indulgence. While doing so he allegedly bumbled into a prominent opponent of the measure and stopped to confide in a whisper 'my heart is vid you'.[17] He need not have troubled his conscience for the Bill was defeated. The more extreme Tories reacted by sneakily trying to 'tack' it to a financial measure that was helping to pay for Marlborough's conduct of the war. Sarah canvassed Anne's views so hectoringly on the subject that the latter bit back, claiming she would stop writing to Sarah 'since everything I say is imputed either to partiality or being imposed upon by knaves and fools'.[18] Sarah responded that ''tis not possible to love you & your interest as I doe, & not say a great many things that I know (by sad experience) is uneasy to you'. She pleaded with Anne not to cast aside 'those that have given proofs that they would dye every hour in the day to serve you' by being dazzled by the self-seeking villains and closet Jacobites who masqueraded under the name of Tory.[19] These were strong words, but Sarah got her way and, in any case, the 'tack' was defeated in the Commons when even many Tories refused to support it.

The huffy tone of this correspondence between Anne and Sarah was an early sign that, even in the sunlit year of the victory at Blenheim, political differences were drifting in to cloud their relationship. When Anne had been a princess, Sarah had never encountered much resistance in giving Anne the benefit of her stridently pro-Whig interpretation of political developments. Instilling such opinions in Anne once she was Queen turned out to be another matter. Anne's self-confidence was developing fast due to the panorama she could now survey from the elevation of a throne. Sarah's failure to make allowance for rank or title, seeing it as her duty to address Anne 'without flattery or dissimulation',[20] had been a breath of fresh air to a princess who had felt herself the prisoner of her circumstances. Now that she was a more confident head of state, the fact that 'dear Mrs Freeman is sincerity itself' was losing its attraction. As Sarah's great descendant, Winston Churchill, was to summarise it, 'she sought to win by argument, voluble and vociferous, written and interminable, what had hitherto been the freehold property of love'.[21] Sarah's failure to adapt appropriately to this evolution led to a series of terrible misjudgements. She later wrote that 'the first important step, which her Majesty took, after her accession to the government, was against my wishes and inclination: I mean her throwing herself and her affairs almost entirely into the hands of the Tories'.[22] Undoubtedly, Sarah believed she was doing the Queen a favour by warning her of supposed evil intent lurking underneath the unctuous bowing of Tory politicians, but Anne had now gained sufficient confidence to trust her own judgement of men and measures. She did not believe that many of the Whig politicians were the high-minded patriots Sarah insisted they were, nor did she share Sarah's suspicions that all Tories were covert Jacobites, intent on treason. The Tories' more strident Anglicanism that pleased Anne meant little to Sarah, a woman who wore her religious conviction more lightly. 'I know the principles of the

Church of England, and I know those of the Whigs,' Anne had told Sarah in 1702, 'and it is that and no other reason which makes me think as I do of the last.'[23] Thus Sarah had been warned which patches to stay off. With breathtaking self-confidence she ignored the hint.

It was not just a question of diverging views on who should be in the government and who should not. Before she became Queen, Anne had depended upon Sarah firstly as a friend in what was so frequently a friendless environment; secondly as a spirited source of conversation and interpreter of the political world around her; and thirdly as an informal go-between with Godolphin and Marlborough. On ascending the throne, Anne had made these two men her principal political servants. Consequently, she no longer needed Sarah to act as intermediary on her behalf. All she really now wanted was for Sarah to revert to her primary role as devoted friend and companion and not to try and set herself up as an additional member of the administration.

At the time they had both shared in thanksgiving for the deliverance of Blenheim, Anne had complained to Sarah of 'the coldness you have used me with of late' while insisting that her love for her remained undimmed.[24] 'I am very sorry to find Mrs Morley and Mrs Freeman cannot yett bring things quite right,' Godolphin wrote to Sarah, 'I am sure they will doe it at last, and when this case happens betwixt people that love one another soe well, it is not impossible but that both may bee a little in the wrong.'[25] It was wise counsel, sensitively conveyed. Sarah, however, was becoming detached in manner and casual about the relationship. The great loss in her life was that of Jack, her son and heir, rather than the decreasing amount of time she spent in attendance to a gouty Queen who was losing her looks and figure. Although she was in her forties, Sarah was determined to have another child, and her failure to conceive (despite her repeated exercises in wishful thinking) was taking its toll on her mental and physical health. Anne was deeply concerned about Sarah's state but found herself shut out from her innermost affections, or, worse, the recipient of strident lectures on the business of politics. Time and again, she wrote to Sarah, volunteering to come and stay with her in her country retreat: 'do but name it [the date to meet] and I shall fly with joy to my dear Mrs Freeman'.[26] Sarah's replies, when they came at all, lacked the intimacy of old. 'I can't help being uneasy that you call me twice Majesty' was one of Anne's concerns after reading a letter from Sarah 'and not once mention your poor unfortunate faithful Morley.'[27]

Events at Westminster following the defeat of the 'tack' should have created an opportunity for Anne and Sarah to turn politics from a barrier to a bridge. No sooner had Anne lectured Sarah on the shortcomings of her Whig friends than she was to be hugely embarrassed by the antics of certain Tories. In Parliament the Tories proposed a motion to invite the house of Hanover – the Electress Sophia and her son George – to settle in England by way of acclimatisation for their likely succession upon Anne's demise. For her part, Anne did not like to be reminded of her failure to produce an heir. The last thing she wanted was to have her German relations decamping upon her, poking around the palace grounds and sizing up the dimensions of the royal bedchamber. The intended targets of the Tory motion were in fact Marlborough and Godolphin – for they would lose Whig support if they rejected the offer being made and would incur the Queen's displeasure if they supported it.

Like so many plans that are too clever by half, it backfired. When Anne arrived in the House of Lords to listen to the debate she was horrified by the tactless disregard of Tory speakers. When Lord Haversham insensitively referred to how secure Anne would have been on the throne if only her son the Duke of Gloucester had survived, she got up and walked out. When she had dried her eyes and recovered her composure sufficiently to return to the debating chamber, it was to hear the Duke of Buckingham (her childhood would-be sweetheart, Lord Mulgrave, who had survived the leaky boat to Tangier) raise the fear that 'the Queen might live till she did not know what she did and be like a child in the hands of others'.[28] These blundering manoeuvres were easily sidestepped by a brilliant countermeasure by the Whig Lord Somers in the shape of a Regency Bill. It invested Lord Justices with authority during the time it would take to bring the house of Hanover over to assume the throne. This settled the matter to Anne's liking and a thankful Queen wrote to Sarah, acknowledging the services done her by the Whigs of whom Sarah had always spoken so highly and admitting that she was at last 'marvellously convinced of the malice and insolence of them that you have always been speaking against'.[29]

Sarah particularly favoured the five most able Whig politicians: the Lords Wharton, Somers, Halifax, Orford and Sunderland, who were popularly known as the 'Junto' (from the Spanish word *junta* for council). Their hand was strengthened by Whig parliamentary gains in the 1705 general election and by Godolphin's desire that he should have their support in the great undertaking with which he was engaged: the Act of Union between Scotland and England. Since 1603, when the Scottish house of Stuart succeeded to the English throne upon the death of the childless Elizabeth I, the crowns of the two ancient kingdoms had been united. But their parliaments were not. There was still a strong whiff of Jacobitism north of the border and combined with anti-English sentiments heightened by the failure of the Darien Scheme (an ill-conceived and financially ruinous attempt to start a Scottish trading post in Panama), there was a clear danger that when Anne died the parliament in Edinburgh might declare her exiled half-brother, James Francis Edward Stuart, their King of Scots. They might even invite the French army over to secure the matter, placing the English realm under threat. After all, Louis XIV had recognised the Stuart 'Pretender' as King upon Anne's succession in 1702.

On personal grounds, Anne could not stand any of the Junto members. She even resisted Sarah's petitions to offer Sunderland (her son-in-law) one of the two positions of Secretary of State in the Cabinet. However, Anne recognised the Junto's importance to securing the Act of Union. The Aliens Act, which they sponsored, shut out Scottish trade and was designed to bludgeon the Scottish politicians into union. There were also no shortage of financial inducements (nationally and personally). In April 1706 negotiations for Union commenced, the Queen rising above another gout attack to attend; Junto Whigs were among the commissioners dispatched to bring off the deal. It was finally completed the following year. The United Kingdom was proclaimed, the greatest and most enduring legacy of the reign of Queen Anne.

But between Sarah and Anne, all was still not as it should have been. In August 1706 Sarah retired to her house in St Albans in order to escape any more court drudgery, writing to her mistress: 'Tho tis easy to see the great change in Your Majesty to me & that I have all the reason in the world to think when I am alone with you tis a great constraint to you, yet having lately received some little markes of kindnesse from you, I can't satisfy myself without waiting upon you, or telling you the reason why I don't do it.' The reason was that she felt that unless Sunderland was made Secretary of State, there was little hope of keeping Godolphin's administration in office. This was an honest assessment of the situation. But disastrously her letter ended by criticising the interference of her Tory brother-in-law, George Churchill, to which she hoped that 'Mr [Prince George] and Mrs Morley may see their errors as to this notion before it is too late; but considering how little impression any thing makes that comes from your faithful Freeman, I have troubled you too much, and I beg your pardon for it.'[30] Unfortunately, Sarah's handwriting was characteristically wild and careless and Anne read the word 'notion' as 'nation'. Consequently she was deeply offended by Sarah's lese-majesty in accusing her of 'errors as to this nation'. Unaware of the hurt that had been caused and feeling snubbed by Anne's failure to reply, Sarah then made matters worse by firing off another letter accusing the

Queen of showing 'great indifference and contempt' towards her for sending no answer to the original letter.[31]

When it was discovered why Anne had broken off communications, the hapless Godolphin was dispatched to broker peace between the two ladies. He tried to explain to Anne the nature of the mistaken letter 'a' (the original letter survives – and the 'o' does look ominously close to being an 'a'). Anne was somewhat mollified by this explanation and asked Sarah to call upon her at Windsor Castle. Sarah, however, had had enough of Anne's failure to follow her advice. Not only did she avoid her mistress, she wrote a note claiming that it was neither here nor there whether she had written 'notion' or 'nation', again berating her for not rushing to appoint Sunderland and making clear that 'I am not very like to trouble you again'.[32] Wearing an expression 'of stiffness and reservedness', Anne told Godolphin that Sarah's behaviour was 'very extraordinary' and when confronted again with whether she would follow Sarah's advice to appoint Sunderland, the Queen suddenly collapsed into 'a passion of weeping'.[33] Coldly, Sarah was to claim that if Anne really still loved her 'she would not have been displeased at the shap[e] of any of my fine letters'.[34]

Despite the devastating blow that Sarah's presumptuous behaviour had dealt her friendship with Anne, Godolphin continued to try and patch things up between the two of them, informing Sarah that at his audience with the Queen:

> I went onn to tell her that I knew very well all Mrs Freeman's complaints proceeded from having lost Mrs Morley's kindness unjustly, and her telling her truths which other people would not, to which she sayd, as she has don 40 times, how could she show her any more kindness than she did, when she would never come near her? I sayd she had tryed that severall times and complained it was always the same thing. Upon that she sayd, Mrs Freeman would grow warm somtimes, and then she herself could not help being warmer than she ought to bee, but that she was always ready to bee easy with Mrs Freeman.[35]

In later life, Sarah explained her conduct. She maintained that she had tried to be with Anne as much as possible. At the very least, it would not have been in her political interest to do otherwise. Anne might continue to write to Sarah to 'be assured when ever you will be the same to me as you was five years ago you shall find me the same tender, faithful Morley'.[36] But it was Anne's increasingly reserved nature whenever they did meet that made certain the demise of the old devotion. At the time Sarah did not know why. Only later would she discover that there was a betrayer in her midst. For the time being she remained in ignorance about the other woman in the Queen's life.

*

In May 1706 Marlborough hammered the French forces so decisively at the Battle of Ramillies that Antwerp, Ostend and Brussels soon fell as well, effectively delivering the Spanish Netherlands (modern Belgium) to the Allies. But for Dutch objections, he would have been made the Spanish Netherlands' Viceroy by the Holy Roman Emperor. For one as avaricious as Marlborough, being unable to accept the position was disappointing for it was worth £64,000 a year. However, at home his victory reaped a new reward. Having passed the Act of Settlement to secure the Protestant throne after the childless Anne's death, Parliament now stepped in to safeguard the future of Marlborough's dukedom in view of the fact that he no longer had a son to inherit it. Permission was thus given for the title to pass down through his daughters' line which would now – after all – be assisted with the £5,000 annual grant that Parliament had previously refused to countenance.

But for all Marlborough's stirring victories, the war appeared to be not much closer to being won – not if the Whigs' slogan of 'No Peace Without Spain' was to be honoured in full. True, the Allies' capture of Barcelona was a positive development, but a problem with trying to foist their favoured candidate, 'Charles III', on the Spanish throne was that the Spanish appeared not to want him. Indeed, the decisive victory of the French army under the Duke of Berwick at the battle of Almanza in April 1707 made the case for seeking a compromise all the more pressing. What was more, as surely as the long war continued to create widows, it drove higher prices and heavier taxes. It was not lost on the critics that while the pro-war Whigs' financier friends in the City seemed to be doing well out of the conflict, the rising tax burden was being felt most heavily by the predominantly Tory landed gentry and squirearchy.

Doubts spread as to whether Marlborough's Continental land strategy was the right one. It might suit his own talents and ego to go marching around Europe at the head of an army in search of a pitched battle to fight, but was this really the best use of British resources? Would it not be more sensible to pay Britain's European allies to do the fighting on the Continent, leaving Britain to pursue a self-interested maritime strategy of relieving the French King of his colonial possessions? The longer the land conflict dragged on without sign of resolution, the more attractive this policy sounded, although in truth the Royal Navy was already far more fully engaged than the 'blue water school', the exponents of using naval power alone, acknowledged. Other critics felt that Marlborough paid too much attention to the Low Countries when he should have been reinforcing the effort to wrest Spain from Bourbon control. To silence these mounting objections, it was in Spain that decisive victory was needed. The problem was that the Allies – the British, the Dutch, the Portuguese and the Holy Roman Empire – could not agree among themselves how best to bring this about or even what, short of the total humiliation of France, would actually constitute a final victory.

The political climate in London was similarly disturbed. Anne despised the ungodly disposition that she believed to be the common factor unifying the five Junto Whigs' private lives. For all his abilities, Lord Wharton – who had penned the words to *Lilli Burlero* – was a militant atheist, Kit-Kat Club rake and debauchee. But it was the Earl of Sunderland, the first of the Junto cabal to enter the Cabinet, whom Anne grew to detest most, a fact that could only damage in her eyes his mother-in-law, Sarah, Duchess of Marlborough. Anne had finally given in to the persistent petitioning and granted the antiquarian-book-collecting Sunderland one of the two Secretary of State posts in December 1706. His father had been one of the most unscrupulous politicians of his age but the son's ideological Whiggery was of such ferocity that to Anne it was virtually indecipherable from republicanism. Like his mother-in-law, Sunderland seemed unable to distinguish between the paths of honesty and rudeness, but he went further, never taking the trouble to disguise his low estimation of the Queen's abilities as head of state.

If nothing else, this was bad politics for there were ministers of potentially greater attraction to Her Majesty who were more skilful in their dissimulations. Two were particularly gaining prominence: the silken-tongued Secretary of State for War, Henry St John, and the second Secretary of State, Robert Harley. Having long since forsaken his early puritanism for what would eventually become an all-consuming devotion to the bottle, Harley had been Speaker of the House of Commons, and as a moderate Tory purporting to desire a government beyond faction, had trimmed sufficiently to enter the Queen's confidence. Seeking a way to find an endgame to the interminable Continental engagement and, in doing so, to oust Godolphin and the Duke and Duchess of Marlborough, Harley began to intrigue covertly against his fellow ministers. Marlborough had long benefited from having a wife who was Anne's first confidante. Harley wanted to find someone equally close who could influence the Queen's thinking in his direction. With this in mind, he set about befriending those in the royal Bedchamber whom he thought might prove to be subtle sources of influence: Samuel

Masham, one of Prince George's gentlemen of the Bedchamber, John Arbuthnot, Anne's doctor and a woman who worked in the Queen's bed-chamber, Abigail Hill.

'It was so long before I suspected I had a secret enemy that was under trust betraying me', Sarah later wrote, 'that it was past helping before I apprehended it.'[37] She might have expected that another woman of refine-ment, perhaps another senior lady-in-waiting at court, might try to form the sort of bond with the Queen that Sarah had so long enjoyed herself. There were both Tory and Whig sympathisers among the ladies of the Bedchamber and Sarah was always vigilant about how much time the Tory women were in attendance. But Sarah never imagined that while she watched out for the comings and goings of senior court ladies like the Duchess of Somerset, the real menace was quite literally kneeling at the Queen's feet.

It was back in the days when Sarah had been living in the Cockpit with the then Princess Anne that she had first learnt that she had a cousin by the name of Abigail Hill. Because Sarah's father had died when she was still a child of eight, she had not known – or had subsequently forgotten – that one of his twenty-one siblings had been married to a City financier who had proceeded to lose all his money in a failed speculation. Upon his death he left four children in destitution. Supposedly, they were virtually in rags. Despite her previous ignorance as to their existence, Sarah was touched by their plight and she decided to help these young cousins as best she could. The youngest girl, Alice Hill, was found a position as a laundress to the Duke of Gloucester. Of the two boys, Sarah clothed and educated the younger brother Jack, eventually getting him a position as a page of honour to Prince George and asked Godolphin to find a job for the elder boy in the Custom House. Abigail was the eldest of the four Hills. Sarah first took her into her own home, Holywell, finding for her things to do there and – if Sarah's own testimony is to be believed – 'she lived with me and my children, and I treated her with as great kindness, as if she had been my sister'.[38] It may even be true that she nursed Abigail through a potentially deadly attack of smallpox.

Like her sister and brothers, Abigail had every reason to be thankful to Sarah in her guise as Lady Bountiful. Yet, however readily they accept the offer at the time, recipients of charity can find the baggage of gratitude rather burdensome. This is particularly the case when they realise that they are expected to remain eternally in debt to their benefactor. It would not be difficult to imagine that Sarah's kindness was undermined in its recipient's eyes by the naturally bossy and overbearing manner in which it was doubtless expressed. If Sarah did indeed put up the pretence of treating the orphaned

Abigail as the equal of her own family, Abigail may have come to question why this foster mother arranged her own daughters' marriages into some of the most wealthy and influential families in England while continuing merely to make use of Abigail's domestic skills around the house. Did such a perception breed in Abigail a well concealed but deep-seated seam of resentment and jealousy? When in 1697 Sarah secured for her a position as one of Anne's Bedchamber women she thought she had done her young cousin a good turn, unaware that exposure to the Marlboroughs' opulent lifestyle might have already given Abigail ideas above this particular station. Women of the Bedchamber were far below ladies of the Bedchamber in the court pecking order, for their tasks were equivalent to those of personal maids. How different this was from the role of the Groom of the Stole and Mistress of the Robes. Sarah could embrace a Queen without it looking contrived. Abigail may have gazed up from the floor she had just scrubbed – the floor across which her more successful relation had just confidently stridden – and contemplated the day when she and the mighty Duchess of Marlborough might swap places.

If this was so, Sarah had no inkling of the hard intent lurking within the breast of the poor relation. Anne rarely mentioned her maidservant in her correspondence with Sarah so there was no reason to think much more about Abigail. Having established the girl's position, duty had been done. Doubtless, the usual solicitations were made whenever Sarah and Abigail bumped into one another, but this was likely to have been an increasingly infrequent occurrence as Sarah's absences from court lengthened from 1704 onwards. On one occasion Sarah had paid Anne a visit 'very privately by a secret Passage' in Windsor Castle. During the course of the tête-à-tête Abigail had 'unlockt the door in a loud familiar manner and was tripping across the room in a gay air, but upon seeing me she immediately stopped short and, acting a part like a player, dropped a grave curtsey when she had gone a good way without making any, and in a faint low voice cry'd, "Did your Majesty ring, pray?"'[39] At the time, Sarah had thought little about so slight an episode. Only later did something about the incident begin to bother her.

It was not until May 1707 that Sarah, writing to her husband who was again away with his troops in Europe, found she had cause to return to the subject of Abigail. It seemed the Queen was starting to rely on her for more than domestic chores and had taken a liking to her company. What was more, Sarah had become suspicious that Abigail was speaking favourably about Harley – even that Harley might be putting her up to promoting his cause in Anne's presence. It was possible, because by a strange coincidence Harley was also related to Abigail, being her second cousin on her deceased

father's side. When the Hill family had been destitute, Harley's helping hand
had been nowhere to be seen, but now that Sarah had found for Abigail a
position that involved regular contact with the Queen, she feared that
perhaps Harley had cynically decided to take a belated interest in his relation's
career development. If so, this had to be nipped in the bud.

In July 1707, Sarah sought an interview with the Queen at Windsor Castle.
She confronted Anne with her suspicions that she was being swayed by
Abigail and Harley. Denying that either exerted undue influence, Anne
effectively told Sarah to mind her own business and suggested that as
monarch she was capable of forming her own political judgements without
being the puppet of others – that she was no longer the sad and helpless
princess, in thrall to her tomboy girlfriend. Sarah left the castle less than
entirely convinced that the devious Secretary of State and the maidservant
were not in cahoots. Anne wrote to assure her that Abigail was nobody's
political tool: 'your Cousin Hill, who is very far from being an occassion of
feeding Mrs Morley in her passion, as you are pleased to call it, she never
meddling with any thing. I believe others that have been in her station in
former times have been tattling & very impertinent, but she is not at all of
that temper.'[40] But Sarah was not so sure. Doubtless acting on his wife's
suspicions, Marlborough was sufficiently concerned to write from his
command post sharing her concerns about the pernicious influence of what
he described in code as '256 [Abigail] and 208 [Harley]'. He believed the
time had come to make it clear to Anne that if she persisted with this
company, she would have to choose between it and his own continuation in
office.[41]

Had Sarah made more of an attempt to spend time with Anne at Kensington Palace and her other residences she would have realised how far
Abigail had already supplanted her in the Queen's affections, for the obliging
chambermaid was more than content to fill the void created by Sarah's
increasingly frequent absences. Like Bagehot's definition of the constitutional
monarch, Sarah had come to believe that her friendship with Anne brought
with it the right to be consulted, the right to encourage and the right to
warn. In short, she was no longer there just to keep Anne entertained. In
contrast, Abigail was both an accomplished harpsichordist and mimic. Laid
low by the concerns of her office and the disappointments of her personal
life, it is easy to see why Anne increasingly found Abigail's skills more
endearing than those of her long-established friend and mentor.

Fatally for Sarah, Anne deliberately chose to hide the extent to which
Abigail had become her boon companion. In mid 1707 she had attended
Abigail's marriage to Samuel Masham, one of Prince George's gentlemen of

the Bedchamber. Quiet ceremonies of this kind were common at the time (Sarah's own wedding had been equally low-key) but the decision to keep the marriage secret from the woman who had once been like a foster mother to the bride suggested there was something peculiar afoot. In her capacity as Keeper of the Privy Purse, Sarah was still scrutinising Anne's finances (to the latter's increasing irritation) and wanted to know to whom a present of 2,000 guineas had been given. The true answer was that it was Anne's wedding present to Abigail.

In September, Sarah first heard the rumours linking Abigail with Samuel Masham. When she approached Abigail and – by way of supposed friendly inquiry – asked if she planned to marry him, Abigail replied with unadorned candour that the wedding had already taken place. Biting back her fury at this lack of courtesy, Sarah offered to notify the Queen about her maid-servant's good news. At this suggestion, Abigail felt the need momentarily to scrutinise the ceiling before prevaricating that she thought the Queen had already been informed about it by another of her Bedchamber women. Sarah was naturally hurt at not having been told in advance of the wedding and chose to mention it to Anne when next she saw her. Unhelpfully, Anne admitted that she did indeed already know all about it and that she had repeatedly urged Abigail to tell her cousin but that she had refused.[42] It was the throwaway line, 'I have a hundred times bid Mrs Masham to tell it you and she would not' that gave the game away. A hundred times? So just how often were the Queen and her maidservant discussing matters, and Sarah in particular? And why had Abigail been so reluctant to tell the woman who had saved her from a life of provincial poverty?

The more Sarah mused over the matter, the more she felt the need to have her suspicions confirmed. She proceeded to gather the gossip of anyone and everyone she could find among the court staff to discover how long Abigail had been on terms of intimacy with Anne. The picture that emerged from these inquiries could not have been more alarming. It transpired that at least since 1704 Abigail's relationship with the Queen had been far more than that of a mere maidservant – in other words, from about the time that the first cracks in Sarah's friendship with Anne had begun to appear. Armed with this information, Sarah convinced herself that her own friendship with the Queen had not withered naturally on the vine, still less that it had been bludgeoned to death by her own imperious nature. Rather, she came to believe that she had been deliberately ousted by the cousin who owed her very position at court to her helpfulness in the first place.[43] Expressing the emotions of one who felt herself jilted, and aware of how singularly intense Anne's devotion could be, she began to suspect that the nature of Anne and Abigail's relationship had gone beyond the natural boundaries of friendship.

On each of the next few nights following her discovery of the extent of Abigail's involvement, Sarah called upon the Queen. Infuriatingly, whenever she eventually opened the door to leave, there in the ante-room already awaiting her departure was Abigail. The two rivals for the Queen's affection would curtsey formally to each other before, without any exchange of words, Sarah would brush past, passing Abigail a flinty look which, as Abigail described it to Harley, was 'not to be described by any mortal but her own self'.[44] After the summer at Windsor, the court returned to St James's Palace and it was there that Sarah requested an interview with Abigail who, for her part, was desperate to put off any such showdown. When it eventually took place, Sarah accused her of poisoning Anne's feelings towards her. Sarah later wrote that rather than answer directly, Abigail merely commented cuttingly 'that she was sure the Queen, who had loved me extremely, would always be very kind to me'.[45] This naturally infuriated Sarah: 'To see a woman whom I had raised out of the dust, put on such a superior air, and to hear her assure me, by way of consolation, that the Queen would be always very kind to me!'[46] It would have taken the character of a saint not to resent such a reversal of fortune and Sarah had never put store by the meek inheriting the earth.

Sarah wrote to Anne on 27 December 1707, 'If Mrs Morley has any remains of the tenderness she once professed for her faithful Freeman, I would beg she might be treated one of these two ways, either with the openness and confidence of a friend, as she was for twenty years; (for to pretend kindness without trust and openness of heart is a treatment for children, not friends).' If this proved too much, she suggested they could merely observe cold civility to one another as the minimum necessary for each of them to undertake their responsibilities.[47] But come what may, Sarah was determined to destroy Abigail. In the attempt, she ensured her own self-destruction, although she believed that pulling her punches would have equally fatal consequences.

The Duke and Duchess of Marlborough liked to reassure one another that what they most looked forward to was to quit their respective state obligations so that they could spend the rest of their lives together in quiet and comfortable retirement. This certainly contradicted the charge of their political enemies that their lust to stay at the forefront of the country's affairs was fuelling their determination to prolong the costly and seemingly unwinnable war on the continent of Europe. But both Marlboroughs continued to believe that the Queen's throne was in danger from the supporters of her usurped Catholic half-brother, backed by the French government with whom Marlborough was at war and the Jacobite sympathies that Sarah believed secretly animated Harley and the Tories in Britain. Such fears were in no sense hysterical. Through the winter of 1708, the French invasion fleet assembled at Dunkirk, ready to convey James Francis Edward Stuart across the Channel to reclaim his father's throne. In March it set sail with the twenty-year-old 'Pretender' on board. In Parliament, edgy legislators voted to suspend Habeas Corpus. Laws were reintroduced restricting the free movement of Catholics and those suspected of being inclined to aid and abet the invasion. Despite the previous year's Act of Union, Scotland was regarded with particular suspicion and Anne blocked a Scottish Militia Bill, fearing it would help recruit a force of Jacobites (this, incidentally, was the last time a British monarch vetoed an Act of Parliament). Indeed, Scotland was exactly where the invasion force was heading. The British fleet failed to intercept the Jacobite armada as it sailed towards its first target, Edinburgh. But, when the would-be invaders reached the mouth of the Firth of Forth and telescopes scanned the coast, none of the signs of support were visible. The wait proved disastrous, for it allowed Anne's fleet under Sir George Byng to locate its target. Forced to take evasive action, the Pretender's ships avoided being bottled up in the Firth of Forth only by setting sail again, first heading north before finally concluding that their only option was to turn around and head back to France.

Even before the Pretender's fleet had set sail, Godolphin had come to share Sarah's belief that Harley was trying to supplant him and that Anne would have to choose between her principal minister and his rival. If Godolphin resigned from the Treasury then Marlborough's prosecution of the war would be threatened. Yet, the spread of Harley's influence meant that Godolphin's power was already being undermined from within. Marlborough decided he must tell the Queen that he was not prepared to wash his hands of Godolphin who was, after all, his oldest friend in political life. Thus, if the Queen was content to lose her Lord Treasurer, she would also lose her military commander – in the middle of a war and with invasion imminent. To this, Sarah also played her hand by intimating that her husband's resignation would be followed by the relinquishment of her own court titles. At first, Anne seemed prepared to keep Harley even if it meant losing Godolphin, and Sarah's departure meanwhile would probably come as a relief. But the Godolphin-Marlborough house of cards had always stood firm because the Queen dared not remove the one card she feared would bring them all down – that of Marlborough. On 8 February 1708 Anne received a deputation. First came Godolphin, offering to resign. Then came Sarah, offering to resign. Finally, back from Flanders, came Marlborough, making the same submission. Most of all Anne felt she could not afford to lose her Captain-General, telling him that 'if you doe my Lord, resign your sword, let me tel you, you will run it through my head'.[48]

It was outside forces that eventually forced the Queen's hand. Harley's popularity – particularly following the damaging revelation that a clerk in his office had been channelling state papers to the French – had very shaky foundations in Westminster. When Harley attempted to speak at a meeting of the Privy Council which Anne held shortly after receiving the offers of resignation from Godolphin and the Marlboroughs, several of the other ministers, led by the Duke of Somerset, made clear they would not serve with him at the expense of Marlborough. Whereupon, the ministers promptly got up and walked out. The Commons rejected a Supply Bill as a mark of its disapproval of Harley. Even Prince George interceded with his wife, with some quiet words about the good of the nation. Thus, on 10 February 1708, it was Harley who was forced to resign the Secretaryship of State. Henry St John left with him, to be replaced as Secretary of War by an ambitious young Whig named Robert Walpole. Godolphin and the Marlboroughs had won a reprieve, however much their position now rested on support in Westminster rather than Kensington Palace.

Harley had gone and the Whigs were jubilant. In May, a general election further strengthened their Commons support and before the year was out Anne had reluctantly been forced to invite the Junto grandees Lords Somers and Wharton into her government. The *bon vivant* playwright and Whig MP, Arthur Maynwaring, effectively now acting as Sarah's secretary, was keen to foster a yet closer alliance between the Marlboroughs and the Junto, playing on a temporary tiff between Sarah and her husband in an attempt to get her to influence Marlborough's political allegiance more actively. The reality of the situation made such a move unavoidable, for Harley's intrigues and the Whigs' predominance had destroyed the notion that Godolphin and Marlborough could serve the Queen in an effective 'above party politics' capacity. But while Whig support for the war hardly placed onerous conditions on the Lord Treasurer and the General, Anne hated becoming the prisoner of a party – and particularly one of a Whig complexion. As a shy and unconfident princess, Anne had found in her 'Mrs Freeman' a force of nature who liberated her from the unloving company of her relations and surroundings. When she had become Queen, she had looked to 'Mr and Mrs Freeman' along with Godolphin – 'Mr Montgomery' – as the triumvirate who would prevent her from surrendering her rule to the dictates of a single political party. Now they had eventually thrown in their lot with the Whig faction and Anne desperately wanted to subvert the captivity into which this formation had thrown her. While Mrs Abigail Masham remained by her side, she retained the covert means of keeping channels open with Harley, the man who promised to keep parties at arm's length. It was little wonder that Sarah remained obsessed with the need to split up the Queen from her cleaner.

In June 1708 Marlborough beat the French at Oudenarde, another famous victory that allowed him to press on into French territory for the first time and in October to capture the great fortress city of Lille. But the laurels the Queen proffered to her brilliant General soon shrivelled on the vine, for in their mutually congratulatory correspondence, she took exception to his suggestion that she could only 'make . . . use' of the victory if she stuck with Godolphin 'who has been so long faithful to you; for any other advisers do but lead you into a labyrinth, to play their own game at your expence'.[49] Sarah too chose to stick a proverbial oar in, claiming that the royal court did not hold her husband in the esteem he deserved and decrying George Churchill's influence upon Prince George at the Admiralty.[50] In her annoyance, Anne mistook this reference to Sarah's hostile Tory brother-in-law for another swipe at Abigail. She wrote back requesting Sarah not to 'mention that person any more who you are pleased to call the object of my favour, for whatever character the malicious world may give her, I do assure you it will never have any weight with me, knowing she does not deserve it nor I can never change the good impression you once gave me of her'.[51] When Sarah wrote back to point out Anne's error of attribution, the Queen replied sarcastically that she would reply more fully when she had 'time to read it over & over againe before I begin to writt, for feare of making any more mistakes'.[52]

In any case, Sarah could not leave off the subject of her fixation. Even when complaining about her brother-in-law to Anne, she soon returned to denouncing the influence of the ungrateful cousin:

but I never thought her Edducation was such as to make her fitt company for a great queen. Many people have liked the humour of their chamber maids & have been very kind to them, but 'tis very uncommon to hold a private correspondence with them & put them upon the foot of a friend & support them in all things right or wrong to the mortifycation of one you had honoured soe long with your kindness & who never ded nor never will doe anything to deserve the change.[53]

This did not end the flow of reproaches. Anne pointedly made clear that 'I may love whom I please'.[54] Unable to contain her resentment at being supplanted, Sarah wrote on 26 July 1708 to contrast this statement: 'how much more easyly your Majesty talks now of this fine passion then you ded not long since; for when I first mentioned it you were pleased to tell me that in your life you had never been half an hour alone with Hill & disownd that you saw her but as a bedchamberwoman'. 'I took her from a broom', Sarah continued on a favourite theme, 'hoping the greatness of the obligations would have made her a faithfull servant to your Majesty & not unmindful of what she ow'd to Lord Marl: & me.' Instead she had betrayed her patrons, and would have been pleased to 'turn out Lord Marl:, for that was really the case, Madam, & will never be forgott; tho the necessity of your affairs & the discontents that were breaking out in both houses of Parliament obliged your Majesty to call him back to your Councill'.

Reminding her of the ridicule that Charles II had suffered because of his supposed subservience to his mistress, the Duchess of Portsmouth, Sarah warned Anne that she was making a fool of herself over her popsy – 'people will only laugh at a queen's forsaking her old servants for such a favorit' – and that Abigail would end up becoming the target of popular loathing. Sarah had already sent Anne a couple of ballads that were doing the rounds, one of which referred – among other innuendoes – to the Queen's 'dirty Chamber Maid' performing 'dark Deeds at Night' with her royal mistress. Sarah insisted that she was concerned only for Her Majesty's reputation 'after having discover'd so great a passion for such a woman, for sure there can bee noe great reputation in a thing so strange & unaccountable, to say noe more of it, nor can I think the having noe inclenation for any but of one's own sex is enough to maintain such a charecter as I wish may still be yours'.[55]

If Sarah wanted to regain the Queen of Great Britain's affections then reprimanding her for bedding her chambermaid was a bizarre form of flirtation. But Sarah could not hold back, incandescent as she was that the Queen who had for so many years expressed to her an undying devotion appeared now to prefer the company of 'a woman that I took out of a garrett'. Yet, even with this letter, full of accusation, reproach and hurt, Sarah appended to Anne a last and touching appeal for reconciliation:

I remember I have formerly desired your Majesty to burn my letters. Now I make it my humble request that you will please to lay this in your cabinit & I wish that all the notams that I have writt to you were there in hopes some accident or other, when I am dead, might make you remember me & think better of me then you doe att this time. Att least sooner or later it would shew that your Majesty had once a very true friend & a most faithfull servant.[56]

The Queen did not reply.

Such a breakdown made matters difficult when on 19 August, Sarah had to be given the honour of accompanying the Queen in her coach for the service of thanksgiving in St Paul's to commemorate the victory at Oudenarde. While the cheering crowds, shouting their exaltations, pressed close to the coach, slowing up its progress, Anne and Sarah – between acknowledging the warmth of the multitude – froze each other out. Sarah was peeved that the Queen had chosen not to wear the jewels she had laid out for her and assumed (despite the fact that Abigail was away in the country at the time) that this was the cursed Bedchamber woman's doing. When they got out of the coach to mount the steps to the cathedral, the untimely altercation continued. Anne's attempts to rebut the accusations that she did not give Marlborough the support he needed were cut off by Sarah who, warning her that she could be overheard by those assembling inside, hissed at her to 'be quiet!'. Insolence of this kind could not be easily forgiven. When, the following day, Sarah sent Anne a letter from Marlborough it was returned with the comment 'After the commands you gave me on the Thanksgiving day of not answering you, I should not have troubled you with these lines but to return the Duke of Marlborough's letter safe to your hands, and for the same reason do not say anything to that nor to yours which enclosed it.'[57]

It might be thought that this was the end. But no, for the following month (9 September 1708) Anne asked Sarah to join her at Windsor so they could talk over their differences. Anne expressed how much she 'shall think my self very happy if that meeting setts every thing right between us'.[58] That Anne still believed the wounded friendship could yet be healed by the balm of better understanding merely demonstrated that she did not perceive the nature of the wound. In Anne's eyes, the Duke and Duchess of Marlborough had little to grumble about. The Duke remained in command of Her Majesty's forces. Even if she should no longer consider herself an *éminence grise* politically, surely the Duchess could learn to live honourably with the titles and riches the Queen had been pleased to shower upon her and her family. Was not Blenheim Palace rising – at vast expense – in Oxfordshire? Could there be a greater proof of her position than that Anne had also permitted Sarah to build a huge town residence, Marlborough House, to Wren's design, next to the Queen's own St James's Palace in London? Could the Duchess point to any other subject in the kingdom who had been shown such favour? By comparison her gifts to Abigail had been decidedly parsimonious. Anne was in poor health, her weight sitting as heavily upon her frame as her realm's troubles on her mind. Was it beyond Sarah's imagination that having someone mentally undemanding but always on hand to provide a massage was exactly what attracted Anne to Abigail's company? Why could the imperious Duchess not accept that Abigail and Sarah occupied different compartments in the Queen's heart?

It is tempting to assume that Abigail had unwittingly become the object of Her Majesty's affections and was rather embarrassed by it – even that her espionage for Harley was a figment of Sarah's imagination. Had the *ménage à trois* truly been so uncomplicated, perhaps even Sarah might have accepted it. But Anne was deceiving herself first and foremost if she thought there was no more to it than that. She did not confide her political intentions to Abigail in the way that she had once sought to share her thoughts with Sarah, but Abigail nonetheless was a political operative, transmitting to Harley everything she managed to discern. Even if Sarah exaggerated it, her assumption that Abigail was conniving to poison Anne's view of the Marlboroughs in favour of their enemy Harley was basically correct. Anne herself could not have been oblivious to this fact. Perhaps Abigail did provide Anne with the relaxing company that Sarah had ceased to offer, but Abigail was not just a playmate, she was Harley's spy. Abigail was actively keeping Harley informed about court gossip, her letters using the code of 'my aunt' and 'Aunt Stephens' for the Queen and 'Lady Pye' for Sarah.[59] Trying to convince Anne that Marlborough was a potential threat, Abigail even took to calling the Duke 'King John' (as Sarah put it when she heard of it) 'in her nauseous bufooning way'.[60]

Sarah could hardly be blamed for not being prepared to share Anne's affections with an opponent of this kind. This is why Sarah was essentially right to insist that Anne had to choose between keeping her oldest friend and her new comfort – she could not have both. After all, if the friendship between the Queen and her chambermaid had been so innocuous, why had they both gone to such lengths in concealing it from Sarah? The problem was that for all Anne's attempts at bridge-building with her oldest companion, she had no intention of letting Abigail go.

Into this world of intrigue and insinuation, the Queen lost the other person for whom she felt a bond of affection. Prince George's health had been even worse than that of his wife. When Sarah received news that his end was approaching, she immediately set off to Kensington Palace to be of what service to Anne – who was tending George at his bedside – she could. His death on 28 October 1708 heralded a lengthy period of official mourning

which touched few profoundly other than the Queen herself. Sarah knelt by
the new widow, trying to express her condolences. But her insistence that
Anne would be better retiring to St James's Palace than remaining with the
body at Kensington was ill received, as was her failure to notify Abigail
Masham that Anne wanted to see her. When eventually Anne agreed to
Sarah's suggestion that it would be better to go to St James's, the two walked
out together, Anne leaning on Sarah's arm for support. Yet, even at this
solemn moment the spectre presented herself: Abigail was spotted making her
way along the long gallery towards them. Sarah recorded that the doomladen
Queen 'had strength enough to bend down towards Mrs Masham like a sail
and in passing by went some steps more than was necessary to be nearere
her, and when that cruel touch was over, of going by her with me, she turned
about in a little passage-room and gave orders about her dogs and strong-
box'.[61] The next few days proved to be a torture. Sarah and Abigail took
turns comforting the widow while – like warring ex-wives at the funeral of
a shared husband – trying to avoid each other's company.

During the spring of 1709, Louis XIV sent out peace-feelers. The terms were
not unreasonable: Louis would seek to persuade his grandson to vacate the
Spanish throne in return for him being given compensatory land in Italy.
The Spanish throne and the colonies that went with it would be transferred
to the Allies' candidate, Charles of Austria. There were still some issues left
unresolved, not least what would happen if the Bourbon claimant simply
refused to switch his possessions, but the Allied negotiators ensured that
any prospect for a proper truce was lost thanks to their obstinacy and
determination to see Louis humiliated. So the struggle continued. The Allied
forces of Marlborough and Prince Eugene moved into French territory. In
September 1709 they claimed victory on the field of Malplaquet. But the
bruising encounter had been won at unacceptable cost: the 20,000 or more
Allied losses (although only perhaps 2,000 of these were British troops)
significantly exceeded those sustained by the French. Victories of this kind
were not worth having. In Britain, unease about the war continued to mount.
    The courtly war of words was also no closer to abatement. At the end of
the month, Anne, cocooned within the protective confines of Windsor, was
subjected to a visit from her principal lady of the Bedchamber. For two
hours Sarah harangued her so loudly that footmen outside had no difficulty
following the discussion. It is not recorded what they made of Sarah's
repeated insinuation that the Queen was having an affair with Abigail, but

it embarrassed Anne sufficiently that she turned her head away from the light of the candle to conceal her profuse blushing.[62] Keen to terminate an interview which she found painful, Anne promised her jilted favourite that she would write her a letter explaining herself. Instead it was to Sarah's husband that Anne wrote: 'I believe nobody was ever so used by a friend as I have been by her ever since my coming to the Crown. I desire nothing but that she will leave off teasing and tormenting me, and behave herself with the decency she ought both to her friend and Queen, and this I hope you will make her do.'[63]

When Sarah eventually received a letter from her sovereign, its criticisms were so acute that she tore it up. She did, however, subsequently make a note of its contents: the attack on her rudeness, the weariness at the constant abusing of Abigail and the statement that 'it is impossible for you to recover my former kindness'.[64] Far from encouraging contrition, Sarah responded by telling Godolphin that 'I would not have more to doe with her then other ladys for all the treasure upon earth, but I will vex her so much as to convince even her stupid understanding that she has used me ill, & then let her shutt herself up with Mrs Masham.'[65] Another lengthy letter was drafted off to Anne, together with a digest of the latest pornography to be doing the rounds including 'stuff, not fit to be mentioned, of passions between women'.[66] With a lot to browse through, Anne postponed her reply.

Anne had indulged Sarah's rudeness for longer than was fitting, partly for the sake of honouring the public debt of friendship past but also because of the hard political reality of retaining the genius of the Duke's military command. But in the light of the blood and guts of Malplaquet, Marlborough's style of leadership looked increasingly like a vainglorious luxury. When he returned to London in November he found that the Queen who had previously been almost girlishly overawed by his manly talents was now intent upon pulling rank. Having been so long in the saddle, Marlborough believed he was better able to judge who was officer material than the Queen and was incandescent when Anne attempted to give Abigail's untested and not obviously talented brother Jack Hill command of a regiment. Repeatedly Marlborough tried to dissuade Anne from insisting upon such folly, to the point of making clear he would resign if Hill was given the command. It was only with the greatest reluctance that in January 1710 she was persuaded to give way on the matter. Later, however, she made Hill a general – and his subsequent incompetence in the abortive campaign against the French in Canada bore out not only everything Marlborough had said about him but also the pitfalls in believing that France would provide easy colonial pickings while bogged down in her own continent's war.

The Queen's new defiance of his advice prompted Marlborough towards misjudgement. He had been seeking to have his tenure confirmed in order to reassure the Continental Allies, but now he feared that under the influence of Abigail and her puppet-master, Harley, he might be stripped of his command just when he felt his presence was necessary to ensure outright victory. He thus pressed Anne to confirm him as Captain-General for life. However much this request was a consequence of his sense of vulnerability, Anne believed those who suggested it was a demonstration of the Duke's megalomania. Here was a General who assumed too much; here, it was argued, was a new Cromwell waiting for his chance, backed by his army, to become a dictator. What was more, Marlborough's Whig allies appeared to be threatening the Queen's prerogatives.

In January 1710 Whig politicians – encouraged by Sarah's 'secretary', Maynwaring – began to organise a parliamentary motion demanding Abigail's banishment from court. It was hardly a new tactic, for Marlborough himself had once backed similar calls to have William forcibly separated from his Dutch cronies just as the parliamentarians of the fourteenth century had united to see Edward III deprived of the comfort of Alice Perrers.[67] But as a princess, Anne had been prepared to accept ostracism from William and Mary rather than accede to their request that she should part with Sarah and she was not going to behave differently when overbearing Whig subjects told her to be shot of Abigail. She won the day by personally corralling influential peers and pleading with them – at the point of tears – not to vote for the parliamentary address. It was emotionally draining and rather degrading for the head of state to have to assert her prerogative to choose her own friends.

This Whig presumptuousness was about to take a fall. For, whatever the intrigues of Sarah and Maynwaring, the political climate was increasingly conducive to a recovery of Tory fortunes, a fact that well suited Anne. Tory squires resented shouldering the burden of the Land Tax that was paying for the war while the Whigs and their (sometimes non-Anglican) financier friends in the City appeared to be profiteering from the conflict's prolongation. But it was when the Whigs sought to impeach the Revd Dr Sacheverell that Tory discontent was accompanied by popular rioting. Sacheverell had delivered the offending sermon – 'In peril among false brethren' – as the guest preacher from the pulpit of St Paul's Cathedral on the anniversary of the Gunpowder Plot and its subsequent publication necessitated a huge print run. It appeared to date the country's moral decline to the people's taking up arms against the anointed King, James II. Sacheverell's trial commenced at the end of February 1710 in the same Westminster Hall where James II's father, Charles I, had been sentenced to death in circumstances equally sacrilegious to the High Tory mind. On each day of the three-week trial, Anne turned up to watch proceedings from behind a screened box in the crammed spectators' gallery. As a Tory zealot, Sacheverell could scarcely lose. Acquittal would have been vindication, whereas a guilty verdict would instantly show that a corrupt Whig establishment was trying to silence a man of God. When sentencing came, he was found guilty. But the leniency of the sentence – a three-year ban on preaching – was not much of a condemnation. The popular reaction suggested that it was the Whigs who would soon be on trial.

It was an inauspicious time for Sarah to seek to tackle Anne again. In light of how she had spoken to Anne at Windsor, Sarah extraordinarily demanded another audience, on the pretext of refuting gossip she believed was being spread about what she had been saying behind the Queen's back. Despite Anne's attempts to avoid another unseemly confrontation, on 6 April 1710 Sarah turned up at Kensington Palace regardless. When Anne tried to leave the room, telling her to put her complaints in writing, Sarah merely advanced to block her exit. Between her tears, Sarah protested her innocence and claimed, even, that she could no more verbally abuse the Queen than kill her own children. This certainly demonstrated how high she placed the threshold for what constituted verbal abuse. She also repeated her claim that she had only ever offered critical advice because she believed it to be in Her Majesty's best interests, which is what marked her out as a friend rather than a sycophant. Anne had heard all this sort of thing too many times before and when Sarah demanded to know what other gossip had been spread against her, she fell back on Sarah's initial assurance that she need not answer. Sarah pleaded with the Queen to speak, but was met only with the stony response 'you desired no answer and you shall have none'. Sarah tried again, and again was rebuffed with 'you desired no answer and you shall have none'. A third attempt hit the same brick wall. Realising that further perseverance would be fruitless, Sarah turned to leave, but not before shooting a parting volley of abuse, informing Anne that 'she would suffer in this world or the next for so much inhumanity'. Anne had the last words: 'that would be to herself'.[68]

As the Duchess banged the door shut behind her, Anne must have thought that was the end of it, although some moments later there was a knock. Anne opened it to find a deflated Sarah standing back in the doorway. She had been on her way out of the palace and, on stopping to dry her eyes and regain her composure, had decided to turn back for one last assurance. She wanted Anne's word that she would not humiliate her in public and that, in return, she would avoid being at Windsor at the same time as her. However appalled that Sarah should dare to show her face again after the exchange that had just taken place, Anne recognised the element of pity and she gave Sarah her word. Upon this, Sarah bowed and was gone. The Queen ensured that they would never meet again.

Sensing that the national mood was turning against the Whigs in the government, and with Abigail as an intermediary with Harley, Anne could now plan her escape from the incarceration of her ministers. First, the Duke of Shrewsbury gained a seat in the government. Next, the Queen started to steel herself to remove Sarah's son-in-law, Sunderland, as Secretary of State. In June 1710, Sarah wrote to Anne, ostensibly to reassure her that Abigail would not be the subject of a parliamentary petition. Sarah, however, was incapable of leaving the matter there, and instead rambled on to warn that Abigail would become a source of trouble if the Whig ministers were dismissed. She also mentioned, in a somewhat suggestive fashion akin to blackmail, that she had kept all the letters the Queen had written to her in the headier days of their friendship.[69] Anne's reply, drafted – ominously – by Harley, announced that:

> Having had assurances from your self & the Duke of Marlborough just before he went into Holland that you would never speake to me of Politicks, nor mention Mashams name again, I was very much surprised att receiving a long letter upon both, but I shall trouble you with a very short answer, looking upon it as a continuation of the ill usage I have so often met with which shews me what I am to expect for the future.[70]

Anne also asked for all the letters she had ever written to Sarah to be returned to her. Sarah refused to hand them over. They were, she no doubt thought, her insurance policy against Anne choosing to have her publicly disgraced and her political allies dismissed. The Queen, after all, would not want her self-debasing professions of love to her first lady of the Bedchamber to end up as a sure-fire best-seller.

At the same time as these final threatening letters were being sent, Anne sacked Sunderland and in doing so wrote to Godolphin that she was delighted to be rid of the 'obnoxious' politician whom she had never wanted in the first place. Now she no longer cared if 'it is true, indeed, that the turning a son-in-law out of his office may be a mortification to the Duke of Marl-borough; but must the fate of Europe depend on that?'[71] There had until quite recently been a time when the mortification of the Duke of Marl-borough seemed to matter rather more. But Anne was now emboldened by a far greater degree of political certainty: Godolphin must go. The Lord

Treasurer had served her honestly and well throughout her reign, but he was increasingly obstinate in the face of what Anne wanted and was, in any case, in Harley's way. Anne had directly and indirectly tried to get him to renounce his friendship with Sarah, but he refused to sunder a bond tightened by years of collaboration and by the ties of his son's marriage to her daughter. Aware of the rumours circulating about his impending sacking, on 7 August Godolphin asked Anne personally to make her intentions towards him clear. Hating awkward conversations, Anne told him, in a moment of cowardice, that he continued to have her confidence. The following day a lowly groom from the royal stables arrived at Godolphin's home to inform him that he had been sacked. The request, dated 7 August, instructed him to snap his staff of office in half so that he would not have to trouble Anne by bringing it to her in person.

It was a shabby way to part with the man who had been her principal minister throughout her reign and with whom she had benefited from a loyal association that stretched back to her days as a bewildered princess. He was never paid the £4,000 a year pension Anne had promised him in her letter of dismissal and – having devoted rather more time to the nation's finances than to his own – the last two years of his life were eased only with the charity of his brother's estate. Anne, it seems, did have qualms about what she had done but her actions were now governed by what she saw as urgent necessity – to bring back Harley and to end the war. In October 1708 the changed political temperature was confirmed by the Tories' winning a landslide victory in the general election on such a scale that, if anything, it acted to thwart Harley's attempts at non-partisan administration. But the key element was that, both in the executive and the lower house of the legislature, the Whigs had been purged of their power. If a negotiated peace with France was to be achieved, it was necessary to oust the embodiment of the war party, the Duke of Marlborough, from his command and to strip his troublemaking wife of the court positions she (albeit *in absentia*) was keen to keep.

Although she retained some affection for the Duke, Anne was ready to humiliate Sarah in public. To be fair, this was the same motivation that lay behind Sarah's threat to publish Anne's personal letters. Anne conceded that the proposed publication, in a compendium ominously entitled *The History of Mrs Morley,* could be damaging. She told her doctor, Sir David Hamilton, that 'when People are fond of one another, they say many things, however indifferent they would not desire the world to know'.[72] But compromise she would not. Instead, it only further increased the Queen's hatred of the woman for whom she had once promised to 'go to the utmost verge of the earth' so that they might not be parted. With Sarah's threat to publish looming, a pre-emptive strike was launched to destroy her reputation first. Thinly disguised accusations by Jonathan Swift appeared in the pro-Harley *Examiner*. They insinuated that in her role as the Keeper of the Queen's Privy Purse, Sarah had embezzled £22,000. Although Sarah's first thought was to bring forward publication of her correspondence in order to clear herself of these charges, she decided, on reflection, that it would be better to retain her court positions by promising not to publish the letters. Anne, however, was not playing that game. In January 1711 it was made clear to Marlborough, back in London, that Sarah's resignation from court was the price the new administration demanded for retaining his services in the field. The deal was non-negotiable – for it was the Queen's settled will.

Friends offered their counsel: the cause of winning the war for the Allies could not be served by the Duke and Duchess choosing to go down together if, by sacrificing herself, Sarah might be able to secure the survival of her husband's command. Sarah was distraught at the effect the strain was having on Marlborough, writing to Anne that he 'cannot live six months, if there is not some end put to his sufferings on my account'.[73] Although Sarah prepared herself for the relinquishment of her position, one last attempt was made to appeal to the Queen's old affections. On 17 January, Marlborough personally delivered a letter from his wife, written at his own instigation, in which she apologised unreservedly for her past behaviour and promised future good conduct. Anne's heart could no longer be moved by such protestations. Instead, Marlborough had to leave asking for a fortnight's grace in which to persuade his wife to jump before she was given the push. Even this request was denied. Anne demanded that Sarah's gold key of office – the key to the bedchamber – be returned within three days. When, the next day, Marlborough tried to discuss military business with the Queen she refused to hear him until he had brought Sarah's key with him. Anne now wanted her pound of flesh in full, and the formal return of the key would adequately symbolise her haughty subject's submission to her. Sadly Marlborough reported the state of affairs to his wife. There was no way out. On the evening of 18 January, he placed the gold key back into the hand of the sovereign. So ended the more than thirty-year relationship between Sarah Churchill and Anne Stuart. The Duchess of Somerset was appointed the new Groom of the Stole and first lady of the Bedchamber. Anne gave Sarah's other office, the Keeper of the Privy Purse, to Mrs Abigail Masham.

Could Sarah's sacrifice yet save her husband? In March the hidden hand of the assassin almost upset everything when, arraigned before the Council, a deranged French refugee with a financial grudge against the British government, for whom he had once spied, lunged at Harley with a knife. Standing close by, Henry St John and the Duke of Ormonde drew their swords and cut the assassin down but not before the less than sprightly Harley had been stabbed in the frenzied attack. For a while his life hung by a thread – almost literally, since it was the depth of his waistcoat's over-elaborate embroidery that had cushioned the dagger's impact. Anne was deeply upset by the incident (she had had a private audience with the Frenchman only the day before he made his attack) and while Harley recuperated she made him Lord Treasurer and elevated him to the House of Lords as the Earl of Oxford and Mortimer.

Slowly but surely he recovered his strength and with it his determination to use his enhanced authority to foreclose on Marlborough's war effort once and for all. The difficulty was that, at last, Marlborough actually appeared to be on the verge of delivering what he had so long promised. With Prince Eugene, he had got through the supposedly impregnable French lines and would be in a position to march on Paris in the new year. The war could be won. But Harley (or rather Oxford, as he was now styled) not only opposed waiting that long with all its attendant risks. He simply did not want the war wound up the Marlborough way, for he could see no gain in replacing the Continental supremacy of the Bourbons with that of the Habsburgs. Far better, reasoned Oxford, for a negotiated peace to create a balance of power, particularly if Britain could gain some commercial and colonial advantages for herself in the process.

To this effect, secret informal negotiations were opened with the French behind the Allies' backs. Thus, with the Queen's blessing, the British government was committing men and matériel under Marlborough's command to fight with the Allies while negotiating with the French a deal that would leave the said alliance high and dry. But this was only the less subtle aspect of the intricate betrayal; for the wily old Oxford was thinking one step ahead with a commitment to *realpolitik* that would have made Bismarck blush. Anne was visibly ailing and would not last for ever – or, more important, for as long as Oxford wanted to remain in power. But the Act of Settlement determined that on her demise the throne would pass to the house of Hanover, who were among the most committed of the German electorates on the Allied side. They were a family unlikely to be forgiving to a politician who had just double-crossed them. Here was a difficulty. Oxford thought hard, cast around, and saw a way out. Compared to saving his own skin, what was the sanctity of a mere political expedient like the Act of Settlement? Behind the Queen's back, he allowed discreet feelers to be sent out to James Francis Edward Stuart, Anne's Catholic half-brother at St Germain, encouraging him to think purposefully about what steps he should take to reassure the British political establishment come the day when the proclamation was read out announcing that the Queen was dead.

Unaware of this second line of subterfuge, Anne was now sure of the rightness of the advice she was receiving – advice to end the war and sack Marlborough. He had led his men across the battlefields of Europe but he could not defeat the campaign of whispers and accusations by his enemies at home. The Commission of Public Accounts charged him with accepting bribes from the army's contracted bakers and for pocketing the 2.5 per cent sundry expenses payments made by the Allies to cover the army's intelligence work. Marlborough had his own reply to these trumped-up allegations, but it was drowned in the howls of outrage whipped up against him. At Oxford's prompting, in November 1711 Jonathan Swift's pen was employed to prove mightier than Marlborough's sword. His *The Conduct of the Allies* repeated and enlarged upon the familiar accusation that Marlborough and his confederates were seeking to prolong the war because of the private profits they were making from it. It was a corpus of falsehood pumped into life through a very narrow vein of half-truth and it sold more than eleven thousand copies in its first month alone.

In the fame and riches it brought, none could deny that Marlborough had had a good war. But he had risked all by it and for it. Throughout the years which his accusers had whiled away, scribbling and squabbling and drinking themselves to the verge of oblivion, Marlborough had occupied himself in the discomfort of the saddle, risking life and limb, within range of musket shot and cannon ball, in the service of a Queen who now turned her back upon him just when he seemed most confident of completing the task she had bestowed upon him. By comparison, what service had her new chosen intimates performed to justify her favour? Yet, as one historian has written: 'there was an ironic symmetry between the beginning and the end of Marlborough's career. As he owed his first upward steps to greatness to his skills as a young courtier, so it was as a discarded courtier, not an unsuccessful general, that he lost his offices.'[74] Armed with the accusations of profiteering, Anne had her excuse. At the start of her reign, Parliament had voted that Marlborough had 'retrieved the ancient honour and glory of the English nation'. As the years went by he had proceeded only to add to that claim, ensuring that posterity remembered the name of Queen Anne not just for the Act of Union and a comely doll's house aesthetic of architecture.

The parliamentary manoeuvres that preshadowed the Duke's removal could not have been more squalid. The Whigs formed an expedient and unholy alliance with the High Tories, conceding the repeal of Occasional

Conformity in return for a House of Lords vote blocking Oxford's proposed peace terms with France. This tawdry bargain was outmanoeuvred when, taking the list of names drawn up for her by Oxford, Anne simply regained her administration's majority in the Upper Chamber by creating twelve new peers. There were peerages for Oxford's son-in-law and his cousin. Another of those Anne elevated to the House of Lords was Abigail's husband, Samuel Masham. The Bedchamber woman was Lady Masham at last.

The list of creations was published on 31 December 1711, along with the official announcement that the Duke of Marlborough had been sacked. When he received the Queen's personal letter of dismissal it was so mean in spirit that he threw it on to the fire.[75] Well might he have reflected upon the words of the Earl of Strafford, the loyal favourite of Charles I, as he learnt he had been forsaken for political expediency and faced the scaffold: 'put not your trust in princes nor in the sons of men, for in them there is no salvation'. Nor in princesses either.

FOUR

The Spoils of Ruined People

No affectionate letter from the Queen or service in St Paul's marked the commemoration of Blenheim Day on 13 August 1712. With building work frequently diverted or suspended altogether, the great and ruinously expensive retirement home of Blenheim Palace remained incomplete. Instead, the Duke and Duchess of Marlborough celebrated the anniversary of the great victory in a marquee erected in the grounds of Holywell House. The pitched canvas was tailored from the magnificent tent the Duke had taken with him on his campaigns. Enterprising as ever, he chose to cash in on the exercise by charging locals 6d each to look round it before the people of quality arrived.[1] But the latter guests were fewer than in previous years. And within a short time, many of the mainstays were no more. In September, Godolphin died while on a visit to Holywell. A couple of months later Maynwaring too, was gone.

There was little reason for the Marlboroughs to linger in England. There seemed no escape from the snubs and insults delivered to them, the accusations levelled in the press and, for a while, even the possibility of politically motivated impeachment proceedings being initiated as a result of the trumped-up peculation charges. When they announced their wish to retire to the Continent the government made no move to block them, being thankful to see what it hoped would be the last of them. At the end of November, Marlborough travelled down to Dover and, a few days later, when the sails of the packet boat were unfurled, he was cast off across the Channel, a voluntary exile. As had been prearranged, Sarah followed him in the new year, wearily confessing that 'I really long as much to bee out of this horrid countrey as I used to doe to come into it'.[2]

Their progress through Europe was slowed down by Sarah's ostentatiously heavy luggage train but more especially by the lavish entertainment laid on for them by the towns and estates through which they passed. From Frankfurt they eventually reached their own Bavarian principality of Mindelheim, the Holy Roman Emperor's gift in gratitude for the deliverance at Blenheim. The locals of Mindelheim were friendly and Sarah liked her pocket realm. It was easy to understand why she confided to her husband's business manager that she was beginning to 'think the whole world is but a sort of a popit shew'.[3] But there was a limit to taking salutes and attending banquets. For all its charm, Mindelheim was a scale model of a state and, as such, emphasised how the mighty Marlboroughs had been cut down to size.

Indeed, by the time Marlborough took the first salute from the guard at Mindelheim, Oxford and St John (who had been elevated to the title of Viscount Bolingbroke) had already extricated Britain from the war. What was more, the Treaty of Utrecht, signed on 31 March 1713, had been reached on terms which were highly advantageous to Britain's self-interest. On top of gaining territories of strategic significance like Newfoundland and Hudson Bay in Canada, Gibraltar and Minorca, Britain was also offered fresh commercial concessions including control of the Spanish-American slave trade. For what his word was worth, Louis XIV at last agreed to mumble his recognition of Anne and Parliament's choice of her successors as the legitimate authority in Britain. Whigs grumbled about the worth of these baubles compared to sacrificing the greater goal of smashing French Continental power. But such complaints were confounded when the Bourbon Philip of Spain voluntarily renounced any future claim to the throne of France. The intended Allied strategy of putting an Austrian Habsburg on the Spanish throne may have been dropped but the substance of the old slogan 'no peace without Spain' had effectively been achieved. Oxford and Bolingbroke had pulled off a diplomatic triumph in every sense other than the perfidious manner in which it had been negotiated.

In the eyes of her (now former) German-speaking allies, Britain had simply cut and run. That she had taken other allies like the Dutch with her only made the betrayal worse. The Emperor's first thought was to fight on – a tactic that was quickly exposed as counter-productive. Anne's rapidly failing health could not be ignored and with it the fear that upon her death either Oxford or Bolingbroke would secure the British throne for the pro-French Stuart Pretender. In this eventuality, the Grand Alliance would indeed have been strategically disadvantaged by what had been agreed at Utrecht. Almost from the moment he had arrived on the Continent, Marlborough had tried to shore up the Allies' resistance to Oxford's and Bolingbroke's machinations. At the same time he sought from the Jacobite court at St Germain an assurance that – if the Stuart Pretender was restored on Anne's death – there would be no retribution for his having betrayed the Pretender's father, James II, and having fought so tenaciously against his protector, the King of France. Since Marlborough's enemies had almost succeeded in impeaching him while he had still been in Britain, it was not unreasonable to assume that they would strip the Duke and Duchess of Marlborough of all their worldly goods and titles as soon as King James III found London worth a Mass. Nonetheless, seeking such an insurance policy rather undermined Marlborough's moral superiority about Oxford's and Bolingbroke's dealings with St Germain – and it is not clear that he let Sarah into the extent of his correspondence. But the evidence does suggest (as the Duke of Berwick always suspected) that Marlborough was playing a double game with the Pretender. He forwarded such information about Jacobite plans as he was able to glean from the exchanges straight back to the Hanoverian Whigs in London.[4]

Marlborough was right to fear a Jacobite restoration and hawkish in the plans he devised to prevent it. Anne's refusal to allow any members of the house of Hanover to reside in Britain while she lived created the real possibility that with help in London, the Jacobite Pretender might reclaim his realm before the Protestant Hanoverians could get anywhere near a Channel port. Marlborough tried to convince the Allies of the need to contemplate a pre-emptive strike, landing troops as William of Orange had done in 1688, ousting the crypto-Jacobites from power in London and thereby making Anne's last days secure for the continuation of the Protestant succession. But it was one thing to act in this way to redress a Jacobite coup that had already taken place, quite another – as was forcefully made clear to Marlborough – while Anne was still on the throne, however much she might be the captive of her treacherous ministers. If only she would rise above her situation, dismiss Oxford and send for Marlborough, her realm might be secured peacefully and without bloodshed. Could anything be said or done to encourage her to put aside her vendetta against the Duke and Duchess who had served her so long?

In March 1714 terrible news reached the exiles – their daughter Elizabeth had died of smallpox. Sarah was deeply upset. Marlborough was devastated, crashing his head against the marble fireplace upon which he was leaning with such force that he collapsed to the ground temporarily unconscious. Having lost their son and heir, now they had lost their favourite daughter. Enough was enough. The Duke decided the time had come to write a letter to the woman who knew most about the pain of losing children. He sat down and began his letter to the Queen.

Riddled with pains, swathed in plasters, frequently too lame to walk, Anne lay almost incapacitated by illness but still incarcerated by her office. She was infrequently seen in public (she had been too ill to attend the celebrations staged for the signing of the Peace of Utrecht) and her face had to be caked in heavy make-up to conceal its worn state. Whom could she trust? She had rid herself of Sarah's carping forthrightness only to find no greater peace in the deceitful obsequiousness of those who now pressed close to her. She distrusted Bolingbroke, not least because his private life bore no discernible relationship to his public evocation of the High Church cause. But she was also losing patience with Oxford. Lifelong adeptness at the art of dissimulation, combined with the effects of the bottle, were making him increasingly incomprehensible. The Queen struggled to understand a straight sentence from him. She knew she did not have long left. She did not have time for this sort of prevarication. What was clear – for they were even bickering in her presence – was how much the Lord Treasurer and the Secretary of State had come to hate one another. Bolingbroke could see how Oxford's grip was slipping and was determined to replace him in time to manipulate the system with a flood of his own appointees, thereby forestalling a Whig recovery when the Hanoverians arrived in Britain. He knew he had to strike quickly and gain Anne's confidence, and he had identified the woman he thought could smooth his passage.

It was thanks to Oxford that Abigail had become Lady Masham. Indeed when he had first suggested making Samuel Masham a peer, Anne had been uneasy about it, telling the Earl of Dartmouth that she 'never had any design to make a great lady' of Abigail 'and should lose a useful servant about her person: for it would give offence to have a peeress lie upon the floor, and do several other inferior offices'. She consented to the elevation 'upon condition she remained a dresser and did as she used to do'.[5] How very different was the language of equality with which Anne had formerly embraced the Sarah Churchill it had been her pleasure to make a Duchess. But perhaps this was the point: she wanted Abigail to be near her as a companion and nurse, not to develop haughty notions as the titled Sarah had proceeded to do. If so, Anne misread the extent of Abigail's aspirations, ambitions which encouraged her to shed feelings of gratitude to her second cousin Oxford as surely as she had rid herself of the claims of her first cousin Sarah.

The disenchantment had started as early as 1711 when the Lord Treasurer's grip on reality was still strong enough for him to regard with derision the notion of putting Abigail's inexperienced brother in charge of that year's abortive invasion of French Canada. Sensing Abigail's displeasure, Bolingbroke had seen his chance and rushed to support the ridiculous appointment. Reports that Oxford had laughed when he heard of the hash Abigail's sibling had proceeded to make of the operation can only have further damaged his credit with her, a damage for which the subsequent peerage failed to make repair. At any rate, Abigail believed in her ability to forecast political share prices. Oxford's value was depreciating fast while Bolingbroke looked like a shrewd investment. And for his part, Bolingbroke knew Lady Masham's price, siphoning off for her both *bona fides* and downright illegal earnings from the South Sea trade.[6] By the time Oxford realised the extent to which he had been duped by the all-knowing Bedchamber lady, it was too late. An attempt to get Anne to patch things up between them in July 1714 ended in ignominious embarrassment for all concerned.

Surrounded by these intrigues, life was becoming a torment to Anne. It was a consequence of her character, her sex and her physical infirmity that she seemed always to be trying – and never quite succeeding – in her quest to break free from being the hostage of her senior ministers. Whether they be Whig or Tory, supposed friend or assumed foe, she always seemed to be trapped by them. Just as, as a blushing girl, she had sought to escape the prying attentions of her guardians by getting her playmates to run errands with her emotionally manipulative *billets-doux* to her nursery sweethearts, likewise as a disappointed queen she entrusted her closest servants with the passage of secret correspondence behind the backs of her official ministers. But could she even trust her personal servants anymore? Abigail, once so helpful in arranging assignations with Harley, had graduated into playing her own game, for she appeared not only to be Bolingbroke's agent of influence but was also rumoured to be prepared to assist the Earl of Mar, stalwart of the Jacobite cause.[7] Anne was even beginning to wonder whether Abigail was, in fact, spying on her.[8] Unsure who was working for whom, in July 1714 Anne instructed her physician, Sir David Hamilton, to initiate covert diplomatic exchanges with the court of Hanover. With death almost upon her she had, it seemed, finally decided to secure the succession. What she did not know was that Hamilton had already been briefing Hanover on her health, using as an intermediary a newly arrived German composer in London by the name of Handel.

The carefully laid plans of Oxford and Bolingbroke had seemingly gone awry, as both were disappointed by their separate dealings with the Jacobite Pretender. All they had wanted was for him to renounce – at any rate publicly – the Roman Catholic faith, so that upon his half-sister's death he could reclaim his father's throne. But he would not. He was a Stuart, no more inclined to have politicians dictate his religious faith than Anne would have been. Westminster's politicians would have to accept him on his terms, or none at all. And thus, it was the latter. With the prospect of the coronation of James III receding, Oxford and Bolingbroke desperately scrambled to rebuild their shattered credit with the electoral family of Hanover. Both independently contacted Marlborough. Suddenly they needed him.

The self-exiled couple had by this time retraced their steps to the Low Countries, setting themselves up in Antwerp – within striking distance of the passage back across the Channel. Sarah was homesick, but there was also the realisation that as events in London approached an endgame, it would be ill advised to be out of reach. Which of the two warring ministers, Oxford or Bolingbroke, they should side with was a difficult decision in view of Sarah's assessment that 'there were never two falser villans'.[9] Marlborough's price was their ability to secure the Hanoverian succession. Oxford said he could oblige, but his claims to leadership of the necessary coalition were undermined by the revelation that the story he had told the Whigs that he was behind the campaign to let Hanover's Electoral Prince take up his seat in the House of Lords was a lie. Meanwhile, rumours spread that Bolingbroke had succeeded in cutting a deal with Marlborough and that the Duke would soon be returning to England, restored to all his offices.[10] With a last throw of the dice, Oxford accused Bolingbroke of embezzlement, claiming indeed that both the Secretary of State and Abigail were illegally profiting from the Asiento slave contract under the Treaty of Utrecht. But this salvo came too late to save Oxford. On 27 July the dying Queen plucked up the energy to sack her Lord Treasurer. Before departing her presence, Oxford warned his sovereign that on no account should she recall the Marlboroughs.

For two days, the Lord Treasurer's stick of office lay unclaimed. It was in the Queen's gift, and as she lay on her deathbed, attended by Abigail and surrounded by her anxious Privy Counsellors, her life could now be counted in hours. Bolingbroke desperately wanted the office. But she did not gesture for him to step forward. The politicians caballed and conspired as the power vacuum grew. Why was Anne delaying her announcement? Who had she in mind? It was known that she had accepted the Duke of Marlborough's letter, written to her after his daughter Elizabeth's death. But what had it said and had the Queen replied? Now she was barely *compos mentis,* drifting in and out of a coma. According to one set of reports, as life ebbed from her body she would momentarily return to consciousness and ask whether Marlborough had reached London yet before slipping away again, only to awake, ask the same question and doze back off.[11]

The answer to the Queen's inquiry was that the Duke and Duchess of Marlborough were frantically trying to get to London as quickly as possible but were kicking their heels out in Ostend, waiting for the sea to calm and the wind to change in the right direction to carry them back. At last it changed, but it did so just too late, for Anne could hold on no longer. She finally caved into the pressure of her Council around her by placing the Lord

Treasurer's stick in the safe hand of the Duke of Shrewsbury. Emergency measures were put into operation in case the Pretender should land. Her head shaved like a convict and her skin blistered from the hot irons applied to it, Anne died in the morning of 1 August 1714, utterly worn out. She was forty-nine. In the view of one of her doctors, 'sleep was never more welcome to a weary traveller than death was to her'.[12] John and Sarah Churchill caught sight of the White Cliffs of Dover the following morning.

Crowds turned out to cheer the Duke and Duchess of Marlborough upon their entry into London. The following month, the Elector of Hanover stepped ashore as King George I of Great Britain and Ireland, assuring the Duke who was there to greet him that he very much hoped his troubles were now at an end. The Whigs were triumphant, the Tories ruined. Lord Dorset cheekily introduced Oxford to the new King with the words 'Here is the Earl of Oxford, of whom your Majesty must have heard.'[13] Fearing impeachment, Bolingbroke fled the country and proceeded – briefly but damningly – to serve the Pretender as his Secretary of State. Crypto-Jacobites left behind at first opted to lie low. One of those who crowded into Westminster Abbey for George I's coronation was Lady Dorchester, who – as the former Katherine Sedley – had once been the mistress of James II and intended wife of the young John Churchill. When the Archbishop went round the throne, demanding the 'Consent of the People', she turned to Lady Cowper who was standing behind her and said, 'Does the old Fool think that Anybody here will say No to his Question, when there are so many drawn swords?'[14]

One who did not hang around to seek favour at the new court was Lady Masham. Unlike more aristocratic ladies at court, her personal credit and financial security were buried with the sole person in whom they had been invested. Anne had died without signing a will and Abigail was thus unable to enjoy the material munificence that Sarah had stored up from the years which she and her husband had passed in the service of the state. It was said that as Anne had lain dying, Abigail had left her bedside 'for three hours to go and ransack for things at St James's' Palace'.[15] Abigail lived out George I's reign in obscure retirement with her husband at their house, Langley, in Buckinghamshire, receding from the public stage as unobtrusively as she had first crept towards it. She died in 1734, a largely forgotten figure. After she had gone, her husband sold Langley. The builders and craftsmen arrived, and the Mashams' residence was transformed out of all recognition behind a façade more to the liking of its new owner, Sarah's son-in-law, Charles, third Duke of Marlborough.

For her own part, Sarah had no desire to return to court. In any case the question of who would be the new Queen's lady of the Bedchamber did not arise – the charmless George having long since divorced his Sophia Dorothea and locked her up in a far-off fortress. Sarah's sons-in-law, however, all received handsome offices from the new regime and her daughter, Mary, Duchess of Montagu, was appointed lady-in-waiting to the Princess of Wales. Conscious of her husband's faltering health, Sarah hoped he would now be left to enjoy retirement, but the King offered him back his old position, Captain-General of the Army, and Marlborough felt obliged to accept. His days in active command, nonetheless, were over, and when in 1715 the fruitless Jacobite insurrection was launched in Scotland, Marlborough was not asked to march towards the sound of the guns. The time had come for others to win their laurels.

And so the British people escaped being ruled by a monarch who did not share their religion by persevering with one who did not speak their language. This, of course, was a state of affairs that well suited the Whig politicians; indeed, it well suited parliamentary government itself. Never easily contented, it was not long before Sarah found fresh reasons to gripe about those in power. Her son-in-law, Lord Sunderland, became Prime Minister, but her arguments with him reached such an intensity that he maliciously told the King that she was a Jacobite sympathiser. Happily, George I was not so ignorant of his adopted country's ways that he took the preposterous accusation seriously, and he readily, if rather clumsily, accepted Sarah's protestations of loyalty towards him. For the Duke and Duchess, compensation came in being able to witness the fate of those who had connived at their fall and who now found themselves washed up by events. With Abigail cut back down to size and the disgraced Bolingbroke absent without leave, Oxford had chosen to stay and face his accusers. Revenge at hand, Marlborough was amongst those who voted for his impeachment. Although the former Lord Treasurer was eventually acquitted, the intervening couple of years in the Tower of London inflicted what physical damage his years of alcohol abuse had not already ravaged upon him. The result was a state of health scarcely compatible with the fashionable London medical practices that later came to congregate around the principal reason his name has remained a household term in Britain – Harley Street.

The truth was that while the politics of Hanoverian Britain held no less a fascination than had those of the house of Stuart, Sarah and her husband were no longer at the centre of it. In 1716, the Duke of

Marlborough suffered a stroke which removed him from active life. Three years later Blenheim Palace at last became habitable and it was in this gigantic mausoleum to his life's work that he died in 1722. Having amassed the greatest fortune of any non-royal in Europe, his final hours were accompanied by Sarah's intense devotion and the background noise of their family arguing.

Indomitable to the last, the widowed Sarah continued to show a sharp eye for managing her finances. With splendid irony she made a fortune from Oxford's speculative venture, the South Sea Company, profitably cashing in her investment before the bubble burst taking with it the fortunes of so many others. She spent her last years comforted by an enormous financial estate, the matriarch of the Spencer-Churchill dynasty, entertaining the likes of Voltaire and railing against the politicians of the day. After going through countless drafts, her memoirs were published in 1742. As expected, they were unforgiving. She died on 19 October 1744 aged eighty-four and was buried next to her husband in the chapel at Blenheim, one of the most impressive private palaces in the world.

But the reason for her fame had withered long before, with the destruction of her friendship with Anne Stuart. Of course its political importance may be contested. After all, it was the Duke of Marlborough, not his Duchess, who with his ally Godolphin provided the backbone of British government for nine of the twelve years of Anne's reign. It was the Duke who commanded the armed forces and sat in the councils of the state. Sarah recognised that this was so. 'I am confydent', she maintained, that 'I should have been the greatest Hero that ever was known in the Parliament Hous if I had been so happy as to have been a Man.'[16] Unable to be a feminist before the word had currency, Sarah – like so many of the other ladies-in-waiting – was first and foremost the political agent of her husband and the unrelenting promoter of his ambitions. In the early years she had done him a great service in this respect for although Anne came to judge the Duke of Marlborough on his own terms, he was, thanks to Sarah, first commended to her as 'Mr Freeman'. Indeed, he might never have gained the opportunity to command the British Army but for the influence of women: it was his sister Arabella who had got him the vital introduction to her lover, the future James II, and it was the Duchess of Cleveland who provided, besides her affections, the finances with which he established himself in James's entourage.

But even after the Duke of Marlborough demonstrated his genius on the battlefield, it could never be said that Sarah was thereafter merely the wife of a great soldier-politician, who for all her opinions and strident posturing

was really as irrelevant to the course of her nation's history as Mrs
Cromwell or the Duchess of Wellington. Those in Whitehall, Westminster
and Grub Street certainly did not underestimate Sarah's influence. They
recognised the extent of her self-belief when it came to possessing what she
told Anne's physician in 1710 was 'a great deal of experience of the men on
both sides, & ... a certain knowledge of a great many facts, which her
majesty could hear from nobody else'.[17] They feared her determination
to make Anne aware of these interpretations, and, at first, the Queen's
receptiveness. Because Anne's own views were often concealed from open
scrutiny by her withdrawal from the public gaze through shyness, frequent
pregnancies and illnesses, there was a widespread belief that she was being
manipulated by the favourite lady of the Bedchamber with whom she was
closeted. Indeed, the intense manner of Anne and Sarah's relationship (to
say nothing of the catty manner of their parting) seemed to fit the misogynist's
notion of powerful scheming females and petticoat government. This is
apparent in some of the language used. 'Is she not a detestable Slut?'[18] wrote
Swift of Sarah in 1713, in the context of regaling how – having first stripped
it of its diamond-studded frame – she had given away a miniature of the
Queen gifted to her by Anne in happier days, to a woman who had fallen
on hard times. One pamphleteer maintained that: 'Her hair was grisled and
adorn'd with Spoils of ruined People. Her neck bare, with Chains about it
of Dice, mixed with Pieces of Gold, which rattling, made a horrid noise; for
her Motions were all fierce and violent. Her garment was all stained with
Tears and Blood.'[19]

The Whigs were equally resentful about Abigail's above-stairs influence,
singing ballads that suggested there was something unnatural about Anne's
feelings for her maidservant whom they uncharitably dubbed 'that Pimple-
faced Bitch'.[20] Still, the level of abuse was mild when compared to the
graphic lesbian dominatrix practices that Marie Antoinette was later to be
imaginatively accused of enjoying with her female friends. It says much
about the extent to which senior politicians believed the head of state was
ruled by her heart that Bolingbroke could support the candidacy of a wholly
unsuitable soldier to lead a British invasion of French Canada because he
was Abigail's brother. Bolingbroke having succeeded in this task (and Abigail's
brother having failed in his), Oxford assured Abigail in May 1714: 'You
cannot set any one up; you can pull any one downe.'[21] Doubtless, as she
nursed and massaged the ailing Queen's body, Abigail was subtly poisoning
her mind. But her original influence as a go-between with Oxford (or
Harley as he then was) was a product – rather than the cause – of Anne's
disenchantment with the Godolphin-Marlborough administration. It was

not Abigail's subsequent favour of Bolingbroke that caused Anne, eventually, to drop Oxford.

In fact, Whigs and Tories both exaggerated the hold of their respective female hate-figures. Those, who believed Sarah was pulling the strings of the royal puppet failed to recognise the Queen's innate stubbornness and, especially as her reign progressed, her own sense of determination. As far as Sarah's ability to promote her own political favourites was concerned, her successes were few and not necessarily directly attributable to her personal intervention. She was, for instance, at first unable to push her son-in-law, Sunderland, into the Secretaryship of State, and, after Anne had reluctantly appointed him, she was unable to persuade Anne not to sack him from that position in 1710. Nonetheless, Sarah was *presumed* to have influence, as the number of requests for royal patronage that were addressed to her testified. This, perhaps, was where she performed the most useful function on behalf of the Crown, sifting out those who had no talent to offer from those she forwarded to the Queen. Not only did this save Anne time and trouble, it meant that those who were turned down could vent their spleen on Sarah's often tactlessly phrased letters of rejection rather than on the Queen. For all Sarah wanted to rule Anne, it was Sarah who served the purpose of the Queen's lightning conductor.[22]

The waxing and waning power of the Queen's bedchamber can be shown by the fact that as late as 1839 a 'Bedchamber Crisis' could still dictate the composition of the government. In that year, Sir Robert Peel, trying to form a Tory administration upon the Whig Lord Melbourne's resignation, sought reassurance that he commanded the young Queen Victoria's confidence by asking her to forsake some of her all-Whig-supporting ladies of the Bed-chamber for one or two identified with the Tory interest. Heavily influenced by her mentor, Melbourne, Victoria dug in her heels on the issue. Peel thus felt this was a sign that he could not count upon Her Majesty's confidence and Melbourne returned as a Prime Minister without a parliamentary majority. Victoria was dismissive of Peel's lack of purpose, noting 'what an admission of weakness!' if he felt 'the Ladies his only support'. Others were more critical of Victoria's stance: as one diarist without much sense of history put it, 'It is a high trial of our institutions when the caprice of a girl of nineteen can overturn a great ministerial combination and when the most momentous matters of government and legislation are influenced by her pleasure about her Ladies of the Bedchamber!'[23] From 1841, when Peel's sweeping general election victory could not be circumvented by courtly preference, a con-stitutional compromise was worked out, but by then Victoria had become far more interested in the company of her beloved husband, Prince Albert.

With this adjustment, the age of bedchamber power-brokers was finally exhausted. The leading ladies of Victorian politics were social reformers, not social climbers.

*

Without empathy for their predicament, it would be easy to reduce the relationship between Anne and Sarah to a tale of a dim-witted and stubborn Queen's struggle to rid herself of a controlling and spiteful shrew. Their falling-out seemed the inevitable *coup de théâtre* in a plot riddled with their betrayals of others: Sarah and her husband deserting their King and benefactor, Anne renouncing her own blood, fleeing from her father and conniving in the disinheriting of her half-brother. Always one to have the last word, Sarah vanquished Anne after her death with the publication of memoirs that did much to colour future generations' views of the Queen.

But empathy is necessary, for it was also a relationship marked by tenderness, loss, and an attempt by those born in unequal circumstances to bond. Anne was propelled out of her depth, separated from her family, and destined to be a mother who lost all seventeen of her children. She desperately sought refuge in friendship from the cares of a Crown that could, at any time, be wrested from her by her Catholic half-brother.

Could the relationship have endured if handled differently? Friendship is about providing stability. Politics is the anticipation of and reaction to constant change. As such, a political friendship is always a vulnerable association. For Anne to have maintained an unaltering devotion to her lady of the Bedchamber would have necessitated divorcing the relationship from the political climate in which it operated – never something that would have interested Sarah. In this respect, a useful contrast is provided by the friendship between Marie Antoinette and the Princesse de Lamballe which was kept for so long in good repair primarily because of their mutual immaturity, indeed ignorance, of the political wolves prowling beyond the palace gates. In the end, the wolves decapitated Lamballe, sticking her head on a pike and waving it high in the air so that the doomed Queen of France could see it from her prison window.

The irony was that Anne's relationship with Sarah deteriorated not only because in becoming Queen she resented Sarah's opinionated treatment but also because the mutually inclusive experiences of continuing pregnancies and motherhood had been replaced by divisive political ones. With the death of her son, the Duke of Gloucester in 1700, Anne had to face up to the stark reality that she would not produce an heir, while Sarah was so overcome with grief by the loss of her only son, Jack, in 1703 that she partly withdrew from court life altogether. Anne, the High Church Anglican, tried instead to become the mother of her nation. Sarah became more ruthless in her opinions and quicker to find fault. What in the bloom of youth was regarded as flair became in middle age the traits of a nag. Set upon this path, love turned to hate, and politics conquered all. Dr Johnson said that Anne seemed born for friendship, not for governing.[24] Little wonder, then, that she died disappointed by life.

PART TWO

REVOLUTIONARIES
Benjamin Franklin, William Franklin and Joseph Galloway

'The coward does it with a kiss,
The brave man with a sword'

OSCAR WILDE, THE BALLAD OF READING GAOL

FIVE

The City of Brotherly Love

The Duke and Duchess of Marlborough considered Britain's exit from the War of the Spanish Succession a shameful betrayal of allies. Their Tory opponents, in grubbing about for a short-term expedient, had rescued France from pending defeat and squandered any hope of fostering the stability of Europe. Events, however, conspired to postpone this reckoning. The death of Louis XIV in 1715 and the failure of his client, James Francis Edward Stuart, to regain his father's throne presaged more pacific times. The Duke of Marlborough would not see war again in his lifetime. While his martial achievements were chiselled on to the stones of Blenheim Palace, the army he had commanded was scaled down to a trifling 17,000 men. Such economising was based upon a presumption of non-involvement in Continental adventure.

For a time, politics proved amenable. Across western Europe expediency became fashionable: new alliances were forged, even between former enemies. Such relationships flowered briefly before buckling at the end of the 1720s when the genetic enmities of Europe's dynasts could no longer be contained. Despite the hopes of the Whig Prime Minister, Robert Walpole, that military entanglement might be avoided, British and Spanish ships scuffled over maritime rights and the French and Austrians again collided, ostensibly over the question of the Polish succession. Nonetheless, these quarrels had to be viewed in perspective. Compared to what had gone before, the quarter-century following the Treaty of Utrecht was a period of comparative peace.

From 1740 onwards, all this was thrown away: the Austrian Habsburg male line died out and, with the Archduchess Maria Theresa struggling to assert herself, France and Prussia were at the forefront of states seeking an opportunity to make gains. The British, with a king who was also the Elector of Hanover, felt unable to stay aloof from the mounting crisis and drew up on the side of the embattled Archduchess. In doing so, George II became the last British king to lead his troops into battle, advancing dismounted and sword drawn towards the French lines at Dettingen, driving them into the enveloping flow of the River Main. By the time Sarah, Duchess of Marlborough finally passed away in 1744, twenty-two years after her husband,

Europe was once again fully engaged in the business of slaughter.

The War of the Austrian Succession was fought out in many places: in Bavaria, Bohemia and Silesia as well as on the Rhine and in Flanders. With the British Army fully committed on the Continent, James Francis Edward Stuart's more glamorous son, Prince Charles Edward, seized the opportunity to land in Scotland and advanced as far as Derby. The road lay open for him to march on London. Instead, the 'Bonnie Prince' retreated and, in 1746, received at Culloden Moor the crushing blow that destroyed the house of Stuart's chances of taking back the British throne. The survival of the Protestant succession in London was but one feature of the engagement. Indeed, the wider war was far from being confined to European soil. On the contrary, it provided an opportunity for Britain and France to intensify their fight for global supremacy.

In this struggle for land and trade rights, there were three main theatres of war: India, the Caribbean and the vast, under-exploited domains of North America. The Treaty of Utrecht had ceded the Canadian lands of Acadia, Newfoundland and the Hudson Bay territory to Britain but the exact border with France's possessions remained hazy. Supported by their Native American Indian allies, the French launched largely unsuccessful attacks into Maine and Nova Scotia. But the most telling blow was struck not by the imported forces of old Europe but by a detachment of New England settlers who captured Fort Louisbourg on Cape Breton Island on behalf of his Britannic Majesty. It was no small achievement, but those who imagined that it presaged France's final downfall in North America were in for a disappointment. Three years later, in 1748, hostilities came to a close through the usual means of the diplomatic exchange of gifts. The colonists were incensed when Britain chose to bargain away the strategically important gateway they had won on the St Lawrence River in return for Madras.

The peace agreement reached at Aix-la-Chapelle left the future of the New World firmly in the balance. Of particular importance was the question of who would ultimately control the Mississippi valley. There, the French had a foothold and they intended to complete a line of fortresses that would link French Canada down through Louisiana and out into the port of New Orleans, encircling and boxing Britain's American colonies into a strip along the eastern seaboard and preventing their expansion westward. Such a prospect was no more agreeable to Virginia's English-speaking settlers than it was to the francophobes of London. Further conflict was inevitable. It came in 1754, without first waiting for Britain's formal participation in the war that had once again broken out across the European continent. An army of British regulars supported by Virginian militia was dispatched to capture

Fort Duquesne on the Ohio River. Success would have severed French lines of communication beyond the Appalachian Mountains. Instead, the mission turned into a disaster when the force was ambushed by French troops and American Indians.

Among the officers narrowly escaping with their lives was a Virginian estate owner named George Washington. Such was a small deliverance for which future generations might ponder the workings of providence. Strategically, it was not until William Pitt – 'Pitt the Elder' – took charge in London that Britain really gained the upper hand. Louisbourg fell and the French abandoned Fort Duquesne. It was renamed Pittsburgh. And, after the initial hesitancy, Britain formally joined the war in Europe as the ally of Frederick the Great's Prussia against France and Austria. Decisive victories came in India and North America. General Wolfe stormed the Heights of Abraham, seizing Quebec. With it, control of Canada was wrested from the French. By the time what became known as the Seven Years' War was formally concluded in 1763, Britain was in an immeasurably stronger position. Not only had she supplanted the French in Canada, France's domains in North America had been confined to the untamed plains west of the Mississippi.

One American who rejoiced at Britain's victory was Benjamin Franklin. Concerned that the colonies were not working together collectively to defend themselves against the French and American Indians, he had attended a congress at Albany in New York State in 1754 as a representative from the colony of Pennsylvania. Assisted by Thomas Hutchinson of Massachusetts, Franklin had presented to the delegates his 'Plan of Union'. It was accompanied in the press by an explanatory woodcut of a serpent cut into slices (each representing a colony) with the exhortation 'unite or die'. It was a powerful image for a potent idea. At the time it was produced, the American colonies had no common assembly. Consequently, the political structure operated linearly between London and each of the thirteen colonies rather than interactively between the colonies themselves.

Franklin wanted to maintain the transatlantic connection. Indeed, it was to enhance it that he proposed that the American colonies should act together in formulating a common defence policy and should settle land disputes (primarily with the American Indians) in consort with British wishes. In Franklin's scheme, each of the lower houses of the thirteen colonial Assemblies would send representatives to a Grand Council invested with the power to raise taxes to pay for the implementation of its initiatives. The Grand Council would forward its proposals to a President-General who would be appointed by the British King. Effectively this Crown appointee would assume the powers of a viceroy and could veto any Grand Council initiative that was not to London's liking.

There was much to commend Franklin's diagnosis. It was no longer fanciful to equate Britain and its fast-spreading Empire with the Rome of Cicero where the institutions of republican government, intended for a city state and its environs, had failed to adapt to the new demands of a sprawling imperium. It was unreasonable to expect British troops to do so much of the defence and frontier policing of the American colonies while the colonies themselves guarded little more than their legislative independence from one another. Franklin's Albany 'Plan of Union' impressed the congress delegates. But when they returned to discuss it in their respective colonial legislatures they discovered the dearth of enthusiasm among the house-proud Assemblymen for an innovation of this kind. Not one of the colonial legislatures was prepared for the sharing of sovereignty that it necessitated. The scheme thus had no future and subsequent events only reinforced the arguments of its opponents. In 1763, the Treaty of Paris confirmed Britain's victory over the French in North America. The colonists could relax in the knowledge that with the external threat virtually removed, there was less, rather than more, need to help shoulder Britain's defence burden. For that matter, there was less reason to need British protection at all. The moment for Franklin's pro-British 'Plan of Union' had already passed. The thirteen colonies saw no gain in convening together in a Grand Council to speak as one.

From London, the perspective could not have been more different. The Seven Years' War may have been won, but at a financially debilitating cost. The national debt soared to the then enormous sum of £129,586,789. The interest charged on this alone was £4,688,177 per annum.[1] Without finding ways of making savings, the pressure would cripple British taxpayers. Inevitably, partners were sought to shoulder the burden. At a time when the average British male was paying twenty-six shillings a year in tax, his Bostonian counterpart was contributing one shilling.[2] Unsurprisingly, His Majesty's subjects in the British Isles grumbled that His Majesty's subjects in America were enjoying the fruits of the military commitment, while escaping paying for its costs. While economising Britons conceded that the expense of policing North America could be greatly reduced because of the diminution of the French threat, it could not be removed altogether. They maintained that if the colonial legislatures were not prepared to act together to provide the means of security, then at least they should pay their share in the burdens of the Empire's defence. The whole relationship between Britain and its American colonies needed to be rethought.

British politicians were casting around for measures to reduce the national debt at a time when the colonists stopped fearing the French threat. This combination of circumstances would later be seen as a fertile condition for the American Revolution. This was not widely foreseen at the time. There was no popular call for independence, a prospect that in 1760 Benjamin Franklin believed could materialise only if Britain embarked upon 'the most grievous tyranny and oppression'. As far as Franklin was concerned, if the American colonies 'could not agree to unite for their defence against the French and Indians, who were perpetually harassing their settlements, burning their villages, and murdering their people; can it reasonably be supposed there is any danger of their uniting against their own nation,' for, ''tis well known they all love [Great Britain] much more than they love one another'.[3] In writing this, Franklin articulated common wisdom. True, there was a receptive audience for John Locke's writings, in particular his argument that there was a natural law that permitted rebellion against any government that overrode its traditional contract with the people. This, after all, was what legitimised the Glorious Revolution that supplanted James II and his Catholic descendants. But, whatever American colonists thought of the chicanery of London's politicians, the idea of replacing the protection of the British Crown with a republic was scarcely imagined, let alone promoted.

It was the relationship with the sovereign that was particularly important. Virginia had been the first territory to become a Crown colony but, during the reigns of Charles II and James II, the Crown made successive assumptions of executive control over the other colonies. Of the thirteen colonies in existence by 1763, nine had become Crown colonies whose Governors were appointed from London. The four that remained aloof were Connecticut and Rhode Island who elected their own Governors, and Maryland and Pennsylvania, where the governorship was determined by their proprietary owners (although even here, the Crown formally approved the process). Whether 'Crown' or not, every colony had its own elected legislature whose rights were codified in written constitutions. But, in the Crown colonies, the executive, in the shape of the Governor and his Council (the upper house of the legislature) were chosen by the King on the advice of his ministers. In this respect, the British Crown, rather than the British Parliament, exercised guardianship over the colonies. Many settlers preferred it this way round. Benjamin Franklin did not care for the way in which 'Every man in England seems to consider himself as a piece of a sovereign over America; seems to jostle himself into the throne with the king, and talks of our subjects in the Colonies.'[4] Yet, by the second half of the eighteenth century, it was increasingly difficult to protest loyalty to the Crown but varying degrees of hostility to Parliament. Over the course of the past hundred years the concept that the monarch ruled through and not over Parliament had been strengthened, even if the new King, George III, who succeeded to the throne in 1760, had ideas about regaining some of his royal dignity. It was to be a supreme irony that a monarch who generally resented Parliament's encroachment on his own authority would proceed to do so much damage by accepting Westminster's sovereignty over his American subjects.

These American subjects were different not merely in their sense of detachment from the shenanigans in the Houses of Parliament. Different colonies, with different characteristics, attracted different immigrants. Some appealed to those seeking freedom of worship or the prospect of owning property. Georgia was founded in 1732 as a haven for those fleeing their debts. In the eighteenth century, the majority who arrived in North America from Britain were Scots and Irish. Indeed, over the whole period of colonial America, most Europeans who settled there came to serve out a term as indentured servants, essentially working as little more than white slaves for a fixed term after which they had their chance to establish themselves in the new land of opportunity. Those forcibly unloaded from Africa were, of course, condemned to a worse – and hereditary – form of servitude.

Wherever they had come from and on whatever terms they had made their passage, most Americans settled not in the small bustling cities on the eastern seaboard but to work on the land where the expanse of rural pasture and abundance of natural materials was the greatest allure. Bare statistics provide a generalised testimony to a myriad of human expectations. The population of British North America swelled from a little over a quarter of a million in 1700 to 1.2 million in 1750. By 1770 it reached 2.3 million. Benjamin Franklin prophesied that by the middle of the nineteenth century there would be more British subjects in North America than in Great Britain. Interestingly, he did not think this would necessarily cause a mighty rupture.[5]

Colonisation had been achieved primarily through private rather than state-organised endeavour, although the pioneers had done so within the latitude granted by royal licences. The situation in Benjamin Franklin's colony was particularly complicated. Charles II had bestowed on William Penn a royal charter of proprietorship over an estate in the New World so vast that it made him the largest single landowner in British history. The King had given Penn the territory in lieu of a £16,000 debt that he owed his father. The latter had certainly done his royal master a favour by capturing Jamaica, a particularly valuable possession for the emerging British Empire. In 1682, William Penn journeyed across the Atlantic to claim his vast domain. He named it Pennsylvania. An admirer of Locke's political philosophy, he intended his new property (which was larger than Ireland) to be a model society structured along Quaker lines and with full freedom of worship to all religions. Optimistically, its capital on the Delaware was given the Greek name for brotherly love – Philadelphia. Unlike in the Crown colonies, where the government in London supervised senior executive appointments, it was to Penn's descendants that the royal charter bequeathed a form of hereditary proprietorship over Pennsylvania's government.

In 1701, Penn drew up a constitution. It acknowledged the legislative role of the Assembly, with its elected lower house. Its members could propose legislation and had tax-raising powers. But Penn's own descendants retained the power to veto legislation through their appointment of the colony's Governor who, in turn, selected the upper house, the Council. In 1712, William Penn agreed a price with the British government for transferring his executive powers to the authority of the Crown. But his health deteriorated sharply and no sale had been transacted by the time of his death. His heirs had no intention of reviving the sale. In 1741, Thomas Penn left the colony in order to settle in England and did not return. Comfortable in his wealth and London society, he retreated from his Quaker heritage and started attending the services of the Church of England. As each year passed, Pennsylvania's absentee proprietor appeared to be less and less in harmony with the political culture of his colony across the ocean.

While the heirs of William Penn counted their wealth and made the most of their privileges in London, their colony developed at an extraordinary rate. By 1750, Pennsylvania had a population of around 120,000. By 1760, it had passed 180,000. Religious tolerance and opportunity for enrichment had a magnetic effect. Philadelphia developed as a port and centre of commerce. By 1760 it had nearly 24,000 inhabitants, making it the largest city in the colonies. The Delaware valley proved a fertile land for growing grain. The mercantile traders of Philadelphia were largely Quakers and Anglicans – although the former constituted most of the city's political élite. English émigrés also formed the predominant culture in much of the land around the capital, especially in Bucks County. Beyond, in the rural communities where most of the colony's inhabitants settled, Ulster-Scots Presbyterians and German Protestants predominated. Nonetheless, Quakers continued to hold most of the reins of local power in the colony even though, by the middle of the eighteenth century, they constituted only a fifth of the inhabitants. The Quaker Party dominated the Assembly in Philadelphia, its power curtailed only at the executive level by the proprietary interest attached to the Penn family.

The wars with the French and American Indians highlighted the stresses in this arrangement. Thomas Penn instructed the Governor of Pennsylvania to veto money Bills passed by the Assembly that were intended to provide for a defensive militia unless the Penns' own estates were excluded from being taxed. Doubtless Penn feared that once he had conceded the legitimacy of having his vast estates taxed, Philadelphia's politicians would proceed to milk him dry. Yet, it seemed that at a time when the colony was threatened, an effective response was being blocked by a combination of the Quaker pacifism of Philadelphia's leading politicians and the Penn family's financial self-interest. Having sat in the Assembly since 1751, Benjamin Franklin started to put together a new coalition in the lower house that was neither pacifist nor in thrall to the Penn 'proprietary interest'. Franklin's group, the Assembly Party, began to bond into an effective unit. When, in 1755, the threat to the colony from American Indians became acute, Franklin and his son, William, were put in charge, successfully relieving the endangered outlying settlements. Not that this brought the gratitude of the Penns. Thomas Penn was suspicious about the nascent threat to his authority implied by the stationing of a popular militia in his colony. The proprietors reacted to Britain's declaration of war on France in 1756 by abrogating Franklin's Militia Act in the colony. Outraged by the behaviour of the proprietors, the Assembly dispatched Franklin as its Agent to London to appeal directly to the British Crown for redress.

What made Franklin's appointment as Agent possible was his Assembly Party's victory in the October 1756 elections. This handed his supporters control of the lower house of Pennsylvania's legislature. In the course of building this power base, he had formed a close alliance with a lawyer turned politician, Joseph Galloway. Together, these two men would become the driving anti-proprietary force in Pennsylvanian politics. For, on the central issues affecting the colony, they were of like mind. No sooner had victory been secured in the Assembly than Franklin insisted on Galloway becoming his chief legislative assistant. Benjamin Franklin and Joseph Galloway were both men of earthly ambition, Whigs by nature, who were familiar with the lessons of the Glorious Revolution and supportive of its curbing of executive power. It was to be a partnership based upon common values and contrasting, but mutually supportive, talents.

Neither Franklin nor Galloway was Pennsylvanian by birth. Franklin had been born in Boston in 1706, the fifteenth child of an English Nonconformist maker of soaps and candles who had emigrated from Northamptonshire almost a quarter of a century earlier. After local schooling, the ten-year-old

Ben Franklin briefly joined his father's business before switching to his half-brother's printing firm. But he did not get on with his sibling and moved to Pennsylvania in 1723. He was seventeen and arrived in Philadelphia with nothing but a Dutch dollar and a copper shilling; however, he was eager and intelligent. These were prerequisites upon which the 'American Dream' – as later generations understood it – was built. Benjamin Franklin had them in unlimited supply.

It was thus ironic that it was this quest for opportunity that initially propelled him, aged eighteen, across the Atlantic to the land his father left behind. His mission was to buy presses in London. There, he found employment with the city's printing companies. The work was hard and he proceeded to lead a life divided between days of honest toil and nights of sordid pleasure. His personal theology led him towards deism. With such unburdensome spiritual beliefs, he adopted the Puritan work ethic without acknowledging the God-fearing constraints instilled by organised religion. This first experience of London life was important for him but it was not his intention to remain there indefinitely. Instead, he returned to Philadelphia in 1726 and it was from then on that he began to make his mark. By 1730 he had taken over the ownership of the printers of the newly founded *Pennsylvania Gazette*. He had also set up home with a common-law wife.

Deborah Read was about the same age as Benjamin Franklin, but it was there that the comparison stopped. She was the virtually illiterate daughter of one of Franklin's former landladies and certainly seemed an odd choice for one of his already evident level of ambition and self-motivation. She had been deserted by her husband, whose subsequent death was rumoured but – unhelpfully – not confirmed. So while Franklin could not marry her legally, she was generally assumed to be his wife. The arrangement almost certainly saved Deborah from the sort of existence an abandoned and unprepossessing woman could otherwise have anticipated. She rewarded Franklin with a daughter who survived infancy and a son, Francis, who to his parents' great sadness died of smallpox in 1736, aged four. Most of all, she demonstrated a quiet adoration manifested by shouldering the sort of practical domestic burdens with which great men prefer not to be troubled.

For his part, it remains unclear what governed Franklin's motivation towards her. It may have been the honourable desire to rescue the 'child' (as he patronisingly called her) to whom he perhaps felt he had incurred obligations. It may merely have been that she was an unfortunate youthful indiscretion he could not shake off. As time progressed, it began to look more like the latter. He came to prefer a relationship with her conveniently divorced by the expanse of the Atlantic. He also fathered two illegitimate children – a daughter and his beloved son, William.

As with his decision to stick with Deborah, Franklin did not shirk his responsibilities to his illegitimate son.[6] Rather than disposing of him permanently to some distant or institutional care where the lad could be conveniently forgotten, Franklin brought him up in his own house. This created difficulties not least because although the boy was encouraged to call Deborah 'mother', she seemingly made little attempt to indulge the pretence, openly doting over Sarah, her daughter by Franklin, instead. But without a surviving son from his union with Deborah, Franklin was more than content to look upon William as his heir. By nature adventurous, William had inherited his father's inquisitive mind. He would have much to live up to.

In the years after William's birth in 1731, Benjamin Franklin reaped the benefits of hard work. As a writer and printer, his great success was *Poor Richard's Almanack*. With their quarry of useful and useless information, almanacs were very popular in colonial America, but Franklin's successive editions led the market. They mixed facts with proverbs, homespun wisdom and aphorisms often plagiarised from various sources and rescripted as if the product of personal observation. *Poor Richard's Almanack* made its author wealthy. Indeed, in due course it accumulated American sales second only to the Bible. Such was the publishing sensation that Benjamin Franklin soon found his appeals to thrift and self-help quoted throughout the colonies. It made him famous. What was more, the homilies had weight because their author practised what he preached. He spent modestly but read widely. He learnt French, Spanish, Italian and Latin. He initiated several Philadelphian civic schemes – a police force, street improvements, a lending library and an academy that would form the nucleus of the University of Pennsylvania. In 1744 he became the first secretary of the American Philosophical Society. Here was the ideal of a renaissance man, but transported to the New World. In word and in deed, he was the most admired man in the colony.

Watching his father's mounting fame and fortune, William Franklin grew up eager to make his own way too. Indeed, Ben Franklin had to rein in his fifteen-year-old son, rescuing him when, hoping for a life at sea, he ran off to join a privateer. But he did not prevent him joining the army. In 1746, William Franklin put on his redcoat uniform and joined the expedition to repel the French-led Indians' incursions in New York colony. It was a perilous adventure, but the young man came out of it well – and with the rank of captain. On his return home, he assisted his father in drilling the Philadelphia Association Militia. He also lent a hand with the scientific experiments that were increasingly preoccupying the senior Franklin's free time. When

William returned to the frontier, he took a gift from his father to another amateur scientist, Governor Clinton. It was a glass tube for experiments. William explained its operation.

William was still only nineteen when he returned from the frontiers of New York and the Ohio to Philadelphia. Arriving home, he found his father had done so well commercially (his income now exceeded that of the Governor of the colony) that he had hired a manager to take over the day-to-day running of his printing firm so that he could devote himself more fully to scientific inquiry. Well versed in the observations of Newton and other European scientists, Franklin was fascinated by electrical current and the development of the condenser. William became his assistant and constructed the kite with which his father's most famous contribution to learning would rest. William ran with the kite, key attached, through a lightning storm, allowing Franklin – allegedly watching from the safety of a shed – to deduce that lightning was indeed electricity. William also sent his father detailed observations on a house struck by lightning, suggesting that electric lightning passed upwards rather than downwards. But as the driving force behind such experiments, it was the senior Franklin who quite properly took the credit. It was Benjamin Franklin's findings that were printed in America, Britain and France. He invented the lightning rod. The university colleges of Harvard, Yale and William and Mary were the first to award him honorary degrees. In 1752 and for many years thereafter, he had a reasonable claim to being the world's most famous American.

If he did not always give his son the public acknowledgement he perhaps deserved, Franklin was nonetheless proud of him. At over six feet, William was a taller, leaner, strikingly handsome version of his stocky and somewhat ungainly father. While Franklin opposed the hereditary authority of the Penn family, he was not averse to nepotism himself. Having become Deputy Postmaster-General of the colonies, he appointed his son the postal system's Comptroller-General in 1754. The position demanded accounting skills that William proved well able to grasp. But it was William's determination to pursue a legal career that had brought him, the previous year, into the practice of Joseph Galloway. The two men were nearly the same age and became friends. It seems that it was through William that Franklin got to know Galloway well and discovered a political kindred spirit. That Galloway was such a good companion of his son could only have further encouraged Franklin to believe that he had found the ally he could trust in public life. Such were the ties that bind.

When Franklin and his Militia Bill came under vicious attack in late 1755, William and Joseph Galloway, together with another friend, George Bryan, issued a devastating reply by publishing *Tit for Tat or the Score Wip'd Off.* Together with subsequent pamphlets by Galloway, it more than returned the invective of the proprietors and their sycophants. William's quickness in defending his father's honour was natural. But the actions of Galloway were particularly noteworthy given that he had recently married into a wealthy pro-proprietary family – a connection that he could so easily have used to feather his own political nest. Here, it seemed, was a man of principle. Franklin became Galloway's friend as well.

Joseph Galloway had been a lawyer in Philadelphia since 1748. Born at West River, Anne Arundel County, in Maryland in or around 1731, he was twenty-five years Benjamin Franklin's junior. An age difference of this scale would normally have precluded a friendship of equals, but Galloway's poise and attainments were sufficient to narrow the gap. He came from a wealthy Quaker family that had crossed the Atlantic before the outbreak of the English Civil War and acquired considerable property in Maryland and Pennsylvania. His father had died while he was still young and the family moved to Kent County, Delaware. He received no formal schooling but did have a private tutor. Once he was old enough, he was encouraged to study under an attorney. Thus his professional course was set and, after moving to Philadelphia, he was licensed, at the age of eighteen, to practise law. It was in Philadelphia that he began, despite his youth, to establish a high professional reputation for himself. His refined, alert features were set off with the accessory of a gentleman, the short, white powdered wig, swept back from the forehead, curled over the ear and tied in a ponytail at the back with a large black ribbon bow.

In 1753, when he was twenty-two, Galloway took a swift step forward. He married Grace Growden. She was by repute the most beautiful woman in Pennsylvania. It was also gratifying that she was the daughter of Lawrence Growden, Pennsylvania's wealthiest man, second justice of the colony's Supreme Court and Speaker of its Assembly. In one exchange of vows, Galloway was thus marrying a trinity of money, legal preferment and political power. The union did involve a sacrifice on Galloway's part. As a Quaker, he had shared the faith and business contacts of the dominant group in Philadelphia. But the Growdens were Episcopalians. Galloway made the necessary conversion. Whatever setback this involved in terms of severing useful professional connections among co-religionists in the Society of Friends, there were alternative worldly compensations. The Growdens had a sizeable country house outside Philadelphia in Bucks County on a fine five-thousand-acre estate they called 'Trevose'. It had been from Trevose Point on the Atlantic coast near Padstow in Cornwall that the Growdens' forebears had left to embark upon their voyage to the New World. They also owned the local Durham iron furnaces. The difference with Franklin's upbringing and marriage arrangements could not have been starker. It was not surprising that the soap-maker's son valued a deepening association with someone who, for want of a better term, had class. For their parts, Joseph and Grace Galloway were welcoming. Philadelphia's most famous citizen was a valued guest. According to one tradition, it was from the grounds of Trevose that Franklin sent his kite and key up into the storm.

If social standing had been all that Galloway offered, the friendship with Franklin would not have endured beyond the first imagined snub or *faux pas*. Franklin was justly proud of having accumulated a comfortable living from his own endeavours and was not one to seek elevated status by grasping at the embroidered coat tails of someone born to privilege who, into the bargain, had bagged a pretty and moneyed wife. That many of Philadelphia's most socially sophisticated families still kept their distance from Franklin did not appear to cause him distress. Instead, he gave every impression that he was more than happy with the existing company he kept – a constant stream of visitors who passed through his door keen to debate the latest political and intellectual developments. The Franklin town house on lower Market Street was a hospitable meeting place that did not grade according to rank. Galloway possessed something that Franklin valued above money and position: he had a well honed mind. True, his was not the sort of intellect that ranged broadly over many interests – the characteristic of Franklin's inquiring outlook. And, while like Franklin he was largely self-taught, Galloway did not have the indiscriminate thirst of the natural autodidact. Rather, he possessed the sharp and focused brain of the lawyer and parliamentary debater. Franklin was a poor public speaker and having a polished advocate of Galloway's ability to put the case was necessarily attractive. What was more, if the Penn family's proprietary power was to be weakened, as both men hoped, it would take a forensic legal mind to establish and order the arguments accordingly.

Franklin did not know how long his mission to London as the Pennsylvanian Assembly's Agent might take. Quite probably it would take years. During this time he would be away from Philadelphia and unable to assert his will among its politicians. What he needed was not only backup from a competent lawyer but also someone who could command the respect of the Assemblymen and hold together his great political creation – the Assembly Party. He needed someone he could trust; someone who would not seek to supplant him in his absence; someone who would not waver from shared political goals. Others had better claim on account of their political experience. Yet, despite having been an Assembly member for a mere five months, Joseph Galloway was the man in whom Benjamin Franklin felt he could place total confidence.

Preparing to board the ship that would take him to England, Franklin wrote to warn Galloway of their enemies' plotting, asking him 'to watch 'em and guard my Reputation and Interest as much as may be from the Effects of their Malevolence. I cheerfully leave my dearest Concerns under that Care, having no Reason to doubt the Continuance of the Friendships I have so long experienc'd.'[7] After he arrived in London, he continued to express the same sentiments. 'I know that the Cannon and Small Arms of the Party consist of great and little Calumnies and Falsehoods, and you may depend on my endeavouring to shield your Reputation wherever I find it attack'd', Franklin assured Galloway, 'as I rely on the like Defence in same case from your Friendship.' So long as they could stay united, Franklin remained adamant that their case against Penn proprietorial power in the colony would eventually prevail: 'God knows when we shall see it finish'd, and our Constitution settled firmly on the Foundations of Equity and English Liberty', he wrote, 'But I am not discourag'd.'[8]

After the three-thousand-mile journey by sail across the Atlantic, Franklin arrived in London – via a quick detour to look at Stonehenge – in July 1757. With him were William and, providing domestic help, two slaves, Peter and King. Father and son rented lodgings at 7 Craven Street (the building still stands), a house that was part of a narrow but handsome terrace, in a reddish-brick 'Georgian' style equally familiar to any boulevardier of the city rising on the Delaware that the Franklins had left behind. Craven Street led down to the Thames. It was only a few blocks further along from the makeshift government offices that had risen from the fire-scorched apartments of the old Whitehall Palace. Agents were not spies. They were, in effect, the colonial Assemblies' ambassadors in Westminster and Franklin intended to get as close as possible to the heart of government. Craven Street was no less practical for William, who enrolled to read for the Bar at the Middle Temple, just a short walk to the east along the Strand.

Franklin's first meeting with the colony's absentee landlords in London demonstrated only that the Penn family were not to be easily moved. They appeared secure in London society. Persuading the British government of the need to bring them to heel was clearly going to prove to be a long and disheartening experience. In the meantime, there would be more happy diversions to keep the Agent in good heart while he remained in Britain. With William as his companion, he ventured to Ecton in Northamptonshire to pay his respects to the plot of earth his father had left behind. An aged relative was discovered and – disconcertingly – found to be living in rather more comfort than had softened Ben Franklin's first experiences of the New World. Father and son located and tended the family graves and examined the parish register which contained the details of two centuries of Franklin descendants. There were also excursions to Wales, Bristol, Bath and even across to the Dutch Republic.

The most agreeable aspect of these peregrinations was the reverential attention received from the country's intellectual classes. Franklin was lionised on trips to the universities of Cambridge, Oxford, Edinburgh and St Andrews. Among those he met in Edinburgh were Adam Smith and David Hume. So pleased was he with the honorary doctorate of law bestowed upon him by St Andrews University that he allowed himself to be known thereafter as 'Dr Franklin'. What would normally be considered something of an affectation stuck because it was patently appropriate for the man; just as it was fitting that Samuel Johnson, who received honorary LL Ds from Dublin and Oxford, would come to be known as 'Dr Johnson' (although it was seldom how he styled himself). Nor was this the extent of Franklin's honours. Three years later, in 1762, Oxford awarded him a Doctorate of Civil Laws and also acknowledged William with an honorary Master's degree.

Adulation from the intelligentsia only sharpened Benjamin Franklin's perception that, by comparison, Westminster's political élite were keeping him waiting in their ante-room. To persuade the politicians to curtail the Penns' power, what was needed was to place before them specific legal precedents rather than abstract notions of proprietorial excesses of authority. For this Franklin depended upon Galloway to forward him intelligence on what misdeeds were taking place on the other side of the Atlantic. But the principles upon which they would make their case also needed to be understood by a wider polity on both sides of the ocean. In Britain, land owned by the Crown was not exempt from being taxed by Parliament, unlike in Pennsylvania, where the proprietors had so contrived matters that they were able to stop the legislative Assembly in Philadelphia taxing large tracts of their estate. Franklin and Galloway proposed that the Penn family should be no more exempt than the royal family.

The second objective was to bring the colony into line with Britain on judicial matters. In particular, instead of judicial terms of office being held at the whim of the proprietors, judges should hold their post as long as they did not bring it into disrepute. It was Galloway who laid out the case in print before the public when in 1759 he published his *True and Impartial State of the Province of Pennsylvania.* It argued that the colony's legislative Assembly should have the same rights as the House of Commons in Westminster. And in executive matters, the British Crown, rather than the proprietors, ought to assume direct control. What had begun as a campaign to trim the proprietors' areas of competence was now turning into an attempt to replace them altogether. Franklin and Galloway were aiming to bring Pennsylvania under the direct rule of the British state.

As far as the Penns were concerned, Galloway was as much of an irritant in Philadelphia as was Franklin in London. It was Galloway who schooled Teedyuscung, the self-styled king of the Delaware Indians, to press for London's arbitration over his claim that the Penns were using forged sale documents to cheat his people out of their land. Galloway got Franklin to join in the chorus. First a Board of Trade inquiry spread blame before passing it on to the Crown's Indian superintendent to adjudicate. He eventually came down on the side of the proprietors. But by then, Galloway had brought about a minor constitutional revolution in the colony. In April 1759, he got the Governor, William Denny, to agree to the Assembly's attempts to tax all the proprietors' lands. Galloway recognised Denny was a man with a price and the Assembly duly voted him a personal financial bonus. What was more, Galloway assured Denny that there was more performance-related largesse for him if he agreed to legislation that would put the colony's judicial appointment procedure on the same terms as existed in Britain. The Penns' preferment powers had kept gubernatorial authority in their pocket. By demonstrating that the Assembly could also satisfy the Governor's venality, Galloway struck a blow for the powers of the elected chamber of the legislature.

Wrong-footed, it was the proprietors' turn to appeal to London for redress. The Board of Trade issued its report in June 1760. It struck down Galloway's legislation as unlawful. Franklin tried to get the Privy Council to overturn the judgment. In the matter of taxing the proprietors' land (to be permitted on a lenient basis) he had success, but not over the judicial appointment procedure. Disappointed with Governor Denny, Thomas Penn replaced him with someone more pliant. This was his nephew, John Penn. In August 1762, Franklin packed together his belongings and caught a ship back across the Atlantic. There seemed little more he could do in London so he would be better returning to support Galloway in the midst of Philadelphia's political fray. There, the Assembly's mandate to demand royal control of the colony had to be won first, before Franklin could return to London as the cause's champion.

While he had been in London with his father, the increasingly sophisticated William Franklin had made a mark in society. One consequence was an indiscretion: he fathered an illegitimate child. The boy was given the name William Temple Franklin. Benjamin Franklin – with experience in these matters and rather better financial means with which to take responsibility – agreed to oversee his grandson's wellbeing. Temple's birth appears not to have created much of a ripple. Such behaviour was scarcely considered scandalous at the time and did nothing to hold back William's advancement. This was continuing apace. Most importantly of all, he had made a favourable impression when introduced to Lord Bute, the Tory Prime Minister. Here was a friend in the highest of places. Bute was evidently charmed by the young American. This, and perhaps the calculation that it would further cement Benjamin Franklin's loyalty, resulted in William being appointed Royal governor of New Jersey colony. It was an extraordinary promotion.

Perversely, this news did not altogether please the senior Franklin. Instead the elevation of his thirty-one-year-old son to the Governor's mansion in Burlington, New Jersey gave the father some apprehension. Perhaps he believed it would impair the reputation he had built for himself as an independent man who could not be bought by official favour. There was, however, little he could do about it. Putting aside his doubts, Franklin joined the welcoming party for William when, in February 1763, he arrived back in America to take up the office. At the young man's side was his new wife, Elizabeth – the charming and well read daughter of a rich owner of plantations in Barbados. By this, of course, was meant that the family money was minted on the backs of slaves. This hard reality did not greatly trouble Ben Franklin and his circle. After all, as a philosopher, Franklin could appreciate the iniquity of slave labour but not to the extent that he yet felt ready to part with his own slaves. To his sister, Franklin rejoiced that his daughter-in-law was a lady 'of so amiable a Character'. Looking at the prospects for his promising son, Franklin boasted 'I have no doubt but that he will make as good a Governor as Husband: for he has good Principles and good Dispositions, and I think is not deficient in good Understanding.'[9] Like Joseph Galloway, William Franklin became an Episcopalian.

Having royal patronage bestowed upon his heir was potentially embarrassing for Benjamin Franklin, coming at the very moment when Galloway and he were trying to win Pennsylvania over to direct Crown rule. Back in Philadelphia, there was no shortage of acrimony to surmount. Critics wanted to know what royal control of the colony would mean in practice. Were Galloway and Franklin hoping to gain further from royal patronage personally, and if so, would they become as deaf to the Assembly's authority as had the Penns? Quakers and Presbyterians feared that with royal control would follow bishops and the official establishment of the Church of England over the colony. German settlers (a large group within the colony) and hardy frontiersmen were suspicious it would lead to a royal standing army being stationed to watch over them. Galloway and Franklin had to be particularly stern in the face of the intimidatory march on Philadelphia by the 'Paxton Boys', a body of frontiersmen who had murdered defenceless American Indians and were pressing for greater representation in the Assembly.

Having so assiduously built up the interdenominational coalition that was the Assembly Party, now Galloway and Franklin witnessed its fragmentation over their conviction that the colony's executive problems could be addressed by being taken out of the Penns' grip and placed into the royal care. When the proposal to ask for direct Crown control was debated in the Assembly, Galloway clashed with an opponent and supporter of the Penns, John Dickinson. As they were leaving the chamber, fisticuffs broke out between them. Forcibly separated, Dickinson mouthed the offer of a duel. Cooler heads prevailed and Galloway and Franklin won a majority vote for the Assembly to petition London for the assumption of direct rule. But before it could take effect, the annual election campaign had to be fought and won. A furious pamphleteering campaign got under way to discredit their plan. Supposed anti-German remarks by Franklin (likening them to pigs) were dredged up and used against him.

For Franklin and Galloway the main problem was that they advocated direct royal rule at exactly the time when the British government appeared hostile to colonial interests. The issue was settlers' rights. Or, in grandiloquent language, 'Manifest Destiny'. Ministers in London – no more than Quakers in Philadelphia – shared the Paxton Boys' exterminatory zeal over the Native American Indians. The campaign of the various tribes in the Ohio valley organised by Chief Pontiac sounded a warning that they would not accept dispossession without a struggle. The result was the 1763 Proclamation Act. It sought to restrict the colonies' expansion west into American Indian territory on the other side of the Appalachians. Franklin and Galloway both valued good relations with the American Indian tribes – a harmony that it was the Act's intention to preserve. But the legislation inflamed all those who hoped to gain or extend their own land into the Appalachians and beyond. They had assumed Britain's defeat of the French would facilitate going west. Now they discovered Britain wanted to restrict the horizon and their dreams. Furthermore, London established an office of superintendents to oversee compliance with the new frontier policy and the proper pacification of the native tribes.

This led to the second source of friction between white Americans and the government in London: tax. The cost of the superintendents' work was £20,000 a year. What was more, they were to be joined by 10,000 troops to help keep the peace. The annual cost, together with the forts and garrisons to maintain them, would run to £350,000 a year. This was unpopular. Franklin and Galloway then made a further strategic error by failing to anticipate the hostility in the colony to London's imposition of the Sugar Tax. Although both men opposed it, they were not perceived to have acted with the promptitude critics demanded. Then London proposed the Stamp Act. Newspapers, legal documents and gambling cards would be among the items taxed not just in Britain, but also in the American colonies. Faced with the crippling cost of financing the debt run up by the Seven Years' War, part of which was incurred in the defence of North America, and the policing of the colonies' frontiers with the native tribes, the British government decided to spread the tax burden more widely. It did not see why the colonists should be exempt from paying their share.

Franklin wrote to a friendly MP in Westminster expressing his hope that the proposed Stamp Act would not reach the statute book. Nonetheless, he remained relatively sanguine about the proposal.[10] In this, he misjudged the mood of his fellow Pennsylvanians. In September 1764, the Assembly passed a motion of opposition to the Sugar and Stamp Acts. In the elections of that year, Franklin and Galloway's 'old ticket' coalition retained a majority of seats in the colony at large, but in Philadelphia, their supposed power base, they were routed. Both city seats went to their opponents as did six of the eight of Philadelphia's country seats. Galloway came tenth. Franklin came thirteenth – second from bottom. So much for being the world's most famous American. Electors, it seemed, preferred the proprietorial devil they knew to a future Crown appointee they did not, especially given Britain's increasing deafness to the colonists' complaints.

Despite their own defeat, Franklin and Galloway were not deterred. According to one political enemy, the two friends continued to meet every night to plan tactics.[11] It was time well spent. Their motion to petition London for royal control scraped an Assembly majority; Franklin agreed to return to London to press for its favourable reception by the British government. He arrived back in the great capital city in December 1764. But his hopes of being able to petition for royal direct rule were hampered by having first to deal with the furore over the Stamp Act. Along with the Agents of the other colonial Assemblies, Franklin met the British Prime Minister, George Grenville, on 2 February 1765. The meeting was not a success. Grenville refused to back down on his proposal to tax the colonies. Franklin accepted that the mother country needed to raise the money somehow and that asking the colonies to contribute their share was not unreasonable. However, the manner in which a direct tax was to be imposed on paper transactions – including newspapers – trampled upon the colonists' sensibilities and was wrong in both principle and practice.

As a printer and publisher, Franklin was never likely to be enamoured of the idea. But he came up with alternatives. He proposed ways in which Britain might receive the necessary sums from the colonies without causing the offence of imposing the Stamp Tax. He suggested a 'paper money' plan. The temporary ban on the colonies issuing their own paper money would be rescinded. This would make currency in the colonies less scarce, which – given the level of colonial indebtedness to Britain and the ongoing desire to buy British imports – would work to Britain's advantage. Westminster could charge interest on the notes. It was not to be. Grenville thought Franklin's proposal impractical. Thus, the Stamp Act duly became law in March with implementation in the colonies scheduled to commence in November.

Defeated but hardly distraught over the matter, Franklin saw no need to orchestrate civil disobedience. Indeed, having failed to win the government over to a different scheme, he accepted his obligations to see Grenville's legislation put into practice. After all, Franklin was not likely to secure royal rule for Pennsylvania by disrupting the flow to His Majesty's Exchequer. He nominated the Assembly Party politician, John Hughes, as the Stamp Distributor in the colony. When Hughes began to fear his appointment had done him great damage with an angry public, Franklin wrote to assure him that 'a firm loyalty to the Crown, and faithful Adherence to the Government of this Nation, which it is the Safety as well as the Honour of the Colonies to be connected with, will always be the wisest Course for you and I to take, whatever may be the Madness of the Populace or their blind Leaders, who can only bring themselves and Country into Trouble, and draw on greater Burthens by Acts of rebellious Tendency'.[12] Far from being a man of the people, Benjamin Franklin was, it seemed, a British government man.

In this, he made a terrible misjudgement. The Stamp Act had its most detrimental effect not in the rural communities where most colonists lived but in the bustling commercial cities of the eastern seaboard where coalitions of dissent naturally had greater leverage. In charging pub landlords to keep licensed premises and placing additional expenses upon the work of newspaper editors, it managed to hit hardest those best equipped to convey their anger to the widest audience. The Act provoked serious riots in Boston and New York. Philadelphia appeared to be next when hotheads threatened to reduce the elegant town houses of Galloway and Franklin to rubble – as they had done to the stately residence of the Chief Justice of Massachusetts, Thomas Hutchinson (Franklin's collaborator back in 1754 on the Albany Plan of Union) in Boston. It was no good looking to the Proprietary Party to assume a restraining influence. It too had jumped on the anti-Stamp Tax bandwagon. From the comparatively calm gardening colony of New Jersey, Governor William Franklin dashed to Philadelphia to rescue his sister Sally and stepmother Deborah from the avenging mob. Sally agreed to flee to the sanctuary of the Governor's mansion in Burlington. Deborah Franklin, however, preferred to brazen it out, boarding herself up inside the family home and announcing she would shoot anyone who attacked it.

It was Galloway who prevented Philadelphia from descending into anarchy. He did so by getting tough. He organised eight hundred volunteers to patrol the streets; their orders were to suppress the first sign of trouble. The display of force worked. But it did not convert. Even those who wanted to protect property were eager to have the tax scrapped. In Virginia, Patrick Henry caused uproar in the House of Burgesses with his violent condemnation of the Act. A congress of representatives from nine of the colonies, including Pennsylvania, convened in New York in October 1765 and passed motions condemning Westminster's right to tax directly the American colonies. In this respect, a distinction was made between Parliament's imperial and domestic role. Westminster might be within its rights to impose taxes as part of the regulation of imperial trade that Americans would have to pay, but in matters of internal taxation Americans should recognise only the legitimacy of their own colonial Assemblies to make such levies.

The strength of opposition frightened Galloway. In August he had penned an article under the pseudonym 'Americanus' in the *Pennsylvania Journal* arguing that it was futile to threaten Britain, a country that had seen off the combined powers of France and Spain. In any case, given that the colonies ought to pay for their defence they should consider alternative ways of raising the money. Galloway revived Franklin's Albany Plan for the creation of a colonial Assembly charged with raising taxes for defence. Alternatively, the colonies could petition to elect MPs directly to the House of Commons in Westminster. That, at least, would end the anomaly in which they could be taxed by a legislature to which they sent no representatives. Writing to Franklin, Galloway advocated his idea for 'the Strongest and most indissoluble Bond of Union that can be invented, between the mother Country and her Foreign Dominions':

Can Brittain, when she duly considers the Ambitious Temper of Human Nature, without this, or some theory like it, expect to retain her Sovereignty over the Colonies longer than they find themselves in a Capacity to separate from her? Should it not be recollected, That the first Settlers of America came over possessed of the highest Ideas of Liberty. That their Posterity have been educated in the same Notions. Several of their Governments are meerly Democratical, and Consequently very liable to discontents and Insurrections. Their Distance from their mother Country will lessen her Awe, and the Idea of her Power, and when in a more Opulent State, and increased in Numbers, will probably prompt them to throw off their Subordination. I do not think this can possibly Happen in our Day, God Grant it never may – I am sure no good man woud wish to see it. But certainly these Considerations indicate the Prudence, if not the Necessity of Uniting the Colonies to their Mother Country by every Prudential Measure that can be devised.[13]

The identity of 'Americanus' was not, at first, common knowledge. But where Galloway had shown himself publicly in the midst of the crisis, he attracted admiration. He profited from this display of leadership under pressure. He had saved the city of brotherly love from burning. Here was the noble Roman who faced down the mob; its citizens responded. In the October 1765 elections, the previous year's losses for the Assembly Party were reversed. Galloway was returned and John Dickinson lost his seat. The city looked at the prospect of mob rule and backed away. Moderate opposition to Westminster's taxes was called for instead; it showed signs of success. In London, Franklin was busy putting together his case to the Privy Council for Crown control of Pennsylvania. Galloway wrote to him impressing upon him the necessity of exerting further pressure on London to repeal the Stamp Act. Reporting the situation in Philadelphia, he stated that 'It is difficult to Describe the Distress to which these distracted and Violent Measures have subjected the People of this Province and indeed all No[rth] America'.[14] It was important advice. Franklin was hopeful that all might be well, believing the change in government presented an opportunity. The Marquess of Rockingham had formed a ministry in July. It looked as if he would repeal the Stamp Act.

The Rockingham administration certainly seemed more interested in Franklin's views on the Stamp Act than on his petition for royal control. The Privy Council put the latter to one side until normality had been seen to return on the far side of the Atlantic. With Galloway drawing up the Assembly's petition to lift the ban on Pennsylvania issuing legal tender, Rockingham was not as quick as Grenville to dismiss Franklin's paper money scheme. Rockingham desired the Stamp Act scrapped. Apart from any other consideration, British merchants wanted it repealed since they were losing out from the embargo on traded goods that the colonists had organised in response.

In February 1766, Franklin was summoned before the House of Commons committee examining the Stamp Act. Asked many questions (of those put, 174 were recorded), he laid out with calm determination the constitutional and practical objections to it. Many of the questions had been prearranged with Franklin by Rockingham's allies, although Grenville and the tax's supporters also waded in. Again, Franklin remained constant to his position. He drew a distinction between indirect taxes that regulated trade (which he accepted) and direct taxes (for revenue) which he did not. Some thought this an arbitrary distinction since either Westminster had the right to impose taxes on the King's American subjects or it did not. Was the distinction a result of a more deep-seated animosity towards the mother country? Franklin gave the impression that it was merely the recent fiscal impositions that disturbed transatlantic relations. Asked to contrast the current unease in the colonies with the situation prior to the Stamp Act débâcle, he stated that the relationship had been 'the best in the world'. Americans had:

> submitted willingly to the government of the Crown, and paid, in all their courts, obedience to acts of parliament. Numerous as the people are in the several old provinces, they cost you nothing in forts, citadels, garrisons, or armies, to keep them in subjection. They were governed by this country at the expense only of a little pen, ink, and paper. They were led by a thread.[15]

Franklin's performance was noted, printed and widely circulated. The following month, the Stamp Act was repealed. Galloway wrote to Franklin to describe the scenes of jubilation in Philadelphia at 'the great News' – adding that he had advised 'more Temperate and Private rejoicing on this great Occasion' and opposed 'the Intended Fire Works Illuminations, firing of Canon &ca'. He was particularly gratified that 'the Numerous Accounts we have of my Dear Friends Integrity and Address in procuring the Repeal give us all the greatest pleasure, and has open'd the Eyes of Many who entertained a Contrary Opinion of you, from the wicked Calumnies of your Enemies'. He continued, 'Some few there are yet, who with unwearied Industry are endeavouring by their Malevolent Falsehoods to injure your Good Name. But it will be without Effect – The Prop[rietor]y Party never will desist from their Abuse of you. Tho they are Dayly put to Shame on that Account.'[16]

Such was the relief that Westminster's assertion – laid out in an accompanying Declaratory Act – stating it 'had, hath and of right ought to have, full power and authority to make laws and statutes of sufficient force and validity to bind the colonies and people of America' was initially passed over as little more than a face-saving pronouncement. The trade embargo had concentrated minds in the administration but the path of moderate opposition called for by Galloway in Philadelphia and followed through in London by Franklin appeared to have been vindicated. Politically, Galloway's standing had never been higher. For the next eight years he would be Speaker of the Pennsylvania Assembly. Franklin was overjoyed at his friend's promotion.[17] It was a position from which, with sufficient force of character, Galloway could do far more than preside over debate. Rather, he could now hope to direct much of the Pennsylvanian legislature's business. He wrote to Franklin, 'I have now no doubt that all Discontent will Subside in America.'[18]

The fiscal quarrels between Britain and her colonies appeared to have been settled, for the moment at any rate. But Franklin did not share Galloway's optimism for the road ahead. His goal as Agent, to petition for proprietary rule to be replaced with royal rule for Pennsylvania, was still going nowhere. He was given to understand that the British government would only be prepared to replace the Penns' executive authority on terms that would reduce rather than enhance the rights of Pennsylvanians. This Franklin could not accept. It was, in any case, not sellable in Philadelphia. During 1768, hope of royal direct rule all but faded away and Franklin's annoyance at London's self-satisfied inertia on the matter hardened commensurately.

His growing truculence was evident in his response to the imposition of the Townshend duties on a variety of goods imported by the colonists including paper, glass, lead and tea. Having made clear there was no con-stitutional objection to external transatlantic trade-related duties being imposed upon the colonies, he could not reasonably complain about the new duties in principle. But Charles Townshend, the Chancellor of the Exchequer, also believed in bringing the colonies under tighter control from London. He wanted the Crown rather than the colonial assemblies to pay Governors' salaries. This had never been Franklin's conception of what royal rule should involve. The arrangement in Pennsylvania (where the Governor's salary was paid by the Assembly) had proved to be one of the most important checks on executive authority that the legislature possessed.

Franklin began to wonder whether the previous distinction he had made between external and internal taxation was tenable. Indeed, he began to question whether London did have any fiscal rights over the colonies at all. To his son, William, Franklin postulated that either 'Parliament has a power to make *all laws* for us, or that it has a power to make *no laws* for us; and I think the arguments for the latter more numerous and weighty than those for the former'. In that eventuality, 'the colonies would then be so many separate states, only subject to the same King, as England and Scotland were before the Union'.[19] Franklin was beginning to think such a settlement desirable, although it was noteworthy that he still imagined North America in terms of constituent colonies and not as a federal United States.

William agreed with his father's latest logic and in November 1768 used his authority as Governor of New Jersey to write on the subject to the Secretary of State for the Colonies, the Earl of Hillsborough. Without exception, every colonial Assembly 'believes that the Parliament has not a right to impose taxes for the purposes of a revenue in America', he assured Hillsborough. Using troops to collect the taxes only inflamed passions, for 'no force on earth is sufficient to make the Assemblies acknowledge by any act of theirs, that the Parliament has a right to impose taxes on America'. Trade boycotts were inevitable, Governor William Franklin continued, and 'the mother country may thereby lose more in her commerce than she can possibly gain by way of revenue'.[20] Assembly Agent Benjamin Franklin meanwhile had thrown himself publicly behind this very cause, writing articles in both the London and Pennsylvanian press condemning the duties and commending the boycott of the items upon which they were to be levied. 'Let us agree', he thundered with puritan righteousness in the *Pennsylvania Chronicle*, 'to consume no more of their expensive geegaws'.[21]

From his chair as Speaker of the Pennsylvania Assembly, Galloway also opposed the new duties. But he did not endorse the boycott. He wrote to Franklin pointing out that there was a potential benefit from the government's scheme because if part of the revenue raised supported 'our Civil Authority will not the Crown name the Governor?'.[22] He steered the Assembly towards petitioning against the duties rather than determining to disrupt their collection. Setting a good example of respect for law and order remained Galloway's guiding strategy – a view relentlessly attacked in the press by John Dickinson. The rivalry between Galloway and Dickinson was not merely political. It was deeply personal. Galloway was never slow to use the press as a tool for his own cause and counter-attacked his tormentor, accusing him of base personal motives for impugning the patriotism of Franklin. This war of words worked in the Speaker's favour. In the 1768 elections, Galloway topped the ballot. Dickinson failed to get elected.

Yet, it was clear that Franklin and Galloway reacted to the Townshend

Acts with different levels of condemnation. In January 1769, Franklin wrote to Galloway suggesting the necessity of a plan to conciliate Britain and her colonies. His suggestion could be 'express'd in a few Words; *Repeal* the Laws, *Renounce* the Right, *Recall* the Troops, *Refund* the Money, and *Return to the old Method of Requisition*'. In a few words he proposed a great change. And the concessions were to be largely one-way, Franklin relenting only so far as to permit Parliament's claim of Right if it was in future to be considered 'in the same Light with the Claim of the Spanish Monarch to the Title of King of Jerusalem'.[23] Responding to pressure, Galloway came to see the necessity of endorsing the consumer boycott of imports carrying duties. But he did not support the campaign advocated by Dickinson being implemented in New York and Boston to order merchants not to import them. Galloway was fearful that this would cause economic hardship for the Pennsylvanian merchant class that was the bedrock of his support. Yet, in February 1769, they chose of their own volition to join the non-importation campaign. Galloway, it was clear, had misread the level of anger.

What was more, the non-importation strategy worked. British trade with the colonies was decimated by it and Parliament repealed the Townshend duties in March 1770. It was a notable triumph for colonial solidarity. Only one duty remained – on tea. Some may have adopted the political gesture of shunning it in favour of coffee, but more often the response was to buy it from smugglers instead. Franklin remained dissatisfied, continuing to press for the comprehensive boycott to continue until Parliament repealed the Declaratory Act stating its legal right to tax the colonies. Notwithstanding his own more cautious approach, Galloway wrote to him in June 1770 encouraging him to keep up the harassment of the government: 'The M[in-istr]y are much Mistaken in imagining that there will ever be an Union either of Affections or Interest between G. Britain and America untill Justice is done to the latter and there is a full Restoration of its Liberties.'[24] His tone had certainly hardened and he was doing as much as possible to keep in step with Franklin.

Although Galloway continued to be the most important politician in the Assembly, it was at this moment that he suddenly found his mastery questioned. He had been instrumental in establishing the *Pennsylvania Chronicle* as a supportive newspaper. But in 1770 he fell out with its editor, William Goddard, who was demonstrating a burgeoning attachment to editorial independence. Galloway objected to his newspaper giving Dick-inson space to air complaints and, by 1770, the number of alternative voices had multiplied in its pages. Goddard responded by publishing his account, *The Partnership*, chastising Galloway and the Assembly Party for interference and accusing them of debasing public affairs. He revealed Galloway as 'Americanus' and portrayed him as a closet supporter of the Stamp Act. These were damning charges. Fearing they had endangered his re-election in Philadelphia, Galloway made a last-minute switch to stand as the candidate in the rural constituency of Bucks County where he had recently inherited his father-in-law's delightful country house, Trevose. The switch was timely and he was successfully elected. But it was hardly a triumph. He came eighth on a ticket where the top eight were elected. He was able to continue as Speaker of the Assembly and to get his business through the lower house with the exercise of preferment that came with the post, but he had lost any claim to being a popular tribune. The Assembly Party was no longer a cohesive group. Galloway's tormentor, Dickinson, was returned and the *Pennsylvania Chronicle* heaped abuse where once it had printed laudation.

Increasingly alienated from the political mood, Galloway was shaken by this sudden reversal of fortune. He appeared to lose stomach for the fight. His health had deteriorated the previous summer. Franklin had offered to put him up in London while he recovered, but Galloway stayed on. He wrote dispirited letters instead. It was clear he wished Franklin would quit London and return to Philadelphia: they needed each other.[25] Fearful that his principal friend and ally was close to resignation, Franklin tried to cheer him by reminding him that, 'We must not in the Course of Publick Life expect immediate Approbation, and immediate grateful Acknowledgement of our Services. But let us persevere, thro' Abuse and even Injury. The internal Satisfaction of a good Conscience is always present, and Time will do us Justice in the Minds of the People, even of those at present the most prejudic'd against us.'[26] A month later, Franklin tried again to raise his ally's spirits: 'I must however beg you will not think of retiring from Publick Business. You are yet a young man and may still be greatly serviceable to your Country. It would be, I think, something criminal to buy in private Retirement so early, all the Usefulness of so much Experience and such great Abilities.'[27] There were hard realities behind these soothing words. To one of his supporters Franklin had written, 'I hope our Friend Galloway will not decline the Public Service in Assembly with his private Business. Both may be too much for his Health.' Yet, 'I do not see that he can be spared from that Station without great Detriment to our Affairs and to the general Welfare of America.'[28]

For years now, Galloway had held the fort back in Philadelphia while his friend traded diplomatic niceties in London. Thanks to the postal system, their relationship had not been damaged by this physical distance. Rather it was perhaps more closely held together by it because it effectively divorced Franklin from so many other Pennsylvanian politicians who might have come between him and Galloway with different views and objectives. The partnership hung, however, on a stark reality. Franklin's accomplishments were broader and more profound, his fame may have stretched further, but to hold on to his commission he was dependent on Galloway remaining in power, not the other way round. To his son, William, Franklin wrote with forced optimism, 'I cast my Eye over Goddard's Piece against our Friend Mr Galloway and then lit my fire with it. I think such feeble malicious Attacks cannot hurt him.'[29]

Galloway was in difficulties in Philadelphia and could have benefited from Franklin's return to fight by his side, especially since the Agent's mission to London appeared to be making little headway. But the absence of the older sage did nothing to dent the affinity William Franklin felt for Galloway. Similar age, similar outlook, both married to attractive heiresses, they continued to see one another when work permitted. Before moving to the socially more exclusive Perth Amboy, south-west of New York City, William had made his principal Governor's residence at Burlington, on the Delaware. There he farmed six hundred acres. But, importantly, he was only seventeen miles away from the cosmopolitan world of Philadelphia. He frequently visited his neglected stepmother, Deborah and his half-sister, Sally. When doing so, he stayed with Galloway, sometimes at his town house and at other times out at Trevose.

For Benjamin Franklin, the temptation to return to Philadelphia to see Deborah and their daughter Sally, to wander the Trevose orchards with Galloway or inspect the improvements to Burlington with his son were still insufficient to induce him home. With the exception of his two-year break in Philadelphia between 1762 and 1764, he had spent the last fourteen years living on the British side of the Atlantic Ocean. He had not seen his son, daughter, wife or best friend for seven years. For much of this time he appeared unwilling to tear himself away from the continuing variety and allure of living in the western world's largest city. But he had also come to believe that by staying on in London he could yet pull off a personal and political triumph that would justify his years of labour there.

Between 1768 and 1770 he thought he was poised to become an American-born member of a British administration. Senior members of the government, he had heard, were speaking highly of him. There was the possibility of being offered an Under-Secretaryship of State. This was no time to be leaving town. On the contrary, he went out of his way to stake his claim. In his correspondence with William, he made it clear he would accept a government position if it was offered. Lord North, the Chancellor of the Exchequer, had talked to him 'very obligingly' and said 'I hope we shall find some way of making it worth your while'. 'I thanked his lordship,' Franklin recounted to William, 'and said I should stay with pleasure if I could any ways be useful to government.' For someone who had only three months previously been fulminating against his fellow Americans purchasing British 'geegaws', it was a remarkable about-turn. To the Secretary to the Treasury, Grey Cooper, Franklin was positively obsequious about the Prime Minister, the Duke of Grafton:

> There was no nobleman to whom I could from sincere respect for his great abilities, and amiable qualities, so cordially attach myself, or to whom I should so willingly be obliged for the provision he mentioned, as to the Duke of Grafton, if his Grace should think I could, in any station where he might place me, be serviceable to him and to the public.[30]

It is hard to imagine that a proud, self-reliant man of Franklin's bearing would have put on such a fawning performance had the expectation of government office not burned so brightly. Not even the news that his long-suffering Deborah had been afflicted by a stroke could tempt him back across the Atlantic. Clearly he thought that he could be of real use facilitating the unity of Britain and her American colonies from an office in Whitehall. But there was also the question of personal enrichment. For this, he needed the government to approve a substantial land grant west of the Ohio River to a company in which he was a major investor. Although nominally French-settled, the area was in the gift of the British Crown and the Board of Trade had begun to question whether the 1763 Proclamation Line preventing westward settlement had been drawn too restrictively.

Investing in the scheme had been William Franklin's idea. The cost of entertaining in Burlington and Perth Amboy far exceeded his Governor's salary, forcing him to borrow from his father. Having also footed the bill for William's study at the Middle Temple, Franklin had a long record of extending credit to his grand-living son (who certainly had not imbibed the simple homilies of *Poor Richard's Almanack*). The father was wearily keeping a careful note of all the transactions, intent on being eventually remunerated. For the son, acquiring the land would bring forward that day, finally freeing him from his debts to his father. William had persuaded Galloway to join his scheme (they were already investing in a silver mine together). When William asked his father to become a shareholder too and to use his influence in London to secure government consent, Franklin gladly agreed to do so. He had already won a land grant in Nova Scotia and believed that investing in this new venture would reap dividends.

When the first proposal faltered, he helped organise a petition for a yet larger twenty-million-acre land grant. It covered a vast tract west of the Appalachians to the Mississippi and south-west to the Kentucky River. This quickly received the support of the Lords in Treasury only to be blocked by the Earl of Hillsborough, the Secretary of State for the Colonies and brother-in-law of Lord North, who was antipathetic to sporadic and ill-considered westward expansion. But Hillsborough's opposition was surmounted when the Privy Council Committee for Plantation Affairs overturned the Board of Trade's opposition. The Privy Council then set in motion plans for the creation of a new colony named after Queen Charlotte's birthplace – Vandalia. Joseph Galloway, Benjamin and William Franklin were all, it seemed, poised to grow immensely rich from it. Working together promised to pay dividends.

SIX

Distant Loyalties

Two years after Franklin had made clear he would welcome a job in the government, he had still heard nothing. During this time, the Earl of Hillsborough adopted the habit of greeting him interchangeably with great affection and total indifference. When Franklin called upon him to announce that he had accepted the Massachusetts House of Representatives' offer to become their Agent as well, he was received by a third expression – outright hostility. Far from acknowledging it as a formality, Hillsborough pulled rank, claiming Franklin could not accept the post without the consent of Massachusetts' Governor, Thomas Hutchinson. Franklin ignored Hillsborough's protestation and proceeded to take up the patronage of the rowdy Boston Assembly regardless. In doing so, he relinquished hope of office in a British ministry.

By 1770, Franklin had become the London Agent of four colonial legislatures: Pennsylvania, Georgia, New Jersey and now Massachusetts. There were the makings of a surrogate ambassadorship here. What was more, in the case of New Jersey, he represented the legislature of a colony of which his son was the Governor. Had a rival been handed such scope for conflict of interest, Franklin might have condemned the set-up as corrupt. But he had a high opinion of his own righteousness and propriety. He was protective of the arrangement that while the Governor was appointed by the Crown, the Agent's loyalty was to the Assembly. Indeed, by accepting the Massachusetts offer, he tied himself to an Assembly intent upon maximising the gulf between the two bodies. Boston was the city of Franklin's birth; it was also the least deferential city in North America. Its popular leaders were now able to press their arguments upon Franklin. In doing so, they weakened Galloway's role as his eyes and ears on the American side of the Atlantic. Although neither appreciated it fully at the time, it would prove a decisive shift in their relationship and in the future of their continent.

The success of the non-importation campaign against the Townshend duties had hastened Boston's gravitation towards mob politics. Sam Adams, the 'Sons of Liberty' and other self-appointed tribunes openly challenged

British authority, or indeed any authority. Ruffians roamed the streets, intimidating those tempted to trade with the mother country. Threatening the troops garrisoned in the city provided sport and in March 1770, drew blood. On the day the new Prime Minister in London, Lord North, repealed the Townshend duties, a group of redcoats were set upon. They retaliated, opening fire on their assailants. Three were killed. It was a gift to the polemicists. Furnished with their first martyrs, the rabble-rousers talked of the 'Boston Massacre'.

The fraught atmosphere in Massachusetts exceeded that felt elsewhere. During 1772, tension appeared to be easing in most of the other colonies. The duty on tea was all that remained of the once sweeping Townshend measures, the non-importation campaign had been largely lifted and Hillsborough was replaced as Secretary of State for the Colonies by the more personable Earl of Dartmouth. But the Massachusetts House of Representatives was far from pacified. Franklin forwarded its petition against the Crown paying Governor Hutchinson's salary to the government. Dartmouth suggested postponing the question, but the Boston politicians were not so easily put off. They encouraged Franklin to persevere. Thomas Hutchinson had been Franklin's collaborator in developing the 'Union' proposals for the Albany Congress in 1754. A wealthy Bostonian by birth, he had been Speaker of the Massachusetts House of Representatives during the 1740s and, like Speaker Galloway in Pennsylvania, believed in order as the prerequisite for a just society. Prior to his appointment as the Massachusetts Governor he had written letters in 1768 and 1769 to one of the Under-Secretaries of State in London, arguing that Boston's rowdy outbursts needed to be met with a firm hand, including the curtailment of some liberties. This correspondence was subsequently stolen and, in 1773, passed to Franklin. The means to discredit the Governor were at the Agent's disposal.

Franklin still held the office of Deputy Postmaster-General of the Colonies. He should not have been dealing in intercepted letters. Yet, rather than return them to their rightful owner, he decided it was his duty as the Massachusetts House of Representatives' Agent to pass them to Thomas Cushing, the House's Speaker. Writing to Galloway, Franklin subsequently maintained that in passing on the letters it had been his intention to 'promote a Reconciliation' between Boston and London because the correspondence demonstrated not the despicable nature of the British government but rather the perfidy of one of its American servants.' This was the same point he made at the time to Cushing, insisting that the 'resentment' he had come to feel against Britain's politicians had 'been considerably abated' now that he had discovered they had been misled by American 'betrayers of the Interest, not of their Native Country only, but of the Government they pretend to serve, and of the whole English Empire'.[2]

To Cushing, Franklin requested that the enclosure should not be published.[3] Unsurprisingly, the appeal was ignored and the letters duly appeared in print. Boston seethed with anger and the campaign to remove Governor Hutchinson became ferocious. Its timing was acute. The non-importation campaign against the duty on tea had not only been good for coffee sales, it had also deepened the pockets of Boston's underworld who had illegally smuggled in untaxed tea with their other contraband. However, when London removed some trade restrictions to assist the struggling East India Company, the result was to bring down the price of taxed tea dramatically. This spelt disaster for smugglers, whose profit margin was the first to be hit. It was this, rather than a campaign against tax (which was actually good for their illicit business), that inspired a band of smugglers and their politically motivated accomplices on the night of 16 December 1773 to board a tea-laden ship moored in Boston harbour and tip almost £11,000 worth of its cargo into the sea.

In London, the petition for Governor Hutchinson's removal was heard by the Privy Council on 29 January 1774. The news of the 'Boston Tea Party' had reached the capital nine days previously and tempers were inflamed at the destruction of the East India Company's merchandise. It was not the best time for Benjamin Franklin, agent of the request and purveyor of purloined letters, to have to face an inquisition. The grilling took place in the Cockpit in Whitehall, where Princess Anne and Sarah Churchill had once whiled away their youth at the card table. With its history of fowl-baiting and Restoration theatricals, it was a perfect location for the spectator sport.

The Prime Minister and other leading members of the government were present, while the Archbishops of Canterbury and London, Edmund Burke and Joseph Priestley were among those who squeezed into the viewing gallery. As he was called forward to take the stand for questions, Franklin must surely have had a premonition that he was in for a hard time. But he cannot have expected subjection to mockery. Grandstanding before his captive audience, the Solicitor-General, Alexander Wedderburn – a Scot with a history of wounding invective – took his cue. 'Men will watch him with a jealous eye', he ridiculed the sixty-eight-year-old man renowned around the world for his contribution to learning and unpretentious wisdom, 'they will hide their papers from him, and lock up their escritoires. He will henceforth esteem it a libel to be called a man of letters.'[4] The guffaws rang out around the Cockpit.

Having made his way in life and achieved such eminence entirely by his own efforts, Franklin stood there, incensed by supercilious jibes intended to make him look a fool before some of the highest ranks of British society. This was not the gown-clad acclamation of an honorary degree ceremony, not the respect he had been shown by the Anglican dons of Oxford or sober scholars of Edinburgh and St Andrews. This corrupting display compared ill with the world he had left behind where earnest persons had passed without advertisement in and out of his old home in Philadelphia, where no rank was recognised but the right to self-improvement and public enlightenment. In fact, Wedderburn's verbal assault was so intense that even the London press preferred to avoid the legal implications of publishing sections of it. But when the mockery was printed in the colonies, opinion was inflamed by Franklin's humiliation. Wedderburn had gone the full rounds in the Cockpit, jabbing and cutting. He had scored a remarkable pyrrhic triumph.

It was the end of Franklin's belief in British fair play. Sacked as Deputy Postmaster-General of the Colonies, he wrote to his son, telling him that as a consequence, 'there is no Prospect of your ever being promoted to a better government [office]'. He advised William to resign the governorship of New Jersey and to take up a more honourable living as a farmer. An ageing man disappointed by the reality of worldly office was returning to reclaim his earlier cause, the rural homespun self-sufficiencies of *Poor Richard's Almanack*. The letter ended, 'You will hear from others the Treatment I have receiv'd. I leave you to your own Reflections and Determinations upon it, and remain ever, Your affectionate father, B. Franklin.'[5] It was an appeal to filial loyalty. However, if Franklin believed that his son should withdraw from public life in protest at the way his father had been forced out of it, he was soon to be disappointed. William had always been in his father's shadow. But he was not about to vacate the Governor's mansion to follow the plough.

At root, Benjamin Franklin had tried to ride several horses at once and inevitably come to grief. He had accepted too many conflicting positions. It was not possible to be the Agent for Boston's brusque-mannered politicians (in addition to representing three other legislatures) while also expecting favour from a ministry against which Boston had hired him to be antagonistic. A man who was the Deputy Postmaster-General of the Colonies could not expect to trade stolen post and keep his job. For all his fame and ability, for all that he had achieved in America, his years spent in Britain on the fringes of Whitehall and power had produced little of consequence. He could be forgiven for becoming bitter against a culture that had failed to exploit his talents. Yet he had assured William as late as 1773 that although he might return briefly to America to settle his financial affairs, he intended to live out the rest of his life in Britain.[6] Such was hardly the attitude of an American revolutionary.

Subjection to a public humiliation changed matters. The degrading manner in which he was treated in the Cockpit did as much as anything else to alienate him from the country whose government and society he had long sought to influence. To understand how much the Cockpit mauling bruised him it is necessary to advance the clock to the midst of the American War of Independence, when Franklin went to meet King Louis XVI at Versailles to sign the agreement between the rebel colonies and the kingdom of France. This would prove to be the deal that would humble Great Britain. For the historic occasion he wore the coat – by then faded and quite unsuitable for the grandiose surroundings – that he had worn back on the day a British minister of the Crown had sought to belittle him in the Cockpit. When asked why, he replied, 'for a little revenge'.[7]

Fractious irritation was now the governing passion of the colonies. Measures were enacted to subdue Boston's insurrectionist spirit, closing her port until restitution for the lost tea was made and extending the Governor's executive and judicial authority and giving him the troops to impose it. Bostonians felt they were coming under a form of military rule, complete with General Gage in place of Governor Hutchinson to enforce it. George III was cast as a latter-day James II, intent on riding roughshod over the rights of corporations and assemblies. Far from subduing tempers, the crackdown succeeded only in inflaming them. Indeed, there was almost nothing London could propose that would fail to rouse indignation in the taverns and meeting halls of Massachusetts. Taxation without representation was the cry taken up at the time that found resonance down through the pages of history. But it was not the only issue. New England's Puritan majority also detested London's intent to appease – rather than suppress – the other groups with whom they shared the eastern seaboard of North America. London appeared unwilling to subjugate Canada's French-speaking (and Catholic) majority in the manner many colonists thought necessary. In June 1774, the Quebec Act became law. It provided for Canada to be ruled by a legislative council appointed by the Crown while guaranteeing the preservation of French law, French custom and the open practice of Roman Catholicism.

Such concessions caused outrage among the (largely Presbyterian) American rebels. In Boston, anti-Catholic feeling was whipped up. Overt Catholicism was not the only target. As if the English Reformation had never happened, it was alleged that Anglicanism was merely a cover for Catholicism's eventual triumph in America. And there was something of concern to the future fortunes of Joseph Galloway, Ben and William Franklin, as well as for a gentleman farmer named George Washington and for all those with hopes of establishing westward plantation. London was drawing Canada's boundaries much further south than these men had hoped, determining her territory south of the Great Lakes and into the plains of Ohio and Illinois where there were a number of small disparate French-speaking settlements. This appeared to bar the prospect of the American colonies' westward expansion there. In particular, it crushed expectations of the land grant in 'Vandalia'. In appeasing the French-speakers of North America, the British government inflamed the English-speakers of the thirteen colonies. For Galloway and father and son Franklin, the prospect of enrichment under the British flag was suddenly in doubt.

A crisis was coming to a head. In the House of Commons, the coercive measures against the colonies were ridiculed by Charles James Fox and Edmund Burke, the latter demanding to know how a situation had been reached where 'so paltry a sum as threepence in the eyes of a financier, so insignificant an article as teas in the eyes of a philosopher, have shaken the pillars of a commercial empire that circled the whole globe?'[8] The government was not listening. Despite his unhappy experience in the Cockpit, Franklin remained in London, exploring options for heading off colonial anger with, among others, the Earl of Chatham (as William Pitt the Elder had become), the senior statesman whose period as Prime Minister had brought the military victories in the Seven Years' War that had fundamentally changed the political realities of North America. The problem was that Chatham had not been in office since 1768. Opposition politicians – whatever their eminence – could achieve little in practice. They were not the government and, unless a disaster occurred, were not likely to be in the future.

From the Governor's mansion in Perth Amboy, William Franklin believed it was those currently holding the reins of office that needed to be made aware of the necessity of a very sharp change of tack. He wrote to the Earl of Dartmouth, Secretary of State for the Colonies, warning of the dangers of colonial representatives forming their own convocations as shadow authorities. At the very moment in which Governor Franklin was writing his letter, just such a gathering, the first 'Continental Congress', was getting under way in Philadelphia, with (mostly self-selecting) representatives from the colonial Assemblies sitting down together to determine a joint course of action to force Britain to back down over her coercive measures against Boston. William Franklin warned that Britain was letting the initiative pass to the rebels. What was needed was to win it back. He suggested the government should call an official congress of its own and invite the more moderate colonial Governors as well as representatives from London and the colonial Assemblies to take part. Together, they should frame a constitution for the American colonies on reasonable and equitable terms before a rabble of malcontents seized the opportunity to do it for them.[9] It was a leap of imagination far too great for what Burke called the small minds governing a great Empire from Whitehall. But if the government would not take the Governor of New Jersey's advice, the Governor had to consider what attitude he should adopt to the forthcoming and possibly rancorous congress due to open in Philadelphia. It was time to seek out his old friend, Joseph Galloway.

William's carriage turned into the Trevose estate, passed the lucrative ironworks, farmland and trees and proceeded up the hill to Galloway's mansion, a solid, classically proportioned building from which to look down over Bucks County below. The Governor of New Jersey and the Speaker of the Pennsylvania Assembly were tied not only by a friendship of over two decades but also by their common bond with the senior Franklin, a triangle of association that had kept them in communication with one another over the years when the cares of office and the gulf of the Atlantic might normally have dulled familiarity. William arrived at Trevose with the idea that the colonies should be represented at Westminster. It was a proposal that failed to foresee the extent of future demographic change. Galloway had a far more structured settlement in mind. And he saw his opportunity to get it accepted by the Continental Congress. Given the likely non-meeting of minds between the moderate colonies' representatives and those, especially from Massachusetts, who were belligerent and pressing to sever links with the mother country, deadlock was likely. This would present him with the chance to spring his plan on the delegates.

The First Continental Congress opened in Philadelphia on 5 September 1774. Galloway had offered the use of the State House, the amphitheatre of so many of his triumphs, only to find the delegates preferring the less haughty atmosphere of the Carpenters' Hall. Every colony, except Georgia, sent representatives. South Carolina had gone to the trouble of electing its delegates while a process of self-selection had propelled the other dignitaries to the fore. But among those who had pushed to the front were men who would determine the course of world history – those who would later be known collectively as the 'Founding Fathers' and accorded apostolic status in the new testament of the New World. George Washington and Patrick Henry arrived with the Virginian delegation. John Jay came with the party

from New York. From Massachusetts came John Adams and his con-
frontationally minded cousin, Samuel Adams. This was a far more significant
gathering than the various solidarity-minded discussion bodies that had
preceded it. What William Franklin had warned London about had become
a reality: America's home-grown politicians were creating their own assembly
to repudiate the distant and assuming petulance of the British Parliament.

The delegates arrived together amid some fanfare and much hospitality.
But they were not of one mind. They were not all as keen to agree with the
Bostonian representatives upon a course that could only lead logically to
outright American independence not just from Westminster but even from
the British Crown. A failure to agree a common line would be highly
injurious to the cause. Here, then, was the opportunity for Joseph Galloway,
Speaker of the Pennsylvania Assembly and leading light of his colony's
representation in the Congress, to propose a constitutional compromise. For
years he had worked in tandem with Benjamin Franklin, but his old colleague
was still in London, officially in disgrace and apparently burned out and
impotent. This was surely the moment for Galloway to push on with his
own ideas for his continent's future. And, like his old friend at Albany back
in 1754, he was going to propose a plan for Anglo-American union.

On 28 September, Galloway rose to address the Congress delegates. It was
the most important speech he would ever give. He had an opportunity to
direct the destiny of North America. The delegates had voted to support
non-importation of British goods in the hope that this would force London
to repeal the coercive acts against Massachusetts. But there were divisions
over whether to endorse non-exportation as well. Deadlock presented the
representative from Pennsylvania with the moment to propose his scheme
of union. Non-importation, Galloway argued, would not work quickly
enough to achieve its political aims while non-exportation would succeed
only in wrecking the colonial economy and making her prey to French
invasion. Instead the Congress should issue Britain with a petition for a new
constitutional devolution of powers.

He proposed the creation of 'a British and American legislature, for
regulating and administration of the general affairs of America'. It would be
administered by a President-General appointed by the King and a Grand
Council elected by the thirteen colonial legislatures. The representatives on
the Grand Council would enjoy the same rights and privileges as members
of the House of Commons in London and would face re-election every three
years. As a branch of the British legislature 'united and incorporated with it',
the Grand Council would devise law for the colonies. The internal affairs of
each colony would remain the preserve of the colonial Assemblies but the

Grand Council would be sovereign over matters of common 'civil and criminal and commercial' concern. The President-General had the power to veto legislation and 'with the advice and consent of the General Council' would be responsible for implementing 'the legislative rights, powers and authorities, necessary for regulating and administering all the general police and affairs of the colonies'. In framing common transatlantic legislation, 'regulations may originate, and be formed and digested, either in the Parliament of Great Britain or in the said Grand Council, and being prepared, transmitted to the other for their approbation or dissent; and that the assent of both shall be requisite to the validity of all such general acts or statutes'.[10] Thus, the Grand Council would have the power to veto Westminster legislation it did not like, invalidating it for North America.

Galloway's union proposals drew heavily on Franklin's 1754 Albany Plan, employing the same Grand Council concept, elected by the Assemblies on three-year terms. But the double-lock between the British and American legislatures was Galloway's idea. Unlike the Irish Parliament in Dublin, Galloway's American Grand Council could veto Westminster law it did not like. Upon the world stage, Americans would remain the King's subjects. But they would be masters in their own house.

Galloway's plan attracted immediate plaudits. It was seconded by the New York representatives John Jay and James Duane and supported by South Carolina's Edward Rutledge. It also had its critics. Patrick Henry argued that any council elected by the colonial Assemblies and not directly by the people would encourage corruption and behind-the-scenes dealing. The plan held no appeal for the Boston radical, Samuel Adams. He, of course, was up for a fight. Notwithstanding the complaints, on 29 September the Congress considered endorsing Galloway's plan. It was put to the vote. Five colonies voted for its adoption. Six voted to postpone the matter. It was desperately close. Galloway had come within an inch of being the Founding Father of America's plan for home rule.

But close was not near enough. It soon became clear that in voting to postpone discussing the plan further, Galloway's opponents had masterfully manoeuvred it on to the sidelines, preventing the delegates from being hastily pushed into accepting a novel scheme designed to avert a bloody rupture between Britain and America. In the time bought by this delaying tactic, the critics regrouped and launched a counter-attack. On 22 October they succeeded in getting Galloway's plan taken off the agenda. To ensure it was permanently ditched, Samuel Adams moved that the references to the debate on Galloway's plan be excised altogether from the official minutes of the Congress. Writing in the third person, Galloway later maintained that he had been gagged, for, 'conscious that it would be approved of by the people at large, if published, and believing Mr Galloway would not venture to make it public, they procured a majority, who ordered it, with the introductory motion, to be erased from their Minutes'.[11] Most humiliating of all, he was put in charge of revising the Congress's minutes – with his own contribution officially expunged.

Within stretching distance of the summit, Galloway had been tripped into a cavernous depth. It was not just in the Congress that he suffered this reversal of fortune. While he was there, the Pennsylvanian elections were held. He was re-elected, but his control of the party machine was no more. After eight years in the chair, he finally lost the Assembly vote to remain Speaker of the House. Edward Biddle, an anti-British Quaker, was elected in his place. Yet, Galloway refused to see this as the end of his scheme for an Anglo-American union. Convinced the Congress delegates did not speak for colonial opinion, he remained confident his plan would enjoy popular backing elsewhere in the colonies. He was determined that the question be put to them. In November he set off to New York to rally support. There, he teamed up with sympathisers and had his case, entitled *Candid Examination of the Mutual Claims of Great Britain, and the Colonies: with a Plan of Accommodation, on Constitutional Principles* published in the new year. It did not pull punches. The Continental Congress was a Presbyterian conspiracy comprised of those predetermined upon transforming legitimate grievances into a bogus campaign for independence from Britain. If this dangerous conspiracy ended not in British reaction or a landing of French troops it would create a civil war between the thirteen colonies. In the event, Galloway was to discover it would lead to all three.

Continuing to gather momentum, Galloway had another trump card to play. He could call upon his illustrious friend. The endorsement of the great Dr Franklin was worth any number of pamphlets and appeals. On 27 October and 1 November, he dashed off letters to Franklin appealing to him to support the union plan. But Franklin was still in London and the details of his old friend's scheme would not reach him until January. In the meantime, he too was exploring whether there remained alternatives to a complete rupture between Britain and her American colonies. In December 1774, Franklin got to know Lord Howe, with whose sister he had started playing chess. While the two players shifted pawns around the board, Lord Howe expressed his abhorrence at the way the government had treated Franklin and encouraged him to put forward ideas as to how London could appease the colonies. The former Prime Minister, Lord Chatham, was also in close contact and even visited Franklin at his home in Craven Street. Whatever imperious behaviour was meted out by some politicians, many of the most respected of them still treated Franklin with the highest regard. Lame and close to death, Chatham even had Franklin escort him on his arm into the House of Lords.

In December, Franklin sketched seventeen 'hints' on a new settlement that he sent, through intermediaries, to the Earl of Dartmouth and Lord Hyde. Parliament should renounce its legislative sovereignty over the colonies' internal affairs as embodied in the Declaratory Act. The Coercive and Treason Acts would not be repealed. The tea duty would be scrapped. Customs officers would be appointed by the colonial Governors and not by the Crown. And the colonies, not London, would operate and profit directly from the Navigation Acts as they applied to them. Franklin appeared to be motivated by a desire to return the situation to what he believed it had been before 1763, when British victory in the Seven Years' War and the costs incurred had made ministers in London eager to extract greater worth from the colonies. Encouraged to rethink his 'hints', Franklin added that it would be necessary to remove all British troops from the colonies and that Britain should formally recognise the Continental Congress.

These were not palatable suggestions to British ministers. It was made clear to Franklin that Parliament would not renounce its rights over the colonies. This, after all, was the substantive issue. The prospects for compromise were dimmed further when, in January 1775, the House of Lords defeated Chatham's proposals to recognise the Continental Congress and to grant the colonies the right to suspend (at any rate, temporarily) legislation they disliked.

In the same month, Franklin received Galloway's proposals. He sat down and wrote his reply:

I cannot but lament with you the impending Calamities Britain & her Colonies are about to suffer, from great Imprudencies on both Sides. Those arising there, are more in your View; these here, which I assure you are very great, in mine. Passion governs, and she never governs wisely. What we can't remedy we must endeavour to bear. But I find it to me more and more difficult. Anxiety begins to disturb my Rest; and whatever robs an old Man of his Sleep, soon demolishes him. I have however generally strong Hopes amounting almost to an Assurance, that tho' we may suffer much for a while, America will finally be greatly benefited by her present Difficulties, and rise superior to them all.

I communicated your Plan of Union to Lord Camden soon after I received it, and to Lord Chatham last Week. They seem'd to think the

Idea ingenious, but the Mode so new as to require much attentive Thought before a Judgment of it could be form'd. From something dropt by Lord Gower the other Day in the House of Lords, accusing the Congress sharply of rejecting a *Plan of Union* with Britain, after it had been received, and ordering the Vote for receiving it to be erased out of their Minutes, I imagine the Ministry are in possession of it; if on Enquiry I find they are not, I shall communicate it to them, as possibly it may bring on some Negociation and stay their Hands from Blood; of which I grieve to say there is but little Prospect. For every thing is hurried with inconceivable Precipitation, & every thing rejected immediately, the Consideration of which might occasion Delay. Thus the Commons would not hear the Merchants support their Petition in the same Committee that was to consider the State of America; nor would they suffer us to be heard in support of the Petition from the Congress; nor would the Lords take into Consideration Lord Chathams Plan, but dismiss'd it upon a slight first Reading. With the greatest Esteem and Respect I am ever, my dear Friend Yours most affectionately

B Franklin

By Read who sails in about a Week I shall give you my Thoughts on the Plan. I inclose Lord Chathams

P.S. Feb 7. By information just receiv'd from good Hands, there is reason to believe, that the Troops will have Orders to act on the defensive only, to avoid Bloodshed: That they are intended chiefly to intimidate; the Ministry depending most on dividing America, and on our Want of Perseverance in complying with the Agreement recommended by the Congress. All our Friends here are of Opinion that if we are steady till another Session, this Ministry must retire, & our Points will be gained.[12]

In his second letter, Franklin elaborated on Galloway's plan. 'I would try any thing, and bear any thing that can be borne with Safety to our just Liberties rather than engage in a War with such near Relations, unless compelled to do it by dire Necessity in our own Defense.'[13] But he did not think Galloway's scheme could work. He believed it would only help spread British corruption to virtuous America and drag her into Britain's 'plundering wars' with the European powers.[14]

Franklin had circulated Galloway's proposals to Chatham and Camden, while, independently, William Franklin sent a copy to the Earl of Dartmouth. In April 1775 a printed text of Galloway's proposals was published in London. But the ideas it contained were not taken up by officialdom. Even if his plan had appeal, its rejection by the Continental Congress suggested it could not form the basis for a successful appeasement of America's malcontents. And yet, it might all have been so different. If only Galloway had succeeded in getting his plan adopted as the Congress's specific demand, it would have become the pivotal proposal upon which war or peace was determined. Instead, it was now just another idea upon which time had been called.

When the British government finally began to think seriously about what might be done to avert a separation, it was all too late. Lord North, the Prime Minister, dangled the possibility of a new arrangement in which London would not tax any colony that raised by its own means the revenue necessary to pay for the cost of its defence. This was what Franklin had been arguing for since the days of his Albany Plan over twenty years ago. But there was a difference. Unlike the schemes of Franklin and Galloway, Lord North thought still in terms of the actions of individual colonial legislatures in their relation to London, not of a pan-colonial assembly representing them collectively. And there was also a likely practical problem. In a debt-ridden Empire, the level of spending London thought appropriate and the amount a colonial assembly thought adequate would not necessarily add up to the same sum. Franklin likened it to a highwayman presenting his pistol at the window of a coach, to whom 'if you will give all your Money or what he is pleas'd to think sufficient, he will civilly omit putting his own Hand into your Pockets'.[15]

In London, Franklin could see at close hand the corruption and arrogant minds running America from Westminster and Whitehall. He wrote to Galloway complaining that Parliament was 'a very expensive Machine, that requires a vast deal of oiling and greasing at the People's Charge'.[16] By comparison, he had developed an expat's rose-tinted view of American political virtues. 'When I consider the extream Corruption prevalent among all Orders of Men in this rotten State,' Franklin assured Galloway, 'and the glorious publick Virtue so predominant in our rising Country, I cannot but apprehend more Mischief than Benefit from a closer Union.' It would be like 'coupling and binding together the dead and the living'.[17] He was not acquainted at first hand with the lawless undercurrent accompanying the revolutionary cause that was all too visible to the nervous occupants of Trevose and the Governor's house at Perth Amboy. His son's letters assured him, 'However mad you may think the Measures of the Ministry are, yet I trust you have Candour enough to acknowledge that we are no ways behind hand with them in Ins[tances] of Madness on this Side the Water. However, it [is] a disagreeable Subject, and I'll drop it.'[18]

There was another matter that William had to tell his father. While

Franklin remained in London, his wife Deborah – whom he had not travelled back to see for a decade – died after a long period of ill health. William's letter, conveying the bad news, reproachfully added:

> She told me, when I took Leave of her, on my removal to Amboy, that she never expected to see you unless you returned this Winter, for that she was sure she should not live till next summer. I heartily wish you had happened to have come over in the Fall, as I think her Disappointment in that respect preyed a good deal on her spirits.

William also took the opportunity to make clear he thought it was time his father came home: 'It gives me great Pleasure to find that you have so perfect an Enjoyment of that greatest of Blessings, Health. But I cannot help being concerned to find that notwithstanding you are sensible that you "cannot in the course of Nature long expect the Continuance of it," yet you postpone your Return to your Family.' William continued:

> If there was any Prospect of your being able to bring the People in Power to your Way of Thinking, or of those of your Way of Thinking's being brought into Power, I should not think so much of your Stay. But as you have by this Time pretty strong Proofs that neither can be reasonably expected and that you are look'd upon with an evil Eye in that Country, and are in no small Danger of being brought into Trouble for your political Conduct, you had certainly better return, while you are able to bear the Fatigues of the Voyage to a Country where the People revere you, and are inclined to pay a Deference to your Opinions.[19]

Clearly, William hoped his venerable father could be of more use talking sense to the colonists than he had been in making appeals to the government. He also believed his relationship with him was such that it permitted a degree of candour. William had thought he had his father's blessing to be true to himself. Before the events of the Boston Tea Party and the Whitehall Cockpit, Franklin had written to his son acknowledging that 'I know your sentiments differ from mine' because:

> You are a thorough government man, which I do not wonder at, nor do I aim at converting you. I only wish you to act uprightly and steadily, avoiding that duplicity which, in Hutchinson, adds contempt to indig-nation. If you can promote the prosperity of your people, and leave them

happier than you found them, whatever your political principles are, your memory will be honored.[20]

However, in the months that followed Franklin's expression of these sentiments his attitude hardened, as did his belief that his son's duty was to stand with his father rather than by his own principles. Yet having occupied the Governor's house for thirteen years, William was, in terms of experience, by 1775 the most senior of all the American colonial Governors. He was not prepared to resign in dudgeon on behalf of a father who, when it came to it, had put his own political career in London before the demands of his family in America. Instead, William chose to make a stand against those who were now being depicted as 'Patriot' politicians. On 11 January 1775, he went to the New Jersey Assembly and begged its members not to endorse the proceedings of the Continental Congress in Philadelphia. Narrowly, he lost the vote. His humiliation was about to begin. When he refused to forward the Assembly's hostile petition to King George, the Assembly got their Agent in London, Benjamin Franklin, to do it instead.

As an Irishman who was the Agent of the New York Assembly, Edmund Burke had the advantage of being a Member of Parliament at Westminster who was capable of seeing imperial ties from a non-English perspective. He had received his university education at Trinity College in Dublin, a short walk from a well crafted essay in classical proportions – the world's first purpose-built parliament house. Perhaps this gave him a familiarity with the rights of the legislative assemblies from more distant colonies. In these last months of peace, he spoke repeatedly and forcefully in the House of Commons urging the path of colonial pacification upon Lord North's administration. In the autumn of 1774 he had delivered his great speech, subsequently published as *On American Taxation*. Westminster had always determined the Atlantic trading laws and, he said, should continue to do so; but, equally, since it had not always taxed the colonists in their own domain, so it ought not to claim the right now. 'If that sovereignty and their freedom cannot be reconciled,' he asked, 'which will they take? They will cast your sovereignty in your face. Nobody will be argued into slavery.'[21] In March the following year he spoke against restricting American trade and in a three-and-a-half-hour speech delivered his thirteen resolutions for conciliation. In awe, James Boswell wrote, 'he must be one of the few men that may hope for continual happiness in this Life, he has so much knowledge, so much

animation, and the consciousness of so much fame'.²² Perhaps. But he did
not have the power to move the minds of those who determined events.

Among Burke's thirteen resolutions were the repeal of the hated duties
and the assertion that the colonial Assemblies should inherit the fiscal powers.
Westminster would be left merely exercising a supervisory role. They were
too much for the House of Commons and were defeated by 270 votes to 78.
They were also probably insufficient to please the delegates at the second
Continental Congress that convened in May, following the first exchanges
of fire between British troops and Massachusetts militia at Lexington and
Concord in April. Benjamin Franklin stated that Americans were 'much
obliged' to Burke for making the effort, an acknowledgement that fell short
of personal endorsement of his proposals.²³ Franklin had written to Burke in
December 1774 requesting that he join the other colonial Agents to discuss
presenting the first Continental Congress's petition to King George III.
Burke had excused himself on the grounds that he had not received specific
instructions from the New York Assembly (he refused to assist the conciliatory 'Olive Branch Petition' in August 1775 on the same grounds).²⁴

In truth, Burke was a Parliamentarian, weary of the influence of the King
and his court. He believed the King ruled through Parliament. He had no
time for the view, espoused by Franklin and other American 'Patriots', that
they could be subjects of the King, but not bound by Parliament. Westminster, according to Burke, 'superintends all the several inferior legislatures,
and guides and controls them without annihilating any'.²⁵ Thus even the
most eloquent exponent of the colonists' cause in Parliament was not really
in tune with colonial 'Patriot' thinking.

During the first months of 1775, Franklin and Burke conversed with one
another on a number of occasions. From these exchanges Burke deduced
that, 'soured and exasperated as his mind certainly was,' Franklin never
proclaimed 'any other wish in favour of America than for a security to its
ancient condition'. But, Franklin had finally accepted his son's logic that
there was nothing more his mission in London could achieve in convincing
the government of its errors. Change could only be brought about by the
actions of the colonists. If he wanted to play a constructive part in the land
of his birth, it clearly meant returning there. The day before he set sail for
America, Franklin paid a visit to Burke. If Burke's subsequent recollection is
accurate, the two men had 'a very long conversation' in which Franklin
'lamented, and with apparent sincerity' the coming separation between
Britain and her colonies. 'America,' Franklin supposedly told Burke, 'would
never again see such happy days as had passed under the protection of
England.' Franklin 'observed that ours was the only instance of a great empire

in which the most distant parts and members had been as well governed as the metropolis and its vicinage, but that the Americans were going to lose the means which secured to them this rare and precious advantage.' They could not hope to improve upon such a settlement but nor could they 'give up so happy a situation without a struggle'.[26]

What was to be made of Franklin's nostalgic recollections of an old order that had passed? In his moments of more righteous fury, he had espoused views on a constitutional settlement weighted far more towards colonial rights than had been the status quo prior to 1763. His son certainly hoped his father would return and talk some moderating sense to the hotheads who threatened a violent separation of jurisdictions. The experience of his friend Galloway at the first Continental Congress was hardly encouraging on this score. The truth was that a point of departure had been reached. British politicians had failed to quell the appetite of the colonial malcontents whose suppression was becoming a law and order issue for the British Army. Franklin could not support that repugnant course of action. So, if he wanted to play his part in the unfolding rebellion, he would first have to join it. Packing up his belongings in Craven Street where he had lived, with one brief interruption, for the past eighteen years, the sixty-nine-year-old self-made man finally turned his back on London on 21 March 1775 and set sail for Pennsylvania. To a correspondent, Burke enthused:

> What say you to your friend and brother Philosopher Franklin, who at upwards of seventy years of age, quits the Study of the Laws of Nature, in order to give Laws to new Commonwealths; and has crossed the Atlantick ocean at that time of Life, not to seek repose, but to plunge unto the midst of the most laborious and most arduous affairs that ever were. Fw things more extraordinary have happened in the history of mankind. These rebels of ours are a singular sort of people.[27]

While Franklin's ship cut its path across the Atlantic, Galloway made one last valiant stand on the floor of the Philadelphia Assembly. Returning from New York, he threw his support behind Governor John Penn's proposal that the Assembly – and not the Continental Congress – should petition King George. Here, at last, was Galloway siding with the Proprietary family that he had built his political career alongside Franklin trying to humble. Until Galloway stood up to speak, Penn's proposal had failed to find endorsement from among the legislators. But Galloway produced one of the sparkling displays of eloquence that had for so long made him such a formidable force in the affairs of the colony. His rhetoric, his lawyer's mastery of the brief, was keenly felt. The Assembly members began to sway back towards their former Speaker. A vote that had appeared a foregone conclusion came to hang in the balance, a vote that stood to uncouple Pennsylvania from the rebel Congress's politics.

But then the same obstructive tactic that had done for Galloway's Anglo-American union plan in the Congress was redeployed to take the sting out of his attack in the Assembly. His opponents managed to get the vote postponed until the following month. When in March the division was finally held, the Galloway-Penn cause was defeated by a margin of sufficient comfort: twenty-two votes to fifteen. It was the end for Galloway. The Assembly had re-elected him to serve on the second Continental Congress due in May, but if he could not impose his will on either body, what was the point? Dejected, he prepared himself for the inevitable resignation and retirement to Trevose. To a sympathiser he wrote, 'I hope I have retired in Time from the distressing and ungrateful Drudgery of Public Life.'[28]

In April, British troops and colonial militiamen clashed north-west of Boston at Lexington and Concord. Any small, lingering hope that the future governance of the thirteen colonies could be settled without the exchange of musket fire was extinguished by these first casualties. On 5 May, Franklin stepped off the boat with Peter, his slave, and Temple Franklin, his grandson. Within a day of his return to Philadelphia, the Pennsylvania Assembly elected him to represent the colony for the second Continental Congress which was about to meet in the city.

On 8 May, Franklin received a letter from Galloway, congratulating him on election to the Congress and asking him to come to Trevose. Galloway offered Franklin the use of his own carriage. 'Being impatient to see you,' Franklin agreed, confiding, 'I am concern'd at your Resolution of quitting public Life at a time when your Abilities are so much wanted.' He ended his letter by reaffirming that 'I am ever, with unalterable Esteem and Affection, my Dear Friend, Yours most affectionately.'[29] Days later, he made the journey. After a decade of separation bridged only by the sail-borne postal service, the two men greeted one another and settled down to discuss the grave situation. Galloway urged Franklin to back his Anglo-American union plan. But Franklin assured him Britain's politicians were deaf to persuasion and begged Galloway to join him at the second Continental Congress. The plea was in vain and, on 12 May, Galloway formally resigned from Pennsylvania's delegation at the Congress. In doing so, he accepted what was already a reality – that Franklin was again the dominant statesman in the colony. But neither man was yet ready to forsake the other. Franklin made a return visit to Trevose in June in the hope of finding a way in which the two friends could continue to work together. Still, they could not find sufficient common ground. At the end of the month they tried for a third time to overcome their differences. And this time, William Franklin came too. It would prove to be the decisive moment in the relationship between all three of them.

The first William Franklin heard that his father had crossed the Atlantic was when he received a letter from him dated 10 May. There had been no communication during the previous six months. On the ocean crossing, Franklin had composed a 196-page letter to his son which he did not deliver. Instead the mighty missive provided the notes for the argument he would lay out over the Trevose dinner table. It was the first meeting between father and son since 1764 when William was thirty-three and still struggling to emerge from his father's considerable shadow. Now, more than a decade later, William was the longest-serving Royal Governor in the American colonies. His presence at Trevose for the third attempt to broker agreement between his father and their mutual best friend was crucially important. Galloway might well have hoped that where the tie of friendship had failed to sway the senior Franklin's mind, the bond of blood might find a way. At the very least, it would start as two minds against one.

The fateful dinner party began convivially enough. A good meal accompanied by the best from Galloway's cellar preceded the serious intent of the discussion. Franklin had experienced at first hand the corruption and smug intransigence of the British governing class. His son and Galloway spoke from having first-hand knowledge of the rebel politicians and the mobs whose passions they stirred, men who were threatening in their demeanour and seemingly deaf to compromise – and of whom Franklin had as yet slight personal acquaintance. Galloway later told Thomas Hutchinson, 'the glass having gone about freely, the Doctor, at a late hour, opened himself and declared in favour of measures attaining to independence'.[30] This was the irrevocable point of departure. Galloway stood his ground, sketching the grim consequences that he believed would follow a campaign for independence. It would succeed only in dividing Americans against one another and uniting Britain's political class since Westminster's fighting bulldogs would put aside their perpetual wrangling and close ranks to tear apart the colonial upstarts. Calling for independence would result only in existing American liberties being crushed by a display of overwhelming force. This was not how Franklin saw it. Indeed, having spent his last days in London with Burke, he drew the opposite conclusion, 'That the friends to the

American cause in Britain, would incessantly maintain and increase that division and distraction, by opposing the measures of government.'[31] Franklin believed the noble venture was worth the risk. Galloway was certain the vainglorious endeavour would end in disaster for all concerned.

Of this final meeting at Trevose, Galloway later recalled that 'the two friends parted as they met, unconverted to the principles of each other'.[32] The gulf of the Atlantic had separated both Joseph Galloway and William Franklin from the uninspiring reality of London politics as truly as it had shielded Benjamin Franklin from the ugly side of the disorder in the colonies. It destroyed the mutual understanding they had once shared on what constituted a desirable polity. It destroyed the Franklins as a family. The Atlantic was too wide to preserve a unity of thought among three men who had been brought together by blood or common outlook. Such was the gulf that equally did for the union of Britain and America.

SEVEN

A Broken Vase

In June 1775, British troops ejected rebels from their entrenched position on Breed's Hill overlooking Boston in an engagement won only at horrendous cost. The encounter, made famous as the Battle of Bunker Hill, demonstrated the tenacity of both sides. Thus the War of American Independence began in earnest, transforming philosophical discourses and academic nostrums into a bloody contest of outrage and slaughter. Despite the disappointment at Trevose, Franklin made a final endeavour to win his son over to the rebel cause before it was too late. In August he journeyed to Perth Amboy. If he could not persuade William with argument, perhaps he could try financial inducement. The Continental Congress appointed Franklin Postmaster-General, an improvement on the deputy office from which the British government had sacked him over the Hutchinson letters controversy. Accepting the position, he used it to offer his son the title of Comptroller-General of the postal service, the sinecure William had previously held – also courtesy of his father – back in the 1750s. It would yield a salary of $320 a year but the offer was conditional: he had first to resign his royal governorship. Franklin also implied that a more relaxed view would be taken on the repayment of his son's remaining debts to him.

Franklin had misjudged his son. William turned the offer down flat. The Governor of New Jersey was not going to cast aside his political principles and his position in the service of a government (whose will could yet be expected to prevail) merely in order to crawl back into the protective shadow of his father's powers of preferment. William did not intend to turn the clock back twenty years. It was a botched attempt to bridge political differences which circumstances had widened into a gulf. Rebuffed, Franklin gave the job to his son-in-law, Richard Bache, instead. He made a last visit to the Governor's house at Perth Amboy in November and then turned away, to guide the revolution against the authority that had installed his son there.

For his part, William Franklin had to weigh up where his duty lay and how his own safety and that of his wife Elizabeth might lie. He chose to prioritise duty. While other Royal Governors sought sanctuary upon British warships, William stayed on, trying to get the New Jersey Assembly he convened at Burlington to disregard the Congress and parley directly with London in the same way that Governor Penn and Joseph Galloway had tried and failed to convince the Pennsylvania Assembly to do. William's efforts were equally in vain. He knew he was putting himself at risk from the rebel militias or a lynch-mob 'tarring' at a time when the British troops necessary to restore order were still on the far side of an ocean. Despite the obvious danger, he continued to send intelligence reports to Lord Dartmouth in London. He was doing his duty – as he saw it – and it was his undoing. His messenger was intercepted by armed rebels and the dispatches discovered. Retribution was immediate. A one-hundred-strong militia marched to the Governor's house. In the middle of the night of 8 January 1776, William Franklin was placed under house arrest.

The terms of the Governor's incarceration were not overly restrictive. But with the rebels taking control of New Jersey politics through a self-appointed Provincial Council of Safety, so his prospects for release narrowed. In June, he was brought before a revolutionary tribunal in Burlington. Regarding the kangaroo court to be without legal authority, he refused to answer the interrogation. The tribunal continued regardless and provided a platform for one of its members, Dr John Witherspoon, to launch upon a diatribe of personal abuse directed at William that made Wedderburn's insults to his father in the Cockpit resemble affectionate teasing. Among other accusations not strictly relevant to proceedings, Witherspoon reminded the tribunal that the grand figure standing before them was merely a brat born from the wrong side of the bed.[1] The tribunal determined that the terms of his confinement should be directed by the Continental Congress which was at that moment in secret session in the Philadelphia State House. On 25 June, William wrote a heart-rending letter to his son, Temple, the tone of which suggested he was in no doubt about the gravity of his predicament:

> God bless you, my dear boy; be dutiful and attentive to your grandfather [i.e. Benjamin Franklin] to whom you owe obligations. Love Mrs Franklin, for she loves you, and will do all she can for you if I should never return more. If we survive the present storm, we may all meet and enjoy the sweets of peace with the greatest relish. I am ever your truly affectionate father, Wm Franklin.[2]

He also wrote to his wife, Elizabeth, who was by now ill with worry. It was to be the last letter she would receive from him.

By July William had been moved first to the house of a rebel officer in Wallingford near New Haven and then to Middletown, Connecticut, where other prominent loyalists to the British cause were being held, including two other Royal Governors. Although the restrictions on her husband remained relatively lenient, Elizabeth Franklin was desperately fearful. On 6 August she took matters into her own hands and pleaded with Benjamin Franklin to intercede to save his son, writing as his daughter-in-law:

> Allow me, Dear Sir, to mention that it is greatly in your Power to Relieve them. Suppose that Mr Franklin would Sign a Parole not dishonourable to himself, and Satisfactory to Governor Trumbull; why may he not be permitted to return into this Province and to his Family? . . . Consider, my Dear and Honoured Sir, that I am now pleading the Cause of your son, and my Beloved Husband. If I have Said or done anything wrong I beg to be forgiven.[3]

But in his mind, Franklin was now a parent of the revolution, not the father of a Tory son. He had to toughen his heart against all appeals. Having urged others to risk their lives for a cause he thought noble, he could hardly be seen to be trying to rescue a prominent servant of the enemy – his own son.

In any case, he was busy. Back in September 1775, Congress had appointed Franklin to a secret committee charged with furnishing the rebel – or 'Patriot' – cause with the arms to prosecute the war and to transform the local militias into a disciplined 'Continental Army'. Congress was determined to seize Canada from British control and in March and April the following year Franklin hazarded a trip to Montreal to report on Benedict Arnold's doomed siege of Quebec. Despite being under guard, William had got to hear of his father's mission and had a letter smuggled out to Lord Germain, Dartmouth's successor as Secretary of State for the Colonies back in London, to warn him of it. Both Franklins had reached the pass where their cause took precedence over all else – where blood was no longer thicker than water. But Benjamin Franklin was in a far stronger position to assert his will over events.

On his return from Canada, he assisted in the drafting of the Declaration of Independence. Although its content was not his work, he did influence Thomas Jefferson in tightening and improving the wording, helping to create passages of lyricism that would inspire future generations well beyond the continent of America. And in July 1776, the month the Declaration was signed by the Congress delegates, Franklin assumed the presidency of the committee charged with drawing up a new constitution for Pennsylvania. Declaring independence from Britain had, at a stroke, invalidated the royal charters upon which the Penns' proprietary powers rested. The great ambition that had brought Franklin and Galloway together had been achieved at last, albeit as a consequence of events that destroyed the friendship between them.

Yet, while Franklin and his colleagues were busy drafting the documents for a new beginning, the reality beyond their meeting hall suggested they had little chance of being implemented. The rebel cause was not prospering on the battlefield. The British expeditionary force had landed and was making solid progress. On 4 July, while Congress delegates were acclaiming the Declaration of Independence, the British pushed into New Jersey and set up their military headquarters in the Governor's mansion at Perth Amboy. The British commander-in-chief was Admiral Howe, who only eighteen months earlier had earnestly talked reconciliation to Franklin while watching him play chess with his sister. On 20 June, Howe had attempted to revive the acquaintance, by writing a letter addressed to 'My Worthy Friend' Franklin. It stated his hope that further conflict could be avoided and offered, on behalf of the King, a general pardon if the members of Congress swore an oath to His Majesty.[4] Franklin did not receive the letter until a fortnight after Congress had approved the Declaration of Independence. In London, he had worked with Howe to avert the clash of arms that had now taken place, but he was not going to recant on what had happened since then:

> Long did I endeavour with unfeigned and unwearied zeal to preserve from breaking that fine and noble China vase, the British empire. For I knew that being once broken, the separate parts could not retain even their share of the strength or value that existed in the whole, and that a perfect re-union of those parts could scarce even be hoped for. Your Lordship may possibly remember the tears of joy that wet my cheek when, at your good sister's in London, you once gave me expectations that a reconciliation might soon take place. I had the misfortune to find those expectations disappointed, and to be treated as the cause of the mischief I was labouring to prevent.[5]

Congress had entrusted command of the Continental Army to George Washington. In August, Washington's men were routed on Long Island by the forces of Admiral Howe's brother, General William Howe and, but for Howe's dilatory sense of urgency, might easily have been finished off there and then. Instead, Washington and the remnants of his force escaped captivity by pulling off a daring nocturnal crossing of the East River. Nonetheless, wars – as Winston Churchill later reminded Britons rejoicing over their forces' miraculous escape across the English Channel from Dunkirk in 1940 – are not won by retreat and the Patriots' predicament remained desperate. Edmund Burke confided the same sentiment to his leader, the Marquess of Rockingham, at the news: 'An army that is obliged, at all times and in all situations to decline an Engagement may delay their ruin, but never can defend their Country.'[6]

Keen not to postpone the agony, Admiral Howe offered Congress terms to end the war. Franklin, John Adams and Edward Rutledge were dispatched from Philadelphia over to Perth Amboy to examine what was being put on the table. They were greeted with the utmost cordiality and, in effect, offered what Franklin had for so long demanded: a return to the constitutional settlement prior to the 1760s. Howe appeared to hold most of the cards. His troops were poised to enter the city of New York, where there was strong Loyalist support. Yet, whatever was happening in and around Manhattan, those who had put their names to the Declaration of Independence could not now take back its words, its stirring, unequivocal phrases and visions. They were not going to recant what was now their common article of faith. There was no going back.

Franklin and his fellow Congress members may have opted to stand by their principles rather than bow to King George but, given the rebellion's precarious fortunes, others might accept Howe's offer of amnesty in return for vowing to become, once again, His Majesty's subjects. Breaching the conditions in which he was allowed movement, William Franklin set about issuing 'protections' to New Jersey's Loyalists as a means of making sure their lives and property were not harmed by the advancing British troops. It was a brave action intended to safeguard those who shared his cause although – given the success of British arms – he might have considered he would not, in any case, be long subject to the dictates of the rebel Connecticut Council of Safety.

While his son awaited liberation by the British, Benjamin Franklin boarded a ship to take him away from America. He was again quitting its shores after a stay of only sixteen months but he did not feel he could refuse Congress's request that he should be one of its three commissioners to the French court. His task would be to appeal directly to King Louis XVI for assistance. There was certainly an irony in this – revolutionaries seeking to shake off their links with a constitutional monarchy by forming an alliance with a king whose despotic power ranged far beyond even George III's wildest dreams. However, desperate times had necessitated a revival of the enduring assumption that an enemy's enemy was consequently a friend. Now the seventy-year-old Franklin, stooped, slow-moving, suffering painfully from gout, was dispatched to work his cosmopolitan charm as the world's most famous American in the cause of a Franco-American amity that, only a few years earlier, he would have thought incomprehensible and detestable. But needs must. Upon the success of his mission appeared to rest the fate of the American Revolution.

Ill-wishers wondered if Franklin's journey was really a pretext for running away from a failed rebellion whose leaders were sure to be rounded up sooner or later. Even to more charitable observers, his expedition to bring the Old World to the rescue of the New appeared a forlorn excursion. Writing to the Marquess of Rockingham, Edmund Burke assumed that the French would not come to the aid of a clearly failing republican movement in America and that, consequently:

> it is to be presumed, that he is authorised to negotiate with Lord Stormont [the British Ambassador in Paris] on the Basis of a dependence on this Crown. This I take to be his Errand; for I never can beleive, that he is come thither, as a fugitive from his Cause in the hour of its distress; or that he is going to conclude a Long life, which has brightened every hour it has continued, with so foul and so dishonourable a flight.[7]

Indeed, Burke even considered going to Paris himself in order to press his own conciliation proposals of November 1775 (which the House of Commons had rejected by 210 votes to 105). He was dissuaded by his friends. In any case, it was doubtful that the British government, with victory seemingly all but assured, would have made the necessary compromises involved.

Before setting sail, Franklin had made one last transaction with Galloway. Despite his opposition to the revolution, Galloway had been uneasy about Britain's counter-measures, in particular the Prohibitory Act permitting the Royal Navy to plunder American shipping at will. If Britain was as clumsy at protecting law, order and property as Galloway had always assumed the rebels to be, perhaps there was little to choose between them. When a four-hundred-strong rebel militia arrived at Trevose, its owner was not minded to make a one–man stand. Instead he presented the troops with colours and provided hospitality. Was he reconciling himself to the Patriot cause, or merely engaged in the emergency expediencies necessary to dodge the incarceration that was William Franklin's fate? At any rate, Ben Franklin was sufficiently moved by his former friend's disillusionment with the Loyalist cause that, in October 1776, on the eve of his voyage to France, he entrusted him with the care of his private papers. Twenty years of correspondence were contained in the great trunk. To their owner – as to later generations of historians – they had a worth weighable in gems and rubies. It was an extraordinary act of trust.

Galloway should not have accepted the responsibility, for despite his irritation at the British, he remained apprehensive and foresaw mounting chaos. He disliked the new radical constitution for Pennsylvania and prayed it could not last. The Patriot forces were falling back towards their capital, Philadelphia. A British assault to dislodge them was imminent. With arrests and reprisals continuing in the meantime, Galloway may have feared for his own life. Samuel Adams had organised mobs to intimidate him. He had received death threats and a noose was delivered to his door, accompanied with instructions for its use. There was also the warning that he would be thrown in hot tar and feathered. These may have been impotent effusions of poison pen writers; or, as many Loyalists had discovered, they were threats to be backed up by violence. On 28 November – with Franklin's ship nearing the French coast and its most important passenger destined perhaps never to return to his native land – Galloway seized his moment for flight. He piled some of his possessions on to a wagon and escaped towards the safety of the British lines. In doing so, he left Trevose unguarded and at the mercy of plunderers. It was duly ransacked. The chest with Franklin's papers was broken open and its contents scattered about the house. Some of the Doctor's letters were thrown outside where they were borne away by the four winds.[8]

In his will, Franklin had intended to leave all his books and papers to William. As a friend of both men, Galloway had been appointed one of the executors. Franklin was long ensconced in France by the time he discovered Galloway had deserted his duty of care. It was from there, five years later, that Franklin encouraged his son-in-law, Richard Bache, to search for the lost testament to his life, lamenting:

> I should not have left them in his Hands, if he had not deceived me, by saying, 'that tho' he was before otherwise inclined, yet that since the King had declared us out of his Protection, & the Parliament by an Act, had made our Properties Plunder, he would go as far in Defence of his Country as any Man; and accordingly he had lately with Pleasure given Colours to a Regiment of Militia, & an Entertainment to 400 of them before his House.' I though he was a staunch Friend to the glorious Cause. I was mistaken.[9]

William, meanwhile, might have wondered whether he had been right to entrust his son, Temple, to the senior Franklin's care. As William had been Franklin's illegitimate son, so Temple was his motherless grandson, conceived back when his father, still a bachelor, was studying at the Middle Temple in London. Upon William's return to America to get married and take up the New Jersey governorship he had left the inconvenient Temple behind. Perhaps childhood memories of growing up with, but never being truly accepted by, Deborah Franklin swayed William against subjecting his own much higher-born wife to the embarrassment – even dishonour – of having little Temple running around the grand matrimonial apartments. He thus left it to his London-dwelling father to become Temple's guardian, paying for his foster care and overseeing his schooling in Kent. While the senior Franklin could hardly take issue with his son for fathering a child out of wedlock given that William was himself such a product of youthful indiscretion, he had at least gone on to demonstrate a better recognition of his responsibilities in that regard. Consequently, he probably thought Temple owed his grandfather rather more loyalty than was due to his distant father.

William was not reunited with his son until 1775 when Temple, by then aged sixteen, accompanied his dejected grandfather back across the Atlantic. But in arriving just at the moment when political divisions were translating into exchanges of gunfire, the boy's hopes of getting to know his father properly were dashed. Nonetheless, Temple did what he could to maintain a link and perhaps become the human agent through which the family could reunite. With William's incarceration, he asked to visit him and even offered to run letters between father and grandfather. He did get to call upon his stepmother, Elizabeth, bringing with him some money from Franklin to alleviate the worst of her situation. But when he showed signs of wanting to stay with her, Franklin quickly summoned him back. He also refused Temple permission to involve himself with his father's plight, supposedly on the grounds that it was too dangerous and that it would interfere with the forthcoming college term in Philadelphia.

That consideration was quickly forgotten when Franklin accepted Congress's request to parley with the French court, necessitating a decision on whether to take Temple with him. Leaving him in a war zone might have seemed careless, although taking him on a transatlantic vessel trying to dodge British warships was not obviously a safer bet. The more practical options would have been to dispatch Temple for a longer period to Elizabeth, his stepmother, or to the more politically reliable care of the boy's aunt and uncle, Sarah and Richard Bache. Instead, Franklin chose not to be parted from him. Thus the college term was conveniently forgotten and Temple voyaged with his grandfather to France, officially in the capacity of his secretary. 'I have rescued a valuable young man from the danger of being a Tory', Franklin later assured Richard Bache, adding, 'It is enough that I have lost my son; would they add my grandson! . . . If I die, I have a child to close my eyes and take care of my remains.'[10]

The tussle over Temple Franklin was symptomatic of his family's torn loyalties between their obligations to each other and their perceptions of duty. William had been happy to keep Temple at a three-thousand-mile distance while he discharged business from the Governor's mansion. Yet, he appeared critical of his own father for effectively doing the same to Deborah, the common-law wife he had abandoned in Philadelphia between 1757 and her death in 1774 in order to pursue his own chosen calling in London. Franklin might have riposted that because Deborah had refused to cross the Atlantic he had decided to put his career first and reside in London without her. If the surviving correspondence is a judge, he did not feel the resulting separation too keenly. Yet, while he had put his public life before his private one, Franklin saw no contradiction in reproaching his son for staying loyal to his post rather than supporting his father in the revolutionary cause. Strong commitment to a cause was as corrosive to the ties of family as, with Galloway, it had been to friendship.

Franklin arrived in Paris in December 1776. To some extent, it must have been a relief. The foreign posting permitted him to serve the revolutionary cause with a philosophical purity uncontaminated by the hard realities faced by those at the sharp end. At any rate, it provided sufficient physical distance from its causalities – his son and his former closest ally. Negotiations commenced with the Comte de Vergennes, the French Foreign Minister, whose support would be crucial in overcoming the doubts of those who foresaw the financial burden involved for France and King Louis XVI who, with equal foreboding, was uneasy about the republican precedents America's revolutionaries were creating. Nonetheless, revenge for the losses of the Seven Years' War burned brightly and the opportunity to discomfort Britain was a powerful one. In the meantime, credit and munitions were extended through a variety of channels to the rebel cause. This was a lifeline for a venture short of matériel and the foreign exchange to pay for it. But the French were nervous about declaring war on Britain. There would need to be clearer evidence that the Continental Army, shivering and shrinking from desertion, was a force seriously worth backing before the might of French arms would be committed to its cause.

While news of any such breakthrough remained elusive, Franklin nonetheless made the most favourable of impressions. His host, the Comte de

Chaumont, accommodated him in the garden house of his magnificent home, the Hotel de Valentinois at Passy. Half an hour's carriage ride from the centre of Paris and on the road to Versailles, the location was as suitable as it was delightful. When, sixteen months later, John Adams arrived at Passy to join the diplomatic effort, he was struck by the breadth of Franklin's popularity: 'His name was familiar to government and people, to kings, courtiers, nobility, clergy, and philosophers, as well as plebeians, to such a degree that there was scarcely a peasant or citizen, a *valet de chambre*, coachman or footman, a lady's chambermaid or a scullion in a kitchen, who was not familiar with it, and who did not consider him as a friend of humankind.'[11]

Franklin encountered none of the reserve or social condescension he believed he had received during his long years in London. When he embraced the eighty-three-year-old Voltaire at the French Academy of Sciences onlookers marvelled at the spectacle. His apparent ease of manner delighted those used to being weighed down by the elaborate artifice of French society. As far as the Comte de Ségur was concerned, 'His clothing was rustic, his bearing simple but dignified, his language direct, his hair unpowdered. It was as though the simplicity of the classical world, the figure of a thinker of the time of Plato, or a republican of the age of Cato or Fabius, had suddenly been brought by magic into our effeminate and slavish age, the eighteenth century.'[12] He sat for the painter Duplessis and the sculptor Houdon. His ubiquitous fur hat was adopted by ladies as the latest fashion.

John Adams was less impressed, seeing little of the republican virtues and none of the frugal aphorisms of *Poor Richard's Almanack* in Franklin's indolence, enjoyment of a vast cellar and – despite being in his seventies – shameless cavorting with younger women. In particular, Franklin made a determined play for the widowed Madame Helvétius. Despite being more than twice her age, he also tried it on with Madame Brillon. The latter, married to an older man enjoying a *ménage à trois* with the family governess, took to sitting on Franklin's lap and calling him 'Cher Papa'. Eager to read more into her flirtation than she was prepared to fulfil, he assured the supposedly devout Catholic that there were in fact twelve Commandments, the additional two being 'increase and multiply' and 'love one another'. It was not very subtle. He admitted, though, that he coveted his neighbour's wife. Furthermore, he wished to consult her about 'the opinion of a certain Father of the Church, which I find myself willing to adopt, tho' I am not sure it is orthodox. It is this, That the most effectual Way to get rid of a certain Temptation is, as often as it returns, to comply with and satisfy it. Pray instruct me how far, I may venture to practice upon this Principle?'[13]

Instead, she consented to watch him play chess with a friend while she bathed in her tub. When she became jealous of his wandering attentions he explained his amours were like a pianoforte recital in which the listeners' pleasure was no more diminished by it being shared by others.[14] French courtiers appeared unperturbed by this late-flowering lust. Not so other Americans. To the censorious Adams, 'the life of Dr Franklin was a scene of continual dissipation'.[15]

While Benjamin Franklin enjoyed the French aristocratic embrace at Passy, William Franklin languished in a tiny, fetid cell. His belief that the rebellion was close to defeat and his liberation at hand had been dashed. Over Christmas and the first days of the new year, George Washington had won victories at Trenton and Princeton, the symbolic importance of which, rather than the scale of the encounter, breathed life back into a cause that had until that moment appeared to be fading fast. In April 1777, Congress deliberated over how to punish the ex-Governor of New Jersey for issuing 'protections' to Loyalists. Taking the view that he had abused the leniency shown him, they voted unanimously to subject him to solitary confinement. The following month he was taken to Litchfield Gaol, a Connecticut penitentiary already crammed full of Loyalists including David Matthews, the former Mayor of New York. Denied all privileges of rank, William was thrown into a tiny unfurnished cell where for months he lingered unable to wash and surrounded by his own excrement (there was no latrine). The best that could be said was that it was not the worst of Connecticut's prison camps. At Simsbury, Loyalists were herded together and winched down a shaft into the abandoned copper mines, a dank and dark tomb of the living. 'In a few months the prisoners are released by death,' wrote one who survived the experience, the Reverend Samuel Peters: 'This conclave of spirits imprisoned may be called, with great propriety, the catacomb of Connecticut. The light of the Sun and the light of the Gospel are alike shut out . . . '.[16]

William's dank fate could not have been more removed from the grand living his father and son were enjoying at Passy. In his official capacity Dr Franklin also dealt with prisoner exchanges. Yet he pointedly refused to involve himself in his son's plight, despite Temple's attempts to get him to intervene. Perhaps he simply did not wish to know the details. It would certainly have looked irregular if so high-minded a philosopher was intervening to save his own son's life while urging the ferocious prosecution of a war against all other traitors to the cause. Furthermore, it was not as if all the cruel degradations were being committed by the Patriots. Thousands were also starving to death in the atrocious conditions of British-run prison camps.

Unsurprisingly, such aloof ambivalence was not the attitude of William's wife, Elizabeth. She had taken separation from her husband badly, but the news that he had been taken to Litchfield Gaol and possible death destroyed her completely. Galloway, having fled Trevose for the British lines, visited her at Perth Amboy in May. He found her distraught. Soon afterwards, the British decided to vacate New Jersey in order to launch their assault on the rebel capital, Philadelphia. This would place Perth Amboy at the mercy of rebel militias again. In the wake of the departing British troops, Elizabeth packed together her belongings and her husband's library and joined the cart train of refugees on their trek to join the Loyalist community of New York City. An asthmatic, her weak constitution collapsed under the burdens of worry and grief. By now her health had almost entirely gone. Her steward succeeded in getting a message through to Litchfield Gaol that she was dying. An appeal was made to General George Washington asking him to permit William – under armed guard – a final visit from his wife so that they could say goodbye to each other.

With the correctness that was his hallmark, Washington replied that he could not override a Congressional order but he nonetheless wrote to Congress advising, as a matter of humanity, that they should allow a visit. Unmoved, Congress turned down the request. By then, the question was in any case academic. Her spirit gone, her health broken, Elizabeth Franklin gave up and died, age forty-three. She was buried under the crypt of St Paul's Church, New York. A week later, her husband learnt of her death. Fifteen years of happy marriage had been snuffed out. It was a devastating blow. Elizabeth, he subsequently wrote, 'died of a broken heart occasioned by our long separation and my ill-treatment'.[17] A decade on, from exile, he managed to have a plaque inscribed in her honour, ending 'this monument is erected by him who knew her worth and still laments her loss'.[18] Meanwhile, Joseph Galloway looked after her effects, together with William's belongings. He took better care of them than he had Benjamin Franklin's archive. In the autumn of 1777 he had to leave New York and, in doing so, deposited William and Elizabeth's possessions for temporary safekeeping in what he assumed was the relative security of a British military warehouse. In the meantime, he had an important mission to fulfil. It involved returning to Philadelphia.

Sailing out from New York with 18,000 troops on 267 ships, General Howe had landed south of Philadelphia. At Brandywine Creek, Washington's army suffered 1,500 casualties, trying unsuccessfully to halt Howe's advance. The men of Congress packed up and began fleeing the city on 19 September, 'chased like a covey of partridges' as John Adams put it.[19] Seven days later, the rebel capital was in British hands. For the second time, the rebellion was on the verge of being delivered the *coup de grâce*.

Galloway returned not only to check on the state of Trevose. He set about assisting the Loyalist cause in earnest. Howe took up residence in the house of the former Governor, Richard Penn, next door to Galloway's town house on the south-east corner of Sixth and Market. He installed Galloway as Superintendent – in effect Philadelphia's civil governor. In this role he took charge of the city's police and port and was manager of imports and exports. He also organised the network of local pickets and surveillance that kept the British garrison's supply lines open cross-country. Galloway even raised a cavalry troop fit for the purpose. They located where rebel uniforms were being cut and seized all the cloth before it could be delivered to Washington's shivering troops at Valley Forge. In these and other skirmishes, Galloway's light horsemen acquitted themselves well, taking nearly two hundred prisoners and disrupting rebel activity between Philadelphia and Trenton.

During the winter and spring, Galloway oversaw the work of around eighty agents and used this spy network to file intelligence reports to Major John André, who was ensconced in Benjamin Franklin's town house in Philadelphia. In April 1778, Galloway sent word that the rebel Governor of New Jersey and his senior circle had set out for Burlington without an adequate armed escort. Galloway proposed leading his horsemen in an attempt to seize them. A low-risk raid promised to reap a high reward. Yet, inexplicably, the order to attack was countermanded at the last minute by Admiral Howe. In cancelling the mission, Howe dashed the best opportunity to trade New Jersey's rebel Governor for the freedom of its ex-Royal Governor, William Franklin.

With the rebellion's capital in British hands and Washington's forces confined to the scant refuge of Valley Forge, Benjamin Franklin's efforts to convince the French government to pour further resources into the rebel campaign were hampered. From almost the first, French supplies had been reaching the rebels but they fell far short of what was needed and the vigilant activities of the British Navy frayed the lifeline. Louis XVI's financiers were right to question how the rebel colonies, as short of specie as of major victories, could be remotely creditworthy. It was difficult to take seriously Franklin's optimistic claim that 'instead of Howe taking Philadelphia, Philadelphia has taken Howe'.[20] 'Le bon Quacker' (as the deist was inexplicably assumed to be) was still making a good impression with men of learning and women of society, but he had yet to convince the hard-hearted practitioners of power politics. His Most Christian Majesty, Louis XVI, may have conveyed his true opinion of the humbly dressed philosopher-sage when he gave a chamber pot as a gift to one of the ladies with whom Franklin was enamoured. The pot's inside base was decorated with the good Doctor's knowing visage.

However, bad news from Philadelphia was accompanied in the same breath by a report of an extraordinary denouement alongside the Hudson River. Hoping to cut Washington's Continental Army off from its supporters in New England, General John Burgoyne had marched down from Canada. But his advance had slowed while his men found themselves assailed by the difficult terrain and constantly harried by rebel militia who did not take kindly to Burgoyne's threat of unleashing the American Indians upon their homesteads. By October 1777 Burgoyne was surrounded and forced into a humiliating surrender at Saratoga. When news of the capitulation reached Paris in December, it immeasurably strengthened Franklin's bargaining position. The rebels had fighting spirit and could humble a large regular army. Realising the threat, British intermediaries approached Franklin with sketches for a settlement. But having past experience of weighing British expressions of good intent in the balance and finding them wanting, Franklin did not take the offers seriously. In any case, he had a valuable supporter in the Comte de Vergennes. In February 1778, France agreed a treaty of commerce and aid to defend American independence. Now she would fight. France's ally, Spain, also declared war on Britain the following year.

The declarations transformed the situation, forcing Britain from the offensive to the defensive. In July 1778, her navy clashed with a French armada in the English Channel in a preliminary to what proved to be France's aborted plan to invade Britain with 40,000 troops. With so many soldiers and sailors on the far side of the Atlantic Ocean, Britain would certainly have been exposed if the French had been prepared to risk the hazards of a larger naval encounter in the English Channel. Franklin was excited at the prospect of seeing England's coastal towns burn and drew up for the French a scale of ransom charges that could be extracted from towns that pleaded to be spared from destruction. It would, he hoped, 'spread Terror' across the country.[21] In the event, they were saved by the weather and a faltering of Gallic will.

Instead, pressure was applied elsewhere by a combination of feints and assaults upon British territory in India and the Caribbean, ensuring that the very extent of the Empire's reach became a liability – for it was never clear where the French or Spanish might attack next. Spain captured Minorca and lay siege to Gibraltar. The Dutch, long a supplier of guns and credit to the rebels, were moving closer to a position of formal hostility as were the nations of the League of Armed Neutrality (Russia, Denmark and Sweden). The

American War of Independence was igniting into a continuation of the Seven Years' War, although on this occasion Britain could not count on Prussia to divert French attention on the continent of Europe. George III's impression that suppressing revolt in North America would involve nothing more than 'a few bloody noses' was shown up for all its arrogant complacency.

In June 1778, the British took the decision to evacuate Philadelphia, partly because of the fear that they could be trapped there by an approaching French fleet able to blockade the Delaware. Already, the involvement of the French was beginning to dictate the strategy of Howe's replacement, General Clinton. The troops were withdrawn to reinforce New York since it could be better guarded from a French naval assault. In Philadelphia the British had suffered little open hostility from its citizens but also witnessed scant evidence of the support that Galloway had originally led Howe to expect. Part of the problem was that the Quakers, who formed the most prominent pro-Loyalist community, were debarred by their beliefs from taking up arms in Britain's cause. For those with a primary interest in self-preservation, circumspection proved to be the most sensible policy. The peripatetic military strategy once again forced those Americans who were helping the British to be constantly on the move or risk the vengeance of the returning rebels. Conscious of the predicament they were creating for their supporters, the British command found places on boats to evacuate them to New York. Three thousand Loyalists clambered on board and were taken off to safety. Among them were Joseph Galloway and his daughter, Elizabeth. There was no time to lose. The Continental Army's vanguard re-entered Philadelphia only hours after the last redcoats had rowed out into the Delaware.

Those unable to escape in time risked imprisonment by the city's incoming rebel Executive Council. Lists of people to be attaindered for collaborating with the British were posted up. To lighten the load of the Chief Justice, an extra-legal body was established intent on expediting business. Accusers would not have to make sworn statements. Fortunately, the vast majority of Loyalists had slipped away while they could and most of those who had stayed behind were spared the noose. But the execution of John Roberts, a sixty-year-old miller, leaving behind a wife and ten children, caused particular revulsion. To no avail, a thousand individuals, including civic figures and prominent Quakers, took the personal risk of signing a petition for clemency.[22] Galloway had little reason to doubt what his own fate would have been if he had fallen into rebel hands. The Assembly had passed an Act in March 1778 specifically naming him and demanding he surrender himself by 20 April or face the confiscation of his property. The likelihood was that, given the extent of his involvement with the British occupation, he would be hanged. A ditty published in *Freeman's Journal* the previous year had expressed the Patriot opinion of him:

> *Galloway has fled and joined the venal Howe*
> *To prove his baseness, see him cringe and bow;*
> *A traitor to his country and its laws,*
> *A friend to tyrants and their cursed cause.*[23]

Yet, while he chose to sail with his daughter for New York, Galloway's wife, Grace, opted to stay behind. Clearly, with the incoming administration declaring him a traitor, there was no hope of holding on to his property but there remained the possibility that if Grace remained in the houses that came with her Growden inheritance, they, at least, might avoid being looted or redistributed. The estate, after all, was worth £70,000.[24] At any rate, whatever the barbarities being committed by both sides, the incoming Executive Council were not going to hang a woman, especially not one of her social standing. It was a brave decision with sad consequences for it ensured she would never see her husband or daughter again.

While Trevose remained at the mercy of the pillagers, Grace Galloway opted to brazen out the occupation in the family's Philadelphia town house. In place of the British General Howe, her new next-door neighbour was the Continental Army's military commander for the city, Major-General Benedict Arnold. Far from this being a misfortune, it was a stroke of luck. Arnold was the true hero of the Saratoga campaign but he was feeling increasingly ill-used by his fellow Patriots and loathed having the French as allies. What was more, he was avaricious and keen to be accepted in Philadelphian society. His eye alighted upon the glamorous eighteen-year-old form of Peggy Shippen. The Shippens were Grace Galloway's in-laws and, despite the family's Loyalist associations and the state of Arnold's leg (a legacy of his Saratoga heroics), the two proceeded to get married.

There were further signs of the Major-General's magnanimity towards the enemy. Arnold intensely disliked the zeal with which the city's Council was hunting down Loyalists and agreed to help Grace by providing guards for her house. Unfortunately, the soldiers appeared to regard their duty there as ceremonial and proved unwilling to stand in the way when the Pennsylvania Executive Council dispatched the militia to seize the property. Grace, however, showed fighting spirit. When Charles Willson Peale, the agent for the confiscation, arrived to orchestrate her removal, it was to find he had to make a forcible entry. Grace recorded in her diary the ensuing contretemps: 'I told them Nothing but force shou'd get me out of My house Smith [one of the eviction party] said they knew how to Manage that & that they wou'd throw my cloaths in ye street.' News arrived that Major-General Arnold was personally sending his coach and four so that Mrs Galloway might be accorded some dignity in the manner of her departure. Eventually the carriage drew up at the front door and the agent, Peele, made his move:

> then with greates[t] air said come Mr[s] Galloway give me your hand I answer'd indeed I will not nor will I go out of my house but by force. He took hold of my arm & I rose & he took me to the door I then Took hold on on[e] side & Look[ed] round & said pray take Notice I do not leave my house of My own accord or with my own inclination but by force & Nothing but force shou'd have Made Me give up possession Peel said with a sneer very well Madam & when he led me down ye step I said now Mr Peel let go My Arm I want not your Assistance he said he cou'd help me to ye Carriage I told him I cou'd go without & you Mr Peel are the last Man on earth I wou'd wish to be Obliged to . . .'[25]

The house was duly confiscated and turned over to Joseph Reed, the Congress delegate and president of the Executive Council who had refused clemency to John Roberts. Trevose was handed over to General Wilkinson, the rebels' Secretary of the Board of War. However, Major-General Arnold had, in offering his coach, made a small sign that the city's military commander was no longer at ease with the lengths to which his cause's supporters were going. It was not until some time later that it would come to look like rather more than a mere chivalrous gesture.

Meanwhile, the wheel of fortune had turned for William. Following his wife's death, his health had deteriorated sharply. Various appeals had fallen on deaf ears until Connecticut's rebel Governor, Jonathan Trumball, fearing the consequences of William's imminent death, moved him out of Litchfield on 31 December 1777 to a more comfortable detention at East Windsor. The prisoner was to be given basic privileges. A sketch by Benjamin West of the drawn and wan former New Jersey Governor that emerged from Litchfield Gaol, compared to the earlier painting of him, graphically illustrated the physical deterioration he had suffered. Months passed until in September 1778 Congress debated exchanging William for John McKinley, the rebel Governor of Delaware, who was being held by the British. The deal was agreed and, on 1 November, William Franklin was finally handed over to the British in New York City. He had been in captivity for nearly three years.

In New York, William found not only the spot of his wife's interment beneath the crypt but also discovered that all their possessions had been incinerated. In August, Patriots had launched a devastating arson attack on the British military warehouse in which Galloway had carefully stored his friends' belongings. All the mementoes of William and Elizabeth Franklin's lives had gone up with it. It was symptomatic of the turning tide of war that New York was no longer a city that felt invulnerable. Instead there was a sense of unease, of encroaching danger. Late in 1778, Galloway's nerve finally snapped. After weighing up the options and his likely fate if he fell into rebel hands, he chose to catch a boat out and to take his daughter with him. They would cross the ocean, as refugees. Behind him, Galloway left the continent where he had not only spent his entire life but for which, at one stage, he had seemed poised to shape its political destiny. Grace had not managed to get through to make the journey with him. She died four years later.

'I had almost determined to follow you', William wrote from New York to the departed Galloway, 'but for an unwillingness to quit the scene of action, where I think I might be of some service.'[26] Galloway felt he would not only be in less danger in London but also that there he might be able to advise and influence the British government in the conduct of the war. In contrast, William decided to carry the fight directly to the enemy, throwing himself into the Loyalist resistance, encouraging the New York Refugees' Club and assuming the position of President of the Board of Associated Loyalists. His plan was to lead his Loyalist volunteers in retaliatory raids on rebel coastal territory. To the British Commander-in-Chief, General Clinton, such guerrilla tactics were a pointless distraction from the main theatres of war and, to William's exasperation, he succeeded in blocking most of the proposed missions. It was not until 1780 that the government in London overruled Clinton and William got his chance to launch his commando raids.

British military policy, meanwhile, had changed again. The army moved south into the rural areas of the Carolinas where there were Loyalist communities ready to rally to the flag. In May 1780, General Clinton took Charleston, the one sizeable southern city and, with it, 5,500 rebel prisoners of war. In August, General Cornwallis defeated the Continental Army at Camden. In November, the apostles of American patriotism were found to count among their number a Judas when Benedict Arnold fled to his British paymasters. The Patriot Major-General had been on the point of handing over the strategically crucial West Point when his treachery was unmasked. Personal rancour with his fellow Patriots, dislike of being on the same side as the French and the pro-Loyalist sympathies of his new wife may have helped dictate his betrayal of the Patriot cause for which he had previously risked life and limb. The fact that he was being paid to be a turncoat proved enough to ensure that future generations would remember his name with contempt.

He made it to New York, where he was given the rank of Brigadier-General. Major André, his interlocutor, did not and – against the dictates of his rank – was hanged. That Arnold would face a similar fate if captured was not in doubt, a reckoning that may have encouraged the viciousness with which he prosecuted his subsequent advance into the rebel heartland of Virginia. Cornwallis moved up to join him, taking Richmond and Charlottesville. None of these manoeuvres brought closer the moment of outright victory. The French, tiring of the expense of a contest seemingly weighted towards stalemate, privately proposed to the British a peace settlement that would have left the American colonies divided with the rebels holding on to their territory and the British holding on to theirs. George III rejected the proposal. Soon after, Cornwallis made the fatal decision to establish his base at Yorktown on the Virginian coast.

George Washington had been planning a long and risky siege of New York, but his French allies opened his eyes to the easier prize suddenly on offer. The French fleet being in control of the Chesapeake Bay, his men could be ferried into position. With decisive boldness, he rose to the occasion, covering four hundred miles to link up with the French and take Cornwallis by surprise. The French fleet blockaded the coast around the Yorktown peninsula, cutting the British garrison off. Attempts by a relief armada to break through failed, not least because of the timidity of the commanding officer, Admiral Graves. Cornwallis was in a trap. Unable to be resupplied by sea and surrounded by a heavily calibred American and French force twice his size, he concluded that he had no option but to surrender or be annihilated by the heavy guns trained upon his crowded nest. On 19 October 1781, more than 7,000 British troops marched out into captivity to the fife and drum of 'When the King Enjoys His Own Again', a tune more presciently known to the Americans as 'The World Turned Upside Down'. Cornwallis, supposedly too ill to make his abasement personally, sent his deputy to surrender his sword. It was offered to the French commander, the Comte de Rochambeau, who indicated that it should be given to General Washington (who duly ensured the martial trinket was passed to his subordinate). It was a humiliating end to the British Second Army. In London, the news hit the Prime Minister, Lord North, 'like a bullet in his breast'. 'Oh, God!' he rasped, 'It is all over.'[27]

In seeking to explain their eventual defeat, much has been written on the fractured and dysfunctional British command. In fact, the Patriots' generals were also of uneven quality and comradeship. Whatever may be said of the native British officers, they at least had no equivalent of treacherous Benedict Arnold. But nor did the British have a galvanising personality of George Washington's stamp to lead them tenaciously through the uncertain fortunes of conflict. London was too far away to give more than vague direction to strategy. If such latitude was a gift, it was not one of which the commanders made best use. Where London did interfere decisively was in denying them the resources necessary to complete the task. The opportunity to overwhelm the rebels was lost between 1775 and 1778.

The entry of France into the war brought threats in the English Channel, the Indian Ocean and the Caribbean that Lord North's ministers understandably felt also needed to be countered. The presence of the French fleet off America's eastern seaboard frustrated a British strategy that had relied on outright control of the Atlantic coast. It was the French naval presence that intimidated Howe and Clinton into evacuating Philadelphia and prevented Cornwallis from escaping safely from the Yorktown peninsula. Rochambeau's gesture with Cornwallis's surrendered sword may have been dictated by protocol (Washington was the senior commander) but it has been remembered primarily for its symbolic significance. French involvement ensured the success of the War of Independence but without the American colonists' tenacity, bravery and self-belief, the war would have been lost before the French thought seriously about getting drawn in. And but for Washington, the course of the American Revolution might have been as directionless as its English predecessor would have been without the steel of Cromwell, its chief of men.

In London, Members of Parliament reacted to the news of the surrender at Yorktown by concentrating their fire upon the government. Lord North came close to losing his House of Commons majority and all thoughts of a fresh military offensive were dispelled. The war party shrank to a small coterie around George III who, never fast to learn from experience, believed victory could yet be grasped. But it was those who paid for the war who were in control and they were determined to bring it to a close. A similar mood prevailed across the English Channel. Although the French were tied to the Spanish (who were hopeful of making gains in North America), Louis XVI's ministers were weary of the expense of further conflict. Negotiation was thus inevitable, with military manoeuvres in the meantime designed primarily to improve each participant's bargaining position.

Those who stood to lose most from a complete sell-out to the Patriots were the American Loyalists. A chilling incident during the fall of Yorktown gave them cause to doubt British fidelity. Attempting an evacuation of the besieged peninsula, the British ship *Bonetta* had not waited to pick up the hundreds of desperate Loyalists trying to row out to it. Their fate was to be captured by Washington's army. This was particularly serious because when Cornwallis surrendered to Washington, he omitted to gain a guarantee that the Loyalists would get the same protection of prisoner of war status afforded the British soldiers. The *Bonetta*'s Captain was subsequently brought before a court martial for his betrayal, but his actions, like those of Cornwallis, appeared symbolic of his nation's attitude in North America – as careless of its friends there as of its enemies.

Given the uncompromising attitude of Patriots who regarded them traitors, those Loyalists still at liberty had nowhere else to turn. It was thus not surprising that, cooped up in New York, a grim determination continued to animate the Board of Associated Loyalists and its President, William Franklin. Reprisal raids on rebel groups and privateers continued. The inter-American conflict had always been more bitterly waged than that between the Continental Army and British regulars. The peripatetic nature of British strategy had not served well those Loyalists they encountered along the way. As soon as the redcoats moved on, the Loyalists were exposed to reprisals from the active network of rebel committees and militias operating throughout the country. Attempts by the Loyalist groups to repay the terror often embarrassed the British high command. In the south, Banastre Tarleton's Loyalist Legion had, like Benedict Arnold's strikes into Virginia and Connecticut, participated in a particularly bloody campaign. Such tactics aggravated more than they intimidated. In April 1782, an attack led by the Loyalist Captain Richard Lippincott escalated into pointless brutality when Joshua Huddy, a Patriot Captain of the New Jersey militia, was hanged after he had surrendered.

The hanging of Huddy had been a reprisal act for a Patriot atrocity committed a few days previously – the death of a Loyalist carpenter, Philip White, who first had his legs smashed, then an arm severed and thereafter an eyeball yanked out. Nonetheless, Huddy's murder was just the sort of counter-productive vigilante activity that General Clinton had wanted the Associated Loyalists to avoid. Brought before a court martial, Lippincott was tried for murder. The more sensitive question was whether he had been acting on the orders of the Associated Loyalists' leader, William Franklin. George Washington was incensed by what he considered to be the war crime of Huddy's execution and held the Loyalist President to be corporately responsible for it. What was more, he threatened to hang a captured British officer if General Clinton did not surrender William. He faced the death penalty.

Much as Clinton had never thought the Loyalist raids a sensible idea, he could not casually condemn the former Royal Governor to be hanged like a common criminal. But the alternative was to see an innocent British officer's neck broken by the noose. Nervously, William awaited his fate. Having survived the ordeal of incarceration in a fetid cell during the most intense period of the conflict, he now had to contemplate the prospect that either he or a blameless officer would be strung up just when the war was all but over. Salvation came from the most unlikely quarter. In desperation, the condemned British officer's wife wrote to Louis XVI and Marie Antoinette. Amazingly, the French King and Queen took up the case and appealed to General Washington to back down. Congress also requested the British officer's release and Washington, perhaps keen to limit what threatened to develop into an ongoing tit-for-tat blood feud, dropped the charge.

The affair was a warning to William Franklin of what he could expect if he was ever captured by his fellow countrymen. On 13 August 1782 he boarded a ship, as his friend Galloway had done before him, that would take him to political asylum in England. He would never return to the land of his birth. Fifteen months later, General Washington entered New York City in triumph.

On 19 March 1782, Lord North tendered his resignation as Prime Minister. A new government was formed with the intention of concluding peace. The Marquess of Rockingham became Prime Minister. He was now old and in poor health; yet, as a Whig who had for so many years been a proponent of conciliating the colonists, his return to office made clear the direction of the new administration even if he might not personally be able to steer it energetically. Although outside the Cabinet, Edmund Burke was brought into the government as Paymaster. Charles James Fox became Foreign Secretary. The Earl of Shelburne was named Secretary of State for Home and Colonial Affairs. As such, he was responsible for negotiating peace with the Americans while Fox oversaw negotiations with the French. With this division of labour came a division of outlook. Fox favoured accepting outright American independence as the stated prerequisite of reaching a settlement while Shelburne – hoping that American home rule need not preclude total separation – adopted a more equivocal position. Rockingham's death in July 1782 and Fox's hasty resignation ensured it was Shelburne who assumed the premiership, under the gaze of a disapproving monarch.

It was not surprising that Shelburne wished to retrieve some wreckage from the ruin. Despite what had happened at Yorktown, the British military presence in North America was far from dislodged. And in early 1782 Britain's negotiating position with her European enemies was greatly strengthened when her navy smashed a Franco-Spanish fleet intent on conquering the British colony of Jamaica. Many in London regarded this as more than recompense for the loss of Yorktown. The sugar islands of the Caribbean were the primary source of Britain's transatlantic wealth; in 1773, the value of the American colonies' exports to Britain was still only worth a fifth of what was being traded from Jamaica.[28] Another spectacular British victory followed with the relief of the long-running Franco-Spanish siege of Gibraltar. There was certainly no need to make concessions to the Bourbon powers. The contentious issue concerned how hard a bargain to strike with the representatives of the American Congress.

In the summer of 1781 Congress had appointed five commissioners (Franklin, John Adams, John Jay, Henry Laurens and Thomas Jefferson) to negotiate peace. They would do so from Paris and since Franklin was the only one of them based there from the first, he naturally prepared much of the groundwork. Congress and Franklin were agreed on two fundamentals: the precondition that the United States' unqualified independence had to be recognised and the inadmissibility of any deal being struck with Britain without French authorisation. Sentiment required a connection between these two points but political reality did not. It was not just the British who found the cost of prolonging the war crippling; the French Exchequer also groaned under the burden. Desperate to end hostilities, the Comte de Vergennes' commitment to outright American independence had waned and his envoy to London hinted that France might agree a peace that fell short of American aspirations. Here was an opportunity to nip the New World's idealism in the bud. If the French were not prepared to fight to the death for what Vergennes had privately told his ambassador in Philadelphia were 'the pretentious ambitions' of a United States,[29] the two Old World powers might cobble together a deal at the expense of the ingénue.

However, the liberties in whose name the revolution had been fought were those that American Patriots shared with British Whigs. Whatever Congress was prepared to do, Westminster Whigs of the stamp of Fox and Burke were not going to dance to the rebarbative tunes of Tories, let alone that of the absolutist court at Versailles. The ascendancy of Britain's political liberals at this time removed the necessity for the American diplomats to be in thrall to France. The hard-headed negotiator John Adams certainly did not feel Franklin's sense of fraternity, arguing that Congress had 'prostituted' its sovereignty to Vergennes.[30] Franklin was persuaded to forget Congress's sense of obligation to its Gallic ally.

In treating with the British, Franklin had originally indicated that he expected them to pay reparations for the damage they had caused to Patriots' property and to surrender Canada to the new United States. It was not clear what right the United States had to annex Canada other than what would emerge as the mystical notion that it was their manifest destiny to colonise all of North America. Franklin, however, wished it might be seen in practical terms: if the British were going to pay for the damage they had inflicted while waging war across the thirteen colonies, handing over Canada was one obvious unit of exchange. Unsurprisingly, British accountants argued that the audit of war was more finely balanced. London made clear it expected Americans to honour their pre-war debts and to recompense those Loyalists they had dispossessed. Franklin was particularly adamant in his opposition to honouring the latter. In his view, honed by bitter personal experience, the Loyalists were traitors who had fought against their families and neighbours. But in July 1782 he drew up a less aggressive list of objectives that would form the basis for eventual agreement: the unconditional independence of the United States, acknowledgement that Canada would stay British, a general settlement of US boundaries and an acceptance of American fishing rights off Newfoundland.

Franklin's poor health ensured that it was John Adams and John Jay (who had originally voted in favour of Galloway's Plan of Union) who shouldered much of the diplomatic burden when formal negotiations with the British government's envoys commenced on 30 October 1782. Adams and Jay had no qualms about selling out on the French. Matters were also made easier by the British attitude. Franklin having been persuaded to drop his demand for Canada, Shelburne proceeded to demonstrate a willingness to allow the United States to push westward at the expense of British Canada's claims south of the Great Lakes. Thus the American settlers were finally able to go west, doubling the size of their territory by redrawing the national boundary on the Mississippi River rather than the Appalachian Mountains. This was a momentous concession, for it ensured that the United States would eventually spread from the Atlantic across the entire continent to the Pacific. On 30 November 1782, Franklin, Adams, Jay and Henry Laurens signed a separate peace with Britain, leaving their supposed French allies high and dry. 'I am at a loss, sir, to explain your conduct, and that of your colleagues in this occasion,' wrote Vergennes to Franklin with mannered restraint.[31]

After further talks, Britain made peace with its European enemies and the Treaty of Paris was signed on 3 September 1783. It returned most seized colonies – primarily in the Caribbean – to their pre-war owners, except of course, in North America, where all parties recognised the free and independent United States of America nine years after the first Continental Congress had convened in Philadelphia and rejected, by one vote, Galloway's plan for Anglo-American union.

The Founding Fathers had realised a remarkable aspiration. They were masters of their own destiny at last. What shape the new nation would take – in particular what powers should rest at state and what at federal level – would be the focus for debate and rancour between them in the years ahead, as indeed it would continue to exercise their descendants in the centuries that followed. But it was, at least, in their hands to decide the matter. No more would Dr Franklin, or any other Assembly Agent, have to sail across an ocean to make his case before ministers whose interest in American life had rarely been sufficient to tempt them west across the Atlantic. In England, and elsewhere, there were those who waited for the whole experiment to fall flat on its face and there were moments when it looked as if the fledgling republic, its economy dislocated and torn by the sort of internal dissent that only the presence of a common foe had temporarily quelled, would do just that.

However, underlying the beliefs of Fox and Burke and the assessment that Shelburne too had come to accept was the fact that the American Republic possessed the potential for greatness. Making peace with it on reasonable terms was not just an expedient means of extracting Britain from a costly and seemingly unwinnable war, but a surety that the two great English-speaking nations would bury their enmities. Ties not only of blood but also of outlook meant that Americans would regain their affinity with Great Britain and cast off a temporarily convenient but ideologically incompatible fraternity with the absolutist France of the Bourbons (they, no more than the Bourbons, foresaw that the revolutionary spirit would so soon conquer Paris too). Back in August 1782, Burke had been impatient to conclude a deal, writing to Franklin in Passy, 'I flatter myself that by this time we might have shaken hands as publick friends as I hope we always should have done as private. In the Latter Case States have no power, though in other respects they may and do put us in odd and awkward Situations.'[32] Now there was the prospect of a new understanding.

In the long view of history, the British government's decision to concede to the secessionists more than the immediate military situation necessitated made obvious sense. But the display of a measure of magnanimity towards an unbowed foe rested upon a decision to betray a deserted friend. Native American Indians and the 400,000 African-American slaves (about one fifth of the new United States' population) lost out as a consequence of the Patriots' victory: the former because London's proclamations reserving their land beyond the Appalachians were now to be brushed aside by Americans who, having freed themselves from colonial status, zealously proceeded to colonise their own neighbours; while the slaves would remain in servitude in the southern states long after slavery was made illegal in Britain and its Empire. Some in Britain, notably the acerbic Dr Samuel Johnson, drew attention to the number of slave-holders who signed the Declaration of Independence and dismissed their protestations for liberty on that basis alone. Yet, bitter though the harvest was to be, it could hardly be argued that the human rights of slaves and Indians had been a central motivation for Britain to fight on. Selling out on the Loyalists – Britain's kith and kin – was another matter. It was one that went to the heart of political and personal sentiments.

At the start of the peace negotiations Franklin had been particularly insistent that the United States would not feel bound to compensate Loyalists who had lost their properties and livelihoods in the struggle. For the British negotiators this had been a problem. The French expected their American allies to honour the rights of property but, ultimately, the fate of Loyalists was hardly an issue upon which the court at Versailles was going to ditch its ally of convenience. For politicians at Westminster, however, the decision to wash their hands of those who had lost everything fighting for King George III was altogether more disagreeable. Having been rallied in war, now the Loyalists were a stumbling block to peace. They were an inconvenience, like France's *pieds noirs* when Paris granted Algerian independence in 1962.

In Parliament, the former ill-starred Prime Minister, Lord North, attempted to regain some moral authority from the loss of political dominion when he appealed against selling the Loyalists down the river. 'They have exposed their lives, endured an age of hardships, deserted their interests, forfeited their possessions, lost their connections and ruined their families in our cause', he reminded his peers. 'Never was the honour, the principles, the policy of a nation, so grossly abused as in our desertion of those men, who are now exposed to every punishment that such desertion and poverty can inflict, BECAUSE THEY WERE NOT REBELS.'[33] Almost two centuries later, American decision-makers would be faced with a similar predicament over what to do about the South Vietnamese allies they were about to desert. A dispossessed Loyalist put it ruefully:

> *Tis an honor to serve the bravest of nations*
> *and be left to be hanged in their capitulations.*[34]

Yet, short of going back to war – a resumption that was clearly to be avoided – there was not much Britain could do to force America to compensate the Loyalists. So the peace treaty set out a face-saving diplomatic nicety in which Congress would recommend to the thirteen state legislatures that they compensate the Loyalists. As Franklin and his co-signatories well knew, the recommendation had no legal force and would never be acted upon. This proved to be the case. The states ignored the proclamation made in January 1784 by Congress to make due restitution. Instead, all thirteen states enforced laws that confiscated Loyalists' property and prohibited them from holding office or practising law or medicine. Many states enforced the exiling of named Loyalists and five states disenfranchised them. In a display of victor's justice, some were hanged, lynched, tarred or roughed up by those keen to display their allegiance to the new regime – and steal a neighbour's property into the bargain. The intimidation did its job. Between 80,000 and 100,000 Loyalist refugees fled or emigrated from the new United States rather than face the consequences of staying. The diaspora spread to Canada, the West Indies and to Britain. Out of a total population of three million, the flight of up to 100,000 was – proportionately – one of the major political exoduses in history.

Those who made it to Britain found they had a worthy advocate already ensconced there – Joseph Galloway. Ever since his arrival in London, Galloway had been championing the Loyalist cause. In 1779 he had appeared before a committee of the House of Commons where he decried what he regarded as the half-hearted way in which Howe had prosecuted the war, believing that he had missed chances for outright victory and imperilled the lives of those who had risked all to serve the King. His arguments helped shore up the resolve of the factions wanting to persevere with the war. Even Lord Shelburne passed on Galloway's memoranda to George III. Such exhortations were not enough, however, to alter battlefield realities. In 1783 he wrote a pamphlet drawing attention to the sacrifices the Loyalists had made and arguing that if the United States could not be prevailed upon to recompense them then the British government ought to do so. William Franklin joined Galloway's campaign. Ruined by war, the British Exchequer was almost as ill-equipped to underwrite such expenses as were the financially shattered American states. Nonetheless, the clamour was too loud to be ignored. Commissioners were duly appointed and examined 2,560 claims.[35]

Inevitably, the recompenses did not make up for what had been lost. The eventual pay-out covered about a fifth of the sum claimed. Shed of the property and position that had given them status in colonial America, many Loyalists who made it to Britain found they counted for nothing in London society. They had pledged themselves to a country that cared little about them in return. A Boston judge like Robert Auchmuty was reduced to asking for handouts. Ladies who had grown up in privileged ease suddenly had to make ends meet through menial labour. Many expats tried to stick together. Bewildered and embittered, they congregated to gossip and read the newspapers in a New England coffee house in Threadneedle Street and the Crown and Anchor in the Strand where James Boswell and the sympathetic Dr Johnson were habitués. Whatever the circumstances they had left behind, all found that the cost of living in London far exceeded what they had been accustomed to at home. In fact, most of the Loyalists were not the positioned or the wealthy but rather farmers, skilled labourers and small businessmen. Many now found themselves having to adapt to life as domestic servants.[36] One for whom there was limited sympathy, not least among the Loyalist community, was Benedict Arnold. The government gave him a pension but few respected the manner in which the turncoat had come over to the redcoat side. One day he was spotted observing a parliamentary debate from the gallery of the House of Commons. An MP had him promptly ejected.

By the time William Franklin had left New York, he told Galloway that he had been reduced to such circumstances that he could no longer afford to entertain a friend to dinner.[37] It was quite a comedown from the Governor's mansions in Burlington and Perth Amboy. In London, he found lodgings in Suffolk Street, west of what is now Trafalgar Square. It was only a few minutes' walk from Craven Street where he had once lived with his father in happier times. Like Galloway, he was dependent on a government pension. Having to prove his Loyalist credentials before the Claims Commission (Galloway spoke in his support) was painful and degrading, especially amid preposterous suggestions that he and his father had connived in choosing to be on opposite sides as a means of hedging their bets. The Commission awarded him compensation only for the loss of his furniture and books. William's hopes of being appointed Governor of Barbados, where 'dear Mrs Franklin was born', came to naught.[38]

Galloway had time to brood on the extent of his loss and it embittered him both against those American colleagues who had fomented the revolution and those Britons who had given in to it. He convinced himself that most Americans had wanted to remain loyal to the Crown. This may well have been true before shots were exchanged in anger. As late as 1774, George Washington was still writing that no 'thinking man in all North America' wanted independence. But modern research suggests that once the war began in earnest, Britain could count on less than a third and possibly only a fifth of colonial loyalties (although, of course, there was no uniformity of attitude governing what the disillusioned majority wished ultimately to achieve). Given how strong Galloway believed loyalty to British America had been before the revolution, he was at a loss to account for the subsequent turn of events. He looked for scapegoats. Benjamin Franklin, he now believed, had been scheming for years to incite rebellion while pretending to act with propriety in London. He had deceived everyone. In prosecuting the war, Howe's lethargy was, to Galloway's mind, a dereliction of duty bordering upon the culpable.

The greatest treason, supposedly, was that of the Patriots' friends in the British Parliament. In this category none stood so prominently as Charles James Fox. In 1781, when military events at Yorktown were fundamentally shifting the terms of debate in Fox's favour, Galloway sought to expose the sybaritic reformer. This he did through the well worn technique of thinly disguised classical allusion. He adopted the persona of Cicero, the great orator and philosopher who warned the Roman Senate of the conspiracy of Lucius Sergius Catilina, the noble-born but profligate radical who mouthed democratic demands in order to further his own ambition (the conspiracy duly suppressed, Cicero found himself banished and his property confiscated for his part in advocating the death penalty for Catiline). Galloway published his attack, anonymously, as *Letters from Cicero to Catiline the Second.*

Having been considered one of the foremost orators in Pennsylvania, if not North America, Galloway piled on the venom. To serve personal ends, 'Catiline' and his faction had conspired sedition. At their eve-of-war attempt at reconciliation at Trevose, Franklin had assured Galloway that the Patriot cause had many friends in Westminster and that, consequently, Britain would be wracked by division if there was any attempt to suppress the American rebellion. Galloway had dismissed this suggestion, holding instead that an insurrection would unite the normally opposed British factions the – 'two Bull Dogs' – who would find common cause in suppressing it. Subsequent events had shown Franklin's interpretation to have been the more prophetic. Galloway now brooded on the possibility that his former friend had been arguing with the benefit of inside knowledge of an anti-government campaign that had actually been carefully planned.

What particularly offended Galloway was how brazenly the conspiracy had been put into practice. The Patriots' supporters in Westminster had called for the British troops to be recalled and had raised funds for the rebel cause even when the rebels had been in league with Britain's arch enemy, France. They had exhorted the American insurgents 'to persevere in rebellion; to "make a solemn, sullen and invincible stand", against the authority to which they had submitted, without a murmur, for more than *one hundred and fifty years*'.[39] But the rebellion's British admirers had themselves been the victim of a deception that encouraged them to overrate the Patriots' popularity in America. Here, Galloway pointed the finger firmly at his former friend, Dr Franklin:

> Not seeing the art and duplicity of this political quack, you suffer him to deceive you again. He now assures you, that the militia in America, disposed to rebellion is vastly numerous; that although Congress have failed in bringing into the field nearly three-fourths of the number stipulated; although no dependence can be placed on the militia; yet that they may be easily drawn forth 'to approach near New York, to enable you, *their friends in Parliament,* during the winter's debates, to hold it up as a place besieged, and to insist on a recal of the British troops'.[40]

He contrasted what he maintained were the Whigs' self-serving motives, to 'usurp' the rights of their sovereign, with that of the Loyalists: 'As a proof of their fidelity and honour, while you are exerting your utmost abilities to overthrow the government which has given you freedom and protection, they have sacrificed their fortunes, and the independent happiness of their families, for its preservation.'[41]

Such intemperate philippics did little to further the debate, highlighting instead only the extent of Galloway's bitterness and disillusion in having to settle in a country where (in his eyes) treasonable self-serving politicians like Fox continued to be fêted by significant sections of society and the populace. They made no secret of their admiration for Franklin, who had helped to bring about one of the greatest reverses in British history, and indifference to Galloway, his one-time colleague, who had lost everything trying to brook a compromise to avert the disaster. The irony of Galloway's allegation was that he had come to see the British political class as mired in corruption and dissipation – exactly what had disillusioned Franklin with the mother country in the last years before the revolution broke. As for Galloway's charge that Franklin had practised the arts of deception, Franklin also had grounds for feeling ill used. He had joined the Patriot cause having understood, or misunderstood, that his old friend would not take up arms against it.

Others felt that Galloway had proved to be a servant neither of the America he had left nor the Britain in which he sought sanctuary. As one of the voices that had urged the British government to fight on by maintaining that the revolution was a conspiracy without widespread support, he had helped to ensure that the war continued to be prosecuted – with mounting atrocities on both sides – well after it would have benefited all concerned to call a truce.

What was certain was that Galloway was stuck in Britain. He could not risk stepping back in his native land until he could be certain he would not be arrested. Some of those who had been named as Loyalists had continued to live there without serious harassment but Galloway was to receive no such assurances. Two petitions via his attorney to the Pennsylvania Assembly requesting the lifting of the attainder of high treason against him got nowhere and in 1790 he was advised to drop the action. His wife, Grace, had died out there in 1789 without managing to get any of their property returned. In 1791, their daughter, Elizabeth, who had escaped to Britain with her father, made the Atlantic crossing back to see what could be arranged. Her journey proved fruitless, and she returned to London to be with a father reconciling himself to life as a permanent refugee. The British government gave him a pension. Elizabeth later wrote an appreciation of his life in exile: 'Few men, in the course of a long life, settled more business for others; and perhaps, seldom any one gave so much advice gratis. His morning-room was often crowded with, and seldom empty of, Americans, who received from him his best services in their own affairs.'[42]

He also made influential English friends in John Wesley and his son, Charles. Having been nurtured in the strong faith of the Quakers before taking the Anglican Communion alongside his wedding vows, Galloway was of political and theological interest to the founder of Methodism. John Wesley was impressed both by the man he befriended and the arguments he put forth. He also liked Elizabeth and assured his niece, Sarah Wesley, that she would enjoy getting to know them both. After dining with them at Twickenham, he wrote of 'that pleasing family and lovely place'. Like Galloway, Wesley's views on North American politics had shifted from supporting moderate reform to outright opposition to the rebellion and the republican ideals it spawned. Throughout the colonies, Methodists had suffered for their overwhelmingly Loyalist allegiances. Many of Galloway's publications were printed by Wesley's press. 'Surely Mr Galloway owes to the world a true account of the American revolution,' Wesley told his niece, 'all the question is whether it should be published during his life.'[43] Galloway's last major act was to write *Brief Commentaries upon such Parts of the Revolution and Other Prophecies as Immediately Refer to the Present Times*, in which he went in search of scriptural revelation against the evils of the age, damning the atheism of the French Revolution. Thus, he ended up on the same side as Edmund Burke.

He did not live long enough to see Loyalists triumphant in Canada. Their migration helped ensure Canada remained loyal to Britain when the United States tried to seize it during the War of 1812. Indeed, it was in Canada that Galloway's arguments for evolution within – rather than divorce from – the

British Empire bore fruit. When, in 1837, London reacted to the antipathy of the French-speaking Québecois and discontent even among some of the English-speaking settlers at the oligarchic rule of the Governors and their social circle, its response was not to insist on the power of subjugation alone. Rather, the Durham Report was commissioned. It led, in time, to the transferral of power from London's tools of executive supervision – the Governor and the Legislative Council – towards those directly responsible to decentralised Canadian legislatures. There was also a nod towards what the American revolutionaries had created: Canada became a federation of states. For all its problems and the separatist tendencies of its French-speakers, a remarkably durable system was created for Canada by the constitutional agreements between 1837 and 1867 that recognised the autonomy of the settlers and retained Canadians under the British Crown into the twenty-first century.

None of this seemed certain when Galloway died on 29 August 1803. Posterity would not be kind to him. His name was without honour in his own land. Despite his role in the first Continental Congress, he was not to be accorded the status of a Founding Father even though his plan for a constitutional settlement had come tantalisingly close to adoption as the colonists' principal demand. Depictions of the profiles of his colleagues would multiply as the decades passed by – above fireplaces, on civic pedestals, in city squares, in town names and on the ultimate embodiment of the independent America's success, banknotes (Franklin ended up on the $100 note). Galloway's fate was to be forgotten or, at best, dismissed as an irrelevant irreconcilable to the inevitable march of American progress. Nor did successive generations of British historians remember his name, except, on occasion, in a footnote. Brought up in the Whig tradition, their heroes, men like Fox and Burke, were on the freedom-loving Patriots' side.

Elizabeth wrote a lamentation for her father:

> *Though many an epitaph of thine was known*
> *To grace the cold, commemorating stone,*
> *Thine own remains, in some neglected spot,*
> *Now lie unsung, unheeded, and forgot.*[44]

Joseph Galloway lies in an unmarked grave in Watford.

✱

Between Galloway and Franklin there had come no reconciliation. But William Franklin could not endure to skulk around London for the rest of his days without attempting contact with his venerable parent. In July 1784, after almost a decade of severance, he wrote to his 'Dear and Honoured Father' – who was still in France – hoping to 'revive that affectionate intercourse and connexion which till the commencement of the late troubles had been the pride and happiness of my life'. The letter also provided an opportunity for him to defend the path he had chosen to walk:

> I have uniformly acted from a strong sense of what I conceived my duty to my King and regard to my country required. If I have been mistaken, I cannot help it. It is an error of judgment that the maturest reflection I am capable of cannot rectify, and I verily believe, were the same circumstances to occur again tomorrow, my conduct would be exactly similar to what it was heretofore.[45]

Franklin replied to his son's appeal. It was, he assured William, 'very agreeable to me' to be back in touch. But, if his son was going to defend his actions, then the father was also going to spell out some home truths:

> Nothing has ever hurt me so much, and affected me with such keen sensations, as to find myself deserted in my old age by my only son; and not only deserted, but to find him taking up arms against me in a cause wherein my good fame, fortune and life were all at stake. You conceived, you say, that your duty to your King and regard for your country required this. I ought not to blame you for differing in sentiment with me in public affairs. We are men, all subject to errors. Our opinions are not in our own power; they are formed and governed much by circumstances that are often as inexplicable as they are irresistible. Your situation was such that few would have censured your remaining neuter, though there are natural duties which precede political ones, and cannot be extinguished by them. This is a disagreeable subject. I drop it. And we will endeavour, as you propose, mutually to forget what has happened relating to it, as well as we can.

The letter was brought across the English Channel and delivered personally to William by his son, Temple. Unaware that William had lost his possessions in the flames of a British Army warehouse, the senior Franklin suggested he should lend his law books to Temple to encourage him to study. The boy 'will inform you that he received the letter sent him by Mr Galloway, and the paper it inclosed, safe. On my leaving America I deposited with that friend for you, a chest of papers ... These are missing;

I hope you have got them; if not, they are lost.' He also felt it necessary to remind William that while showing Temple around London, 'I trust that you will prudently avoid introducing him to company that it may be improper for him to be seen with.' This was probably a reference to Loyalists rather than low life. 'You may confide to your son the family affairs you wished to confer upon with me, for he is discreet' wrote Franklin in a tone that emphasised the dysfunctionality of the three generations of the family.[46]

In May 1785, Benjamin Franklin, America's greatest expat, received Congress's instructions to return home. He packed up his belongings with mixed feelings. Having enjoyed life among the French, 'a people that love and respect me', he had reconciled himself to the prospect of ending his days with them, 'for my friends in America are dying off, one after another, and I have been so long abroad that I should now be almost a stranger in my own country'.[47] Taking his leave, he crossed the English Channel to Southampton where he intended to catch a ship that would take him across the Atlantic. Awaiting the wind that would bear him back, he booked in with Temple at the Star tavern and received visitors. It was there that William Franklin called to see him for what, with the old man's return to their homeland, would clearly be the last meeting. William would never be allowed back into the country of his birth, so it provided an opportunity to settle various financial matters, including the transferral of his property in New Jersey and New York to Temple. But in other respects, it was an awkward and unsatisfactory send-off. The Star tavern, with its stream of transitory clientele, was not the place for intimate soul-searching and quiet confidences. Perhaps the senior Franklin preferred it so. In the early hours of 27 July 1785 his ship lifted anchor and set sail. With Temple by his side, Franklin had boarded it without waking William to say goodbye.

Franklin's ship reached its final destination in September, two years after the Peace of Paris had pronounced international recognition for the United States of America. Philadelphia responded enthusiastically to his return. Hailed as a national sage and Founding Father, he was made President of the Pennsylvania Executive Council. In May 1787 he was sent as a representative to the Constitutional Convention established to determine the legal framework of the new republic. His ideas for a unicameral Congress with an executive committee served by unpaid officials were not taken up. He did, however, help broker the compromise over state voting shares and, despite his doubts, spoke in favour of accepting the proposed Constitution unanimously.

Franklin finished the first volume of his autobiography. It was a magnificent work. In the first draft, written back in 1771, the book's opening words had been addressed to his 'dear son'. In 1788 he completed the next section, rather more impersonally, for the benefit of mankind.

Despite the respect in which he was held, Franklin never established the rapport or longevity of fraternity with any of his fellow Founding Fathers that he had for so many years – even when separated by the Atlantic – with Galloway. He lived on, infirm and in pain, but lively to the last in his mind, residing in some state at Franklin Court, attended by his daughter Sally – the dutiful offspring. Pride of place was given to the Louis XVI portrait the King had presented him as a leaving gift, encrusted with 408 diamonds in its frame. Franklin lived long enough to hear of the first rumblings of the French Revolution. Not unnaturally, it produced in him mixed feelings, but he chose to hope it would have beneficial consequences, writing to a British friend:

> The convulsions in France are attended with some disagreeable circumstances, but if by the struggle she obtains and secures for the nation its future liberty and a good constitution, a few years' enjoyment of those blessings will amply repair all the damages their acquisition may have occasioned. God grant that not only the love of liberty but a thorough knowledge of the rights of man may pervade all the nations of the Earth, so that a philosopher may set his foot anywhere on its surface and say, 'This is my country'.[48]

Having freed his slaves, he accepted the presidency of the Pennsylvania Abolition Society. He died on 17 April 1790, aged eighty-four, having urged a memorial to Congress to abolish slavery, the issue that would tear the Union apart seventy-one years later and cause a yet bloodier war on the American continent. Temple Franklin was the chief beneficiary of his will. To William he left only an out-of-date land claim in Nova Scotia – land that had been resettled to Loyalists – and the rebuke, 'The part he acted against me in the late war, which is of public notoriety, will account for my leaving him no more of an estate he endeavoured to deprive me of.'[49]

Perhaps part of Franklin's resentment over William's behaviour was given edge by musing on what his other son, Francis, might have developed into if only he had not died of smallpox back in 1736. Temple was certainly a surrogate. He was an unworthy one. Benjamin Franklin's gifts to America and to the world fructified in the decades and centuries that followed. It was his relations who dismantled his personal estate. Temple left America for good. With the family patriarch in his grave, there was a family reunion in 1792 when Temple, Sally and Richard Bache arrived in Britain. With William as their guide, they toured the country together, retracing some of the steps William had taken with his father in happier times.

William married again, to Mary D'Evelyn, a member of the Irish gentry in a seemingly happy union that also put an end to his money problems. But Temple's wayward behaviour, although within the family tradition, caused his father great upset. After siring an illegitimate daughter, Temple deserted the mother and went off to live a life of dissipation in Paris. William brought up the abandoned girl, Ellen, as his own and paid for her education. There was symmetry in this inter-generational passing of responsibility. In the ensuing decade there was no communication between William and his estranged son. In 1808, Mary's health collapsed and he devoted himself to her care. She died three years later, making William a widow for the second time. With Galloway long in his grave, William's loneliness was kept at bay by Ellen, on whom he lavished his aged affection and hopes.

After all the years of acrimony aggravated by his fruitless attempts to secure the return of the money and property the American Republic had seized from him, William Franklin died on 16 November 1813 deludedly believing his luck had suddenly turned for the better. It was the news from his homeland that cheered the eighty-two-year-old, now suffering from angina pectoris and influenza. The United States had invaded Canada. The attack was a flop. Émigré Loyalists had rallied to the British defence of their land and the assault was repulsed. What most cheered the ailing former Royal Governor was the news that British troops had pushed south into the United States and occupied the Illinois territory. At last, it seemed, William would realise the old Vandalia land grant to which he had staked a claim back in 1766, before all the troubles commenced. His Illinois Company had struck it rich. After so long and bitter an odyssey, he would die fabulously wealthy, with an inheritance he could pass on. It was important he acted fast. The day before his death, he overcame his encroaching ailments sufficiently to leave his house, 28a Norton Street in Marylebone. From there he headed for the United States Consulate. There, he began filing his deposition.

Although he had decided to make Ellen the chief beneficiary of his will, he remained adamant that half of this supposedly fabulous Illinois inheritance should pass to the errant Temple who had recently got back in touch. Anxiously, he waited for his son to cross the English Channel. In a letter to his cousin, William expressed a parting desire to tidy up his unfinished business before it was too late. Halfway through writing it, illness overcame him. Ellen picked up his pen and continued it for him while he, pain overwhelming his senses, stammered out a dictation. The arguments of the past should be buried. Blood was thicker than water. 'Not being able to bear the thoughts of dying at enmity with one so nearly connected,' he desperately wanted to see Temple again. 'My best wishes', he concluded, 'will ever attend every branch of our family.'[50]

Fitzharding,

Sarah Churchill (on the right), killing time with Barbara, Viscountess Fitzharding.

Above: The old Whitehall Palace, viewed from St James's Park.

Right: The other woman: Abigail Masham.

Left: Anne, looking very much the Stuart princess, aged eighteen.

Left: Benjamin Franklin.

Below left: William Franklin.

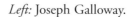

Left: Joseph Galloway.

Below: John Adams, Thomas Jefferson and Benjamin Franklin lead the Declaration of Independence drafting committee in the Pennsylvania State House, 1776. Jefferson appears to be treading on the foot of his rival, Adams.

Above: The Last Roman - Herbert Henry Asquith.

Right: The face of Liberal Imperialism - Richard Burdon Haldane.

Venetia Stanley, aged twenty-seven, at the peak of her hold over the Prime Minister.

Preparing to switch mentors? Edwin Montagu takes a walk with David Lloyd George.

PART THREE

LIBERALS

Herbert Henry Asquith and Richard Burdon Haldane

*

'Since an untimely blow has borne away a part of my soul, why do I still linger on less dear, only partly surviving? That day was the downfall of us both.'

HORACE, *Odes 2:17*

EIGHT

Getting On

Benjamin Franklin and the American colonists could have set a precedent for Britain's political reformers to follow. But the chances of their revolution's principles returning home to lay claim to the mother country were scuppered by a second popular insurrection that broke out in 1789 across the English Channel. Horror and alarm were the primary reactions to France's rapid passage from monarchical absolutism – via a brief spring of liberalism – into 'The Terror' of arbitrary rule by demagogues and ideologues from which salvation came only through the military Caesarianism of Napoleon Bonaparte. By comparison, King George III's ministers governing through Parliament appeared a safer guarantee of the rights of liberty and property. Benefiting from this patriotic reflex, the Tories strengthened their grip on power under the sprightly leadership of William Pitt the Younger. With one transitory interlude, they remained in office under successive administrations until 1830.

These events dented Whiggery's confident certainties. Whigs who had toasted the cause of revolution in America found little to cheer when news spread through London's chop houses of the French Revolution's excesses. Here were tales of atrocity that were, for once, scarcely distorted by the uneven varnish of the popular press. The fate of French nobility demonstrated to Whig grandees what little security a country estate really offered against the impulses of the mob and populist tribunes who expropriated under the slogans of liberty and equality. On the other hand, there were some for whom the cause could never be polluted. Charles James Fox remained doggedly positive about events in France, even when doing so necessitated turning a blind eye to chaos. By this means he kept the measured illiberalism of domestic opponents in court and Parliament in focus. In contrast, his great collaborator in the defence of American freedoms, Edmund Burke, viewed matters very differently. He prophesied disaster from the first, foreseeing bloody turmoil rather than hope in the mob's storming of the Bastille and the ominously insulting glances levelled at Marie Antoinette. The Fox-Burke relationship foundered on this ideological divide as assuredly as colonist aspirations had come between Franklin and Galloway.

In his new guise as a Tory philosopher, Burke repudiated Fox, dying his irreconcilable opponent.

The French convulsions ensured that it was not until the 1820s that those preaching reform began again to direct the course of debate in British politics. In 1829 the Tories were divided by their government's decision to grant Catholic Emancipation. Power passed back to the Whigs. It was a significant moment, for in broadening the franchise and sweeping away the worst anomalies of constituency distribution and the corruption that sprang from it, the 1832 Reform Act heralded a long period of Whig ascendancy. This brand of aristocratic liberalism was as high-minded in tone as it was self-serving in execution. It struggled to avoid disdain for those whose supposed lack of thrift and enterprise made them ineligible for the confidence of the franchise. At a time when Britain was emerging as the first industrial nation, much of its social legislation was coercive in nature. Workhouses were the terminus for those broken by the nation's efforts to become the workshop of the world. The Tories adapted to the changed environment quicker than might have been imagined. Under the tutelage of Sir Robert Peel, they adopted the tag 'Conservative' yet forsook the path of automatic reaction in favour of constructive legislation.

Within the Houses of Parliament, the landed interest continued to pre-dominate without prejudice to party label. However, during the 1840s two radical mass movements from outside Westminster threatened to change this settled arrangement. The first, the 'Chartists', with brazen demands for mass democracy, was the voice of those mostly outside the political process demanding inclusion in it. It peaked in 1848, the year in which Europe was engulfed in revolution and Britain made do with public meetings. The second great campaign was the Anti-Corn Law League which was established in 1839 and led by two radicals, Richard Cobden and John Bright, whose years of collaboration afforded an example of successful political partnership. Opposing agricultural protectionism, the Anti-Corn Law League was a free trade movement that represented the new industrial, commercial, entre-preneurial and more frequently (although not exclusively) Nonconformist interests that were rising in the Midlands and the north to challenge the entrenched élite of landed Anglican old money. With member subscriptions, local agents, regional offices and unity of purpose and propaganda, the League was organised like a modern party. In this it was unlike the interests that returned most MPs at the time. Indeed, the League was soon getting its representatives elected to the Commons.

To its champions, free trade assumed the mantle of a law of nature, a self-correcting mechanism beyond the whims of tyrants and self-serving corporations, crossing boundaries to promote international comity and rewarding the hard-working and enterprising. Recognising that they drew the mainspring of their support from urban rather than countryside electors, Whigs and Radicals combined to fight the 1841 general election on a free trade programme of reforming the Corn Laws. They lost. But the Conservatives proceeded to tear themselves apart over Peel's commitment – in the face of famine in Ireland – to abolish the Corn Laws and combat the scarcity and high prices agricultural protectionism had ensured. Peel took with him one hundred of his followers, including the young William Ewart Gladstone, into a centre ground that risked becoming political limbo. Most were not quite ready to be subsumed into liberal ranks, but nor were they at ease with their former colleagues now comprising the Tory rump.

The result was a lack of stability in mid-nineteenth-century British politics. As the historian Alan Sykes has put it, 'The self-styled Liberals more closely resembled a shoal of fish, a swirling mass forever changing shape and composition, fragmenting and recombining but never a single unit.' Unlike the Conservatives, 'They did not split because there was no party to split.' This amorphous state was not to remain indefinitely, for a major step in becoming a unified party was taken in 1859 when the Whig, Liberal, Radical and Peelite factions united in a meeting at Willis's Rooms to oust a minority Conservative administration run by the Earl of Derby. From this point on, to speak of a Liberal Party was more than convenient shorthand.

With Lords Palmerston and John Russell as well as the untitled Gladstone and Bright on its benches, this Liberal Party was not lacking in talent. Yet, it was still an uneasy coalition of interest groups in which Cabinets predominantly staffed by landed Whigs had little in common with the enthusiasts and 'faddists', shopkeepers and tract publishers, who were active in the constituencies. For the latter, fortified by the burgeoning campaigning journalism of radical newspapers, politics was less a question of dispassionate management than of crusading mission. These ranged from temperance initiatives to limit or abolish the alcohol industry – 'the demon drink' – to the disestablishment of the Church of England. Here was a second Puritan revolution in the making, reinforced by the narrowing gap between the number of active Nonconformists and Anglican churchgoers in England and Wales. Some had no desire to pollute their personal spiritual journey with the worldliness of political involvement, but the overwhelming majority of Nonconformists voted Liberal even though as late as 1868 only fourteen per cent of Liberal MPs were themselves Nonconformist.

There had been good historical reasons for maintaining this trust. As 'Broad Church' Anglicans, the Whigs had long supported religious liberty.

However, the increasingly confident radical argument was now pressing on towards a greater aspiration, that of religious equality. By this was meant breaking down the high walls of institutional Anglicanism. The campaign was a long one, not least because the perceived ultimate goal of disestablishing the Church worried those for whom the Tory cry of a 'Church in danger' – an election slogan dusted down repeatedly since at least the reign of Queen Anne – still had resonance. Numerous attempts at legislation to remove the ancient and compulsory levying of church rates for the upkeep of local Anglican churches faltered until finally reaching the statute book in 1868.

The Church of England's primacy in educational institutions was the other great target of the radical Liberal assault. Religious restrictions were scrapped for students at Oxford and Cambridge in 1856 and further legislation in 1871 removed the remaining limitations for fellowships at Britain's two oldest and most prestigious universities. Although himself an Anglican, Gladstone also undermined his Church's supremacy in elementary schooling when, in 1870, his government introduced an Education Act creating nondenominational schools funded by local rates and administered by elected school boards. This did not totally satisfy those Nonconformists who resented the continuance of public grants for existing Anglican foundations and there was certainly an irony in a chapel-goers' campaign that resulted in the greater secularisation of education. But a victory had been won over Anglican supremacy all the same.

Until these changes took effect, the dissenting tradition had been kept alive in self-funded schools, clubs, Sunday schools and colleges. These were the nurseries of the Nonconformist conscience where self-help was a necessary precondition for maintaining a distinct identity in a land dominated by Anglican institutions. Not surprisingly, they were most numerous in areas like Wales, Lancashire and Yorkshire where Nonconformity was especially strong. A typical product of this upbringing was John Bright, a Rochdale Quaker whose personal integrity and commitment to policies of peace, retrenchment and reform were axioms of mid-nineteenth-century radical liberalism. This, too, was very much the environment in which Herbert Henry Asquith was born in 1852 into an unpretentious, Nonconformist Yorkshire family. His maternal grandfather, William Willans, was one of Bright's enthusiastic disciples and had stood – unsuccessfully – in the 1851 general election. The Asquith family home was a robust stone house overlooking the small town of Morley, near Leeds. In this county of hills and dales, having a house on higher ground was frequently a subtle mark of being, socially, from the 'better sort'. This area of Yorkshire was textile country and Joseph Asquith, Herbert's father, sold cloth to the nearby mills.

The family attended the local Rehoboth Congregationalist chapel, another indicator of respectability. Joseph Asquith gave Bible classes in his spare time.

Respectability is no guard against misfortune. Joseph and Emily Asquith had five children. Herbert – or Bertie, as he was known in the family (Henry, his second name, was added at a later date) – was the second son and gifted with good health. The rest of the family were not so lucky. His elder brother, William, suffered an injury playing sport that stunted his growth and prevented him developing beyond five feet tall. Of three sisters, two died in infancy. Then, when Herbert was eight years old, his father twisted his intestine while playing cricket and died. To make matters worse, Herbert's widowed mother, suffering from a weak heart and the onset of lung disease, was a virtual invalid.

Thus, Herbert Henry Asquith's childhood was one of adversity and genteel poverty. This was a predicament that moulded him into a stronger and more determined person. Of the twenty-four prime ministers of Britain between 1809 and 1937, fifteen – sixty-two per cent – suffered the loss of one or both ,parents in childhood. Most frequently they lost their fathers. Of the prime ministers that Asquith would come to know in his own political life, Rosebery, Balfour and Lloyd George had as children lost their fathers and Salisbury and Bonar Law had lost their mothers. Even accounting for higher general rates of mortality during the period, this was – by a vast margin – a disproportionately high figure.[2]

What Asquith's mother lacked in health and physical vigour in bringing up her children, she made up for in character and ambition for them to succeed. Despite her ill health, Emily Asquith loved books and encouraged her children to share her passion for learning. Both her sons profited greatly from this early exposure to words and ideas. Furthermore, alleviation from the sort of outright poverty that would have crushed the wherewithal to self-betterment came from grandfather Willans, who paid for Herbert and his brother to attend schools in Huddersfield and Fulneck. But in 1863, Emily Asquith decided that the only hope for her debilitating bronchitis was to remove herself from Yorkshire's cotton towns and breathe, instead, the sea air of the south coast. Taking her one surviving daughter with her, she settled in St Leonards in Sussex. Her two sons, meanwhile, were deposited with her brother in London so that they could attend as day boys the City of London School. It was their ticket to a better life.

Asquith was twelve when he arrived at the City of London School, housed in the shadow of the dome of St Paul's Cathedral. Fees were cheap and, in contrast to the Anglican environment of the great boarding schools, the ethos was non-denominational. Both points were important given Asquith's circumstances. When his uncle moved back up to Yorkshire, he found himself and his brother bundled off to lodge with London Congregationalist families who were paid to take them in. Although hardly a hothouse – for the boys were expected to graduate into the office environment rather than the great professions – the City of London School's orientation was more academic than sporty and this suited the bookish Asquith. Given the incidents that had afflicted his brother and father on the sports field, his general avoidance of mud and flannels was explicable. Instead he excelled in other ways. Self-motivated and precociously intelligent, he became head boy and won the school prizes for Classics. The headmaster commended him for 'keeping up the tone, as well as the intellectual standard, of the higher classes' and concluded that because of his precocity he needed little extra teaching. All that could be done was 'simply to put the ladder before him, and up he went'.[3]

A contemporary noted the peerless quality of his performances in the school debating society: 'the style of his speeches differed from that of the ordinary schoolboy's as that of Macaulay's history differs from Little Arthur's ... it was not fire or passion, not so much powers of persuasion or of sarcasm, but the fine phrasing, the elaborate periods, the ambitious rhetoric that impressed us.'[4] He was aiming for the top. Balliol College, Oxford offered two Classics scholarships. Asquith won one of them. It was more than anyone from his school had achieved before. How much this meant to him can be gathered by the boldness of his claim, looking back more than fifty years later, about this first proof of promise. Winning his place to Balliol was, he maintained, 'the proudest moment of my life'.[5]

Balliol was establishing itself as Oxford University's primary claim to worldliness when the eighteen-year-old Asquith arrived there in 1870. The editor of Plato, Benjamin Jowett, had just taken up residence in the Master's Lodge. He was determined to further the college's transformation into the training ground for the leaders – political, administrative, philosophical and moral – of the British Empire, or, as he put it to his long-term confidante, Florence Nightingale, he was looking 'to govern the world' through his pupils.[6] His plan bore abundant fruit. By 1906, there were thirty-one Balliol-educated MPs sitting in the Palace of Westminster, four of them in the Cabinet and one of whom was Asquith. Yet, in his undergraduate days, Asquith's level of acquaintance with the worldly Jowett was comparatively slight. When it suited him, Jowett could be the sort of Master who pronounced 'good morning' as a method of ending rather than commencing a conversation.

Instead, the Balliol don who made the greatest impression on Asquith was

T.H. Green. A low-church (some questioned if he retained faith at all) Yorkshireman who was still in his mid-thirties when Asquith arrived in college, Green promoted the widening of educational access and the broadening of Oxford's philosophical curriculum beyond its Aristotelian obsessions. He included the study of Kant and Hegel. What was more, he argued that there was no necessary contradiction between individual liberty and the active use of state institutions to broaden the common good. A teetotaller, Green had such measures as restricting the supply of alcohol in mind. But the drift of his thinking extended far beyond the saloon door. Here, indeed, were the philosophical seeds of the 'New Liberalism' that would take the Liberal Party away from the non-interventionist outlook of *laissez-faire* and towards more assertive social legislation and, ultimately, a welfare state. Green would influence not just Asquith, but the political generation in which he was to interact for the rest of his life.

Asquith did not give the impression he felt encumbered by his relatively obscure social origins or that his chapel-going background was much of a handicap amid the Gothic Revival trappings of High Anglican Oxford. The experience of six adolescent years in London had undoubtedly made him comfortable with the world he encountered at Oxford, one that was far removed from the local schools of his northern childhood. This ease and composure appears clear from his precocity. He did not retreat behind his books, like a gauche scholarship boy using the college library as a sanctuary from the hooted salutations ringing around the quadrangles beyond. When he later coined the self-reverential phrase about the 'effortless superiority of the Balliol man' he had his own experience with which to back up the claim. He worked diligently rather than excessively. He gained a First in both Mods and Greats. The latter was all the more impressive for the fact that he had been elected, at the second attempt, President of the Oxford Union in his final term. Outside the examination hall and sporting distinction at the Parks or on the Isis, mastery in the great debating chamber of this student club was the greatest mark of distinction an Oxford undergraduate could make. It was already the world's most famous debating society. Asquith ascended a presidential chair that had been graced by the likes of A.V. Dicey, T.H. Green and the current and future Prime Ministers, Gladstone and Salisbury. Importantly, he had got there through the power of his debating skill rather than on the back of some well organised and well connected social clique.

Upon Asquith's graduation in 1874, Balliol offered him a Fellowship. The path to a life in academia lay open to him. But because he was determined upon making his way into politics, he believed becoming a barrister provided both the best apprenticeship and the funds towards this end. He accepted the Fellowship – which provided a modest stipend – before proceeding to London to commence his legal studies. He was called to the Bar a couple of years later and joined chambers at 6 Fig Tree Court. He was a pupil of Charles Bowen, another former Balliol Fellow and past Oxford Union President, but, away from the cosseted undergraduate environment, Asquith discovered that reward was no longer automatic. He had few connections and found it difficult to attract briefs. When his Fellowship expired in 1881, he tried to supplant the lost income with jobbing work as a lecturer, school tutor and exam marker. He also began writing pieces on a wide range of subjects for *The Spectator.*

The sudden lack of progress – after the early promise of an Oxford dream fulfilled – was not only a frustration to one of Asquith's natural ambition, it was also a financial worry. He had got married in 1877 and was starting a family. The woman he had fallen for was Helen Melland, the pretty and unpresumptuous daughter of a Manchester doctor whom he had met while staying with his mother in St Leonards in 1870, just before making the transformation from schoolboy to undergraduate. At the time of this meta-morphosis he was eighteen, she was fifteen and the divergence of their paths while he went off to immerse himself in Oxford's opportunities might have been reason enough for the relationship to have died a natural death. Yet it did not. For seven years they had maintained a long and secret courtship, meeting infrequently, during which time Asquith's male-orientated world shielded him from a wider acquaintance with the opposite sex. Indeed, it seems that Asquith opted to marry the first and only girl he dated. Sweet-natured, Helen gave in her correspondence the impression of being slightly overawed at having attracted the attention of a young man who was inescap-ably her intellectual superior. Her father gave his consent: the Mellands, like the Asquiths, were Congregationalists so there was no incompatibility on that front – Asquith had married within the family faith. Their first child, Raymond, was born after a year of their marriage and a second son, Herbert ('Beb' to his parents), three years later in 1881. Three more siblings – Arthur ('Oc'), Violet and Cyril ('Cys') – followed in 1883, 1887 and 1889.

Asquith's home life was unquestionably a happy one, but professionally he had still not had the success that was his principal motivation in life and which Oxford had seemed to foreshadow. He had been at the Bar for five years and was still making little headway when he met a fellow barrister who was to become the most important male friend in his personal and political life. The man was Richard Burdon Haldane, 'a rather clumsy young Scotsman of twenty-five'. Their meeting appeared to be one of those accidents triggered by the random seating of diners on the benches under the great beams of the hall at Lincoln's Inn. One day, Haldane found himself next to Asquith and began to make conversation. The acquaintance immediately deepened into something more valuable. 'A great friendship arose between us,' Haldane later wrote. 'He and I used to dine together once or twice a week, and we saw each other almost every day. . . . We both had a passion for law, and liked to discuss the few cases each of us had.'[7] When Haldane was first offered a brief, he was so excited that he raced off to find Asquith, waving the documents above his head in triumph as he approached. It concerned a basement infested with beetles. Asquith spent the evening and night going over the legal arguments with him. Shortly after their friendship commenced, Haldane fell ill. Asquith let him stay for what transpired to be a lengthy period at his house in John Street (the current Keats' Grove), Hampstead. It was during this time that the bond of friendship tightened.

Haldane was four years Asquith's junior, although that was where any subservience had its limit. He came from a more prosperous background. Rather than the Croft House above Morley, he had been born in his father's Edinburgh town house in Charlotte Square. Designed by Robert Adam, it was one of the most elegant addresses in the city's Georgian new town. Unlike Asquith's father, Haldane's father came from the professional classes. In Edinburgh, the centre of Scots law and of one of the world's foremost medical schools, this was almost a prerequisite for exerting influence. He was a solicitor who held the distinction within the Edinburgh legal fraternity of being a Writer to the Signet and provided conveyancing work for many of the great Scottish landowners, some of whom were his relations.

The Haldanes' principal family home was set in the rolling Perthshire countryside. The Haldane name was a corruption of 'Half Dane' and the family were Scots lairds, a position in rural society approximating to that of the much-deferred-to squire in the English shires. Called Cloan, the Haldane country seat was a manorial castle in the Scots baronial style with steep gables and turrets and borrowed detailing from Loire châteaux, not wholly dissimilar to Queen Victoria's Speyside fantasy at Balmoral. Near Auch-terarder, it was an idyllic spot, set within an estate of hills and wildlife. As Haldane grew up, so his rambles became more arduous, taking him to the top of distant mountains in the Grampians and back within the day.

Yet, for all the rugged grandeur of Cloan, his family was, temperamentally, as earnest as the Asquiths of Morley. Having started out as a mariner with the East India Company, Haldane's great-uncle devoted the better part of his life to Christian missionary work in India. Haldane's mother was from the well established Northumbrian Burdon family and, in her son's opinion, the less theologically dogmatic of his parents. Nonetheless, she had intended to become a missionary until she met Haldane's father who was a Baptist and widower with five children. Marrying him and helping to bring up his family became her purpose instead, adding to it a second set of four sons and a daughter, of whom Richard was the eldest surviving son. Christian faith was the central feature of life and work. Of his father, Haldane later wrote that he 'was very devout, and had fitted up a barn where he used once a fortnight to preach to a considerable audience of old-fashioned Scottish country folk who came to hear the Word of God in all its strictness'.[8] It was thus a moneyed background but not one given to complacency or soft living. Unpromisingly, the Haldane motto was 'Suffer' – an injunction chiselled deep into the stone above the fireplace at Cloan and at the family memorial at Gleneagles.

When he was old enough, Richard Burdon Haldane had been sent to the Edinburgh Academy, a private day school providing a sound but certainly not a flash or challenging education. In this respect it was like the City of London School but transplanted to the Athens of the North. It left him cold. Nonetheless, at sixteen Haldane passed under the great Adam-designed archway of Edinburgh University to study Latin, Greek and English literature. His parents regarded this as a preparation for going up to Balliol, but they had last-minute fears that an Oxford education might corrupt their son by exposing him to Anglican temptations. Had they been able to overcome this apprehension, he would have presented himself at the Balliol Porter's Lodge at the end of the summer of Asquith's graduation. It was not to be. In theological matters his parents were not risk-takers. Instead, they were persuaded to send him to Göttingen to study philosophy and geology. Haldane arrived at the historic – if by the summer of 1874 rather decrepit – university ill-equipped with little German, a language he found himself having to learn quickly as of necessity. Göttingen was a strange and somewhat underwhelming experience. He soon discovered that the undergraduate body was not especially serious-minded, being much preoccupied by beer and duelling – a reputation for dissipation his parents had overlooked in their zeal to save their son from the possible whiff of incense on the Isis.

Indeed, his parents' hope that sending their son to Germany would protect him from Anglican ritual proved something of a pyrrhic victory. Whatever his bemused opinion of the undergraduate body, Haldane made friends with some of the more learned professors at Göttingen and they whetted his appetite to pursue an intellectual quest that led him to question the very tenets of his parents' fundamentalist beliefs. After continuing his studies at Dresden, he returned to Edinburgh where he graduated with a First Class degree. His father – in following Baptist practices – insisted that the time had come for his son's full immersion. Haldane had no desire to perform this significant ritual but he realised how much it would worry his parents if their son went to his grave without doing so. Eventually, he consented on the condition it was carried out in a low-key manner. However, when he arrived at the Edinburgh chapel, he discovered not only his parents waiting by the font but also surrounding pews filled with rather more of their friends and sundry onlookers than he had understood would be invited to admire the spectacle.

Privately fuming but thinking it too late to back down, Haldane stepped uneasily towards the font and was duly baptised. But as he emerged, dripping, he announced he had something to say. The congregation waited expectantly for his spiritual testimony. They were in for a surprise. For the earnest young man's intellectual quest took him sharply, and inconveniently, in a different direction. He announced that he had had enough. He had only undergone the ceremony to please his parents, and henceforth he would have no connection with the Baptists, their teaching, or, for that matter, with any other church. With that, he changed his clothes and walked out, the clanking of the door behind him punctuating the funereal silence that had descended upon the congregation. There was oppressive silence too when, some time later, the rest of his family returned home. The incident was not referred to by them then, or ever again.

In 1877, the year of his diabetic father's death, Haldane had left Scotland for London to read for the Bar at Lincoln's Inn. Despite his non-English education and his family's links to the Scottish legal profession, it had always been assumed he would go to the English Bar. Family legend had it that as a six-year-old boy visiting relations in London he was being shown round the chamber of the House of Lords when his nanny had seized an opportunity to plump him on the Woolsack and announce sagaciously to its startled guardians that 'the bairn will sit there some day as of right'.[9] Having a Lord Chancellor, Lord Eldon, as a great-great-uncle on his mother's side doubtless played its part in the sense of expectation that he might himself eventually dignify the historic cushion.

He lived simply while reading for the Bar, although he did briefly attend dance classes with the pioneering female medic, Elizabeth Garrett Anderson. He found she was, like himself, 'desirous of making up for the deficiencies of a somewhat restricted upbringing'.[10] Generally, though, the law consumed his time and energies. In 1879 he was called to the Bar, taking chambers at 5 New Square, Lincoln's Inn. Attracting lucrative conveyancing work at first proved difficult. As a Scot who had not passed through the usual social and scholastic institutions of his English contemporaries, he knew few London solicitors and found himself largely dependent on Scottish clients. It was not until 1881 that his annual fees even cleared the £100 mark.

Thus Asquith and Haldane found themselves in similar circumstances. They were both from God-fearing families, the confines of which no longer suited their own outlook. They were both possessed with precocious intellectual abilities, both anxious to succeed at the London Bar and both finding the going difficult. But with family money providing a financial safety net and without a wife or family to maintain in comfort, Haldane, at least, was never in danger of falling into straitened circumstances. What was more, shortly after his friendship with Asquith deepened, his legal career finally started to gather momentum. In 1882 he began appearing in appeals being brought before the Privy Council's judicial committee and the House of Lords. By 1883, he was doing well and earning £1,000 a year. Two years later, when he was still only twenty-nine, he was earning around £2,000 a year.*

The extent to which both men had drifted from their abstemious roots was evident in their increasing enjoyment of good living. For the next twenty years and beyond, they would dine together several times a week, developing a taste for wine of quality in quantity. They also spent their holidays together. At Easter, they went to Paris with Alfred Milner, who had been up at Balliol with Asquith and had followed in his footsteps as President of the Oxford Union. After Paris, Haldane and Asquith proceeded on to Monte Carlo, Pisa and Florence. On another occasion they went on a tour to Ireland together. There, Asquith impressed Haldane with the way he 'cross-questioned' Nationalists about 'matters of fact'.[11]

Back in London, Haldane was especially welcome in Asquith's home. Still a bachelor, he devoted himself to Asquith's family. He liked and got on well with Helen and was particularly fond of the Asquith children, who delighted in his affable and eccentric manner. He was once amused to be greeted by the three-year-old Violet Asquith who assured him she had seen him 'in the Nonsense Book'. She had mistaken what she later described as 'his spheroid figure, his twinkling benignity and pneumatic bulk' for 'those familiar and dearly loved figures the "old men" of Edward Lear'. Since Haldane was aged thirty-four at the time this was not necessarily a compliment, however much it may have been intended. 'He was', Violet reflected in her own middle age, 'a constant presence in our home and life and seemed a natural part of both.'[12]

---

* For comparative purposes, it should be noted that by the end of the nineteenth century, a General in the British Army could expect to earn £1,095 per annum and a senior clerk in the Home Office £800. By 1902, the average wage was £72 8os.

In physical build, Haldane was certainly a weighty figure. He never grasped the point of competitive sport. A great hiker, he preferred striding around Perthshire's rolling terrain. It was a pastime at odds with those who looked at his physique and assumed his hobbies were entirely sedentary. His fattish face and expanding girth gave the impression that he was taking the pleasures of the table too much to heart. After one particularly onerous dinner in London, his place at the table well marked by drained champagne flutes, brandy balloons and charred cigar stubs, his companions teased him about his unhealthy lifestyle. He rose to the challenge, proposing, despite the lateness of the hour, that he should walk that night all the way to Brighton. This he duly did, triumphantly promenading on its seafront thirteen hours later. It was rather more than Asquith would have cared to perform at any time or season. Asquith preferred to confine his exercise to the golf links. His other recreation – which suggested even greater withdrawal from his Nonconformist roots – was the card table. Before his mother died in 1888, he had even encouraged her to backslide sufficiently to permit him to teach her how to play whist, albeit on the condition that the sanitising precaution was first taken of substituting chess pieces for cards.

There may have been a debate as to who was the more intelligent, but there was none as to who was the more intellectual. Haldane was a great lover of Wagner. Asquith's musical tastes were middle-brow. Indeed, he later claimed that Gilbert and Sullivan's comic operas were 'almost the only form of music that has ever given me real pleasure'.[13] There were other differences of emphasis. Haldane's intellect was more concerned with abstract notions than was Asquith's (which was finely honed to the practicalities of material advancement). In 1883, Haldane's first book was published – *Essays in Philosophical Criticism*. It was co-authored with a friend from his Edinburgh student days, Andrew Seth, and was dedicated to Asquith's inspirational mentor at Balliol and prophet of a new social liberalism, T.H. Green. It was soon followed by a translation of Schopenhauer, *The World as Will and Idea*. Indeed, Haldane's lack of Asquith's all-consuming personal ambition made a clash in their professional careers less likely in the future. Asquith, with a passion for worldly success and thrusting self-confidence that early manifested itself on the debating floor of the Oxford Union, could not have reflected upon his undergraduate days as Haldane later did of his time at Edinburgh University:

It was the *De Rerum Natura* of Lucretius that fascinated me most, when I heard Sellar [the University Professor of Latin] lecturing on it. It is more than fifty years since I listened while he declaimed to us his favourite

passages. The lines at the beginning of the Second Book still remain in
my memory, and I often repeat them to myself when alone:

'But sweeter far to dwell remote, aloof
In some high mansion, built on Wisdom's hill:
Thence watch the errant crowd go to and fro,
Matching their wits, striving for precedence,
Toiling and moiling, hurrying night and day,
To rise to fortune and possess the world.'[14]

Thus the two men, one driven by personal ambition, the other by the
promotion of ideas rather than the clash of personalities, seemed mutually
compatible to work together rather than compete for the political heights
they now set out to climb and conquer.

Asquith never concealed his desire to become a politician as soon as a viable
opportunity presented itself. Nor did he betray any doubt that it was to the
Liberal Party that he would pledge his allegiance. With a grandfather who
had stood for Parliament the year before his birth, Liberalism was in his
blood and a feature of his background. His friend's commitment to the
Liberals was equally natural. Before Gladstone's support for Irish home rule
changed everything, the Scotland of Haldane's youth was overwhelmingly
Liberal. In the 1880 general election, Scots had returned fifty-four Liberal
MPs and only six Tories. Seventy per cent of Scottish votes were cast for
Liberal candidates.'[15] Involvement with the natural party of Scotland was
automatic for someone of Haldane's background, temperament and ambi-
tion.

   In the race to enter politics, as with the progress of their legal careers, it
was the younger Haldane who had a head start over his older friend. Having
become politically active in 1880, he was also better connected in the political
world that Asquith aspired to join. As its secretary, it was Haldane who
secured for Asquith membership of the Eighty Club – a dining club named
after the Liberals' 1880 election victory – to which influential Party figures
were invited. It was Haldane too who was the first to be adopted as the
Liberal candidate in a winnable seat in time for the 1885 general election.
Members of Parliament were still unpaid and thus his decision to stand was,
as he later confessed, a considerable risk to take for a barrister who, despite
improving income, was still a Junior at the Bar and who did not have

immediate access to substantial private means (his widowed mother had inherited the family estate).[16]

The constituency for which he was selected was East Lothian. This was a predominantly rural seat east of Edinburgh in which the major town was Haddington, an elegant burgh of stone houses dominated by its parish church, the largest in Scotland. Like so many small Scottish towns it was haunted by the spirit of John Knox, the seventeenth-century Calvinist firebrand who had been born there. It was the next-door constituency to Midlothian, the seat of the greatest advocate of moral force in the politics of his own time, the Liberal Prime Minister, William Ewart Gladstone. Haldane, despite being four years younger, had stolen a march on Asquith.

The general election of November 1885 was the first to be fought since the passage of the 1884 Reform Act had increased the number of voters on the electoral role from 3.1 million in 1883 to 5.7 million and, in doing so, ensured that nearly two-thirds of adult males (but still no females) possessed the vote. What effect this new enfranchisement would have was eagerly awaited, not least by Gladstone's radical colleague, Joseph Chamberlain, who resigned from the Cabinet before the dissolution of Parliament in order to promote his own 'unauthorised programme' of graduated taxation against the rich, land and social reform, local democracy and devolution throughout the United Kingdom – measures that went far beyond the official party line. The result on the British mainland was a convincing Liberal victory and an endorsement of Gladstone's leadership. Haldane was successfully returned to Parliament. Asquith immediately wrote to congratulate him on a 'magnificent and decisive victory' which was 'the most gratifying event in this depressing election'.[17] For, in winning 334 MPs to the Conservatives tally of 250, Gladstone's majority of 84 was two short of the number of Irish Nationalist MPs returned.

When the prospect of a bipartisan solution to Irish demands for devolution broke down, Gladstone grasped the thorn and introduced the Bill to grant Ireland home rule, re-establishing in Dublin a parliament that had been persuaded to vote itself out of existence in 1800. But his plan soon came adrift due to opposition within his own party. In June 1886, the Bill was defeated in the Commons by 341 to 311. Another general election thus became a necessity and this time the Liberals were heavily divided over their leader's adoption of the Irish Nationalist cause. Vehemently opposed to granting home rule for Ireland, 93 Liberal MPs, led by leaders from different wings of the party (the radical Joseph Chamberlain and the Whig Lord Hartington), opted to form a rival Liberal Unionist Party that would campaign against Gladstone's new cause.

The provisions to place Ireland's Protestant minority under the domestic rule of a Catholic-dominated parliament in Dublin was particularly repugnant to many of the Calvinist-minded Liberal voters of Scotland. Amid the resignations and recriminations, Haldane saw a chance to lever Asquith into a seat. The East Fife constituency's Liberal MP opposed Gladstone's commitment to Irish home rule and determined to stand as an independent Liberal Unionist candidate instead. His local association refused to follow him and appealed, at extremely short notice, for a new candidate. Haldane put forward Asquith's name. The nomination was important because Haldane had extensive family connections in the area. Indeed, there was probably no exaggeration in the later assertion that Haldane 'arrange[d]' his selection.[18] With only ten days to go, Asquith was shoehorned into the seat.

Haldane's assistance presented Asquith with a great opportunity. But was he well placed to grasp it? Since switching chambers in 1883, Asquith's income from the Bar had begun to creep up, but he was by no means in a position of comfort. What was more, he was an unknown outsider fighting the sitting MP in a straight Liberal versus Liberal Unionist battle – the Conservatives having prudently decided not to field a candidate in the hope that the Liberal Unionist would win. East Fife was a rural constituency which faced Haldane's East Lothian seat across the choppy gulf of the Firth of Forth. It was pocketed with small villages like Ladybank and Auchtermuchty. It included farms and fishing villages, and some small-scale weaving industries, but excluded the only two urban areas of importance, Cupar and the university town (because of its ruined cathedral, technically a city) of St Andrews. Asquith had enjoyed a leisurely six weeks with Oxford contemporaries in St Andrews in 1876 where he had learnt to play golf on its historic links and he retained fond feelings for the locality. He was standing on a loyalty-to-Gladstone platform. The vote, when it was declared, was close. Yet, amazingly, Asquith won by 2,862 votes to 2,487.

Asquith had been lucky. The massive disaffection of Scottish Protestants with Gladstone's appeasement of Irish Nationalists had manifested itself far more powerfully in the west of Scotland, leaving the rate of defection less pronounced on the eastern side of the country. Haldane too had been returned. But the picture nationally was a disaster for the Liberal Party. The House of Commons now comprised 316 Conservatives, fortified by 78 Liberal Unionists, against 191 Liberals and 85 Irish Nationalists. Although they did not command an outright majority on their own, the Conservatives could now form a government and while the Liberal Unionists would sit on the Opposition benches, on the most important divisions they would vote to sustain the new Conservative administration against their former colleagues.

The new Liberal Unionist bloc had attracted some of the party's most senior figures. The electoral axe had claimed others. Although Gladstone clung on to the leadership, the Liberal Party had received a drubbing. Yet, a defeat of this scale offered opportunities and, in this sense, the Parliament of 1886 could not have been more welcoming to ambitious young politicians in search of a lucky break to shine by attacking the Tory government. Nonetheless, Asquith waited for over eight months before delivering his maiden speech. It was a success and marked him out as a Westminster new boy of promise. It even got him noticed by Gladstone. 'After that,' recalled Haldane, 'half a dozen of us younger Liberal MPs began to draw together under his leadership.'[19] They were responding to a commanding self-confidence that had manifested itself at school, at the Oxford Union and now at the greater debating stage of the House of Commons. That Haldane, despite his own hopes, should so readily fall in behind his friend without reproach was a mark of maturity. He recognised that he was not personally a charismatic speaker: his vocal pitch was too high and his content too convoluted. But he had ideas that he wanted promoted and Asquith was the star advocate to put them across. It seemed an ideal basis for a relationship in public life – a bond between two politicians in which the one recognised the superior claims of the other to lead without hindering the nature of their equality.

Others soon rallied. In Westminster, Haldane and Asquith formed small dining clubs of like-minded backbenchers. Among them were Tom Ellis and Sydney Buxton, both elected for the first time with Asquith in 1886, and Arthur Acland and Sir Edward Grey who were elected with Haldane in 1885. Under the auspices of the Articles Club (so called because it had thirty-nine members), Asquith and Haldane gathered MPs together in dinner parties at the Savoy Hotel and the National Liberal Club. They also organised annual dinners at the Blue Posts, a Mayfair pub off Cork Street, between 1888 and 1892 to which eminent politicians were invited, regardless of their political persuasion. The guests were a roll-call of the great figures of the day and included Arthur James Balfour, Joseph Chamberlain, Lord Randolph Churchill and Edward Carson as well as those from other fields of distinction like the artist Edward Burne-Jones. They were also opportunities for remarkable displays of one-upmanship. On one occasion, Haldane was sitting at the end of the table between Lord Rosebery and Lord Randolph Churchill, trying to keep his head out of the way of their brilliant conversational gymnastics. Never quite as verbally dextrous, Chamberlain made the mistake of trying to get a word in edgeways. Churchill merely beckoned a waiter over and, pointing at the spot on the table between him and Chamberlain, ordered, 'Waiter, put a flower-pot there.'[20]

There had been much in Joseph Chamberlain's radical programme to attract Haldane and Asquith. They shared his progressiveness in domestic affairs as well as his commitment to an interventionist foreign and imperial policy – in marked contradiction to Gladstone, whose interventions in world events aspired to be dictated by moral convictions rather than national interests. Yet, neither the Member for East Lothian nor for East Fife were tempted to follow the former Birmingham mayor and screw manufacturer into the Liberal Unionist grouping and the eventual embrace of the Conservative Party. Indeed, by teaming up with the disaffected Whigs, Chamberlain had deserted the Liberal Party just at the moment when its parliamentary representatives were moving in a more progressive direction. Yet, he could not return to the fold while Gladstone remained at the Liberal Party helm and to this the 'Grand Old Man' proceeded to cling until 1894. By then, Chamberlain was far too implicated in a Tory alliance that would shortly be offering him a place in government – something the Liberals would be in no position to do for the next decade.

In fact, Haldane and Asquith were never tempted by the Liberal Unionist cause. Both supported Irish home rule in principle. At the 1887 National Liberal Association meeting in Nottingham, Asquith even proposed the motion pledging the party to the cause. But neither man shared Gladstone's obsessive zeal with a policy that was always likely to end up being vetoed in the House of Lords. Of the two, it was Haldane who was thinking most about the direction of future legislation beyond the Irish logjam. Liberalism's traditional objectives had been concerned with removing legal, political and religious restrictions – widening the franchise, sweeping aside religious hurdles to joining institutions, disestablishing the Church of Ireland. This was the Liberalism of reform. Building upon the critique of philosophers like T.H. Green, Haldane wanted to go further. For this progressive doctrine he later coined the phrase by which it would become known – 'The New Liberalism'.[21] But he put it best in an article on 'The Liberal Creed' for the *Contemporary Review* in 1888. 'The doctrines of Bentham, the Mills, and the old Radical school of the *Westminster Review,* have been practically accepted', he noted, and because Liberalism had extended political rights by removing legislative impediments, it 'has passed from the destructive into the constructive stage in its history'. Haldane meant that the state and its agencies should improve the lives of the many by investing in education and other forms of personal advancement which the masses could ill afford on their own. This would be costly, but 'those who have got more than an equal share of the good things which British civilization has created, should pay something for their advantages by contributing towards the improvement of the condition of that population out of which they have made their fortunes'.

This was a positive means of expressing the former radical Joseph Chamberlain's rhetorical question, 'What ransom will property pay for the security which it enjoys?' But Haldane did not wish to go as far as the socialist creed of confiscation, in which the state 'is in some position different from that of individuals, as regards the moral obligation to observe its own engagements and guarantees'.[22] He also reaffirmed his commitment to the great Liberal shibboleth of free trade in a biography on Adam Smith which he squeezed in the time to write in 1887.

The preoccupations of Westminster did not prevent Haldane and Asquith continuing to build upon their legal careers. Indeed, professionally they were both flourishing. Asquith was starting to fight high-publicity cases. He successfully acted for the prosecution against the British publisher of Zola's novels for obscene libel. In the commission set up to report on the 'Parnell forgeries', he demolished under cross-examination the manager of *The Times* for accepting uncritically the authenticity of forged documents the paper published that appeared to show that the Irish Nationalist leader supported terrorist outrages. By 1890, both Haldane and Asquith were making good money and decided to take silk. Yet, despite the burdens of work, they continued to find time for each other. They still holidayed together, with Asquith accepting Haldane's regular invitations to go up to Cloan. Then, in March 1890, when he was thirty-four, Haldane made a decision that would psychologically mark him for the rest of his life. He got engaged to an aspiring romantic novelist. The object of his affection was (Emma) Valentine Munro Ferguson. She was, he related in his dotage, 'a remarkable girl of distinguished quality and of good position'. Her 'good position' was impeccably Liberal. Her father had been MP for the Fife constituency of Kirkcaldy and her brother, Ronald, was the Liberal MP for Leith and private secretary to Lord Rosebery. The Munro Fergusons had long been friendly with the Haldanes. It seemed a perfect match.

Valentine was Haldane's first and last love and he was clearly ecstatic when she agreed to marry him. They went off together for a holiday in Dorset. Haldane was blissfully happy, as high a state as it seems he would know in his whole life. Yet, he was to suffer for it. The following month, after he had returned to London, he received a letter from her breaking off the engagement. It was 'as a bolt from an unclouded sky'.[23] She claimed to have misunderstood herself; whatever that meant. At any rate, she made clear to him that she was not open to persuasion, her decision was final. In his autobiography, Haldane wrote:

> Only once or twice again in the course of my life did I see her, and then only momentarily and casually. After five weeks of uninterrupted happiness, happiness, to the best of my judgement then and now, for her as well as for me, all was changed and at an end.
>
> My grief was overwhelming, for I had a strong sense of the irrevocableness of the decision. The shock upset me. I could find relief only in constant work, and for long not much even in that. Sleep, when it came, was the only deliverance from black depression. But there was no moment in which I either blamed her or pitied myself. My feeling was that somehow I had failed.
>
> To this hour I treasure the memory of these five happy weeks, and bless her name for the return she made in them to my devotion to her, and for the feeling inspired apparently in both of us. I came to realise afterwards, when the pain was past, that my love for her, though it failed, had brought to me not loss but great gain. For it enlarged the meaning and content of life for me. All is now over.[24]

Asquith reacted magnificently. He left his own work in order to tend to his heartbroken friend, taking him abroad for a holiday and the chance to readjust. He also invited him to stay at his house in Hampstead again with Helen and the children until he felt well enough to return to the solitude of his bachelor apartments in Whitehall Court. Responding to this care, Haldane gradually improved. He regained the ability to sleep.

In the summer he wrote to a confidante, Mrs Humphry Ward, maintaining that he was finding solace in his philosophical studies:

> When a soul has missed the goal towards which it was striving, and is still staggering, it naturally, in recovering its balance, seeks to restore the prop which it knows of old and has never found to fail. It is more relief to me than I can express to find myself again engrossed in the old searchings, and to be able to believe that they will mean, even in a practical life where they are supposed to be remote, an amply sufficient future to me.

But he could not conquer his emotions through philosophy alone. In the autumn of 1891 he confessed to an aunt, 'Old feelings surge up now, feelings which I had suppressed but could not destroy.'[25]

What lay behind this crushing reversal of fortune? Valentine Munro

Ferguson was an active suffragette but given Haldane's support for the cause of women's rights it could hardly have been politics that divided them. At five weeks, the engagement had been exceptionally short and, as far as Haldane was aware, broken off by nothing of which he had a premonition. The truth, when he discovered it, was perhaps not something he felt able to discuss. His fiancée ran off with another woman. The object of her affection was Mary Wakefield, an accomplished singer and lecturer. By all accounts, the two women were devoted to one another.[26]

This was not the only slap in the face for Haldane. Valentine proceeded to use her experiences with him as the basis for *Betsy*, a short novel she wrote in 1892. It was so clearly drawn from their impotent romance that, for all intents and purposes, it was a 'kiss and tell' publication given a happy – or at any rate conventional – ending. The rather thin plot revolved around Betsy Yarborough, a generous-spirited heiress from Chicago, Evelyn Vernon, the daughter of a stuffy Tory baronet and Edward Howard, the son of a Scottish Borders landowner with ambitions to be a Liberal MP. Evelyn finds herself drawn to Howard, who 'had a curious old-young face which had now and then a sort of solemn, sad look about it as of one who had seen or at any rate mentally realized the sad side of human life'. When he proposes to Evelyn, she accepts. But her father disapproves of her choice and, to please the old curmudgeon, she writes Howard a curt letter calling off the engagement. Unaware of the reason, Howard writes back, assuring her she has destroyed 'a human life' and making clear he could not forgive her. He then throws himself into his political career, the reader assured that 'now and then he left a hall with the applause still ringing in his ears, and thought that life was full of possibilities still, and that he would go forward ... would brazen it out with life and show that if knocked down he could get up again ... So on, then, to the reform of everything – except human nature – the most needed reform of all!' Eventually, Evelyn falls out with her hypocritical father and Betsy Yarborough tells Howard he should stop being so proud and stand-offish, and call on Evelyn. Eventually, he does. And of course, reader, she marries him.[27]

Given the author's lesbian inclinations, there was no such happy ending awaiting Haldane. Yet, Valentine gave the impression of being as obsessed with the man she jilted as he, in turn, remained constant to her memory. Having cannibalised her heterosexual relationship for the benefit of *Betsy*, she was trawling her own experiences again two years later when she wrote *Music hath Charms*. One of its central characters resembled Haldane. In 1897, she wrote *Life Again, Love Again*. Once more, one of its central characters resembled Haldane. She died in September 1897, insane.

The experience appears to have psychologically damaged Haldane out of all proportion to the length of time in which he was engaged to her. He had departed from his world of reason to embrace his emotions, only to be rejected by someone who opted, instead, to follow her own nature. Asquith's daughter Violet later wondered if 'this emotional convulsion left its mark on his whole life and that he emerged from it the man I knew – cauterized, calm, courageous, sustained by a philosophy which seemed to meet his every inner need'.[28] He never married.

The year after Haldane's engagement and disappointment with Valentine, it was Asquith's turn to suffer an emotional torment. In August 1891 he went for a family holiday to the Isle of Arran. A week into the vacation, his ten-year-old son, Herbert ('Beb'), went down with a dose of 'flu. Two days later Helen also took ill. The presumption was that she too had gone down with 'flu. Assuming there was nothing to worry about and that the passage of time would do all the healing necessary, no action was taken. But after five days, during which Helen's condition got worse, a doctor was finally called. His diagnosis was far more serious. She had typhoid. With childhood innocence, Beb tried to cheer his bed-stricken mother up, drawing for her pictures of ships. For three weeks Helen suffered and struggled and on Friday 11 September, she succumbed. On the Monday she was buried on the island. Two days later, the widower and his five children – the youngest, Violet, a babe in arms at only eighteen months – boarded the steamer to take them off the island before making the solemn journey back to Hampstead.

Asquith buttoned up his feelings. All he could bring himself to commit to his diary on the day he left Arran was, *'infelix atque infaustum iter'.** Haldane naturally reciprocated in the offer of support. Asquith's loss, after all, was of a rather greater magnitude than his own brief unhappy flirtation with love. Yet, Asquith was far more self-contained, preferring to grieve alone and to get on with his work as a means of distraction from what had happened. Towards the end of 1892, he sold the family home in Hampstead and rented an apartment in Mount Street. His elder children were now of an age to be off at preparatory and boarding school while the younger children could be brought up by nannies in Redhill, Surrey – a place to which he had been introduced by Haldane when he took Asquith to meet his literary friend George Meredith. Despite his cares and his concerns, Asquith made the time to visit his children regularly.

What he really felt about losing his wife was perhaps best expressed in a letter he wrote to Mrs Frances Horner, one of his female friends, on the first

---

* A barren and unlucky journey.

anniversary of her death. Describing Helen's sweet temperament and her character 'which everyone who knew her intimately (Haldane for instance) agrees was the most selfless and unworldly that they have ever encountered', he continued 'I was only eighteen when I fell in love with her, and we married when we were little more than boy or girl.' She 'cared little for society, shrank from every kind of publicity and self-advertisement, hardly knew what ambition meant' and was not anxious for her husband's political advancement. 'What has happened to me lately would have given her little real pleasure' was how he believed his improving standing in the Liberal Party would have struck her. 'When the sun went down it was in an unclouded sky.'[29]

In July 1892 there was a general election. The result was difficult to predict. In East Lothian, Haldane was returned, but with a reduced majority. Even Gladstone was run close in Midlothian. In East Fife, Asquith's majority was slashed to a perilous 294. Still suffering from grief over Helen, whose Arran grave he returned to sit by as soon as the campaign was over, he confessed that, 'I was more pleased with my boy's [Raymond's] election than my own' for 'on the day that I was returned he got a scholarship at Winchester'.[30] Here, though, were signs of advancement: his son was going to one of the great (Anglican) public schools, while he was on the verge of entering the government. Nationally, the Conservative bloc – now rebranded as the 'Unionists' – won 313 seats (of which 45 were Liberal Unionists) while the Liberals won 272 and the Irish Nationalists 81. Thus the Conservatives were again the largest party but there was a Commons majority for the Irish home rule cause. Rather than cede defeat immediately, Lord Salisbury opted to meet the new parliament. Seeking a backbencher to propose the vote of no confidence, Gladstone asked Asquith to rise to the occasion. This he did and the Liberals formed the new government with the support of the Irish MPs.

Asquith entered the Cabinet as Home Secretary. He was aged thirty-nine and had been an MP for six years. This was an extraordinary leap, and a clear sign that the eighty-three-year-old Gladstone really was marking the young man out for the highest office. His under-secretary was Herbert Gladstone, the Prime Minister's son. When his appointment was imminent, Asquith had written to one of his female confidantes recalling how, 'When I was a boy I used to think that to get into the Cabinet before one was 40 was, for an Englishman who had to start on the level of the crowd, the highest of achievement. I shall not be 40 until September'.[31] There were also positions in the government for his contemporaries: Sir Edward Grey became Under-Secretary at the Foreign Office, Sydney Buxton filled the same position at the Colonial Office, Tom Ellis became Deputy Whip and Acland was made Vice-President of the Council. But for Haldane, there was nothing.

In the space of a very short period of time, Asquith, despite being by no means the most regular of Commons performers, had developed a commanding professional lead over the best friend who had first led him into the parliamentary bearpit. Haldane was able to rationalise his Cabinet exclusion on the grounds that 'I did not want to take office, for I had, in 1890, taken silk and had an uncertain future before me at the Bar.'[32] In 1894, he wrote to a friend that, 'Political success is not to be an admired Minister surrounded by a devoted group of adherents. It is to have a belief that is true and leads others to follow it. I do not propose to leave the Bar. I must live by it. Besides, I like it ...'[33] Yet, it is hard to believe he would not have accepted a suitable position if Gladstone had prevailed upon him to do so. In later life, he articulated the difference between Asquith and himself in the run-up to the 1892 election rather more tartly than he would have at the time:

> Asquith's splendid gift of speech recommended him to Sir William Harcourt and the other official leaders. Moreover, he had fewer views of his own than most of us. But his judgment was wise and his gifts in debate made him popular with the older men. Distinctly he would have office before very long ... I myself was not so popular with the leaders or the Whips. I was not only independent but I was rather impulsive, and had the reputation of persuading my friends to take courses which they might not have taken apart from me. I was looked on by the official group as an intriguer.[34]

As Home Secretary, Asquith certainly gave the impression he was governed by meeting contingencies rather than a coherent Liberal philosophy. His term of office was dominated by taking strong lines on public order offences against unruly demonstrations in Trafalgar Square, unrest in the Yorkshire collieries and Fenian terrorist atrocities. In these matters he displayed toughness. Yet, he was also responsible for the passage of legislation that would disestablish Anglicanism in Wales, although this had still not reached the statute book by the time the government fell. He remained at the Home Office when, in March 1894, Gladstone finally resigned and Queen Victoria passed over Sir William Harcourt's claims in favour of Lord Rosebery. This choice of the new Prime Minister was potentially good news for Haldane, who had already pinned himself to Rosebery's camp. He had hopes that the new Prime Minister would offer him the Local Government Board or the Scottish Office. In the event, he had to contend with the 'old radicals' forcing their own claims upon the junior Cabinet posts and thereby keeping him out. The administration would prove of too brief a duration for him to get a second chance. Rosebery had touted the possibility of putting him up for Speaker when the position fell vacant. But this was not a tempting offer, Haldane later writing that 'I considered that I had neither the voice nor other requisite gifts for the work. Asquith agreed with me in thinking that there was quite different work for me to do in the future.'[35]

Rosebery's style was very different to that of Gladstone or Harcourt and his demeanour was certainly not shared by typical party activists in the Liberal heartlands. By the time he was forty-seven, one of his horses had won the Derby, he had married and lost an American heiress (although retained her money) and he had become Prime Minister. But despite his abilities, the great political prize proved too burdensome for one of his intermittent stamina. Indifference and insomnia, the troubles of office and the loss of a much loved wife pressed heavy upon the seemingly lightly worn talents that had made him so attractive a personality. Later placed next to him at a dinner party by Haldane, the acerbic Beatrice Webb confided to her diary that 'he aggravated and annoyed me by his ridiculous airs: he might be a great statesman, a royal Prince, a beautiful woman and an artistic star all rolled into one'.[36]

Rosebery's assumption as Prime Minister ensured that Irish home rule – already vetoed in 1893 by the House of Lords – was effectively shelved for the Parliament. However, this did not free up the administration to pursue new and exciting avenues. The parliamentary Liberal Party had the problem of being led by a Prime Minister in the House of Lords and a Leader in the Commons (Sir William Harcourt) who were scarcely on speaking terms. Socially, Asquith got on better with Rosebery, although he was drawn to the abrasive Harcourt's more progressive domestic agenda. With its Irish Nationalist allies disappointed and without a Commons majority of its own, the government was on borrowed time. Harcourt described it as 'hanging on by the eyelids.' The radical wing of the party was disaffected and disliked the way in which Rosebery listened to Asquith and Haldane rather than to the activists; internecine ill feeling was what best animated the government benches. 'It is war to the knife now', Haldane had assured Beatrice Webb 'impressively' shortly after Rosebery had assumed the helm, adding 'either they or we have to go down!'[37] By January 1895, Haldane was even driven to such despair that he wondered if it would be better for them all to go down together – that the party's best hope would be to fight and lose a snap general election, after which it could go through a necessary period of adjustment and reconstruction.[38]

Such were the musings of a politician who put ideas above power. At any rate, he soon got the first part of his wish. When in June 1895 his government was defeated in the House, Rosebery resigned. The subsequent general election rewarded Lord Salisbury and the Unionist cause. The Conservatives were returned with a majority of 152. Their Liberal Unionist allies accepted office with them, Joseph Chamberlain becoming Colonial Secretary. The Liberal Party, it seemed, was not just divided but severed. The laid-back and disconnected double act of Rosebery and Harcourt reduced the Liberal Party to a rump of 177 MPs. The electors of East Lothian returned Haldane, and in East Fife Asquith was rewarded with an increased majority from 294 to 716. But elsewhere the returns were dismal. Harcourt lost his seat. Appropriately, Rosebery was at sea when the results came in. From the deck of his (rented) yacht he wrote with insouciance to Asquith that 'my only interest has been in individual elections like yours' before adding 'for the general catastrophe was under the circumstances certain and inevitable'.[39]

NINE

All for One

Asquith was still married to Helen when he first met Margot Tennant. The occasion, in 1891, was a dinner in the Palace of Westminster organised by Lord Battersea. The host's younger brother, a keen huntsman named Peter Flower, had – at nine years – been by some margin the longest term of Miss Tennant's love interests. As the diners assembled, the seating plan indicated that it was Asquith's lot to be seated next to the irrepressible huntswoman and socialite. In temperament and interests, there was no reason for them to hit it off. However, Margot subsequently claimed to have been immediately struck by her dining companion's easy conversational manner (a trait she found absent in most men of public distinction) and by his 'clear Cromwellian face'.

It was not that she had gone out to attract him intentionally for, until that moment, she had not even heard of him. Yet, after the formalities of dinner, the party drifted out on to the House of Commons Terrace with its view across the Thames, Westminster Bridge and the orderly pavilions of St Thomas's Hospital on the opposite bank. Margot was flattered to find that, rather than use the perambulation as an excuse to mingle with other guests, Asquith remained at her side. Even the 'noisy and flamboyant' interjection of the host proved only a temporary distraction before the honourable Member for East Fife and Miss Tennant managed to retire to what she subsequently described as 'the darkest part of the Terrace where, leaning over the parapet, we gazed into the river and talked far into the night'. It must have been a very secluded spot for the host and the rest of the party eventually left, under the impression the evening had drawn to a close and the guests had all gone their separate ways. 'When we finished our conversation the Terrace was deserted and the sky light,' Margot remembered. 'It never occurred to me that he was married.'[1]

Margot was the youngest of five surviving daughters of Sir Charles Tennant, a Scottish Liberal MP. The self-importance attached to the baronetcy with which he was rewarded in 1885 may be gauged by the fact that even his own family came to refer to him as the 'Bart'. Like the Asquiths, the family business had been in textiles, but that was where the resemblance

ended. The grandson of a weaver who had made his fortune by patenting a
new means of bleaching cloth, the Bart's factory at St Rollox in Glasgow was
the largest chemical plant in Europe. He also purchased a four-thousand-
acre estate in Peeblesshire, south of Edinburgh, complete with a Georgian
house he converted into a Scots baronial castle in a style that resembled the
Haldane pile at Cloan. Accomplished in the saddle, Margot had grown up
with the hunting set. But through her father's political career she had early
come into contact with Gladstone, who enjoyed her breezy conversation and
was sufficiently smitten to compose for her a poetic eulogy which included
the stanzas:

> *When Parliament ceases and comes the recess,*
> *And we seek in the country rest after distress,*
> *As a rule upon visitors place an embargo,*
> *But make an exception in favour of Margot.*

> *For she brings such a treasure of movement and life,*
> *Fun, spirit and stir, to folk weary with strife.*
> *Though young and though fair, who can hold such a cargo*
> *Of all the good qualities going as Margot?*[2]

Another serious-minded man who took delight in this sprightly girl was
Benjamin Jowett, who descended from the Balliol Master's Lodge to advise
her sternly that she should concentrate on improving the lot of the less
advantaged rather than the fast thrills of the hunt. In the meantime, she
frequented the same country house parties as the precious and self-regarding
social set known as 'the Souls', among whom she came to count the Conservative politicians Arthur Balfour and George Curzon as her confidants.
Fools she did not suffer gladly. Supposedly, Lord Randolph Churchill once
pompously asked her if she knew any politicians. She replied coquettishly
that with the exception of himself, she knew them all intimately. In the year
in which she met Asquith, her name had even been linked in the press to
the widowed Lord Rosebery – who was irritated by her insufficiently strident
denial of the story.

Months later, after some matchmaking by Jowett, Alfred Milner, the new
financial Under-Secretary to the British administration in Cairo, proposed
marriage while riding with her in the evening light near the Pyramids. His
choice of setting could not have been faulted. Yet, after some thought, she
rejected him. She had, in any case, begun a correspondence with the by now
widowed Asquith, who wrote to assure her, 'You tell me not to stop loving

you, as if you thought I had done or would or could do so.'[3] The widower was clearly smitten and, it may be assumed, it was an infatuation that had come rather quickly for the taste of those who were closest to him and his late wife.

Sensibly, Margot kept Asquith waiting before agreeing to get engaged (it also gave her time to weigh up rival offers). He was twelve years her senior. When in early 1894 she did agree to marry him, she asked to be reminded of his sons' names. Given that she had been in regular correspondence with him for well over two years, it was a telling confession of ignorance. It certainly suggested she was going into marriage without much of a plan as to how she would assume the other prerequisite role of stepmother. Names, indeed, were a problem for her. She did not care for Asquith's Christian name, Herbert. Thus, Herbert was no more. Henceforth, to her he was always known by his second name, 'Henry'.

Two 'Souls' who did advise her that Asquith was right for her were the Tory politicians Balfour and Curzon. But not everyone was convinced the marriage was a good idea. Many of Margot's friends, conscious that she loved hunting and affluent, carefree company, wondered about the wisdom of her settling down to what she admitted was 'a ready-made family of children brought up differently from myself, with a man who played no games and cared for no sport, in London instead of the country, with no money except what he could make at the Bar'.[4] Nor was there any shortage of senior Liberals wading in to warn her away from their party's rising hope. Even the Master of Balliol proffered her his opinion that she would have to change her ways, for 'It is not possible to be a leader of fashion and to do your duty to the five children.' By way of encouragement – although phrased in a manner short of confidence – he added that if she did consider herself equal to the struggle of this 'nobler manner of living' then 'I can only say, "God bless you, you are a brave girl"'.[5]

The marriage took place on 10 May 1894 at St George's, Hanover Square in Mayfair. The groom asked Haldane to be his best man. Pavements were lined with well-wishers as much to see the socialite Margot Tennant on her wedding day as the proud Home Secretary. Despite the cares of his duties, Haldane noted how nervous the bride looked. In truth, she was having last-minute doubts.[6] But the momentum of the ceremony carried her along regardless. The register was signed by William Ewart Gladstone, Lord Rosebery, Arthur James Balfour and the bridegroom. As events transpired, these were to be the signatures of four prime ministers. The Herbert Asquith who had been brought up to attend a Nonconformist chapel in Morley had not only pledged his troth on one of the more fashionable altars of Anglicanism, he had very publicly entered Society. He had gone from Herbert to Henry. He had come a long way. His Puritan forebears might have wondered if he had taken a wrong direction.

The new matrimonial London home said it all. Asquith took out a lease on 20 Cavendish Square. Like the Georgian house in which Haldane had been born, it had been designed by Robert Adam. Almost palatial in scale, he set about peopling it with the mobile furniture of fourteen servants. Not one but two footmen were employed and there were stables for Margot's horses. The contrast with his previous home life could not have been more marked. Shortly after he had first met Margot he had introduced her to Helen. Having moved among rich and ambitious people all her life, Margot was astonished to discover that Helen

> told me that . . . she did not think that she would ever care for the sort of society that I loved, and was happier in the circle of her home and family. When I said that she had married a man who was certain to attain the highest political distinction, she replied that that was not what she coveted for him . . . I wondered if my ambition for the success of her husband, and other men, was wrong.[7]

Margot's temperament was very different from Helen's. She was a doyenne of London society, haughty of manner and worldly. She was over-fond of finding things and people 'commonplace'. After she had suppressed in her mind the thought that she should have married one of her previous lovers, she became her husband's champion, spurring on his ambition. Her spiky, fault-finding manner made her a difficult personality. She had a stormy relationship with her stepdaughter Violet. 'She was never of course the least like a mother,' Violet pronounced in later life, 'nor was she like a stepmother, wicked or otherwise. She just flashed into our lives like some dazzling bird of paradise, filling us with amazement, amusement, excitement: sometimes with a vague uneasiness as to what she might do next.'[8]

Ever the hospitable host, Haldane invited Margot to join him and Asquith for a late-summer house party at Cloan. Also invited was the young Liberal MP, Edward Grey. But privately, Asquith's best man had second thoughts about his choice of partner. This may have been guided by a feeling of loyalty to the first Mrs Asquith. From the safe distance of old age, Haldane compared Helen's 'beautiful and simple spirit' with the very different effect Margot had on his best friend's character. 'London Society came', he noted, 'to have a great attraction for him, and he grew by degrees diverted from the sterner outlook on life which he and I for long shared.' This contrasted with the

Asquith he had first come to know and admire. 'In his earlier political days he was a very serious person. I remember once passing along the Horse Guards with him. He touched my arm and pointed to the figure of John Bright walking in front of us. "There", he said, "is the only man in public life who has risen to eminence without being corrupted by London Society."'[9]

Yet, it is possible to overdo the sense in which Margot detached Asquith from his Nonconformist moorings and set him adrift in her material world. In fact, of the two, she was the more pious. She was appalled to discover that he had never had his children baptised. What was more, Asquith did not need Margot to make him ambitious – he had ample self-motivation of his own. But whereas Helen might have been a restraining hand, Margot fuelled her husband's drive. She was also responsible for bringing out his social skills and a nascent delight in female company that his male friends, Haldane in particular, came to believe retarded his seriousness rather than rounded his personality. Perhaps the bachelor Haldane – hardly a gifted operator in mixed company – resented too the manner in which Margot came between her new husband and him in a way that the shy and retiring Helen had never interposed herself. But Asquith showed every sign of wanting the high life Margot brought with her and to which by birth and background he had been denied. The Roundhead was finding Cavalier company to his liking. The problem was that he could not really afford to live in the style to which Margot was accustoming him. The running costs of 20 Cavendish Square and the socialising that came with it were to prove greater than the annual £5,000 allowance that Margot brought with her into the marriage. The Calvinist ancestral voices nagging Haldane told him that this was not right. Worse, he found himself entrusted with his friend's dirty work. In 1898, Asquith asked him to approach Rosebery and Balfour to see if they would suggest to the plutocratic 'Bart' that he might like to up his son-in-law's allowance. To Haldane this was an embarrassing, not to say disagreeable, commission. But he did it all the same.

Making money thus became a pressing concern for Asquith. He was forty-two when in 1895 he departed the Home Office for the Opposition benches and in the following seven years, with the prospect of being in government far from imminent, he decided to focus on earning a decent income again by returning to 1 Paper Buildings. He did well, although he did not attract the high-profile cases so beloved of his illustrious contemporaries. This was a high challenge. The late-Victorian and Edwardian period has been celebrated as a golden age for the Bar, when Edward Carson, F.E. Smith, Edward Marshall Hall and Richard Burdon Haldane were at the peak of their advocacy. The latter, indeed, was making steady progress as a QC, shining in cases before the Privy Council's Judicial Committee. Beatrice Webb described his 'vital energies' at this time being 'divided between highly skilled legal work and the processes of digestion – for he is a Herculean eater'.[10]

When the affairs of the Free Church of Scotland came before the Law Lords, Haldane showed extraordinary philosophical and theological grip (aided by scriptural fact-checking provided *pro bono* by his mother). The case proved a long and bitter one in the history of the periodic tussles in which rival groups of 'United Free' and 'Wee Free' Presbyterians attempted to wrest control of their Church's considerable wealth by demonstrating a firmer adherence to the 'true' interpretation of its Spartan doctrines. Haldane's theological disputations were accepted in court but the 'Wee Frees' won the legal argument on trust deeds. However, Haldane, the politician, helped persuade the Tory government to pass legislation stripping them of the gains made by their temporal covetousness. For his own part, he was not doing so badly. By 1905, his legal work was earning him £20,000 a year.

When Asquith and Haldane wanted to get away from the material cares of London, they seized the opportunities provided by the long recesses to go to Scotland. Not that this isolated them entirely from the passing Liberal traffic. Besides Haldane's constituency in East Lothian and Asquith's in East Fife, Campbell-Bannerman was MP for Stirling Burghs and had his own Perthshire estate, Belmont. Also in Perthshire – and not far from Haldane's baronial pile at Cloan – was the 'Relugas' lodge where Edward Grey retreated to go fishing. Residing in greater opulence, Rosebery retained his country seat at Dalmeny overlooking the Firth of Forth west of Edinburgh. Asquith once recalled an occasion when he was staying with Haldane and the Liberal MP for West Fife, Augustine Birrell, as guests of Ronald Munro Ferguson at Raith. 'We strolled up one morning to an elevation on his property which commands a fine view of the Firth of Forth and the adjacent territory. We all admired the prospect, but the only articulate ejaculation came from Birrell: "What a grateful thought, that there is not an acre in this vast and varied landscape which is not represented at Westminster by a London barrister!"'[11]

Asquith's marriage to a Tennant brought him into the Scottish country house fraternity and when not staying with his in-laws or their friends, he rented Dalquharran Castle in Ayrshire in 1904 and Glen of Rothes in Moray for the following couple of years. Margot's elder brother lent Archerfield between 1907 and 1912, a Robert Adam enlarged house in East Lothian with a private nine-hole golf course. There were also regular invites to stay with Haldane at Cloan. There, they were often joined by Edward Grey. A keen angler and ornithologist, Grey's book *Fly Fishing* was published in 1899. He did not share Asquith's and Haldane's embrace of metropolitan life, preferring the relaxation of his beloved Northumberland countryside, for which Perthshire offered an adequate surrogate. Indeed, while other allies of convenience had fallen away, Grey had emerged as the most important of Asquith's and Haldane's political companions. In some respects, this was surprising. The son of a baronet, he had displayed none of Asquith's youthful ambition and mastery of facts. Nor had he demonstrated Haldane's studiousness and earnestness of purpose. After his school days at Winchester, he had gone up to Balliol six years after Asquith had graduated. There, he had displayed the famous effortlessness but without justifying the presumption of superiority. He was sent down for impenitent idleness.

This proved no barrier to advancement, even in the supposedly more meritocratic Liberal Party. With the advantage that comes from being the son of a nearby landowner, he managed in 1885 to become MP for Berwick-upon-Tweed at the tender age of twenty-three. Yet, once elected, he showed himself more able than his youthful prospectus suggested. He was quick to acknowledge his debt to friendship. 'If it were not for you, I do not think I should have even the hold on public life which I have now', he assured Haldane as early as 1890, adding 'that Asquith owed some of the very best of himself to you'.[12]

In analysing what made Haldane so attractive a figure to those with whom he felt the bond of loyalty, a perceptive assessment was written in 1897 by his socialist-inclined friend, Beatrice Webb:

> He attracts confidence where he is at all liked; once on friendly terms, you feel absolutely secure that he will never use personal knowledge to advance his own public career to the detriment of any friend. The rank and file of his own party dislike him intensely, partly because he detaches himself from party discipline ... and partly because he seems dominated by some vague principle which they do not understand and which he does not make intelligible. His bulky awkward form and pompous ways, his absolute lack of masculine vices and 'manly' tastes (beyond a good dinner), his intense superiority and constant attitude of a teacher, his curiously woolly mind would make him an unattractive figure if it were not for the beaming kindliness of his nature, warm appreciation of friends and a certain pawky humour with which he surveys the world. And there is pathos in his personality. In spite of the successful professional life ... he is a restless lonely man – in his heart still worshipping the woman who jilted him seven years ago ... He was made to be husband, father and close comrade.

He has to put up with pleasant intercourse with political friends and political foes ... [13]

As a politician, Haldane lacked the rhetorical gifts that punctuated true oratory and separated it from the mere unloading of ill-assorted information. This, indeed, was a rare example of his failure to take on board the requirements of others – in this case a long-suffering audience. He was never a star turn on the stump. As a parliamentary performer he was adept at emptying the House, one of the proverbial 'dinner bells'. He was no more commanding when addressing the voters. John Buchan overheard a couple of Scottish farmers leaving the hall after a Haldane speech on Chinese labour in South Africa. 'Was he for it or against it?' queried the first farmer. 'I'm damned if I ken' shrugged his perplexed friend.[14]

Political opponents and colleagues alike had fun at Haldane's expense. 'In figure, features and demeanour,' alleged the Tory Leo Amery, 'there was something about him of the old-fashioned family butler.'[15] By this, it can be assumed, it was meant that he was emotionally repressed and at the service of those governed by stronger desires. In fact, his demeanour misled those who did not know him. For all his absence of a passionate temper, Asquith's daughter Violet particularly rated Haldane's 'gift for friendship, his sympathy, compassion, and generosity were limitless'.[16] What made it unusual in a politician of his range was that it was almost guilelessly unconditional. When Oscar Wilde dramatically fell from grace, those with positions in public life to maintain stayed well away. Although more an acquaintance than a close friend, Haldane nonetheless visited the disgraced playwright in Holloway jail. Finding Wilde miserable and uncommunicative in his cell, Haldane assured him that his misfortune 'might be a blessing for his career, for he had got a great subject' after years of squandering his talent on 'a life of pleasure'. He brought Wilde pen and ink and later persuaded the Home Secretary to transfer him to Reading jail. On his release, Wilde sent Haldane a bound volume of the work he had duly composed, *The Ballad of Reading Gaol*.[17]

Nor was Haldane so earnest that he could not mix with ease in gilded salons. He was friendly with both the British and French branches of the Rothschild family, and enjoyed pre-Christmas visits to the Prince and Princess Wagram's château at Grosbois, outside Paris. He shared Asquith's friendship with Sir John and Lady Horner and was also on the fringes of the 'Souls', getting on especially well with Balfour whose country house, Whittingehame, was in Haldane's East Lothian constituency. To some of Haldane's rather humourless left-wing friends, his penchant for dining with the enemy was perplexing. Watching him entertaining the 'Souls' to tea, Beatrice Webb noted how he prided 'himself on hovering between a fashionable "paradise" represented by the "Souls" and the collectivist state represented by the Fabians'. Mrs Webb prided herself on being socially unseducible. 'To me', she maintained, 'the "Souls" would not bring the "peace that passeth all understanding" but a vain restlessness of tickled vanity'.[18]

Despite his failure to find love, there remained two women in Haldane's life. The first was his mother, who lived to be a hundred. Haldane wrote to her several times a week, keeping her abreast of his doings and the excitement of London life. The other was his sister Elizabeth, whose interests in social welfare provision and German philosophy made her his natural match. He often invited her to dinner parties with his political friends, the latter being divided between those who admired her intellect and those who – unwilling to adjust to her mental strengths – found it easier to brand her a prim 'bluestocking'. Her publications included a three-volume translation of Hegel and a two-volume translation of Descartes. Later, in 1920, she became the first woman to become a magistrate in Scotland. But always, those who knew Haldane perceived an underlying sadness at his romantic loss and consequent absence of a wife and children of his own. Clever, wilful, precocious and charming, the Asquith children were a worthy substitute. Violet remembered that as she grew up her impression of Haldane 'was of a being of imperturbable serenity and calm. He was at once unworldly and ambitious, austere in purpose, yet a *bon viveur* in practice. He had an insatiable appetite for work and a formidable mastery of detail. His mind was always totally immersed in some great theme.'[19] As a young girl she enjoyed going for walks with him, ascending the steep climbs around Cloan. 'While I panted breathless in his wake he ambled rapidly ahead reciting Goethe and Emily Brontë without a pause for either word or breath. The line "Changes, sustains, dissolves, creates and rears" still conjures up for me the vision of Haldane's back topping the skyline.'[20]

Haldane had a similar effect on the other Asquith siblings. Nineteen-year-old Raymond, writing to a school friend, Harold Baker, during the holidays before going up to Balliol in 1897, could not contain his admiration for his father's friend: 'My only amusing visit was in Perthshire with the Haldanes – Richard Haldane is the greatest philosopher and the greatest politician now alive, though he comes little before the public, being ill to look at and modest by nature.' Besides his philosophical writing, 'He also does all the brainwork of the Liberal Party, and though not in the cabinet thinks for those who are. In the domestic circle he is the most amusing creature I know: he is a great humorist and thorough-going Epicurean with the finest cellar and the best table in Scotland.'[21] Young Raymond's opinion of Haldane's political contribution doubtless echoed what he had heard from his father on the subject.

Not even a year at Balliol could dent Raymond's esteem and the following summer vacation brought with it another invitation to Cloan. Afterwards, Raymond relayed to his friend that 'As usual I had a most amusing time with old Haldane in Perthshire, he will be a very great man, if not prematurely cut off – like so many of our English sovereigns – by a surfeit of lampreys, or some other unpalatable delicacy, his appetite is quite prodigious – especially for a Hegelian – and seems to increase every time I see him.'[22] Happily, Haldane was not prematurely cut off and in July 1900, from a country house party at the Horners' home, Mells Park, in Frome, Raymond Asquith wrote to Baker of the impression Haldane created when he went for a bathe with the host's eldest daughter. For the quality of the picture it paints, it is worth quoting in full:

> About ½ past 4 – just before tea Haldane suggested a bathe: no-one but himself and this lovely girl seemed keen about it: however we all went down to the lake as spectators and were amply rewarded. Haldane is an imperfect but courageous performer in the water and to see his immense but stately figure clad in a very scanty bathing dress and recklessly precipitating from dizzy altitudes into this green and flowery pond was really exquisite: the quiet slowness and dignity with which he put himself in the most ridiculous situations proved to me more conclusively than anything else could have done the real bigness of the man – to see this vast white mass with the brain of Socrates and the shape of Nero executing his absurd antics from a thin plank which bent double under his weight and sporting fantastically in the water with a divinely beautiful girl no whit abashed recalled the sunniest days of the Roman decline. Finally he came out and after lurking coyly in the bushes for a few minutes reappeared clad in nothing but a bath-towel and a panama hat and joined us at tea on the lawn where he was soon explaining the theory and history of Buddhism – its superiority to Christianity and its weaknesses as a practical religion – to a host of local spinsters who had flocked in for food and gossip. It was magnificent. At 11-30 p.m. he left in a carriage for Bath 15 miles off having to be in the courts at 10 tomorrow and in the train all tomorrow night and the night after – on his way up and down to Edinburgh where he is pleading on Tuesday. He is a marvellous man.[23]

The 'lovely girl' was Cicely Horner, whose younger sister, Katherine, Raymond would marry seven years later. Following the birth of their daughter, Perdita, Haldane – putting aside his theological doubts – happily stood as godfather.

The law, politics, philosophy and education – Haldane's interests were wide and weighty. In 1902 he accepted the invitation to deliver the Gifford lectures at St Andrews University which were duly published with the confident title, *The Pathway to Reality*. Had it not been for the pull of legal and political life that kept him in London, he would have been tempted by St Andrews' offer of the Chair of Moral Philosophy. Less onerous commitments he gladly accepted. Having been defeated when he first stood in 1896, he was elected Rector of Edinburgh University in 1905. Although this was a largely ceremonial post that involved making a high-profile address, it was elected by the students and attracted some of the foremost figures of the day as candidates (predecessors included Gladstone, Carlyle and Rosebery). As such it had become a party political tussle that attracted widespread interest and entertainment. Haldane's election ended a quarter-century of rectorial domination by the Conservatives.

Until the 1880s, Scotland's four million inhabitants were furnished with four ancient universities while England had the same number to cover a population of thirty-five million. Beyond Oxford and Cambridge, this meant making do with the then rather weedy foundation at Durham and with London University, which consisted of two teaching colleges and an examination body that could award degrees to outside students attending colleges in the provinces. After 1884, a fifth degree-awarding university was created, the Victoria University, which was a federal institution comprising colleges in Manchester, Liverpool and Leeds. This level of higher education provision was totally inadequate for a world superpower and Haldane was at the forefront of the campaign to improve matters.

In this campaign he was entirely non-partisan, working with whomever could best realise his objectives. In Westminster, that meant Arthur Balfour. Both bachelors, they had many common interests. Balfour was the author of *A Defence of Philosophic Doubt,* written when he was aged thirty-one which he followed up with *Foundations of Belief* in 1895. It was a useful collaboration that cut across party boundaries. Balfour not only supported Haldane's campaign to give the colleges at Liverpool, Leeds and Manchester charters of full university status, he even sent him to Ireland to draw up proposals that – some years later – would emerge in new universities in Dublin and Belfast, the former on lines agreeable to Catholics and the latter cheering to Protestants.

Haldane was Liverpool's advocate when its appeal to break away from Victoria University came before the Privy Council in 1902, an action that precipitated its metamorphosis, as with Manchester and Leeds, as a separate university. Haldane was also central to the campaign to expand and transform the faculties and functions of London University, helping to cobble together the compromise that ensured the passing of the University of London Commission Bill in 1898. In these matters, he also worked closely with Beatrice and Sidney Webb, with whom he helped to establish the London School of Economics in 1895 and the foundation of Imperial College London. Active in securing Imperial's funding, he envisaged it as a British version of the *Technische Hochschule* he so much admired at Charlottenburg. In 1912, he was elected Chancellor of Bristol University.

Truly, his role in the development of higher education in Britain demonstrated that he was no philosophical dreamer, but rather a practical man with clear aims who was able to work with a diverse range of individuals to achieve the desired ends. As the historian H.C.G. Matthew noted, 'Haldane's achievements during his opposition years would have been substantial for a cabinet minister'.[24] This fact was even recognised at the time. In 1902, Balfour secured him a place on the Privy Council. It was a remarkable honour for a politician who had never been in the Cabinet, indeed never held any government office.

In domestic politics, Haldane was much influenced by his friends in the Fabian Society, Beatrice and Sidney Webb and George Bernard Shaw. But, unlike them, he was also a committed Imperialist. The latter view was of a flexible, rather than unyielding, type, for Haldane's belief in Irish home rule found its mirror in his commitment to an Empire that was held together because rather than despite the fact that its dominions enjoyed autonomy over their affairs. He had given particular study to the constitution of the 1867 Canadian federation. He even toyed with killing two birds with one stone by proposing the conversion of the House of Lords into an Imperial Senate serving the British Empire.

Like Asquith, he found it difficult to get on with Sir William Harcourt, the Liberal leader in the Commons, but Haldane went far further in personally attaching himself to Rosebery's overall leadership. Indeed, at times he behaved as if he was Rosebery's Eton fag, running errands, doing his dirty work and reporting back to him on what was happening in the political world. It should, perhaps, have occurred to Haldane that Rosebery's failure to have a sense of what was going on was a sign that he lacked vigour. But Haldane was certain that Rosebery understood the need to move the party beyond the tired orthodoxies of Gladstonianism. 'The process of pulling down the ancient and somewhat dilapidated Temple of Liberalism proceeds apace', he assured him with evident delight during the summer of 1897.[25]

In 1898 Harcourt announced his resignation in the letters column of *The Times*. Here was an opportunity. There were only six former Cabinet ministers sitting on the Commons benches and Asquith was one of them. Without a formal mechanism for being elected, it was essentially up to a gentlemen's agreement among the six as to which of them would rise to the challenge. 'The best thing for us, far and away,' one increasingly friendly Liberal MP, Sir Edward Grey, told Haldane on 16 December, 'would be for Asquith to give up the Bar & take the lead in the House.' Asquith discussed the prospects with Haldane and Ellis, the Chief Whip, over lunch at 20 Cavendish Square. Both assured him that he was the leader they wanted. But did Asquith want it at this particular juncture? It would mean forsaking his income at the Bar for the gamble of leading a fractured party that was by no means certain to form a government in the foreseeable future.

Haldane sketched a scenario in which the leadership in the Commons would be offered to Sir Henry Campbell-Bannerman who, it was hoped, would refuse it whereupon it would fall into Asquith's lap. But after discussing the options at length, Asquith concluded he should sit out this tilt at the leadership. Campbell-Bannerman would make a far better caretaker during a period in which the party appeared to be going nowhere. On 19 December, Asquith wrote to Campbell-Bannerman, sixteen years his senior, to offer loyal support not just on behalf of himself but from 'all of us'.[26] The parliamentary party duly filed into the Reform Club to elect Campbell-Bannerman as their new flag-carrier. But it was clear who had established himself as the leader-in-waiting.

The thankless task presented to the new leader soon became manifest. The outbreak of the Boer War in 1899 threatened to divide the Liberals as publicly as had Irish home rule. Some, like the scrupulously Gladstonian John Morley and a strident but gifted young Welshman, David Lloyd George, did not conceal their sympathies for the Boer. Asquith and Haldane, however, like Rosebery and Sir Edward Grey, were strongly anti-Boer. They endorsed the Imperialist doctrines both of the renegade Liberal Joseph Chamberlain, who was organising policy from the Colonial Office in Lord Salisbury's Unionist (Conservative) government, and of the equally unflinching High Commissioner in South Africa. The latter was Alfred Milner, Asquith's Oxford contemporary and Margot's onetime suitor in the Egyptian moonlight.

Although personally opposed to the war against the Afrikaners, Campbell-

Bannerman found himself trying to hold his divided party together. It was essential that the Liberal Party did not split again before a general election was called, possibly on the issue. The war had started off badly, but in February 1900 Ladysmith was relieved after a four-month siege and, in May, Mafeking was also reached by the British forces, amid much rejoicing. Salisbury gambled on this as a moment to call a snap poll – a 'khaki election' as it was known on account of the backdrop of mobilisation against which it was fought. The extent to which the Liberal Party put up a united front was nominal. Fifty-six candidates formed themselves into a pro-war body (by inference distancing themselves from the official leadership) called the Liberal Imperial Council. At the forefront of the names were Asquith, Haldane and Grey.

Salisbury had picked his moment with care and was duly rewarded by the electorate. His Unionists – as the Conservative Party was now known in collaboration with its Liberal Unionist allies – had a majority of 134. In Haddington, another slice was cleaved from Haldane's slim margin of victory, his majority shrinking from 580 votes to 378. This was far too close for comfort. Asquith, however, bucked the trend, doubling the size of his majority in East Fife to 1,431. In the months ahead, the fracture the war caused within the Liberal Party was to widen dramatically.

The Commander-in-Chief, Horatio Kitchener, was turning the war in South Africa in Britain's favour by means that were far removed from liberalism or, indeed, that were widely considered the laws of war. He met the highly successful Boer guerrilla tactics with a scorched earth policy. Boer women and children were evacuated from the war zone and put into concentration camps that, while not the extermination camps of Nazi devising, nonetheless were unsanitary and disease-ridden, resulting in the deaths of 20,000 of them, the majority children (also succumbing to disease there were a largely forgotten number of coloureds). It was a dreadful neglect that would run deep in the Afrikaner consciousness if not in the conscience of those mishandling its implementation. Campbell-Bannerman protested at what he described as 'methods of barbarism'. In contrast, Asquith was horrified at such a slur on the British Army at a time when national unity was necessary. He made speeches that all but disassociated himself from his leader's supposedly unpatriotic stance. In this he was joined by Rosebery, who roused himself from his slumber to attack the Liberal programme root and branch. He called, in effect, for it to shed its Gladstonian isolationism, learn from the legacy Disraeli had gifted the Tories, and become an Imperialist party.

Twenty Cavendish Square was now a centre of intrigue in which Asquith,

Grey, Haldane and his would-have-been brother-in-law, Ronald Munro Ferguson, planned co-ordinated action against their own party's leadership. During the parliamentary recess, they reconvened in their respective Scottish boltholes. They styled themselves 'Liberal Imperialists'. Others shortened this to the less majestic 'Limps'. Haldane dubbed it 'the Asquith committee'. But they were more than just an impatient clique. They were also joined by the Methodist Robert Perks, who was important in attracting Non-conformist support for this party within a party. The division was serious. Grey went so far as to assure Campbell-Bannerman that he could not count on his support unless he stopped giving succour to the Boer cause.

On 5 January 1902, Haldane wrote to Asquith arguing that the party should drop its commitment to Irish home rule. On 23 January, Asquith, having been involved in framing the Opposition's amendment to the Address, even abstained in the consequent vote. This was extraordinary behaviour and a sign that he appeared to be searching for a means of remoulding British politics by unifying the Liberal Imperialists with Joseph Chamberlain's Liberal Unionists. In February, *The Times*'s letters column re-emerged as the favoured forum of Liberal infighting when Rosebery used it to repudiate Campbell-Bannerman. The Liberal Imperial Council was upgraded into the Liberal League with Rosebery as its President. In a vice-presidential capacity, Asquith, Grey, Fowler and (soon after) Haldane served as his altar boys. In March, Asquith told the Liberal Party that the majority on the mainland simply would not accept Irish home rule and that 'to recognise facts like these is not apostasy, it is common sense'.[27]

Yet, no sooner had the Liberal Party looked like shattering than the conditions were created for it to rally around old familiar tunes. In March 1902, the government introduced its Education Bill to abolish elected school boards (which had become fiefdoms of local Liberal activism) and transfer funding to local government. For Nonconformists, this seemed the worst of both worlds in that the school boards would disappear but taxes would still be levied to prop up Anglican and Roman Catholic foundations. In April, the Budget chipped away at free trade by opening the way for a duty on imported corn. In May, the Boer War ended. These were all good reasons for Liberals to reunite. In July, Salisbury retired as Prime Minister and was succeeded by his nephew, Arthur Balfour. The transforming event in British politics took place ten months later.

On the morning of 16 May 1903, Asquith bounded into Margot's bedroom in Cavendish Square. 'Wonderful news today,' he exclaimed by way of salutation, holding a copy of *The Times* aloft. The paper contained the details of a speech Joseph Chamberlain had given the previous day in Birmingham.

Asquith sat on his wife's bed and read to her the joyful details. Decrying Cobden and Bright's adherents as 'Little Englanders', Chamberlain had implied that the repeal of the Corn Laws had been a historic mistake and had called for a new policy of protectionism – which he styled Imperial Preference. Producers at home and in the Empire should be helped and foreign imports taxed. Believing this meant the end of cheap food, Asquith assured his wife, 'it is only a question of time when we shall sweep this country'.[28]

Chamberlain's new crusade redrew the political battle lines. Almost overnight, the factions of the Liberal Party were drawn back together again in defence of free trade and 'the cheap loaf'. The Unionist front fragmented. Chamberlain's Liberal Unionist partner, the Whiggish Duke of Devonshire (as Lord Hartington had become), was horrified. There were deep misgivings in Salisbury's family, the Cecils. In May 1904 the late Lord Randolph Churchill's precocious and promising son, Winston Churchill, crossed the floor and joined the Liberals. Other Tory free traders might have followed him, reversing the flow of 1886 over Irish home rule, but for their detestation of the radical, supposedly pro-Boer sentiments of Campbell-Bannerman and, in particular, David Lloyd George.

Balfour tried to prevent a total schism in his party by refusing to come down totally on one side or the other. It was an unhappy attempt reminiscent of John Major's 'wait and see' policy over joining the euro in the 1990s. As a political tactic, it did not work. Chamberlain resigned, as did Devonshire and C.T. Ritchie, the Chancellor of the Exchequer (who was replaced by Chamberlain's son, Austen). The Secretaries of State for India and Scotland also tendered their resignation. The possibility of the Liberal Imperialists fusing together a new centre party with the Liberal Unionists was destroyed by Chamberlain's protectionist pronouncements. The 'Limps' were free traders to a man. In particular, Asquith lost no time in re-embracing the bosom of the Liberal Party. Chamberlain launched a speaking tour of the country only to find Asquith in hot pursuit, countering his claims about the benefits of protectionism and pouring scorn on the arithmetic that underpinned it.

Haldane, the biographer of Adam Smith, was equally certain of his opposition to Chamberlain's remedies but was less adept in ridding himself of Limpish tendencies. Almost alone among Liberals, he had supported the 1902 Education Bill because he believed – regardless of the sensibilities of Nonconformity – that it would put primary and secondary schools on a firmer financial footing. He even abstained on the issue of the exploitative use of Chinese indentured labourers in South Africa when the rest of the party was railing against what it portrayed as 'Chinese slavery'. In these matters, he was in danger of identifying himself as a maverick. By contrast, Asquith remained on good terms socially with Rosebery while recognising that the laird of Dalmeny's chance of being a power broker had passed. The Liberal Party was reunited again, reinvigorated and hungry for government while Balfour's administration had run out of steam and was riven by the divisive issue that Chamberlain, having resigned from it, was now so zealously promoting. Asquith knew that these were not the circumstances in which to play the rebel.

The recovery in Liberal Party fortunes was at one level an opportunity for Haldane and Asquith but also a setback since it was taking place under the leadership of a man neither of them liked. The dilemma they faced was thus whether they should build bridges with Sir Henry Campbell-Bannerman or seek to oust him before his leadership became unassailable. Partly, the breach had been political. Differences over the Boer War had highlighted their opposing concepts of how far the Liberal Party should embrace British imperialism. Campbell-Bannerman's apparent orthodox rather than progressive approach to domestic legislation also demonstrated the generation gap between him and Asquith and Haldane. As Haldane put it, their leader might be 'genial' but 'he was not identified in the public mind with any fresh ideas, for indeed he had none'.[29] The division was also personal. Campbell-Bannerman made no secret of his dislike for Haldane. He especially deprecated the top-heavy philosopher's addiction to gossip and intrigue, observing that he 'always prefers the back stairs to the front stairs; but it does not matter, for the clatter can be heard all over the house'.[30] There was some truth in this, for Haldane certainly had a donnish taste for backbiting and mischief. But as Beatrice Webb, who knew Haldane far better, recognised, there were mitigating circumstances, for his 'intrigues are always to promote a cause, never to push himself'.[31]

Helping Asquith was a central goal of Haldane's manoeuvrings. On 5 October 1903, he wrote from Edinburgh to Asquith to tell him that he had been to see Rosebery at his country house at Dalmeny and that Rosebery was determined to support an Asquith ministry rather than exert himself to the effort of forming one himself. Haldane reiterated his personal pledge that he would not serve under Campbell-Bannerman. 'You must lead us, accordingly', Haldane begged his friend.[32] Grey wrote similarly two days later.[33] Even more encouraging news came after three weeks, when private information arrived to suggest that the leadership might fall into Asquith's

lap without him having to take unnecessary risks. Campbell-Bannerman's
wife was in poor health and her husband appeared to be losing his appetite
to persevere in the political front line. Herbert Gladstone, the Liberal Chief
Whip, wrote to Asquith enlightening him that he had been over to see
Campbell-Bannerman at his Perthshire home, Belmont. From there, the
weary leader had indicated that he did not think he was up to shouldering
the heavy burdens of senior office if called upon to form an administration.
'A peerage and some office of dignity like the Presidentship [sic] of the Council
would be what he would like' Herbert Gladstone suggested, encouragingly.[34]

However, during the summer of 1905, Campbell-Bannerman's energy and
sense of self-worth picked up. Balfour's administration was disintegrating by
its own accord. The effort involved in winning a general election would not
be so titanic. In August, while taking his annual holiday in Marienbad, he
had met King Edward VII and, to his surprise, got on very well with him.
So he had little to fear on that score either. The Liberal leader, it seemed,
now fully intended to form a government if Balfour resigned and to go on
and win a subsequent general election too. This was bad news personally for
Asquith and especially for Haldane. It also portended a Liberal government
clinging to old-fashioned remedies rather than adopting the prescriptions of
Liberal Imperialism. Over the dinner table to his friend Edward Gosse,
Haldane vented his frustration at the official leadership, suggesting a good
use could be put to Lord Rosebery's four empty villas at Naples: 'if they
could be fitted up, and Ld Spencer, C.B., John Morley and Ld R. himself
could be deported thither, with orders to the Syndics of Naples to allow
them every luxury, but to keep them there, the Liberal Party would be in a
perfectly healthy condition'.[35]

Haldane was now impatient for the party to be taken over by 'a body of
men with life and energy and a new outlook on the problems of the state'.[36]
He knew well the candidates he had in mind. In September 1905, while
Parliament was still in recess, Haldane ventured from Cloan to Glenrothes,
where Asquith and Margot were staying, in order to discuss what to do.
They decided to bring Grey – who was only fifteen miles away at his 'Relugas'
fishing lodge on the Findhorn – into the conspiracy. Together they were
determined that their bond of friendship should not be rent asunder by their
mutual political ambitions. Cosseted together at Relugas, they agreed to
proceed, like Dumas' three musketeers, on the basis of one for all and all for
one. If Campbell-Bannerman tried to form a Cabinet, they would all refuse
to serve in it unless he was removed to the House of Lords. Haldane imagined
for him a suitably dignified title – perhaps Viscount Belmont would be
sufficient to tempt him 'upstairs'. From there, he could retain the party

leadership if he wanted (because of his support in the party, it would be difficult to wrest it from him). But handed the Treasury, Asquith should lead the party in the House of Commons and secure for his two mates the jobs of their choice – the Foreign Office for Grey and the Lord Chancellorship for Haldane. For the latter, with no ministerial experience, it would be a rapid elevation.

Could they pull off such a plot? Individually, they were sure that this 'Relugas Compact' had secured their political ascendancy. After all, Campbell-Bannerman could surely not hope to form a government without the talents of any of these three bright stars. However, it was important that the King – whose task it was to call whomever he thought could form a government – was aware of their ultimatum. This Haldane neatly described as placing the Relugas Compact 'on a sure foundation'.[37] In the course of his campaign for expanding London University, he had become acquainted with King Edward VII and it was decided that he should make the most of this entrée by venturing over to Balmoral to inform His Majesty of the situation. For someone of Haldane's love of covert conspiracy, there could have been few more exciting tasks than to embroil his sovereign in one. In fact, this was, in some ways, the less delicate of the two missions. Asquith was deputised to see Campbell-Bannerman as soon as he returned from his holiday in Marienbad so that he too was left in no doubt about his options.

On 15 September, Haldane wrote to Lord Knollys, the King's private secretary, setting out the position. The letter was frank – making clear that none of the three would serve unless Campbell-Bannerman was kicked up to the House of Lords, Asquith given the Treasury and the leadership in the Commons and 'either the Foreign or Colonial Office for Grey, and the Woolsack for myself. As to this last I am merely recording for you the wish of the others.'[38] This was, in several respects, a rather ambitious epistle for someone who had never held office to send to the King's private secretary. Nonetheless, Knollys replied at once, assuring Haldane that his letter would be placed before the King as soon as he arrived at Balmoral but also suggesting that what was most important was that Haldane and his confederates served as a moderating influence in any future, potentially radical, Liberal administration; after all, at Campbell-Bannerman's 'age it is not probable that he would be able to stand for long the combined duties of Prime Minister and Leader of the House of Commons'.[39]

With the King's ensconcement at his Grampian retreat, the royal invitation duly arrived and on the evening of 5 October Haldane was summoned there and directed to sit next to King Edward at dinner. The conversation did not go quite according to plan. The King assured him that, having met Campbell-

Bannerman at Marienbad, he found him not as awful as his speeches suggested. This was not what Haldane wanted to hear. However, on the third and final day of his stay at Balmoral, he got a last chance to press the matter again when he was invited into the King's private apartments. By the time he was ushered back out, he was under the impression that His Majesty was fully on board. Haldane duly wrote to Asquith, apprising him of all that had passed, concluding that the royal party 'are fully alive to the importance of secrecy and reticence' and that 'if only tongues are held (and I have done all that can be done to secure this) I think ... that we have secured very cordial and powerful assistance'.[40]

Campbell-Bannerman returned from Marienbad on 11 November. Haldane had advised Asquith to see him as soon as possible and no time was lost in trying to secure an appointment. Two days after his return, the Liberal leader showed Asquith into his library at his home in Belgrave Square. Even to those sure of purpose, conversations of this kind are attended with social awkwardness. On his arrival Asquith was somewhat nonplussed. He had always been an assiduous examiner of *The Times* for every nuance of political climate change. Now, having at last got within adjectival distance of power, he was surprised to find the man who could deliver it reading not *The Times* but *The Week's Survey*, a newspaper of which he had not heard. It was not at all what he had expected. The chat was at first somewhat stilted. But after a brief survey of world events, Campbell-Bannerman proceeded to the issue that had enticed Asquith into his library – the likelihood of the government's fall and the royal summons for Campbell-Bannerman to form its successor. This was an astute move. Rather than await his visitor's ultimatum, Campbell-Bannerman was determined to take the initiative and, in doing so, wrongfoot him.

Asquith relayed to his wife the ensuing course of the conversation. 'What would you like?', proffered Campbell-Bannerman, 'the Exchequer, I suppose?' To this, Asquith said nothing. He was keen not to be detached from Relugas's united front by agreeing to a plum office at the first time of asking. But his silence might have been taken as acquiescence when the offer of the Home Office elicited from him an immediate 'Certainly not!'. Campbell-Bannerman then toyed with him further, 'Of course if you want legal promotion what about the Woolsack? No? Well then, it comes back to the Exchequer.' Having boxed his guest into a corner, the Liberal leader then twisted the knife: 'I hear that it has been suggested by that ingenious person, Richard Burdon Haldane, that I should go to the House of Lords, a place for which I have neither liking, training nor ambition. In this case you would lead the House of Commons. While Lord Spencer was well and among us, nothing under Heaven would have made me do this! Nothing except at the point of the bayonet.' It was clear from this line of attack that the party leader had worked out the plot against him.

Campbell-Bannerman was not the pushover imagined by the intriguers of Relugas. Asquith did his best, and pressed the case for Haldane to go to the Woolsack and Grey to the Foreign Office, only to find the leader minded to send the former to the Home Office and the latter to the War Office.[41] This was not at all what either had in mind. As for the crucial issue – telling Campbell-Bannerman he would have to go off to the Lords – Asquith felt unable to force home the bayonet.

It was Rosebery who made the next move. On 25 November, he delivered a well publicised pronouncement urging the party to drop its commitment to Irish home rule. Although Asquith had made a similar speech three weeks previously, he suddenly affected to be outraged by Rosebery's impertinence. Chancing to 'come across' Morley (who he knew would repeat it to Campbell-Bannerman) in the Athenaeum, Asquith, pretending to be furious, assured him that he had never heard 'anything so disloyal' and that this 'bombshell' ruled out Rosebery from a Liberal government. Sure enough, Morley duly repeated this confidence.[42] With Rosebery sidelined, the path for translating Campbell-Bannerman to the leadership in the Lords was thus made smoother. Meanwhile, Asquith, perhaps feeling he had not stood up for his friend sufficiently at the last meeting, wrote Campbell-Bannerman a lengthy screed in which he pleaded Haldane's case for the Woolsack.[43] But Campbell-Bannerman doubtless took Asquith's refusal to commit over the offer of the Treasury as a tacit acceptance, sensing that he could be bought with it and the hint of the prime ministership thereafter. With Asquith successfully decoupled from his fellow conspirators, it was no longer essential to have Grey or Haldane in the Cabinet too, or at any rate not in the offices for which they had measured themselves up. To his ally Tom Buchanan, Campbell-Bannerman confided that he wanted Sir Robert Reid for the Woolsack and did not see why the forty-three-year-old Grey was entitled to the Foreign Office given 'his ignorance of foreign countries and foreign language: only once been outside U.K. and that was two days in Paris'.[44]

Rosebery's statement did more than merely clarify power-broking questions in the Liberal Party. It encouraged the demise of the Unionist government too. Balfour believed that in resigning as Prime Minister he would show up Liberal divisions that ran so deep they would be unable to form a workable administration. This caught the intriguers by surprise. Indeed, the Balfour government's termination, on Monday 4 December, came at a singularly inconvenient time for Asquith, just when he was about to board a steamer for Egypt to act on behalf of the former Khedive's family for the princely sum of 10,000 guineas. The money would have come in handy, but its timing meant Asquith had to forgo such riches. The rectitudinous Liberal Party did not summon its leaders from the cushioned luxury of Arabian palaces.

Campbell-Bannerman had been in Scotland and returned to London on the same day that Balfour tendered his resignation. What decision he had come to about accepting the Relugas conspirators' plan (and the advice of his doctor) he kept to himself. That evening, Grey assured him that unless he removed himself to lead a new government from the House of Lords he (Grey) would not serve in his Cabinet. This was the threat that Asquith had been supposed to transmit but had not felt able to after Campbell-Bannerman spiked his guns. The next morning Asquith came calling again. Yet once again he flunked the opportunity to be frank, intimating that the matter was almost too personal for them to discuss but suggesting delicately that nobody could accuse Campbell-Bannerman of being a coward if, given his health and that of his wife, he went to the Lords. Keeping his own counsel, the Prime Minister-in-waiting then went off promptly to Buckingham Palace. There, the King played his part, suggesting that he should accept a peerage and be Prime Minister from the Upper House. Campbell-Bannerman, however, sidestepped the proposal by suggesting that although he thought it was a good idea, it was important that he at first led the administration in its early months of teething from the Commons. The King could not deny the logic of this proposition.

It was only the following morning, Wednesday 6 December, that Asquith gained another interview and found the courage of his friends' convictions. 'It is no use going over the ground again, my dear C.B.,' he said, at last coming to the point, 'I make a personal appeal to you, which I've never done before; I urge you to go to the House of Lords and solve this difficulty.'[45] To reinforce the point, he mentioned that *The Times* was saying the same and that there was no other way of getting Grey to change his mind. He even proposed a new idea dreamt up by Grey, that if Campbell-Bannerman insisted on staying in the Commons, Haldane should become Lord Chancellor and Liberal Party Leader in the House of Lords. This did not appeal. As to his own choice of chamber, Campbell-Bannerman said he would have to consult his wife, who would be returning to Belgrave Square from Scotland that evening. This may have been a stalling tactic, but at any rate Lady C-B's advice, when it arrived, was to tell her husband to stick his ground.

Whether Asquith would do likewise was now the issue. His friends recognised his predicament. Grey assured him that given Campbell-Bannerman's apparent determination to form a government without any of them, it would be understandable if Asquith chose to put his 'personal position' first.[46] This was easier said than done. 'If I stay out, Asquith will have to decide what he does,' Grey confided in his wife. 'If he goes in without me his position will be horrid and people will say he has abandoned me in order to have office.' However, in view of the lack of a Liberal majority in Parliament, Campbell-Bannerman's decision to form a government before calling a general election put Asquith, Haldane and Grey in a difficult position. If they refused to serve, they would play into Balfour's hands by weakening the public image of the Liberal Party. Since a general election could not be far postponed, this risked potentially calamitous consequences for themselves and for the party. Standing aloof would look sordidly self-interested. It was little wonder that Grey ended his news update to his wife, 'Your very much harassed and highly wrought E.'[47]

Campbell-Bannerman then got back to Asquith, making clear he would not do as he wished, but that there were places for him, Grey and Haldane in the Cabinet on a take it or leave it basis. He offered Asquith the post of Chancellor of the Exchequer. With this wholesome fruit dangled before him, Asquith was led into temptation (after all, Campbell-Bannerman was an old man, not likely to last the full term; Campbell-Bannerman was an elderly sixty-nine, Asquith a sprightly fifty-three ... biding time would reap a reward). But he also saw the difficulties of hasty acceptance, pacing up and down the room in Belgrave Square and admitting that 'they will say at once this man deserted his friends and crawled back into office'. Campbell-Bannerman gently twisted the knife, reminding him 'that it was not he that had put Asquith in this dilemma'.[48]

It was clear who had won. Asquith felt unable to reject an offer that made him heir apparent. He dashed off a note to Haldane, explaining why he had felt compelled to tear up the Relugas compact and accept office unilaterally. 'I stand in a peculiar position which is not shared by either of you,' he pleaded. If he refused Campbell-Bannerman's offer either 'the attempt to form a Govt. is given up' or 'a weak Govt. would be formed entirely or almost entirely of one colour. In either event in my opinion the issue of the election would be put in the utmost peril.' Given these circumstances he suggested that Haldane and Grey should also abort the plot and join the Cabinet, 'But I need not say what an enormous and immeasurable difference your cooperation would make to me. Whatever happens nothing can change our affection and confidence.'[49]

Haldane received Asquith's letter in the afternoon. At the same time a note arrived for him from Campbell-Bannerman offering the Attorney-

Generalship. It was a responsibility outside Cabinet rank. As such, it had no appeal to him. Haldane wanted either to be Lord Chancellor or in a position where he could further his great interests; he did not want to forsake his legal career – generating an annual income in the region of £20,000 – merely to be 'a Law Officer'.[50] He was thus determined to reject the offer. However, on his way home he called in at the London home of Lady Horner, an old friend in whose lake at Mells his bathing antics had so delighted the youthful Raymond Asquith. She told him – in effect – that he was being self-indulgent and should put first the needs of shoring up a Liberal administration that was all that stood in the way of Britain erecting trade barriers against the outside world. These blunt words had an effect on him and he returned to his flat on the Thames Embankment, 3 Whitehall Court, with Asquith's plea and Lady Horner's views ringing in his head and Campbell-Bannerman's offer folded in his pocket.

After turning the key in his lock, he walked into his drawing room, where he found Grey 'reposing on the sofa with the air of one who had taken a decision and was done with political troubles'. Doubtless this meant his mind was ranging over happy thoughts of a Northumberland fishing stream. Haldane, however, was now in earnest. He set about trying to reawaken his friend's political ambition. True, the Relugas compact had collapsed, but that was no reason for a worthless act of self-immolation, he argued. The Liberal fight against protectionism had to be won and, if they refused to play their part, 'were we not thinking too much of ourselves and too little of the public?'. Lady Horner's advice had clearly had its effect on Haldane. But Grey was not entirely convinced by this sudden reversal of sentiment and wanted to defer a decision until he had eaten some food. Apart from anything else, his refusal of office had already appeared as reported fact in *The Times*. Haldane, making clear he would do as Grey did (in itself a form of applying pressure), duly booked a private room in the Café Royal, hoping that this would do the trick. It did and by the time the waiters removed the fish course, both Grey and Haldane had talked themselves into following Asquith into the Cabinet. Grey accepted the Foreign Office. Rejecting the Home Office, Haldane accepted the War Office which Campbell-Bannerman assumed nobody would touch 'with a pole.'[51]

Thus, ten years after the last Liberal government had broken up in a state of ennui, the party was back in office with Asquith, Haldane and Grey entering Campbell-Bannerman's Cabinet and intending to act together to prevent it succumbing to the risky thrills of radicalism. In agreeing to serve in what promised to be a short tenure before the inevitable general election, they were effectively turning their backs on the schismatic Liberal League of which they had been Vice-Presidents but whose President, Rosebery, would not join them round the Cabinet table. The lost leader, indeed, felt aggrieved that his Limpish acolytes had not included him in their schemes and had consequently led him into foolishly ruling himself out of contention by speaking out. But most of all, the machinations of the past few days had demonstrated that, when confronted by an obstacle, Asquith would act unilaterally: he accepted the Treasury without enforcing the terms he had agreed with his friends.

That it had worked out reasonably well in the end was not directly down to him. It was only because Lord Cromer, the new Prime Minister's first choice for Foreign Secretary, declined the post that Campbell-Bannerman found he did need Grey after all. Asquith was particularly fortunate that he had friends who understood and excused his change of tack – although it is safe to assume they committed it to memory. He was rightly thankful to Haldane. 'No words of mine can express what I feel', he assured him on 8 December, 'by your action during the last two days you have laid the party and the country and myself (most of all) under an unmeasured debt of gratitude.' It was not the moment to mention whether or how there would be a payback. Instead, he added, somewhat defensively, 'More could not have been accomplished, and there was a real risk of losing everything.'[52]

It was Margot Asquith who summed up the situation most succinctly. 'So we are all in, and not *one* of us has got what we wanted!'[53]

TEN

Liberal England

A deep smog hung low over London on the day Asquith, Grey and Haldane received their seals of office from the King. The walk from Buckingham Palace through St James's Park and across Horse Guards to their respective Whitehall departments would normally have been a pleasant stroll and an opportunity for press photographers to snap images of the new Chancellor, Foreign Secretary and Secretary for War striding purposefully towards their responsibilities. But so dense was the fog that Haldane opted to travel the short distance from the palace in a brougham cab. As he did so, Grey and Fowler (the Chancellor of the Duchy of Lancaster) jumped in to cadge a lift. Only partway down the Mall, the cab came to a halt, its driver unable to see the road in front of him. It was a pea-souper. The three Cabinet ministers got out and began edging one foot in front of the other with wafting arms outstretched, tentatively feeling their way towards their departments. It was not a reassuring image. When Haldane, muddied and confused, eventually arrived at the War Office he asked an attendant for a glass of water. 'Certainly, sir,' came the reply, 'Irish or Scotch?'[1]

There was no time to settle in for the lack of parliamentary majority necessitated calling an almost immediate general election in the new year. Expectations of a Liberal victory were high, but the result, when it came, was beyond wildest hopes. Having dominated politics for a decade, the Conservatives were swept away in a landslide. Returned from the once mighty frock-coated legions were a mere 132 Conservative and 25 Liberal Unionist MPs, making a Unionist total of 157. Among the humiliations, Balfour lost his seat. In mocking contrast, the government benches were tightly packed with 377 Liberals, excited by the opportunities opened up to them and jubilant at the thought that they had saved the cause of free trade. Their satisfaction was understandable. The result was one of the great triumphs in British parliamentary history, greater than Clement Attlee's achievement for the Labour Party in 1945 and comparable with the scale of victories recorded by Lord Grey in 1832 and Tony Blair in 1997. With an enviable overall majority, the Liberals were freed from past constraints. At last, they were not dependent on Irish Nationalists. The tortured subject of home rule legislation – destined in any case for emasculation in the Lords – could be deferred while domestic legislation took precedence. Yet, few governments can really do as they please. This was especially the case given that the House of Lords retained veto powers on legislation and, as had happened during the 1892-5 administration, it was soon clear that its Unionist majority would not let controversial Bills pass without challenge.

The fears of the vanquished were nowhere more evident than on the issue of national defence. The isolationist and even pacifist sentiments of large numbers of Liberal activists greatly concerned those who worried for the guardianship of the world's greatest empire. These alarms were intensified by the new Prime Minister's past attacks on British 'methods of barbarism' during the Boer War and the opposition to that conflict of the Welsh radical he appointed President of the Board of Trade, David Lloyd George. Liberals seeking to sustain the Gladstonian orthodoxy of limited commitment abroad and retrenchment at home were insistent that the money needed to fund social provision should be taken out of the armed forces' budget. It was a symptom of the party's disdain for the subject that so few Liberals wanted even to be considered for the office of Secretary of State for War. When Campbell-Bannerman granted Haldane's wish for the job, he took satisfaction from the fact that he was probably damning a colleague he did not like with the gift of a department over which he could only fail. 'We shall now see how Schopenhauer gets on in the Kailyard,' the new Prime Minister sniffed derisively.[2]

It was certainly a billet of hard practicalities for a man of Haldane's philosophical mind. The Army Council doubtless feared the worst when he sought to reassure them with the confidence that the sort of force he was aiming to construct was 'a Hegelian Army'.[3] The look of bamboozlement around the room can be imagined. Given that he could have held out for the Home Office and that he was a politician devoted to the Bar and the cause of expanding education, his decision to mix with the brass hats was certainly surprising. But here his Liberal Imperialist instincts came to the fore. He had supported the Boer War and he wanted to steer the Army's fortunes not least because he feared the sort of pacifist-inclined Liberal who might otherwise be pressed to the task. What was more, it was one of the most challenging departments. For Haldane, this was a recommendation and an invitation.

The British Army had spent the last quarter of the nineteenth century facing opposition rarely more serious than tribesmen with spears (not that such foes had been overcome without difficulties and loss). There was not even a General Staff. When at last an opponent was found worthy of respect –

the Boers – the results were initially calamitous. Nothing did more than the bitter war in South Africa to show up better the shortcomings of British military planning (and indeed social conditions – a third of potential recruits had to be rejected at the outset because they were deemed physically unfit to serve).[4] Balfour's government had started to act on the damning evidence thrown up by the conflict and a Committee of Imperial Defence was created. But there was still plenty left to do when Haldane arrived at his desk. His response was prompt. He quickly read the French and German military theorists and got down to business. In September 1906, he established the German model of a General Staff. In the following year, this was expanded into the Imperial General Staff, the development of which Haldane entrusted to a promising Scot of similar social background to himself named Douglas Haig.

The Royal Navy remained the champion of the seas, but the ancient aversion to standing armies ensured that – compared to the mass conscript armies being drilled across the European continent – Britain made do with only a small professional soldiery. This inferiority of numbers at a time of rising tension in Europe fuelled demands for conscription at home. There was support for this within sections of the Conservative Party* and, in particular, from the main pressure group for compulsory military service, the National Service League, over which no less a hero than Lord Roberts VC assumed the presidency. Conscription smacked of the strong state and its domination over the rights of the individual. As such, it was anathema to the Liberal creed of volunteerism. It also ran against Haldane's thinking. France and Germany might have massed armies, but they did not have the sizeable navy that patrolled Britain's moat.

Instead, he set about recasting the Army so that it benefited from economies of scale. The old force was organised at brigade strength and backed up by ancient but inadequate volunteer, militia and yeomanry regiments for home defence that could be plundered in time of war. Haldane replaced these historic but ill-co-ordinated bodies with a new formation: the Territorial Army. This was not all. He feared that the 'blue water school' analysis that the Royal Navy could prevent an invasion of Britain was sound only so long as Germany did not seize the French Channel ports. To prevent this and to reinforce the French generally, he constructed a six-division-strong British Expeditionary Force (BEF) that could be deployed on the Continent within fifteen days.

---

* Which, in keeping with contemporary usage, will henceforth be described in the text as the Unionist Party.

Theoretically, the BEF could be used anywhere, but the assumption (if not stated explicitly) was that it would be sent across the English Channel to fight the Germans. The foreign policy implications were that Britain could be drawn into making what it had long avoided: a Continental commitment. For this to have value, holding military staff talks – 'conversations' in the parlance – with the French made sense. The groundwork for this had already been laid. Paris-Berlin relations were at a particular low, exacerbated by assertive German gestures in Morocco. The French Ambassador sought reassurance from Grey at the Foreign Office that in the event of hostilities breaking out, his country could count upon British support. Grey gave a personal opinion that Britain would not stand aside but insisted he could give no *carte blanche*. When, in reply, the French suggested initiating staff talks, Grey discussed what to do first with Haldane and subsequently with the Prime Minister and the Leader of the House of Lords, the Marquess of Ripon. They gave the go-ahead. Yet the matter was not discussed in Cabinet. Doing so would have been problematic given that the Liberal Party fissure between its imperialist and semi-pacifist wings ran across the Cabinet table too. In the circumstances, it was an extraordinary omission from the Cabinet agenda.

In the Commons, however, the passage of Haldane's Army reforms had been a personal triumph for their author. Besides an Imperial General Staff, a Territorial Army and a British Expeditionary Force, Haldane also established Officer Training Corps at universities and a Combined Cadet Force in schools, fulfilling his expectations for future officers who were scholars. If not a Hegelian army, then at least it would be one led by those for whom the German philosopher was not a closed book. Backed by the Unionists, there was never much difficulty in ensuring these reforms were carried through both houses of Parliament. This, in itself, demonstrated how far Haldane had gone in quelling the fears of the country's more reactionary elements who had assumed the nation's defence was not safe in Liberal hands. But his trump card was played in confronting opposition from his own party's quasi-pacifist wing. By enhancing efficiency and trimming the Army's size by 16,600 men, his reforms reduced the cost of the Army Estimates from £30 million to £28 million. While it was recognised that he was a poor public speaker, his high-minded obfuscatory style, which many found difficult to follow, had its uses. Asquith commented, only partly in jest, 'He has got the most contentious measures through the House of Commons without anyone understanding what they were about. I believe that in his hands the People's Budget would have gone through without a ripple!'[5]

By contrast, Balfour – who had returned to the Commons with a new seat – wryly observed, 'Asquith's lucidity of style is a positive disadvantage when he has nothing to say'.[6] As Chancellor of the Exchequer, Asquith had taken to the Treasury with remarkable self-assurance. He delivered his first Budget speech in April 1906. His Permanent Secretary regarded it as having been spoken with 'such lucidity and fluency as if he had been making Budget speeches all his life'.[7] He looked at first to maintain the shibboleths of Gladstonian rectitude, free trade and retrenchment of public finances. The first task of an administration assumed to be radical was to provide reassurance that it was orthodox. But in his second Budget the following year, Asquith created a distinction between the rate of taxation on earned and unearned income.

His real accomplishments, though, were to create the climate for his successor's yet more aggressive programme. Asquith softened up the Treasury for the prospect of progressive, graduated, income tax. He also established the proposals for old age pensions although he underestimated the cost to the Exchequer that they would soon involve. Asquith laid out these proposals in his 1908 Budget speech. As one of his biographers, Roy Jenkins, has pointed out, 'The terms in which he did so were typically non-emotional. There were no references to the secure and contented evening of life which he was promoting for an indefinite series of idealised old couples.'[8] By the time the old age pensions measure was enacted, the Chancellor taking the credit was the great Celtic phrase-maker, David Lloyd George. This was because Asquith had reached his ambition and become Prime Minister.

Campbell-Bannerman had proved a more able performer than the confederates sitting up late in the Relugas fishing lodge had conceived possible. However, in a principal respect they were right. The burdens were too great for him. During 1907 his attentions were increasingly directed towards nursing his dying wife rather than carrying out his responsibilities as Prime Minister. These tasks increasingly fell to Asquith, whom he dubbed, on account of his effectiveness, 'the sledgehammer'. No sooner had Lady Campbell-Bannerman died than her husband's health began to crumble too. After a succession of heart attacks, the stricken Prime Minister summoned his sledgehammer to his bedside and assured him, or so the latter remembered it, that 'You are the greatest gentleman I ever met' and added, by way of a parting reassurance – whether for this world or the next – 'This is not the last of me; we will meet again, Asquith.'[9] A few days later, on 3 April, he resigned.

Unfortunately, King Edward was in Biarritz and had no wish to cut short his holiday just in order to have his hand ceremonially kissed by the new

Prime Minister. Rarely, indeed, had there been less need for the monarch to play more than this most ceremonial of walk-on parts. The choice was so obviously Asquith that there was no need for the King to be in London to take soundings on the appointment. Indeed, he had assured Asquith back in February that he would be sending for him in the event of Campbell-Bannerman's resignation. Thus rather than the monarch going to meet his new Prime Minister, Asquith travelled to Biarritz to kiss hands, the ceremony taking place in the King's hotel room on 8 April (the King had to be dissuaded from expecting all the Cabinet members to venture down to Biarritz to receive their seals of office). In whatever manner Asquith may have imagined the moment of his elevation, a French hotel was doubtless not in his thoughts.

When he stepped back out of the train carriage at Charing Cross, his family was there to greet him. After a courtesy call on Campbell-Bannerman who was still occupying 10 Downing Street (he died on 22 April), Asquith was driven to Cavendish Square with Margot, Vaughan Nash (his new private secretary) and Haldane. A party meeting subsequently confirmed him as leader of the Liberal Party as well. Staying on initially at Cavendish Square was no hardship. When the move was finally made, Downing Street seemed almost a come-down, Margot describing the most famous private residence in Britain as 'an inconvenient house with three poor staircases'.[10]

In forming his new Cabinet, Asquith kept Haldane and Grey, his two closest colleagues, in their existing portfolios. Despite the Liberal Party's supposed disinterest in the hereditary principle, there were three sons of famous statesmen in the new Cabinet: Winston Churchill entered, aged thirty-three, as President of the Board of Trade; Herbert Gladstone became Home Secretary and Lewis 'Loulou' Harcourt First Commissioner of Works. Of this triumvirate, only Churchill was a success. The junior Gladstone proved ineffectual. A menace to schoolboys, 'Loulou' was always one fly-button away from scandal.[11] Asquith had initially contemplated being Prime Minister and Chancellor simultaneously, a burden William Ewart Gladstone had shouldered. After considering the matter, however, he instead sent Lloyd George to the Treasury. Having publicly disagreed on the Welsh Disestablishment Bill, the Boer War and, to an extent, over the 1902 Education Act, Asquith and Lloyd George had a divided political pedigree. Haldane, in particular, did not trust the Welshman. But the elevation of Lloyd George as Chancellor of the Exchequer would prove to be the key appointment. It appeased the Left in the party and promoted a dynamic figure to implement the great programme of social welfare provision.

During his own term as Chancellor, Asquith had set in motion new spending commitments – in particular for old age pensions which Lloyd

George now found himself having to raise taxes to fund. Added to this, the naval race between the British and German fleets was proving increasingly expensive to maintain. In April 1909, Lloyd George unveiled the response, provocatively branded as the 'People's Budget'. The measures included a 'supertax' in supplement to income tax and a land tax. There was outrage from those expected to pay. The City was in uproar. Landowners, their revenue long depressed by agricultural recession, believed this latest assault was motivated by malice. The Unionist majority in the House of Lords decided it was tantamount to a social revolution and in November, after a pause for thought that never went beyond a gulp of indignation, decided by 360 votes to 75 to veto the Budget. In doing so they instigated a constitutional revolution. The House of Lords had not vetoed a finance Bill of this kind for two hundred and fifty years, more than long enough to create a settled precedent on the matter. Nor was it just a historic nicety. Denying an elected government the means of financing its measures made its life impossible.

The peers came up with a novel pretext for their actions, arguing that they could not pass a Budget of this magnitude unless it had been specifically endorsed by a referendum. From his dispatch box in the House of Commons, Asquith gave the peers' presumption short shrift, accusing the Upper House of 'new-fangled Caesarism' in its attempt to morph 'into a kind of plebiscitary organ'.[12] Referendum there would not be, but from a general election there was no escape. A snap poll was called, with the Liberals united under the slogan, 'Peers versus the People'.

It was an eight-week campaign. For Haldane the timing could not have been worse. He was detained in London with a serious eye infection. At one stage the doctors thought he would lose the sight of one eye. As if this was not enough, he had also been diagnosed as a diabetic – which had killed his father. Special diets were the only medicine available at the time and this was a regime that could not have been to the epicurean's liking. In consequence, Haldane was laid up and had to rely on his sister, ably bolstered by guest appearances from Asquith, to help run his constituency campaign in East Lothian. As for the Prime Minister, Asquith was so exhausted by the electioneering that, at the close of the campaign, he departed for a quick holiday in Cannes, forgetting that he was supposed to dine with the King at Windsor. When made public, this oversight encouraged accusations of prime ministerial lese-majesty.

Yet, while Asquith's stamina proved unequal to the demands of the election stump, Lloyd George revelled in the fight. The easily caricaturable attitude of reactionary peers suited perfectly his powers of radical invective. To a mass meeting in Newcastle back in October 1909, he had described them as five hundred 'ordinary men chosen accidentally from among the unemployed'. It was a theme he returned to during the election campaign. Whether such powerful irreverence won converts or convinced waverers that the Chancellor was a class revolutionary was moot. But what was not in question was that the election, and the Budget that had caused it to happen, propelled Lloyd George to the centre of attention. Here was an early warning that despite having friends running the Foreign and War Offices, Asquith had a potential rival in his midst.

The contest certainly captured the public imagination, or at any rate that of the seventy per cent of adult males who were entitled to vote. Indeed, the general election of January 1910 recorded the largest turnout – ninety-two per cent – of any election in British history. But it was not a repeat of the 1906 landslide. The innovations and alarms of the intervening four years had chipped away at the government's breadth of appeal. Asquith and Haldane were returned comfortably, but their party was reduced to 275 MPs while their Unionist opponents recovered to 273. It was thus a hung Parliament and Asquith would now stay on in office thanks to the support of 82 Irish National and 40 Labour MPs. This meant that Irish home rule would have to come back on to the agenda. But given that neither of these two minority parties had any intention to work with the Unionists, Asquith's government remained relatively safe, provided for with what most prime ministers would have craved – a three-figure majority.

On 28 April the House of Lords backed down on the Budget and, acknowledging the verdict of the general election, passed – without a division – the Finance Bill. But the government were now determined to introduce legislation that would permanently clip the Upper House's veto powers and, with it, their ability to block Irish home rule. Such a measure would first have to be accepted by the peers, who saw no reason to perform an act of self-immolation. To circumvent their veto, Asquith discussed with King Edward the appointment of new peers in order to secure a majority for the Bill. There was a precedent: Queen Anne had created twelve Tory peers in order to get the Treaty of Utrecht passed into law. Yet, to ensure a Liberal majority in 1910 it would require over four hundred new peers. All peerages were hereditary and to do this would produce a massive and unwieldy upper chamber as well as encourage accusations of gerrymandering, bringing the monarchy into divisive politics and creating peers out of some with questionable credentials. From June to November, a constitutional conference was convened at Downing Street where the Liberal and Unionist leaders tried to broker a deal. Surprisingly, given his radicalism and rhetoric, it was Lloyd George who drew up proposals for a coalition, a concept that was

attractive to Grey. But Balfour feared that such an unnatural entity would
ensure schism within the Unionist Party. The party had already self-inflicted
grievous wounds over protectionism and he had no desire to repeat the fate
of Sir Robert Peel. In November, the conference broke down. Asquith called
a second general election. This time it would be a short, whirlwind campaign.

The result was all but a replication of the January contest, the main parties
tying on 272 seats and the Liberals again forming a government with the
support of the Irish Nationalists and Labour Members. It was a sufficient
mandate for Asquith to proceed. Even he was astonished how badly the peers
had played their hand, squandering their ancient power in the space of a
year. By January 1911 he believed 'the House of Lords, as we have always
known it, is as dead as Queen Anne'.[13] The Parliament Bill was duly introduced in the Commons. It set out to remove the Lords' veto on finance Bills
and also on other legislation that had been passed three times in the
Commons (so long as two years had elapsed between the initial second
reading and the last third reading).

Haldane, meanwhile, had come to feel that he had achieved what he had
set out to do at the War Office and was ready for a change. When he turned
down the offer of Secretary of State for India, Asquith made him a new
offer – Leader of the Liberal peers in the House of Lords. It would mean
taking a peerage but this was an elevation Haldane was more than ready to
accept. In March 1911 he became Viscount Haldane of Cloan. More important than the title were the duties that came with it. He was charged with
marshalling the Liberal peers just as the great showdown in the House of
Lords was about to reach its denouement.

In July, it was revealed that Asquith had secured the consent of the new
King, George V, to create the necessary peers if the upper chamber vetoed
the legislation. This concentrated minds. There were ugly scenes in the
Commons, Asquith having to endure a barracking from the Opposition
benches – including the undignified sight of Privy Counsellors hurling abuse.
The ferocity was such that he eventually gave up the attempt to speak and
sat down. No past Prime Minister had ever been treated with so much
disrespect on the floor of the House of Commons. But the animus was
poisonous, particularly because it at last looked as if he was winning the
battle of wills. On 10 August, the House of Lords accepted the Parliament
Bill by 131 votes to 114. Its bluff called, the official Unionist position in the
Lords was to abstain. The Government got its way because 37 Unionists led
by Lord Curzon voted with Haldane's Liberals. Asquith had won a major
victory. The aristocratic safety valve on popular democracy had been prised
open.

For Haldane, their Lordships' House was a natural home. He had no desire to be Prime Minister and thus any hindrance that a peerage made towards this goal was wholly immaterial. Yet, while he had achieved his objectives at the War Office, his mind was still preoccupied with matters of defence and he would gladly have accepted responsibility for the Admiralty had Asquith not believed the Navy's cause would be better defended from a performer in the Commons of Winston Churchill's unflagging stamina. In this, the timing was crucial. Franco-German tension had again flared up over Morocco, leading the French to suggest a new round of military 'conversations' with Britain. Amazingly, Grey had omitted (or forgotten) to brief Asquith when he became Prime Minister on the 1906 decision he had taken with Campbell-Bannerman and Haldane to initiate Anglo-French staff talks. Asquith was no dictator and he let his colleagues run their departments with a minimum of prime ministerial interference. The downside of this relaxed attitude was that it reduced collective accountability and co-ordination. Thus, it was not until April 1911 that Asquith, by then three years into his term of office, learned about the 1906 'conversations'. When the matter was finally brought up in Cabinet, several members around the table were horrified. Asquith insisted that no staff talks could be entered into that committed Britain, directly or indirectly, to naval and military intervention without the prior sanction of the Cabinet. This was not, as such, a ban on further conversations.

Although Asquith had decided it was best that Churchill assumed responsibilities as First Lord of the Admiralty, he recognised that Haldane could still lend important ballast from the Liberal peers as well as personally at Cabinet meetings. For these reasons, Haldane remained on the Committee of Imperial Defence and was relied upon by Asquith to advise, and, where necessary, lend support to Churchill's new cause in what had become a full-scale naval arms race with Germany. In 1905, the Royal Navy had launched the 'Dreadnought' class, a faster and more heavily armoured warship. The problem was that by starting again with this revolutionary new standard, the technological development gave latecomers to armada-building a chance of catching up with the previously indomitable Royal Navy. The Dreadnought's obvious superiority effectively consigned much of the world's existing warships – the multi-funnelled flotillas of the White Ensign – to the breakers' yards. What was more, construction of this new class of warship was expensive and cut into funds that might otherwise have been allocated to the government's social reform programme. Yet in 1909, bowing to professional and public opinion, the Cabinet was browbeaten into agreeing to build four Dreadnoughts at once and a further four the following year.

It was not in Britain's interest for this arms race to keep accelerating. Following the 'Agadir incident' that so enraged France, the Kaiser sent out conciliatory feelers to London, suggesting his senior ministers should meet with their British opposite numbers. It was a proposition worth considering but such public parleys, with their reliance on managing popular expectation and national pride, were tricky affairs. In Haldane, Asquith believed he might have an answer. In February 1912 the Prime Minister secured the Cabinet's backing to send Haldane on a private mission to Berlin. There, he would talk directly to the Kaiser, the Chancellor, Theobald von Bethmann-Hollweg and also the chief exponent of German naval expansion, Alfred von Tirpitz. His brief was to see if they were responsive to a suggestion that Britain would slacken off Dreadnought construction if Germany did likewise. These were high stakes. So that hopes were not built up and nobody ran the risk of losing public face, it would be made clear that although Haldane travelled with the government's blessing, he would behave as if he was on a private mission. For a secretary, he took his brother John, the distinguished Oxford physiologist. The (incredulous) press were assured that the trip concerned the Haldane brothers' university interests. So that the pretence was kept up, Haldane casually scattered some educational pamphlets around the Berlin hotel room in which he received some inquiring British journalists.

Haldane already knew the Kaiser. He had accepted his invitation to observe the German Army manoeuvres in 1906 and had reported back to King Edward VII, holidaying in Marienbad, on what he had seen and learnt. When, the following year, the Kaiser visited Britain, Haldane had been duly dispatched to keep him company at Windsor Castle. They had met again in 1911, when the Kaiser and his staff visited London following King George V's accession. Haldane had taken the opportunity to invite the senior German generals to lunch in his home at 28 Queen Anne's Gate. The Kaiser promptly invited himself along too. Haldane had bought the property in one of London's most desirable residential streets, conveniently close to Parliament Square, when he became a Cabinet minister. It was a substantial town house. He had his study on the second floor somewhat self-consciously decorated with the portraits of philosophers and statesmen. His Imperial Highness was duly amused by the Haldane residence, which he christened the 'Dolls' House'. The dining table endured the weight of Edwardian cookery; above it a fine collection of moustaches mixed with the clean-shaven minority, the Kaiser and his generals sitting shoulder to shoulder with the likes of Lord Kitchener, Lord Curzon, John Singer Sargent and Edmund Gosse. Also there was Ramsay MacDonald, the Labour politician Haldane had invited along by way of adding eclecticism to the guest list. After lunch, the Kaiser, hearing that his host's sister was upstairs playing with Asquith's youngest son Anthony, climbed the stairs to say hello to them.[14] It was a good start. There was every reason to believe that if anyone could exploit personal goodwill from the German Emperor, it was Haldane.

He arrived in Berlin on 8 February 1912. He had carte blanche to speak freely and openly but not to conclude any agreement without referring it first back to London. In the course of a succession of meetings, he repeated Britain's treaty obligations to defend Belgium, Portugal and Japan. The Kaiser showed him an advance copy of the new Fleet law. Haldane assured him that Germany could build as many battleships as it liked so long as it understood that Britain would construct double the number. Haldane left Berlin generally optimistic but by no means euphoric. His hosts were not, he thought, planning on war, but he retained the apprehension that Tirpitz was a hawkish influence on the Kaiser. This contrasted with the more cautious Chancellor, Bethmann-Hollweg, 'but he was not strong enough to be able to dispel the atmosphere with which the Emperor was surrounded'.[15] The truth of the matter was that the Germans only appeared open to a deal to curtail the naval race if Britain confirmed it would be neutral in any war between Germany and France. This was a restriction on its options that the government would not countenance. Haldane had tried his best. As the carriage doors slammed shut on the train drawing him out of Berlin he could have had little notion what trouble his efforts to foster Anglo-German understanding would eventually brew for himself and his own future on the front line of politics.

Back in London, Haldane's stock reached a new high. In June 1912, Asquith secured for him the post he had always coveted – Lord Chancellor. The vacancy was created by the declining health of Lord Loreburn. Haldane's qualifications to squeeze into the buckle shoes and robes had long been recognised by almost every senior Liberal apart from the late Campbell-Bannerman. To Haldane, the study and practice of law had never been a means to a personal end and a political fulfilment, as it had for Asquith. Rather, to become Lord Chancellor was the summit of his professional ambition. He would sit on the Woolsack once so illustriously occupied by his great-great-uncle, Lord Eldon. That his mother (Eldon's descendant) was still alive to see this family piety honoured only added to his justifiable sense of fulfilment. Asquith had granted his friend's greatest wish. Writing to express his gratitude, Haldane's mind ranged over their long friendship and the deal they believed they had struck back at the Relugas fishing lodge:

More than six years ago you fought a hard fight for your old friend over this great office and now you have yourself bestowed it on him. My feeling I will not try to express. You know how deep it is. My mind goes back to the past, to the days when we travelled together to the Law Courts from John Street, Hampstead, days which I am not likely to forget and are very present to me now. I cannot easily write more.[16]

ELEVEN

Cutting the Rope

Asquith had a supreme advantage for a man in his position. He could switch off. A politician for whom the ideological struggle of politics was all-consuming could have been broken by the multidirectional battering to which he was subjected. Diehard peers threatening a constitutional crisis, militant suffragettes disrupting public order, mounting tensions in Ireland, the distinct possibility of a war with Germany – all assailed his government and his tenure upon Downing Street. But Asquith was not one to give the impression it was all too much for him. Indeed, his very insouciance became a fault in the eyes of his detractors. It was a trait that looked like supreme indifference verging on sheer laziness or even dereliction of duty. What in his own estimation was 'effortless superiority' appeared as detachment to the point of insincerity to those less impressed by the Balliol approach to problem-solving. More properly, it was an example of his ability to transact business efficiently and to compartmentalise. His Cabinet colleague Winston Churchill concluded that Asquith's mind 'opened and shut smoothly and exactly, like the breech of a gun'.[1] Thus armed, he made being Prime Minister in difficult times look effortless. Some found this irritating.

After dinner Asquith enjoyed nothing more than to ease himself round the bridge table, preferably in mixed company. Cards, gambling – the shudder of disapproval from Nonconformist Liberal activists at such heresies can almost be felt. Their leader appeared not to care. He had dropped such baggage at the Balliol front gate. By contrast, Lloyd George remained attuned to chapel sentiments, at least in public. His disinterest in card games was only one of the reasons why the Prime Minister and the Chancellor of the Exchequer seldom socialised despite (or because of) being separated only by a connecting Downing Street door. After Asquith had finished his business for the day, he liked to unwind. He did not want to talk politics with Lloyd George.

Family life, which Haldane lacked but tried to make up for through godchildren and educational initiatives, greatly assisted Asquith's ability to relax. This is not to say that the picture was entirely without blemish. In particular, Margot's health was poor and, as the years passed by, her insomnia became a torment. She had produced two children, Elizabeth and Anthony (Puffin), but pregnancies had proved difficult and dangerous. Her illnesses cost the lives of three children in 1895, 1899 and 1902 and almost ensured her own demise. But her husband's children from his first marriage were meanwhile growing up and proving cause for tremendous pride. Raymond, Beb, Oc and Cys had been sent to Winchester for their schooling and each proceeded from there up to Oxford. Winning the top Classics scholarship to Balliol, Raymond's undergraduate career was even more impressive than that trailblazed by his father. He was President of the Oxford Union, played football and rowed for Balliol, got a Double First in Classics, won the Ireland Prize for Classics (his father had made do with runner-up) and scooped up the Derby and Eldon law scholarships. In 1902, he was made a Fellow of All Souls and went off to the Inner Temple to train as a barrister.

Beb followed in his father's and brother's footsteps to Balliol, also won the presidency of the Union but went down with a Second in Greats, before following on to the Bar. Oc also made the seamless transition from Winchester to Oxford. Perhaps wisely, he decided to plough his own furrow, opting not for Balliol but for New College (although this was hardly a daring choice for a Wykehamist) and took time out before switching to read Arabic. Thus armed, he journeyed to Khartoum where he joined the British administration of Sudan. By the time Cys arrived up at Oxford, winning the same Classics scholarship to Balliol that his father and eldest brother had, he gained the highest Classics distinctions of the family, a First in Mods, the Ireland Prize and the Hertford Prize. Taken collectively, these were Oxford achievements without parallel.

Asquith's interest in his children went beyond distant pride in their intellectual promise. He particularly enjoyed the company of their friends. Their youthful zest and freedom pepped up his (surprisingly lengthy) hours of leisure. When in later years Lady Diana Cooper (as she had by then become) reflected upon her childhood among this social set, she admitted, 'I really loved Mr Asquith. He delighted in the young and the young's conversation, and would talk of poetry and people and weddings and jokes, and he wanted to hold one's hand and feel equal and comforted.'[2] Country house parties and holidays provided the setting for this inter-generational fusion. Indeed, his preference for parties involving sprightly and glamorous youngsters began to replace the hours he had previously spent comparing Bordeaux and pondering the meaning of life with Haldane. The friendship had endured remarkably well but Asquith could not trump securing for Haldane his life's ambition of the Lord Chancellorship. In this respect, the relationship had reached a level of satiation after which there were no greater spoils to offer and share. The mutual esteem was unchanged, their personal and professional reasons for being bound to one another remained. But the increasingly frivolous means by which Asquith found relief from the burdens of office meant that he no more hoped to draw the evening to a close with a weighty discussion on German metaphysics with Haldane than he wanted to talk political shop or sing hymns with Lloyd George. Apart from anything else, philosophy was a subject upon which Haldane could outgun Asquith.

Rather, from 1913 onwards, when Asquith ventured the short evening walk from Downing Street to Queen Anne's Gate, it was increasingly not to call upon his old friend at Number 28 but rather to present himself at the house of Number 24. There lived his acolyte, Edwin Montagu. Almost immediately after the young man's election to Parliament in the Liberal landslide of 1906, Asquith had chosen him to be his private secretary. The relationship was not one of different yet complementary equals as had so long existed between Asquith and Haldane. Montagu was twenty-seven years the Prime Minister's junior, a gap that, together with their difference in seniority upon becoming acquainted, ensured that Asquith's attitude towards him was primarily protective and paternal rather than based upon recognised equality. Having disliked his early schooldays at Clifton College, Montagu had transferred to the scene of Asquith's first minor triumphs – the City of London School. From there he arrived into the peer group of Asquith's children. While an undergraduate, he had been President of the Cambridge Union the term before Beb Asquith had ascended to the presidency of the Oxford Union.

Montagu's peculiarities strengthened the almost paternal affection that Asquith felt for him. There was something of the ugly duckling about him that made him strangely endearing. He had a large head, with pockmarked skin and a moustache. His eyebrows arched down into the bridge of his nose, giving his face an intensity made more eccentric whenever he screwed a monocle into his left eye. For relaxation, he enjoyed ornithology, donning tweeds to scramble over rocks and loiter concealed in bushes with binoculars poised for a fleeting glimpse of something rare and exquisite. He possessed a charm that was tempered by black moods of depression and sensitivity to real or imagined slights.

His background was privileged, with all the complications that status involved. His father was the millionaire Jewish financier, art collector and Liberal MP, Samuel Montagu; the eponymous bank he founded having helped confirm London as the clearing house of the international money markets. This conferred upon the old man – who became Lord Swaythling – a certain hold over others. Edwin Montagu had tried to escape his father's strict adherence to his Jewish orthodoxy, but not entirely successfully: under the terms of the paternal will, he would be disinherited if he married a gentile. In the circumstances, this would be a considerable hardship. For his part, Asquith found the social predicaments of such a background faintly amusing. This was attested in his frequent jests about his eager private secretary's Jewish Middle Eastern ancestry. It might be added that such repeated observations also demonstrated the less enlightened limits of the Prime Minister's liberal creed. He enjoyed referring to his young amanuensis as 'the Assyrian' and to the Queen Anne's Gate residence he purchased in January 1913 – on account of the curtain material – as 'the Silken Tent'.

The Prime Minister and his private secretary remained close even after Montagu moved on and up to his first government post as Under-Secretary of State for India. He was also on hand for holidays. Margot stayed behind but Montagu made a happy companion when in January 1912 Asquith went in search of some winter sun to Sicily. Together they made their way to a hotel on the Mediterranean coast, the Villa Igeia, with its fine marble balcony covered in purple bougainvillaea. There, they were joined by Asquith's daughter Violet and her friend Venetia Stanley. Accompanied by his twenty-six-year-old valet, the sixty-year-old Prime Minister thus chose to rejuvenate with a thirty-three-year-old member of his government and two girls aged twenty-five. Until that moment he had known Venetia Stanley only slightly. She was the youngest daughter of a Liberal peer, Lord Sheffield, at whose two country houses, Penrhôs in Anglesey and Alderley in Cheshire, Asquith was an occasional guest. As such, he had taken a polite and kindly interest in his host's daughter, but nothing more. This was about to change.

Despite the gaps in ages, the trip to Sicily proved a great opportunity to unwind. Armed with their *Baedekers*, the party enjoyed trots in an open carriage over the narrow mountain roads in search of ancient churches. 'We go down to the Crypt – then on through some catacombs,' Violet noted in her diary, 'Montagu pales at the skulls, shivers at the cold – Venetia and I rally him – we re-emerge covered with cobwebs & drippings into the warm sunlight of the friars' garden – full of the smell of Cherry Pie.' The two girls particularly enjoyed teasing Montagu, jumping out at him in the dark to give him a scare. 'He is so frightened – & so frightening', Violet trilled.[3] He took this mickey-taking in good part, mistaking Venetia's playful attention for a sign of possible romantic interest. This, at any rate, may have encouraged his proposal of marriage to her seven months later. There was something worthy of *A Room With A View*'s Cecil Vyse and Lucy Honeychurch about this proposal. Taken aback, Venetia accepted, wavered, then politely turned him down. The truth was that she found him physically repulsive, but sweet.

For Asquith, the holiday in Sicily was a brief but rewarding one, the respite it provided from political reality sharply exposed by a suffragette demonstration assailing his returning train as it pulled into Charing Cross station. The excursion had been important, not just as a brief escape from such cares. Something deeper had happened on the island. A bond had been formed although not, as Montagu imagined, between himself and Venetia. It was Violet who noted that her father was 'bird-happy'. He was certainly *sans souci*. As he pointed out to Venetia three years later when recalling their holiday together, Sicily had been the 'first stage in our intimacy (in which there was not a touch of romance, and hardly of sentiment) ... we had together one of the most interesting and delightful fortnights in all our lives'.[4]

It may be assumed that Asquith had not just been captivated by the Sicilian bougainvillaea. The ageing Prime Minister was clearly attracted to his daughter's friend and his acolyte's futile object of desire. How attracted Asquith was remains a matter of debate. He was, in the pejorative meaning of the observation, old enough to be her father. But care should be taken before jumping to conclusions. Venetia was an unusual girl. This unorthodox appeal is clear from the description given of her by another of her admirers, Lawrence Jones:

> Venetia had dark eyes, aquiline good looks and a masculine intellect. I delighted in her, and we were close friends, but she permitted herself, in the morning of her youth, no recourse to her own femininity. She carried the Anthologies in her head, but rode like an Amazon, and walked the high garden walls of Alderley with the casual stride of a boy. She was a splendid, virginal, comradely creature, reserving herself for we knew not what use of her fine brain and hidden heart.[5]

Asquith began to see her not only at the house parties of his wife's and children's friends. With increasing regularity, he set aside time for her on Friday afternoons when she was staying at her parents' London house in Mansfield Street. Asquith's preferred form of recreation with her was to go for a drive (he was an enthusiast for the open road, although with Horwood, his chauffeur, at the wheel), taking her to Richmond or Hampstead and back. The public nature of these afternoon jaunts does not suggest the Prime Minister was bent on impropriety.

Yet, there is evidence by the postload that the Prime Minister was forming a reliance on the young girl that had obsessive tendencies. The survival of around five hundred and sixty letters from him in Venetia's private papers, written over a mere two-and-a-half-year period, testifies to his devotion.

Although the flood of epistles was certainly not one-way, none of the letters Venetia sent to him have survived. What may be construed by their destruction is entirely conjectural, although it is important to state that Asquith was not a natural archivist – he appears to have disposed of a great deal of correspondence generally. Nonetheless, his letters to her are revealing enough. During 1912, he began replacing the salutation 'Dearest Venetia' with 'My Darling'. This was certainly affectionate, although for much of the following year he was not writing to her much more than once a week. It was thereafter that he became more ardent. By 1914, the Prime Minister was in daily correspondence with the twenty-seven-year-old girl. Some of his expressions raise even the most placid of eyebrows. On 22 March of that year he ventured to assure her, 'I never wanted you more'.[6]

To modern tastes, such a relationship has sexual connotations. Yet, there is no substantive evidence that Asquith's feelings for Venetia were fully consummated. With so much of their time together spent in the company of others, the opportunities for canoodling were minimised. In any case, Asquith's natural pleasure in socialising with his children's friends helped mask the reality that he was increasingly hanging around with one of them in particular. The Prime Minister liked young people. He liked young women. Such traits had long been understood and thought unremarkable by those who knew him well. At any rate, the Stanley family demonstrated few qualms about Venetia's closeness to the Prime Minister. 'I always feel V. is very safe, which is the main thing,' Venetia's eldest sister told their mother, 'as it is her cleverness and intellectual side that is involved much more than her affections, though no doubt she is very fond of P.M.' Although even here the mask of insouciance slipped slightly with the scribbled afterthought '– But you don't think there are signs of her being too fond of him, do you?'[7]

What Venetia did think of him is now anyone's guess. It is not necessary to paint her either as a flirt or the innocent victim of an older man's advances. Many a young girl from a politically aware family would have been innocently thrilled at the prospect of becoming the Prime Minister's confidante. What, indeed, could be more reassuring and perhaps intoxicating? The destruction of her correspondence to him means that the exact nature of her feelings is lost to posterity. Denied this direct insight, the prurient chronicler will naturally turn to the second-guessing of her friends. According to one of Venetia's intimates, Lady Diana Manners (subsequently Cooper), Asquith did have a lecherous streak. Indeed, if she is to be believed, he was in the habit of fondling young women whenever the opportunity presented itself. Intriguingly, Lady Diana saw no contradiction in assuming that the relationship 'must have included some sexual contact', despite recording Venetia's assurance to her that she was still a virgin on her wedding night.[8]

Venetia was, like the Prime Minister's increasing recourse to alcoholic refreshment, a solace and a means of relaxation. As his defenders have been quick to point out, despite the voluminous quantity, most of the notes were short and, given Asquith's speedy dispatch of paperwork, probably took up only a few minutes of his day. This, of course, assumes that he was not spending the intervening hours fantasising about her. He was not though, by nature, a daydreamer. Although his choice was unwise, it was hardly surprising that he sought temporary escape from the poisonous political environment. But his home life was also not without its vexations. Margot, for all her intense loyalty to her husband, was difficult to live with, her constant acerbity sharpened by ill health and insomnia. She was struck by oppressive headaches and, even in an age of wasp-waist corsetry, looked painfully thin. Apparently, there were even periods in which she found speaking difficult, an affliction that could only have surprised those who wearied of her unremitting opinions. In the past, she had always been relaxed about her husband's 'harem' of young female admirers. But by the spring of 1914 she was increasingly anxious about his relationship with Venetia.

Unable or unwilling to order him to desist, she vented her spleen to – of all inappropriate people – Edwin Montagu. She wrote to him accusing Venetia of being a 'deceitful little brute' who 'is even teaching Henry to avoid telling me things. My step-family think all this very good fun and that I would be a fool to mind. I'm far too fond of Henry to show him how ill and miserable it makes me, it would only worry him at a time he should be free.' Margot continued that she wished Venetia could be married off even if she could not understand how Montagu had once wanted to be the groom: 'Good God! To think you proposed to her! A woman without refinement or any imagination whatever'.[9] To which it might be added that, in expressing herself thus to the rejected suitor, Margot displayed her own customary want of tact and human understanding. These were traits that did not endear her to her husband's oldest and increasingly rarely seen friend. But in the circumstances, she could be forgiven for feeling vulnerable.

Asquith's women problems were not confined to his private sphere. He grasped neither the significance of, nor the desire for, female suffrage. The more desperate and violent the suffragette campaign became, the more unreasonable he found it. The tactics were certainly not designed to appeal to his outlook. There were attempts to strip him of his clothes while he played golf at Lossiemouth. On that occasion, his dignity was ably defended by his daughter Violet swinging a golf club at his assailants. She shared his distaste for the women's cause. Other assaults were more serious. His car was ambushed in an attempt to attack him with dog whips. On another occasion a hatchet blow aimed at him instead struck the ear of the Irish Nationalist leader John Redmond. Like husband, like stepdaughter, Margot was also vigorously anti-suffragette. Conjuring the most unnatural deficiency she could imagine, she described them as 'wombless'. The suffragettes responded in kind: Downing Street's windows were regular targets for their stones. But Haldane also had his windows broken. In this he was unfortunate, since he supported the women's message, if not their mode of delivery. He had, after all, lost his heart to a doomed suffragette.

The campaign's resort to violence was not likely to shift the mind of a Prime Minister proud of his intellectual problem-solving. Yet, he had opposed votes for women at least since 1882, long before violence spoke louder than argument. Partly Asquith's calculation was party political – it was (correctly) assumed that women would be more likely to vote Conservative. To others, he fell back on tired arguments, such as that he doubted there was much real enthusiasm for the franchise among most women. Eventually, in July 1912, he agreed to bring forward legislation to extend the male franchise further, allowing for an accompanying Private Member's amendment to be intro- duced that would include votes for women. However, in the new year, the Speaker ruled that such a fundamental change in the meaning of legislation necessitated a new Bill, not an amendment. Privately, Asquith was thankful, writing to Venetia, 'The Speaker's *coup d'état* has bowled over the Women for this Session: a great relief.'[10] But 1913 was not the finest hour of Liberal England. At the Derby, Emily Davison charged on to the race track and was felled by the King's horse. Violent protest invited prison sentences. Hunger strikes were met with the 1913 'Cat and Mouse' Act permitting forcible feeding.

These were far from being the government's only civil order concerns. Syndicalist action by increasingly powerful trade unions threatened not only faltering economic productivity but was also feared to be a direct challenge to capitalist-parliamentary representative society. Trade union membership rose by more than sixty per cent between 1910 and 1914. Forty-one million working days were lost to strikes in 1912. This compared with an average of seven million during the preceding five years. Strikes on the railways and the coal mines were especially serious for an industrialised country that relied on the former for transport and the latter for energy. Worse was the prospect of an armed insurrection in Ireland. In removing the House of Lords' absolute veto, the 1911 Parliament Act's passage had cleared the way for the completion of Gladstone's unfinished business – the granting of Irish home rule. That this enjoyed the majority support of the Irish Catholic population was no more in doubt than that it was vigorously opposed by the island's Protestant minority. For the latter, home rule foreshadowed 'Rome rule'. What was also clear was that the Unionist alliance in Parliament was willing a showdown that would spill beyond Westminster's Gothic Revival precincts.

In 1911, the Unionist Party leadership had passed out of Balfour's languid hold and into the unyielding Calvinist grip of Andrew Bonar Law, a Canadian-born Scot whom it endlessly amused Asquith to put down as a man who had been fashioned not by God but by Glasgow. The extent to which the new leader threatened civil disobedience was clear when he addressed a mass meeting in the forecourt of Blenheim Palace in July 1912. Effectively disavowing the Liberal government's legitimacy, he claimed it was 'a revolutionary committee which has seized upon despotic power by fraud'. Thus he felt able to assure his listeners that 'I can imagine no length of resistance to which Ulster will go, which I shall not be ready to support, and in which they will not be supported by the overwhelming majority of the British people.' It was not unreasonable to assume that this included armed insurrection. Having recently taken the salute before 80,000 members of the Ulster Volunteers, the north's would-be paramilitary defenders, Bonar Law was playing with fire.

He had also put his finger on an important point, for he said 'Ulster', the predominantly Protestant northern counties of the island, and not 'Ireland' in its entirety. Various proposals for giving Ulster limited devolution or temporary exclusion from a Dublin parliament were canvassed. But all either solved one problem by creating another, failed to appease the Irish Nationalists or were rejected by the Unionists. Asquith, in any case, suspected that the Ulster card was being played cynically in order to scupper the creation of a tenable politico-economic entity in the rest of the island. Secret negotiations with Bonar Law in 1913 failed to reach a compromise. Asquith used Montagu's Queen Anne's Gate home for private talks with the Irish Nationalist leader, John Redmond. Redmond ruled out Ulster's exclusion, temporary or otherwise, but indicated that autonomy for the northern province within a home-rule Ireland might be possible.

In January 1914, the Irish Unionist spokesman, Sir Edward Carson, was also summoned into the 'Silken Tent' for talks. He rejected what Redmond appeared prepared to concede. In this unyielding environment, Asquith stood accused of having no plan beyond 'wait and see', an expression he had used in 1911 with which his detractors soon came to hound his every inaction. As far as Ireland was concerned, it meant that if no agreement could be reached before the legislation granting home rule for the whole of Ireland was due to be implemented in the summer of 1914, only the creation of a crisis could force normally irreconcilable foes to draw back and reach a workable compromise. This was a risky reading of the human condition.

In January, the Cabinet decided that legislation passed in Dublin would not apply in Ulster if Belfast's politicians vetoed it. By February, the position had changed. Redmond was prevailed upon to accept Ulster's temporary exclusion from Irish home rule, but the Unionists were not content with what Carson described as a 'sentence of death with a stay of execution for six years'.[11] On 20 March, Asquith was dining with Venetia and her parents at Mansfield Street when he received news of the 'Mutiny at the Curragh'. Around sixty British Army officers were courting dismissal rather than be ordered to suppress the north. Was the government losing control of the Army? The situation was certainly grave. The immediate casualty was J.E.B. Seely, Haldane's successor at the War Office. Asquith assumed the War Secretary's responsibilities in tandem with those of Prime Minister. There could be no more propitious moment for him to take a close look at military affairs. Indeed, the Army's role was now a key consideration with a potential civil war imminent.

In April, the Ulster Volunteers smuggled in a massive consignment of German arms. The Nationalist Volunteers responded with their own gun-running. Ireland was awash with guns and two paramilitary groups ready to start a civil war if the concessions to their camp were too small or those to their opponents too great. In July, a conference held in Buckingham Palace failed to break the deadlock. The legislation granting all Ireland home rule finally passed successfully through all its parliamentary stages in September 1914 (albeit with an amendment coda that foreshadowed a special arrangement for Ulster). But by then, both Redmond and Bonar Law were in rare agreement that the legislation's enactment should be suspended for the duration of the war that had broken out across Europe. How long that conflict might last was unclear.

On 28 June 1914, the heir apparent to the Austro-Hungarian throne, the Archduke Franz Ferdinand, and his wife were assassinated while on a drive through the streets of Sarajevo. It was not the first regicidal murder in recent years, not even the first to strike the house of Habsburg. But most of the assassins of recent years had been anarchists and other disaffected individuals. This time the conspirators were Serb nationalists. In view of this, Franz Ferdinand's uncle, the Austro-Hungarian Emperor Franz Joseph, was not prepared to let the matter rest. Given the pan-Slavic solidarity animating

Russian politicians in support of Serbian honour, this boded ill. How serious, remained to be seen. After all, there had been trouble in the Balkans before without the peace of an English summer being greatly disrupted. Cooler heads saw no reason to believe that this unfortunate incident in the Bosnian capital need stop the clocks across Europe. Indeed, three weeks later, on 23 July, Lloyd George assured the House of Commons that Britain's relations with Germany were better than they had been for years and that he could foresee in the not too distant future an opportunity to cut the defence budget.[12]

It was the last possible moment that such a claim could have been made. The following day the situation darkened considerably when news was published of Austria's punitively harsh ultimatum to Serbia. From this moment on, Asquith feared that a European war was a serious prospect, although he confided to Venetia the optimistic prognosis that, 'Happily there seems to be no reason why we should be anything other than spectators.'[13] Haldane was making similar forecasts to his aged mother, reassuring her that although the situation was critical, 'there is no power that really wants war'.[14] These assumptions were quickly overtaken by events. Hoping to prevent a Balkan conflict embracing armies other than those of Serbia and Austria, Grey had sent out invitations to Italy, France and Germany for them to attend a conference in London to discuss the crisis. Italy and France accepted but Germany refused to attend. Come what may, Berlin had decided to aid and abet Vienna and on Tuesday 28 July, Austria duly declared war on Serbia. After dinner with Churchill and his wife and the Russian Ambassador and his wife, Asquith ventured over to the Foreign Office and sat up late discussing the situation with Haldane and Grey. The next morning the Cabinet agreed to put the armed forces on a state of readiness.

Despite their recent *rapprochement*, Britain was not absolutely honour-bound to enter any war in which France got involved. Precedence was certainly against helping out: Gladstone's Liberal government had not declared war when Germany had last invaded France in 1870. But Britain had an 1839 treaty commitment to defend Belgian neutrality and this would be breached if (unlike in 1870) the Germans marched through Belgium on their way to Paris. Whether Britain would honour this undertaking – or say she would – became a test of brinkmanship. 'Of course we want to keep out of it,' Asquith wrote reassuringly to Venetia on Wednesday evening, 'but the worst thing we could do would be to announce to the world at the present moment that in no circumstances would we intervene.'[15] Equally to be avoided was too bellicose a statement from London which might only encourage French and Russian military optimism, thereby making war more, rather than less, certain. In the early hours of Saturday morning, King George

V was persuaded to make a personal appeal to his cousin, Tsar Nicholas II, begging him to delay the provocative Russian Army mobilisation.

Avoiding doing anything to upset the hyper-sensitivities of the two German-speaking Emperors in Berlin and Vienna was the paramount concern. If this failed and a European war ensued in which Asquith decided upon British involvement, the pacifist tendency within the Liberal Party would have to be circumvented. Asquith knew that about half of his twenty-man Cabinet were contemplating resignation if Britain declared war. Probably an even larger share of the backbench Liberal Party and its activists in the country were against British involvement in the clash of European empires. They did not care to join France. They certainly did not want to wind up on the side of the Tsarist autocracy in St Petersburg. Like much of the Liberal press, the *Manchester Guardian* was appalled at the prospect. The radicals of the backbench Liberal Foreign Affairs Committee wrote to Grey making clear their opposition to war, and to Asquith their spokesman even suggested they would withdraw support for the government if any attempt was made to engage Britain in the Continental squabble.[16]

Unless Asquith could shift his party's opinion on this, an attempt to join the war would bring down the administration. He would then have to consider whether to press ahead with war by leading a coalition made up of a cadre of Liberal Imperialist friends like Grey and Haldane supported by the Unionists. The latter's support for war looked increasingly likely but recent battles with Bonar Law made Asquith disinclined to attempt a coalition at this time if it could possibly be avoided. Jotting a note to Venetia on 2 August, Asquith assumed that 'a good ¾ of our own party in the H. of Commons are for absolute non-interference at any price. It will be a shocking thing if at such a moment we break up – with no one to take our place.'[17]

At such a moment, the Prime Minister had need of his friends. And they were the same colleagues who had been with him throughout his career, who had plotted a path of mutual advancement at the Relugas fishing lodge a full nine years previously and who, before that, had stuck together as 'Liberal Imperialists' opposed to the official Liberal Party line criticising British actions in the Boer War. Now, in 1914, Asquith, Haldane and Grey found themselves again painted as a 'war party' and as unreformed Liberal Imperialists augmented in Cabinet by the support of Winston Churchill, an ex-Conservative. Grey and Haldane were acting in concert. Indeed, from 27 July onwards, Grey even took up living at Haldane's house while the crisis lasted. Asquith had found the Lord Chancellor 'diffuse' and 'nebulous' during the Cabinet discussions over the weekend but such, as Asquith had long come to recognise, was Haldane's manner.[18] There was no doubt that, at the crunch, he could always be relied upon to be staunch, even if he had a woolly way of expressing it.

The key player now though was unquestionably the Foreign Secretary. Asquith recognised that if Grey resigned, he too would have to go with him. For his part, Grey made clear he would resign if the government made a firm commitment *not* to intervene under any circumstances. There was, however, another pivotal figure in the shape of the Chancellor of the Exchequer, and he looked like resigning if a commitment to intervene *was* given. This, too, was a huge problem. Yet, while Lloyd George certainly appeared to be counted among the non-interventionists at first, as the days went on he showed some signs of movement. By Monday 3 August, with Germany and Russia at war and with four resignation letters from Cabinet ministers pending, the Chancellor's shifting position towards accepting the possibility of a British declaration of war was especially helpful in persuading other waverers to hold back from walking out. That day, Germany went to war with France. Its method of doing so was via Belgium.

It was the decision of Belgium (now 'plucky little Belgium') to resist the massed German forces mounting on her border that stiffened resolves in Whitehall and at Westminster. In the Commons chamber, Bonar Law announced Unionist support for going to war. More remarkably, Redmond announced Irish Nationalist support. As he passed between Downing Street and the Houses of Parliament, Asquith noticed something odd. He was beginning to be cheered by the sort of people who had never saluted him before. There were crowds, expectant and excited, gathering at the gates of Buckingham Palace too. A tide in the affairs of men, and of nations, seemed to be at the flood. In this strange atmosphere, the Prime Minister began to see how he could keep his Cabinet together and rally the nation at the same time. The Fleet was mobilised to stop the Germany Navy using the English Channel to attack France. A decision on dispatching the British Expeditionary Force could not be long delayed – for such was the projected rate of German advance that there was not much point in the Tommies arriving after Prussian generals were already ordering around Parisian waiters. On the morning of 3 August, Asquith asked Haldane to go to the War Office, convene the Army Council, and see that the necessary mobilisation procedures were being put in motion. It was clear whom he trusted in this moment when the intentions of other colleagues remained unclear.

If Germany had backed down and war had been averted, Asquith would have been as relieved as his colleagues. As is clear from his initial attitude, he was not seeking war. Yet, even he could see that if it did prove impossible to stay out, it might solve some of his existing problems. To his colleague J.A.

Pease, with whom he played an after-dinner rubber of bridge on the evening of 3 August (Asquith's equivalent of Drake's game of bowls as the Spanish Armada approached), the Prime Minister confided that the forthcoming 'hateful war' at least had 'one bright spot' if it brought the antagonistic forces in Ireland together in the nation's hour. Quoting Cowper, he added wistfully, 'God moves in a mysterious way, his wonders to perform'.[19]

At the Cabinet meeting the following morning, the confirmation of the invasion of Belgium was received. The Germans were breaching international law and violently occupying a neutral country on the back of a quarrel started by the assassination of an Austrian by a Serb in the capital of Bosnia. Such outrageous behaviour even offended much Liberal, never mind bulldog, sentiment. Thus, a Liberal Party that had appeared ready to bring down its own government rather than shore up the deadly vanities of European power politics suddenly became convinced that British bayonets were needed if liberal values were to be defended from Prussian militarism. Where only days earlier, half the Cabinet had appeared destined to resign rather than go to war, in the event only two members – John Burns and John Morley – proved irreconcilable when the moment arrived.

That moment came on the evening of 4 August. Handed Britain's ultimatum, Germany was given until midnight Berlin time (11 p.m. in London) to back down from invading Belgium. Failure to comply would be met with a British declaration of war. Shortly after nine o'clock, Lloyd George was summoned to the Cabinet room where he found Asquith, Grey and Haldane already sitting together and 'looking very grave'. 'As the hour approached,' Lloyd George later wrote, 'a deep and tense solemnity fell on the room. No one spoke. It was like awaiting the signal for the pulling of a lever which would hurl millions to their doom – with just a chance that a reprieve might arrive in time. Our eyes wandered anxiously from the clock to the door, and from the door to the clock, and little was said.' And then, the familiar chimes of Big Ben started up, introducing the solemn tolling of the appointed hour. 'A shuddering silence fell upon the room. Every face was suddenly contracted in a painful intensity.' Outside, in Whitehall and down the Mall, patriotic crowds began cheering. In retrospect, Lloyd George believed the great bell was actually tolling a terrible portent. With each strike of the hammer it foretold 'Doom!' 'Doom!' 'Doom!'[20]

✻

Ninety-nine years had passed since victory at Waterloo. Ninety-nine years in which British troops had not seen action in western Europe. Was it a wonder that the effect of this lengthy interval had been to shrink the Regular Army into little more than an order-keeping force for India and the colonies? That it was unfit for the twentieth century had been ably demonstrated in the South African veldt, where it had initially struggled to contain a guerrilla force of Boer farmers. True, some had spent the first decade of the new century drawing far-reaching conclusions from that near-embarrassment. The crusty zealots of the National Service League had campaigned to introduce conscription so that Britain, whose power was at sea, might also project its will by land. But such schemes, however loudly advocated, failed to alter a popular sentiment convinced that while the European powers might compel their citizens to serve in their armies, the trueborn Briton was not an indentured serf at the beck and call of the state. So core was this to liberal values that no plan of Army reform based upon mass conscription could have made headway in the years before August 1914. This Haldane had recognised and it had been his achievement as Secretary of State for War between 1905 and 1912 to come up with a workable alternative – a volunteer Territorial force to guard the mainland and provide a reserve plus a small but highly professional Regular Army capable of rapid reaction and deployment on the Continent at short notice. It was for this that, a few days after the outbreak of hostilities in August 1914, Asquith assured Haldane, 'If the country is prepared for this war, it is to you more than to any other person that it owes it.'[21]

Speed was certainly of the essence. German war plans envisaged a quick knock-out of Belgian resistance in a wide enveloping arc that would outflank and then crush the French armies. This quick victory was needed so that there was time to turn east to confront the lumbering menace presented by a fully mobilised Imperial Russia. In the years before Haldane's reforms, so ambitious a stratagem might have been achieved before the old British Army had negotiated the ticket barrier at Victoria station. But Haldane's British Expeditionary Force was far more nimble. Its problem was not efficiency but size. It numbered only 160,000 men. When, on 5 August, the first full day of war, the Imperial War Council met, Haldane argued that there was no time to be lost and that all six divisions of the BEF should be dispatched across the English Channel immediately. Unfortunately, Lord Kitchener's mind moved less dextrously. The conqueror of the Sudan had been invited to attend the meeting and – despite the existence of the Territorials – expressed his concern about leaving homeland defences under-protected. He insisted that only four divisions should be sent initially. The politicians bowed to the military man's supposed knowledge.

The following day, four divisions of the British Expeditionary Force under the command of Sir John French went in. Nothing had been done by the Germans to disrupt the Royal Navy's command of the Channel and the troops were ferried across in secrecy and without mishap. Sir John was leading a force somewhat smaller than that at the disposal of the King of the Belgians. But it was not, as the Kaiser was minded to pretend, a 'contemptible little army'. Although the British could not turn back the seven armies of 1,500,000 men spearheading the German invasion, they were far from being mere spectators. Rather, the BEF proved, in Basil Liddell Hart's phrase, 'a rapier among scythes'.[22] Its superior marksmanship was displayed when, on 23 August, six divisions of the German First Army, seeking to turn the left flank of the Allied defence, instead smashed straight into two divisions of the BEF south-west of Brussels at Mons and were given a bloody nose. After this hopeful display, the British fell back in good order, moving south to support General Joffre's army as it prepared for a massive counter-attack against the Germans on the Marne. There, only forty miles east of Paris, the German advance was finally halted. The victory was not decisive but it was enough to deny the quick conclusion to the war envisaged by the German High Command. Their operational plan now in tatters, the invaders instead fell back and took up new defensive positions by digging trenches along the Aisne.

With apparent stalemate in the main theatre of war east of Paris, both sides raced to outflank each other to the north in a succession of moves and counter-moves that soon consumed the fast-diminishing stretch of land left between the front and the English Channel. It was there, in Flanders, that the BEF proved its mettle and met its end. Ground down, almost out of ammunition and with gaps plugged by French support, it held out against a month-long German assault at Ypres. The town was far too strategically important to concede but by 11 November, when the attack relented, its defenders had been boxed into a narrow and vulnerable salient from which they would later seek to break out at devastating cost. This first battle of Ypres set the tone for what was to come. The Germans' failure to break through effectively ended the prospect of the war being swiftly won by an enveloping march and the turning of the defenders' flank. Military technology had advanced far enough to deliver withering fire but not yet to the extent of producing mechanised fast movement or precision strikes from the air. It was thus a form of killing favourable to those defending rather than those on the offensive. Both sides quickly recognised this and dug in, creating an unbroken line of trenches and barbed wire from the English Channel to the mountain frontiers of neutral Switzerland. For the BEF, Ypres was its graveyard. With half of the men who had crossed the Channel three months earlier now dead or wounded, Haldane's small but professional army had gone down fighting. From 1915 onwards, its place would pass to the volunteers of the 'new armies' that Lord Kitchener was recruiting at home.

This switch of emphasis had been foreshadowed in the first days of the war in Whitehall. A temporary consequence of the Curragh mutiny crisis, Asquith was Secretary of State for War when the conflict began and, with enough on his plate as Prime Minister, had asked Haldane to deputise for him at the War Office. This Haldane had gladly done and there was speculation that he might return to the role permanently. But it was not a prospect deemed sufficient for the hour. The *Daily Express* snarled that 'this is no time for elderly doctrinaire lawyers with German sympathies to play at soldiers'. The *Express,* and its larger-selling rival, the *Daily Mail,* joined the public clamour demanding Lord Kitchener's appointment. He was the hero who had seen off the Mad Mahdi of Khartoum and could be expected to treat the Kaiser with equal disdain. At any rate, in the war of public relations, it was a comfort that he alone could out-moustache the haughty Hohenzollern. This was a campaign to which Haldane quickly surrendered without a fight.

Kitchener's arrival at the War Office certainly sent out the clearest signal at a time when maintaining national confidence was imperative. However, the press, like the public, had got it wrong. Kitchener's reputation was high and he looked the part. What he was not was an organisational and strategic genius. He had been out in India and Africa too long to comprehend the changes that had taken place in military reorganisation at home. Unlike Haldane, he had a poor grasp of this reality and was not given to seeking elucidation. He singularly failed to grasp the worth of the new Territorial Army and would listen to no reason on the subject. This failure may have been costly. At any rate, it was the subsequent verdict of General Edmonds, the British official historian of the war, when writing about the period immediately following the battle of the Marne that, 'had some of the fourteen British Territorial Force Divisions and fourteen mounted brigades, with the Sixth [BEF] Division still in England, been landed at the Channel coast ports to fall on the German communications and rear, a decisive tactical result might have been obtained and the war finished'.[23] This chance – if it was a chance in a conflict that was full of 'might have beens' – was missed due to Kitchener's inability to comprehend the worth of the forces Haldane had placed at his disposal. Instead he (correctly) calculated that the war would be a long one and that what Britain therefore needed was a mass new army. His appeal for volunteers duly rang out. And for this, the bold features of Horatio Kitchener made a better recruiting poster than the moon-like demeanour of Lord Haldane of Cloan.

Indeed, the response to Kitchener's appeal for men was instant and over-whelming. By the end of September, three-quarters of a million volunteers had enlisted and the flow continued at the rate of 125,000 a month until the summer of 1915. Britain could have it both ways – a mass army but without conscription. Or so it initially seemed. In common with families across the length and breadth of the country, the Asquiths answered the call. Thirty-one-year-old Oc was the first to volunteer. He was soon followed by his brothers, Beb and Cys – who was recovering from typhoid. Raymond preferred to see out one last summer before enlisting. Those who believed the Prime Minister had resolved to go to war with the same insouciance he displayed in determining domestic affairs had, at least, to concede that his sons were prepared to pay the consequences.

That price was already coming home to other senior politicians. When Margot accepted an invitation to visit the Belgian King's headquarters, she took with her a makeshift cross that Lord Lansdowne, the Unionist leader in the House of Lords, had given her. The old man, who as Foreign Secretary in Balfour's government had negotiated the *entente* with France, asked if she could try to find and mark the spot where his son had fallen. In doing so, she was also able to witness at first hand the terrible devastation around Ypres. After years of riding her luck on the hunting field, coming within range of the enemy guns did not cause the indomitable Margot to flinch. Other members of the family confronted the dangers with their own brand of *sang-froid*. When, in the war's eighth month, Cynthia Asquith received the news that her husband, Beb, was finally being sent to the front, she confided in her diary, 'It is very difficult to believe that history will interfere in one's private life to such an extent.'[24]

To be fair, this was no more than the outward mantra of her father-in-law's administration. It was a policy described as 'business as usual' and although the term was not one of the Prime Minister's coining (it was, uncharacteristically, Churchill's), critics soon latched on to it as emblematic of Asquith's overly detached style at a time of national crisis. At first, these grumbles existed but were largely suppressed. The government had been greatly assisted by the declaration of a party truce on 30 July 1914. Parliament, like the nation, had come together to meet the great challenge, as politicians who had been spitting venom at one another days previously over home rule for Ireland suddenly put aside their differences in order to stand shoulder to shoulder in defence of an alternative expression of nationhood – the neutrality of Belgium. Opposition to the war was confined to a few Labour and radical mavericks, among them the future Labour Prime Minister Ramsay MacDonald. In fact, once the emergency legislation was passed, there was not much more for the legislature to do in the first months of a war that was primarily a matter for the executive and the military. Some MPs went off to the front. The party leaders prepared for the consequences by agreeing that by-elections would not be contested.

Beneath this surface of united resolve, the former hostility to Asquith was not entirely extinguished. The bulldog wing of the Unionist Party was unconvinced that the government had the energy and resolve to win a war for which they had inadequately prepared. True, Winston Churchill at the Admiralty showed fighting spirit, but also a reckless streak that was sure to end in trouble. Sir Edward Grey, the Foreign Secretary, could also not be faulted for his commitment to the struggle. But as for the others, Unionists doubted they had the stomach for what increasingly looked like being a long and bloody fight. The appeal to patriotism made it impossible to call for the Prime Minister's head so soon. This did not prevent some backbenchers, aided and abetted by gung-ho journalists' rapid-firing column inches from the secure redoubts of Fleet Street, from undermining him by attacking his colleagues. Haldane, they decided, should be the first scalp.

Haldane's influence over the war effort was far greater than might have been expected for a Lord Chancellor. In the first three months of hostilities, the full Cabinet convened most days of the week. Haldane participated in these meetings and also in the less frequent convocations of the Committee of Imperial Defence. Furthermore, Grey, who was in poor health and plagued by fading eyesight, frequently had to take time off from his duties. During these absences, Haldane filled in as acting Foreign Secretary. This arrangement troubled Tory diehards. Under the misapprehension that it was Haldane rather than Kitchener who had blocked the early deployment of the BEF in its entirety, they were convinced the Lord Chancellor was less than fully committed to the struggle. Ignoring the evidence that he had helped persuade reticent Cabinet colleagues of the case for going to war, Haldane's critics even suspected he was actually pro-German.

In a sense, it had long been a fitting description of his attitude. Nor had he been alone in expressing it. 'What — fools we have been believing that Germany would never go for us!' Margot Asquith sighed to Lord Rosebery after three weeks of war, adding how sorry she felt for 'Poor Haldane and all the pro-Germans among whom I have always counted myself.'[25] She might have phrased her words more carefully but it was true nonetheless. Neither Haldane nor Margot had been of the scaremongering tendency that for many years had preached the inevitability of an Anglo-German war. Instead, theirs was a respectable and honourable internationalism but one that the arrival of conflict made dangerously unfashionable.

With war, jingoism descended into xenophobic loathing of all things German. Fear that the country had been infiltrated by spies gave those sitting idly at home a purposeful feeling that extreme vigilance was a form of war service. But in the slow-beating heart of Liberal England, a more relaxed attitude persisted. For fourteen years, the Asquiths had employed Frau Mayer as a governess for their children. At first, it did not occur to any of the family that housing a German in Downing Street during a war against her homeland was, if not actually a security risk, then at the least sending out a rather casual signal to the nation at large. It fell to Grey to explain the hard reality to the Prime Minister. Reluctantly, he agreed that she would have to return to Munich. Nobly, Margot went to the station to wave her goodbye.

But in the popular imagination, it was the Lord Chancellor who was suspect. As the press relentlessly pointed out, Haldane was, by his own admission, the politician who knew Germany best. Who, then, could be more responsible for failing to forewarn his colleagues of the impending danger of Prussian militarism? The assumption, depicted in prose and cartoon, was that his head had been buried, if not in the sand, then at least in a tome of Schopenhauer. What was worse, Professor Oncken of Heidelberg claimed unhelpfully that while attending a private dinner back in April 1913, he had overheard Haldane describe Germany as his 'spiritual home'. The claim was picked up and given maximum publicity in England. In fact, the quote had been taken out of context. What he had actually said in the course of remembering affectionately his Göttingen student days was, 'Yes, I consider Lötze's classroom was my spiritual home'.[26] This qualification was overlooked in the outburst of indignation that met the revelation that the mind of a senior figure in the British war effort reposed with the enemy. Haldane's plight was made worse in October when *The Times* mischievously printed a letter from Professor Quidde, a Munich academic, to a colleague in Italy praising Haldane for continuing in the Cabinet where he could best exert pro-German influence. In fact, Haldane had never even met the Munich professor. Be that as it may, what the letter's publication demonstrated was that a concerted campaign of character assassination had begun.

Extreme and unfair though the picture they painted of him was, Haldane's assailants had correctly identified what events had conspired to turn into a personal weakness. He did love Germany. Hobnobbing with the Kaiser had given him a wonderful sense of self-importance. So excited was he that he had even, and somewhat unfortunately, named his own dog 'Kaiser'. Haldane's detractors would have been further delighted if they had got hold of a private letter he had written to his mother from Göttingen in May 1912 where he boasted, 'I find myself in Germany more popular than in England. It reminds me of the sort of reception Lloyd George gets when he travels in Wales.'[27] In June 1912, he had assured Lord Northcliffe, proprietor of the *Daily Mail* and *The Times*, that there was no more need to worry at the threatening language of the Kaiser, 'an impulsive and rather excitable man,' than there was to print the rather sharp private musings of the late King Edward VII.[28] Doubtless it was an assessment Northcliffe recalled now that the Kaiser had proved himself as good as his word. In newspaper polemics and cartoons, Haldane started to be mocked for his admiration of German 'Kultur'. His esteem for his intellectual 'home' was contrasted with representations of the German Army's torching of famous Belgian towns and its destruction of the libraries of great Flemish universities. German 'Kultur', in other words, was no more than the triumph of Prussian militarism and the worship of brute force.

The defendant, it has to be said, did not always aid his own cause. His woolly and diffuse mode of expression was no guard against the acutely phrased charges hurled at him. Addressing a local Scottish audience in Auchterarder in aid of Belgian refugees, he may have thought he had struck a homely tone when he compared Germany to a much treasured dog that had once uncharacteristically gone off in the night and attacked sheep. 'That was a sudden outbreak in an otherwise blameless career,' he reassured his surprised audience, 'and what was true of him was true of Germany.'[29] When the quaint analogy was duly reproduced in the national press it appeared lame to the point of offensive. In any case, given what he had christened his dog, Haldane might have been better keeping clear of canine anecdotes. To some, it appeared all part of a pattern. He was speaking at a time when scare stories spread rapidly and a campaign was being mounted to intern foreign aliens. It was in this fevered environment that he frequently found himself restating traditional civil liberty arguments from the Woolsack. That he did not pander to extremist conspiracies was laudable but by making this stand, he further convinced detractors that he was not taking the threat seriously.

The critics believed that, despite the provisions of the Defence of the Realm Act, the unhurried demeanour of Asquith and Haldane indicated that they shrank from the methods necessary to defeat the Prussian military's brutality. It was an irony, given the support for the British Army's 'methods of barbarism' that Asquith and Haldane had professed against their own Liberal Party line during the Boer War. Unimpressed, cartoons published in the *Daily Express* showed Haldane as a fat lawyer whose sizeable salary as Lord Chancellor hung around his neck in the shape of a medallion inscribed with £10,000. To its opponents, the Liberal government contained far too many clever lawyers for its own good. Were men whose profession was to argue a brief for money really the stalwart patriots upon whom national deliverance depended? Asquith was a supreme exemplar of this tribe but the salary drawn by his well fed friend reposing comfortably on the Woolsack appeared excessive when boys up from the mines were making the ultimate sacrifice, alone, cold and screaming in agony from shrapnel lacerations in the cratered hell of No Man's Land.

The snipers zeroing in on the bulky target of the Lord Chancellor were mostly gentlemen of the press. Their shots rang out from several directions. He had few admirers at the palaeo-conservative *Morning Post,* a newspaper still appealing to the throne-and-altar sentiments that had been fashionable when it was founded in 1772. But, as its dwindling circulation demonstrated, the paper was past its best and its aim was shaky. Nor, despite its temporary popularity, did he have to duck too much from the blunderbuss marksmanship of *John Bull,* a xenophobic scandal rag produced by Horatio Bottomley, a sometime Liberal MP, fraudster and self-promoting proto-fascist who was himself riding for an almighty fall. Another irritant was the *Daily Express,* which, although not yet brought under the guiding genius of the future Lord Beaverbrook, had a circulation of a quarter of a million and unceasingly fired cracks at Haldane.

More concerning still was the hostility displayed by Lord Northcliffe's two greatest titles, the *Daily Mail* and *The Times.* Supposedly written by office boys for office boys, the *Mail* with a circulation of one and a quarter million proved, *pace* Napoleon's shopkeeping jibe, that England was now a nation of office boys. As such, it spoke for a sizeable proportion of the lower middle class – patriots who were not to be patronised. An early exponent of airplanes, Northcliffe had a particular grievance against Haldane, whom he held responsible for failing to take the military possibilities of airpower sufficiently seriously. In this shortcoming, the former War Secretary was hardly alone. At the start of the war, Northcliffe had wanted Britain's contribution restricted to naval action and had to be talked round to letting his papers endorse sending the BEF to France.[30] No matter, he now decided that it was Haldane's judgement that was to be questioned. Northcliffe interfered less persistently with the editorial policy of *The Times,* still held up as the greatest newspaper in the world, but on the issue of Haldane he did not need to assert himself. The paper's editorial 'Blackfriars' had taken against the former friend of Germany on their own accord. True, *The Times* sold less than 150,000 copies a day, but, unfortunately for its target, they were all the most influential people in the country.

However, Haldane's most virulent critic was the editor of the right-wing *National Review.* French-educated (and imbued with a Gallic hatred of

Haldane's supposed 'spiritual home'), Leo Maxse had run a high-profile 'Balfour Must Go' campaign that had helped force Balfour from the Unionist leadership in 1911. He hoped now to repeat a similar feat by seeing off Haldane, who he believed was equally ineffectual. A scourge of fey intellectuals and a gifted polemicist, Maxse could have been a great Fleet Street columnist in any phase of the twentieth century. He disparaged Haldane's efforts to set himself 'up as an authority upon Germany on the strength of his having been annually bamboozled by German professors in his earlier days'. Indeed, according to Maxse, Haldane had spent the last years of peace at the head of a British 'Potsdämmerung' of 'ex-Ambassadors on the stump, Cocoa Quakers, Hebrew journalists at the beck and call of German diplomats, soft-headed Sentimentalists, cranks convinced that their country is always in the wrong, [and] Cosmopolitan financiers domiciled in London in order to do "good work" for the Fatherland'.[31] The various demons in Maxse's head rose up as one, and reassembled themselves in the guise of the Lord Chancellor.

Some of the popular charges were simply absurd, the fiction of hacks' imaginations. It was put about that Haldane was the Kaiser's illegitimate half-brother. Another story had it that the Scottish bachelor actually had a wife in Germany. Those who imagined that Haldane's student days at Göttingen and Dresden tainted his patriotism did not draw the same conclusions about one of Bonar Law's sons. Nor was there a proper understanding of his past dealings with the Kaiser. That Haldane had thrown open his own home to entertain Wilhelm in May 1911 looked bad in the light of subsequent events. It pealed the same ring of society appeasement that tarnished the reputation of the 'Cliveden Set's' efforts to understand and excuse Hitler in the 1930s. The fact that Lord Kitchener, Sir John French and Sir Ian Hamilton – Britain's senior warriors – had also joined the Kaiser around Haldane's dinner table that day was conveniently overlooked. This was as nothing compared to the reawakened suspicions about what Haldane had been up to in his mission to Berlin the following year. Fearing that sending the Prime Minister or Foreign Secretary would only raise stakes that the Kaiser would take delight in ruining, the Cabinet had sent Haldane. whose annual holidays in Germany and trips there on education business provided a pretext for anonymity. Haldane had generated further suspicion at the time by assuring the *Daily Mail*'s Berlin correspondent that he could tell his paper 'unequivocally' that his trip 'is of an entirely non-political character. I am here for quite private reasons. I have many friends in Berlin, as you know, and I shall see them, I hope, as well as other interesting persons, but I am not here for politics.'[32] This was a lie and its exposure added to the belief that Haldane had been up to something about which he did not want the British public to find out.

Challenged to do so in a House of Lords debate, Haldane refused to release the details of a private letter he had received on the eve of war from Albert Ballin, a German interlocutor who had helped arrange his 1912 mission to Berlin and who had dined with Haldane at Queen Anne's Gate only days before hostilities were declared. *The Times* had alerted its readers that such a letter had been sent. In fact, it had been unsolicited and Haldane had not replied to it. But his commitment to old-fashioned confidences appeared suspicious, especially since Ballin was reportedly claiming Britain had not made clear it would stand by Belgium. The *Daily Express* offered any reader one hundred pounds who could obtain details of what 'Bal' had written to 'Hal'. When, many years later, the letter was eventually published post-humously, its contents were found to be wholly innocuous. However, the more the press and the public became convinced that the government had failed to comprehend the nature of the German threat in the years leading up to August 1914, the more they blamed Haldane, with his supposed understanding of the German psyche, for failing to provide them with the warning. This was the same man, they now decided, who should have pressed for a mass army rather than the small professional BEF. How damaging these charges were was clear when, in late 1914, Haldane was spotted easing himself into his seat in a West End theatre. Sections of the audience began booing and shouting unhelpful suggestions about where he should take himself.

In January 1915, Churchill wrote to Haldane encouraging him not to 'allow this trash to worry you even for an hour'.[33] Trying to be helpful in her artless fashion, Margot Asquith wrote to Maxse of the *National Review* – 'Dear Mr Leo' – a typically long and rambling letter that, while seeking to defend Haldane, only made matters worse by concentrating on point-scoring on irrelevancies while conceding the major ground that Haldane had 'striven for peace' with Germany.[34] The truth of the matter was that there had been nothing shabby, incompetent or unpatriotic about Haldane's actions in the years leading up to the war. The problem was that neither Asquith nor Grey wanted to reveal details of the 1912 negotiations. Had they done so, popular suspicion over Haldane's role might have abated. Of course, it was perfectly understandable why, during a war, a government might not wish to publish details of past diplomatic overtures, but the silence made it look as if there was something to hide and that the person being covered up for was Haldane.

In fact, all that the government needed to do was to publish what amounted to a twenty-page memorandum covering the Anglo-German discussions which had been drawn up in September 1914. But Grey reportedly believed doing so would only give 'the Germans fresh opportunities for misinterpretation' and he did not wish 'to give himself or his department the extra strain of preparing papers and having to deal with all the questions which would at once be raised here and in neutral countries'.[35] To be fair, there was a war on and the Foreign Office was busy. But the minor inconvenience was as nothing to the misinformed animosity building up against one of the government's most important figures. 'If my full story could have been made public I think that the attacks would have been destroyed', Haldane later wrote in his autobiography. In the event, he was to receive no such support and 'I had therefore to remain unshielded'.[36]

He certainly had good reason to worry. For the campaign building against him existed not just in Fleet Street but also in the Palace of Westminster. In February 1915, one of his most dedicated assailants in the press, Arnold White of the *Daily Express,* assured Maxse that he had talked the matter over with the Unionist triumvirate of Bonar Law, Edward Carson and Walter Long. They had 'no desire to abandon the campaign against Haldane just as the scent was burning' and were equally 'anxious to be present in Whitehall and St James's Street when the plump body of the Member for Germany swings in the wind between two lamp posts'.[37] With enemies like these, the Lord Chancellor had urgent need of his friends.

Asquith had problems enough of his own. By November, the full Cabinet's regular meetings had been scaled back to once a week so that the main decisions could be taken by a more streamlined body, the War Council. This was the Committee of Imperial Defence rebranded and it was chaired by Asquith with Grey, Lloyd George, Lord Crewe, Churchill, Balfour, Kitchener and the Chiefs of Staff in attendance. Haldane joined this pivotal group in January. At the beginning of 1915, various options for breaking the deadlock on the Western Front began to be seriously canvassed. Lord Fisher, the First Sea Lord, wanted landings on the German Baltic coast. Lloyd George was interested in fighting up through Salonika. Churchill, the First Lord of the Admiralty, was formulating an idea for a naval campaign against Germany's Turkish ally with the objective of forcing open the Dardanelles Straits and capturing Constantinople.

Great claims were made for this plan. Supposedly it would knock the Ottoman Empire out of the war. It would open the route to supplying Russia and provide a springboard to march through Austria-Hungary and – at a stretch – on to Berlin. Where either the supplies or the troops were to come from to achieve these ambitious feats was never properly explained. However, in terms of producing immediate results, it was much more tempting than sending more men to burrow fruitlessly like moles in the waterlogged earth of Flanders. The Straits were but lightly defended and gaining control of the Bosporus thus appeared well within grasp. Yet, having claimed the operation would need the landing of 150,000 men to succeed, Kitchener changed his mind and concluded the Straits could be forced by naval guns alone. Thus in February when the operation began, it merely took the form of a naval bombardment of the Ottoman defences. This alerted the Turks to what was afoot and they quickly made good their defensive deficiencies. By the time in late April that troops were eventually deployed to follow up the bombardment, the key advantage of surprise had been squandered. Instead of a rapid advance, the Allied troops found themselves pinned down on narrow landing grounds along the Gallipoli peninsula, unable to seize the strategic cliffs from where the Turks poured down an unremitting torrent of fire and invocations to Allah. The British, Australian and New Zealand troops responded by digging trenches. The great punch on the rear of the Central Powers duly descended into the same defensive tactics that had immobilised movement, but not death rates, on the Western Front. Gallipoli was not to be the springboard. It was scarcely a bridgehead. Rather, terrible losses piled up in defence of a foothold.

Fast descending into fiasco, the Dardanelles campaign touched the Prime Minister personally. In May, it was the turn of Oc Asquith's battalion of the Royal Naval Division to go ashore. He had already lost *en route* his good friend, the poet Rupert Brooke, to blood poisoning. Brooke's corner of a foreign field among the olive trees on Skyros represented a loss that shook the whole Asquith family. The Prime Minister had been moved to ponder whether his daughter Violet's friendship with Brooke might have developed into 'something more' if only the poet had survived and that the death had given him a terrible premonition for 'my much beloved Oc – or Beb, who went off to-night to the front in France'.[38] Sure enough, it was not long before Asquith received bad news – Oc had been hit. But soon afterwards, it became clear that he had in fact been the beneficiary of a stroke of extraordinary fortune because the bullet had passed cleanly through his left leg, narrowly missing his kneecap. The medics concluded there was no need for amputation. Asquith was especially cheered to discover that his son had been spotted as he was being carried away from the battlefield remonstrating with the stretcher bearer to put him down so that a wounded private who was in greater pain could be picked up instead. Few products of Asquith's life ever reflected so well on him as the character of his children.

With his children's friends, the Prime Minister also remained close and, in the case of Venetia Stanley, far too intimate. By the outbreak of the war, Asquith was writing to her daily. Sometimes he wrote several times a day. On one occasion he managed four in a day. For a sixty-two-year-old man writing to a twenty-seven-year-old girl, this was excessive and open to misconstruction. That the middle-aged man should be the Prime Minister in the midst of an increasingly calamitous war was distinctly unusual. True, it did not take Asquith long to compose these missives and many were tossed off in brief moments of respite. As such they were a form of therapy. Within London, the postal service was so efficient that it operated like a slower form of email, allowing several messages a day to be sent and replies received. But not only were many of Asquith's notes considerably longer than the average early twenty-first-century email, his tendency to write to her during Cabinet discussions of war policy suggests that a degree of infatuation had unbalanced his sense of priorities. Was he giving his mind fully to the grave peril of the British forces, or was he smiling to himself while composing *billets-doux?* Amazingly, he actually added to his troops' peril because he sought to impress Venetia by disclosing highly secret information about military strategy in his correspondence. For anyone in his position, let alone one with four sons in harm's way, this was a scandalous gamble with national security for the sake of showing off to a young girl. Given that Asquith regularly posted them in the letter box outside the Athenaeum Club on Pall Mall, the risk of their being intercepted was not insignificant.

Within three weeks of the war starting, Asquith was writing to Venetia that 'It will be 27 years to-morrow since you opened your eyes on this sinful world, and it is not yet quite 3 since I made my great discovery of the *real* you. I sometimes wonder, looking back, whether you would rather that I had *not* made it, and that things had continued between us as they were in the early days of the Venetiad.'[39] Exactly what he had discovered was one of the few secrets he did keep in these letters. But such heartfelt expressions suggest that Venetia was certainly more than a pen pal for a lonely Prime Minister. It may not have been a physical relationship, but it certainly involved psychological solace.

The abundance of letters in the first months of the conflict were partly a consequence of the fact that Venetia was at her parents' country house in Alderley and there was little opportunity for her to spend time with Asquith. But at the end of 1914 she returned to London in order to train as a nurse. Whenever time allowed, which it did to a surprising extent, Asquith resumed their Friday afternoon rides in his motor car. What was more, the letter-writing continued at a furious pace. He sent one hundred and forty-one missives in the first three months of 1915. Some were extraordinarily fulsome in their praise and again cast doubt over which matter the Prime Minister's mind was most firmly fixed upon. The prospect of Venetia helping the war effort as a nurse in France filled him with despair. 'My darling, I was so oppressed to-day by the terror of losing you that I am afraid I was rather a gloomy companion,' he confided from the Athenaeum on 12 February 1915, before reassuring her, 'I love you more than ever – more than life!' Two days later he was reminding her that it was the third anniversary of her becoming his 'pole-star. My allegiance has never wavered – and never will.' While on 18 February he was promising her, 'I can honestly say that not an hour passes without thought of you'.[40]

In March, after spending 'a heavenly hour' with her, he wrote while on the car journey that:

> If by some *coup foudroyant* in this solitary drive I were to come to an end, I should die happy in the thought & love of you, who have enriched & redeemed my life. Moses was ready to be blotted out of the book of life for the sake of the Chosen People. Danton said 'que mon nom soit flétri, que la France soit libre'. Sadly futile aspirations both of them – judged by results; in the one case a scattered & unattractive tribe: in the other, the most disappointing experiment in the annals of freedom. But I should be more than content if I could think that I left behind me, in your heart, the memory of devoted worship & undivided and unconquerable love. That at any rate you will always have.
>
> . . . Most precious, you are all the light of all my days – the love & glory of my life.

And when he got back that evening, he found time to fire off another cloying missive, assuring her that while 'Darling – I don't want to seem exacting or greedy or overbearing', the thought of her ever moving away from him would crush his spirit, like 'the tragic pall of black unrelieved midnight darkness'.[41]

This infatuation was causing distress to his wife and on 13 April, after Margot felt unable to withhold her apprehensions any longer, Asquith reassured her that his feelings for her were unchanged while admitting, 'I am reputed to be of serene "imperturbable" temperament' even though the truth was that 'these last 3 years I have lived under a perpetual strain, the like of which has I suppose been experienced by very few men living or dead'. Margot was relieved by this response, which she enclosed in a letter she promptly dashed off to Edwin Montagu. The latter had been promoted to the Cabinet as Chancellor of the Duchy of Lancaster in February and Margot believed he was the colleague who had her husband's best interests at heart (it was no good writing to Haldane, for whom romance with young girls had long since ceased to be a subject for discussion). To Montagu, Margot was disarmingly frank. 'I have as you know often wondered if Venetia hadn't ousted me faintly – not very much – but enough to wound bewilder & humiliate me', she admitted to the thirty-seven-year-old bachelor before proceeding to suggest with spectacular lack of subtlety that 'Your part to play is to persuade both Violet & Venetia that if they dont marry they will be miserable formidable egoists and amateurs.'[42]

At the same moment, Asquith's over-intense relationship with Venetia was coming under strain. He wrote on 22 April pleading to know 'the real truth at once. However hard it may be to me.' He had been upset at a throwaway remark she had made about 'cutting losses' and was anxious to be spared 'suspense & uncertainty', signing himself 'Your own lover'. Four days later, when briefly things appeared to brighten, he wrote, 'to see you again, & be with you, & hear your voice, and above all to feel that everything is unchanged, has made a new creature of me. You are the best and richest of life-givers.' Within days, though, his fears that he was beginning to bore her increased. He spent the first weekend of May with her and her parents at Alderley, and while there he composed to her a note confessing the fear, 'I thought once or twice yesterday, for the first time in our intercourse, that I rather bored you'.[43] He had taken to walking across the thoroughfares around Downing Street in virtual despair, by his own account, nearly being run over countless times. This appeared to be due to Venetia, rather than the war situation.

Venetia was supposed to go to France on 10 May to help out behind the lines as a nurse. At the last moment she was prevented from doing so by a sudden onset of a fever that confined her to bed at her parents' London home in Mansfield Street. Accompanied by Montagu, Asquith paid her a quick visit before walking with his colleague back to Whitehall. When he returned to his desk, he wrote to Venetia, explaining that Montagu and he: 'had (as always) good conversation. I don't honestly believe that, at this moment, there are two persons in the world (of opposite sexes) from whom I cd. more confidently count, whatever troubles or trials I had to encounter, for whole-hearted love and devotion than you and he: of course, in quite different ways & senses.' The following day he went again to see the recovering patient, but, on arrival, was told it was best not to disturb her. The next day, Wednesday 12 May, he received a curt letter from Venetia. She had something important to announce. She was engaged to be married – to Edwin Montagu.

Asquith was stunned by the news. Two friends with whom he had spent so much time in recent years were getting married to one another and he had known nothing about it. Although he was aware that Montagu had once proposed to her before, she had rejected him outright and there was no suggestion that she had revised her impression that he was not good-looking, even in an unconventional way. A shared interest in bird watching hardly compensated for this handicap. In any case, unless Montagu was to be disinherited, Venetia would have to convert to his Jewish faith. Was this a likely course for the daughter of Lord Sheffield? Her rejection of Montagu and his failure to make any subsequent attempt – as far as the Prime Minister knew – to persuade her otherwise had long killed any gossip about the prospect of their getting together. It can be assumed he did not know that Margot had been goading Montagu to risk just such a leap again. But Venetia had now said 'yes' and this her aged admirer found impossible to accept. Distraught, Asquith could only bring himself to reply to Venetia's letter with a three-line response. It said, simply:

> Most Loved –
> As you know well, *this* breaks my heart.
> I couldn't bear to come and see you.
> I can only pray God to bless you – and help me.[44]

If he could not find the words for his lost confidante, Asquith did manage to express his despair in a succession of letters to her elder sister, Sylvia. Given the promising lives being smashed up on the Western Front at that very moment, with telegram boys bringing missives far more grave than anything flowing from Venetia's nib, Asquith's expressions of self-pity were remarkable. 'I don't suppose there is in the kingdom at this moment a much more unhappy man', he protested.

> I don't believe there are two living people who, each in their separate ways, are more devoted to me than she and Montagu: and it is the irony of fortune that they two shd combine to deal a death-blow to me ... I am really fond of him, recognise his intellectual merits, find him excellent company, & have always been able to reckon on his loyalty & devotion. Anything but this!
> It is not merely the prohibitive physical side (bad as that is) – I won't say anything about race & religion tho' they are not quite negligible factors.

But he is not a *man*: a bundle of moods & nerves & symptoms, intensely self-absorbed, and – but I won't go on with the dismal catalogue … She says at the end of a sadly meagre letter: 'I can't help feeling, after all the joy you've given me, that mine is a very *treacherous* return.' Poor darling! I wouldn't have put it like that. But in essence it is true: and it leaves me sore and *humiliated*.[45]

When Asquith entered Margot's bedroom with the news of Venetia's betrayal, he looked so crestfallen that she assumed Beb had been killed.

The silence from Venetia was unendurable. At midnight on 14 May, Asquith could take it no longer and – after what he described as 'the two most miserable days of my life' – he wrote a note pleading, 'This is too terrible. No Hell can be so bad. Cannot you send me one word? It is *so* unnatural. Only one word?' Finally, on Monday 17 May, she wrote Asquith what he described as a 'most revealing and heart-rending reply' although it, like all her correspondence with him, has not survived to tell the tale. In the end, he managed to see her for half an hour before she left for France. 'You were the centre & mainspring of my life: everything in it hung on you: there was not an act or a thought (as you know) wh. I did not share with you', he wrote in a lengthy exhibition of hurt feelings on 11 June, adding:

Look back on the whole time we have spent together, in the most perfect & heavenly intimacy that could exist between man & woman. Was it ever clouded for a moment by suspicion, or jealousy, or doubt, or even a shadow of reserve? You know well, *it never was*.

But how can you think it possible – you don't, I know – that things can ever again be as they were? I had the *best* that a man had or could have. Don't, for God's sake, think me selfish or exorbitant, if I shrink from the second best. I told Montagu the other day in the only talk I have ever had or wish to have with him on the subject that I don't care what happens to me or to him – that I wouldn't lift a finger to save either him or myself from instant death if I could be sure that in that way you wd. be happy … Don't force me to sadder & adamantine resolutions. Don't think me hard if I seem for the time to stand aloof. Don't press me now to say anything – except that I love you – always, everywhere.

Signing himself 'Your heart-broken and *ever devoted*,' he added the desperate postscript, 'My very dearest – I hope this won't give you as much pain to read as it has given me to write it. I love you.'[46] To her intended, Venetia mentioned this latest exchange of sentiment from the Prime Minister, claiming that she had 'shown him more clearly than anything else I've ever written how little I really cared for him'.[47]

She was married on 26 July. Asquith sent a wedding present (two small silver boxes) but, emotionally crushed, it was effectively the end of his relationship with her. There were a handful of brief notes exchanged in the ensuing five months, after which, a long silence.

Venetia had agreed to marry Montagu on 28 April, fourteen days before she summoned up the courage to tell Asquith. She clearly was not in love with her husband-to-be. They had not yet kissed. This was indicative. She stipulated that once they were married she should still be permitted to carry on affairs with other men. Montagu agreed these humiliating terms, which were not the obvious basis for a happy marriage. And so it proved. In order to safeguard his inheritance, she did agree to convert to Judaism. Not that she meant a word of it – as she blithely assured him: 'I go through the formula required because you want it for your mother's sake, and also (I'm going to be quite honest) because I think one is happier rich than poor ... Religion you know I care nothing about and shan't attempt to bring up my children in any ... I shall never think of myself as a Jew, any more than I think of you as one.'[48] But more than this, it was a desperate search for security that drove her into Montagu's nervy embrace. With potential suitors her own age being mown down at the front, Venetia may have settled for the notion that if she was to escape Asquith's increasingly possessive attention, Montagu was the only safe port in the storm. Time was short, she was poised to go off to France and perhaps Montagu deemed that if he did not seize the moment, it might always elude him. Like many major decisions in life, it appears to have been taken in a state of panic and desperation.

Whatever assumptions are made about the match, one consequence was certain. Its timing ensured it was not a marriage convenient to Asquith. Venetia and Edwin Montagu had chosen a particularly sensitive political moment to drop their bombshell upon the Prime Minister. As a government minister, this should have been apparent to Montagu and it should certainly have occurred to Venetia, who thanks to her long years as Asquith's pen pal was even better-informed. Just at the moment when Asquith was preoccupied by the loss of his emotional crutch, he had to deal with a pressing political situation. Two days after Venetia broke her news, a report in *The Times* flatly contradicted statements Asquith had made that the British Army had sufficient quantities of shells. The following day the First Sea Lord resigned.

Although taken together the effect was decisive, the shell scandal was the first and greater of the converging storms engulfing the distracted Prime Minister. There had been rumours gathering for some time that the British forces on the Western Front were running dangerously short of shells. But the report that appeared in *The Times* on 14 May was authoritative – the details had been leaked to the newspaper's military correspondent, Colonel Repington, by no less a figure than the BEF's Commander-in-Chief, Sir John French. Frustrated by his failure to make the decisive breakthrough on the front, French may have clung to the belief that a few more shells would have done the trick. In this he was doubtless mistaken, but the revelation that his men had to ration their firing, looked – and was – bad. It completely discredited the assurance Asquith had given on the subject in a speech at Newcastle on 20 April. He had done so on the basis of what he had been told by Kitchener, within whose department supply matters ultimately rested. But given the public's insistence that the War Secretary was a decisive figure while the Prime Minister's attitude was summed up in the relaxed 'business as usual' axiom, it was clear to whom the opprobrium was going to attach.

At this sensitive moment, the histrionic slamming of doors at the Admiralty echoed across Whitehall. Recalling Lord Fisher to serve as First Sea Lord had been a mistake (he had been appointed after the witch-hunt to remove suspect Germans in high places had driven Prince Louis of Battenberg from the post). Fisher's ego ranged more freely than his Dread-noughts – although his armour plating was thinner. Tied to the bulk of his equally obstreperous political master, Winston Churchill, damage was inevitable. Although many lesser fiascos might have brought matters to a head (he had threatened resignation nine times), it proved to be the disastrous Dardanelles campaign that sparked Fisher's determination to make a scene. Indeed, he appeared to have all but taken leave of his senses, flouncing out in a manner that Asquith told King George's private secretary was 'almost traitrous'.[49]

Fisher sent in his letter of resignation on Saturday 15 May. After tracking him down to a locked room in the Charing Cross Hotel, Asquith intervened to get him to reconsider. Fisher's terms for staying on were so extreme – in effect allowing him to run the Admiralty – that the attempt would prove futile. This did not make the situation any less dangerous. Hoping to do maximum damage to Churchill, Fisher was briefing Unionists against the First Lord of the Admiralty. There were many on the Unionist benches eager to hear the worst. Their front bench had taken the terms of the 'party truce' so seriously that the House of Commons had not debated the conduct of the war since August 1914. To backbenchers, seeking a purpose and anxious about a war that appeared not to be going to plan – if there was a coherent plan – this self-denying gag had become intolerable.

During Sunday, while Asquith was searching for his sense of swing on the golf links, Bonar Law was trying to hold back and divert a powerful force of anger within his disillusioned party. They were demanding a debate. They wanted to ask difficult questions. Given the chance, they would clobber the insouciant Prime Minister with his own putter. At the very least, they thought that if Fisher was going to go down, he ought to take Churchill with him. This was all at a particularly inopportune moment. Britain was involved in delicate negotiations to bring Italy into the war on the Allied side. It was not the moment to rock the boat.

Anxious to gain confirmation about Fisher's departure, Bonar Law went to see Lloyd George early on the morning of Monday 17 May. The Chancellor of the Exchequer confirmed that the First Sea Lord had effectively gone AWOL and, according to Bonar Law, 'burst out passionately', claiming that 'Kitchener had "put lies into his mouth" as to the supply of munitions and that the situation was altogether intolerable'.[50] Whether or not Lloyd George actually advocated the formation of a cross-party coalition during this conversation, such was what Bonar Law was now drawn to conclude was the only means by which angry Unionists could be bridled a moment longer. He returned to his office and, joined by his colleagues Austen Chamberlain and Lord Lansdowne, began drafting a letter to Asquith. It was intended to give warning that he would have to tackle him in the Commons in the afternoon unless 'some change in the constitution of the government' was made. This opaque term replaced the word 'coalition' that Bonar Law had written in the first draft.[51] But before he could deliver the letter, he received a telephone call from 10 Downing Street asking if he could come round to see the Prime Minister immediately. From Asquith, Bonar Law understood that Kitchener was the problem – indeed that the shell shortage had been his fault – and that a coalition government would indeed be one way of overcoming the likely outcry caused if Asquith, in seeking to ride out the storm, dismissed his iconic War Secretary. By the time Bonar Law was ushered out of Downing Street he had understood that the Liberals' monopoly of power was over and that he would soon be entering its replacement – a coalition government.

This was an extraordinary turnaround. Asquith had responded to a question from a Liberal backbencher during Prime Minister's Question Time the previous week, on 12 May, by confirming that a coalition government was 'not in contemplation'. Nor, behind the scenes, was there evidence to suggest he was moving towards just such a realignment. Balfour aside, Asquith felt nothing but antipathy, even contempt, for the Unionist front bench. It was the convulsions of the intervening days that rocked him fundamentally. All of a sudden, he had to contemplate sacking Kitchener – nationally the most popular member of the government – in order to save himself over the shell shortage issue at a time when he was also probably losing his First Sea Lord and possibly the First Lord of the Admiralty with him. Simultaneous change at the top of the departments running the Army and the Navy in the middle of a war was no minor matter. Instead, a highly controversial reorganisation had become a pressing necessity.

Added to this uncertainty, the Liberal Party was rife with rumours (false, at it transpires)[52] that Lloyd George and Churchill were briefing Northcliffe and plotting to break up the government to their own advantage. Asquith had to seize the initiative. With the (increasingly disillusioned) Irish Nationalist and Labour Members, he could still win in a Commons division but a showdown of this kind and at this time would be a bruising affair. By-elections between 1910 and 1914 had tipped the scales and there were now twenty-eight more Unionist MPs than Liberals (although a large number were away serving in the forces). By law a general election was due by the end of the year and he needed to keep Unionist consent to the party truce if – as he earnestly desired – the poll was to be postponed.[53]

The turnaround was no less of a surprise for Bonar Law. On 10 March he had been invited to a meeting of the War Cabinet to discuss the Dardanelles campaign. He decided against repeating the exercise on the grounds that doing so threatened his hold on his own semi-mutinous party. His decision to excuse himself from future inclusion did not greatly upset Asquith or Churchill, who believed he had little worthwhile to contribute in any case. Although Bonar Law had acted with great constraint and responsibility since (if not before) the outbreak of war, he had no desire to serve in an Asquith-led administration. He was desperate neither to join a coalition nor to bring it down in order to replace it with a new Unionist government which would have been an even more divisive prospect. However, on the Monday morning of 17 May, he was in danger of losing control of his backbenchers and agreeing to enter a broad-based coalition was the best way of bridling their attack. Thus, if there was a personal dimension at all, it was motivated by a fear that he might fail to contain his party's assault against the Liberal government, an assault that might end the party truce and perhaps with it his own claim to remain Leader of the Opposition. His predicament was summed up by his colleague, Austen Chamberlain, who wrote to him on the evening of 17 May pointing out that:

If our help is asked by the Govt. we *must* give it. God knows each one of us would willingly avoid the fearful responsibility; but the respons-

ibility of refusing is ever greater than that of accepting, and in fact we
have no choice. If Govt. tapped any one of us on the shoulder and
said: Go to the trenches, we should go. If they asked us to dig trenches
here or work as labourers in the factory we should do it. We cannot
shirk this job because we don't like it or because we think the risks to
ourselves too great.[54]

Asquith had to consider how a new Cabinet should be balanced between
Liberals and Unionists, how power should be rearranged among his increasingly fractious Liberal colleagues and whether the new formation should be
used as the reason for sacking Kitchener or retaining him as a hostage in the
event of a future reverse. He also had to keep in mind that Bonar Law would
make demands as the price of his own party's compliance. The Unionist
leader was not necessarily committed to shoring up Asquith as Prime Minister
at all costs. However, Lloyd George, the man of action whom Unionists
might have favoured at the head of a coalition, refused to put himself forward.
Four years previously, Asquith had stood by Lloyd George when the latter
had faced public allegations of insider dealing and a conflict of interest in
buying shares in Marconi when its British sister company had won a major
government contract. Lloyd George refused to take the Unionist bait and
this declaration of loyalty to Asquith immediately suppressed a nascent palace
coup.[55] So with Asquith, for the moment, safe, the personnel changes Bonar
Law did want to see could be arranged without the Prime Minister risking
his own neck. It was the heads of close colleagues that the Unionists would
demand on the block.

Asquith did not have much time between concluding his lunch on
Monday 17 May and rising to face questions in the Commons chamber in
the afternoon. There was certainly not time to take his senior colleagues
aside for a private chat, let alone submit to detailed horse-trading with Bonar
Law. Instead, a printed memorandum was sent to each member of the
Cabinet requesting their resignation. Naturally, this took them by surprise.
Charles Hobhouse and Reginald McKenna were the first ministers to receive
the memorandum. The latter hurried off to see Grey, who had no idea what
was coming. Shortly afterwards, they were joined by Haldane. 'Have you
heard the news?' they asked him. 'No,' Haldane replied curious, adding
quickly and perhaps hopefully, 'from the Dardanelles?' 'No,' came the instant
reply, 'from Downing Street.' When told what Asquith was demanding, the
Lord Chancellor was seen to turn 'his usual ghastly colour and nearly
collapse[d]'.[56] He was right to be fearful. Distress over Venetia had transformed Asquith from the apostle of delay to the agent of decisive and bold

action. In the space of a morning's work he had just dissolved the last Liberal government of the twentieth century.

✳

Asquith sat down to shuffle the cards. It was soon clear that the Unionists were prepared to be junior partners in the new administration, but this would still involve some Liberals having to make way. However, there was one politician central to the conduct of the war with whom the Unionists made clear they would not work. This was the First Lord of the Admiralty. The partisans in the Unionist Party had long detested a man who had deserted their benches for the Liberals and proceeded to take such an active part in the campaign to enforce Irish home rule. Mounting failure in the Dardanelles and the resignation of Fisher was the final straw. Bonar Law was insistent that if his colleagues were going to join the government then Winston Churchill had to be removed from the Admiralty. It was non-negotiable.

Churchill scrabbled around to find ways of staying, but Asquith had no option but to be deaf to his appeals, answering his letters of complaint with 'I am sure you will try to take a large view of an unexampled situation. Everyone has to make sacrifices.'[57] Eventually he found him a junior position in the new team by offering him Montagu's job as Chancellor of the Duchy of Lancaster. For Churchill, it was a bitter disappointment. Such a sinecure failed to satisfy a man determined to give his all for the war effort and in November he did the decent thing, donned the uniform of the Royal Scots Fusiliers, and went off to command a battalion at the front. The sort of headstrong and reckless officer certain to get himself killed, it could be assumed Churchill would not trouble the pages of history again.

There was one other change Asquith knew the Unionists wanted to see made. Although there is no contemporary record of Bonar Law demanding Haldane's head as the price of coalition, Asquith knew that this was what the Unionist leader wanted. After all, it had been the shrill demand of right-wing politicians and the jingoistic press since the moment war had broken out. But whether Asquith needed to accede to the dropping of his longest and most loyal friend in public life was open to question. To sack him was to show weakness. The campaign of denigration against Haldane had been absurd and misplaced. 'We have to search our memory in vain for an attack on a public man which has been more ungenerous, more ungrateful and more unfounded,' the *Westminster Gazette* had vainly stammered in January when trying to defend him against the torrential downpour of abuse hurled by more effectual newspapers.[58]

Whatever the inconsistent Northcliffe might think, Asquith knew how much the country owed to Haldane's Army reforms. He knew how Haldane had pushed for the rapid deployment of the BEF to counter the German advance at a time when Northcliffe had been telling his journalists to argue that Britain's war contribution should be confined to the sea and that no troops should be sent to the Continent. It was Northcliffe who had miscalculated and been forced to change tack, not Haldane. And, in any case, who, indeed, was the press magnate to dictate matters anyway? With Churchill, whose conduct of Admiralty affairs had helped cause a crisis, the Unionists and their Fleet Street friends at least had a case. But with Haldane they had none.

Having failed to release information that would have proved Haldane's innocence of the pro-German charges levelled at him, it was Sir Edward Grey who stood up for him now. He wrote to Asquith:

> I think Bonar Law should be told that it is at least doubtful whether I shall stay if Haldane goes; that the injustice of the mad and malicious attacks upon Haldane in the *National Review* and Harmsworth Press have cause more resentment to Haldane's friends and those who know the truth about him than any political question has ever aroused; and that now when these attacks have come to a head in this way, it is impossible not to show how one resents them.
>
> If Bonar Law is really pressing the point, I think I had better see him and any of his friends who share his view, and tell them what I think, and how the matter stands.
>
> If you don't object, I will write to Bonar Law and save you further trouble on this point.[59]

Late in the day, the Foreign Secretary had come out fighting for a colleague. But at this vital moment, Asquith showed no such resolution. He was not prepared to risk a political impasse (and one at so critical a moment, with Italy perhaps days away from entering the war). Haldane had been Asquith's best man at his wedding, he had secured Asquith his East Fife seat in Parliament, he had been a loyal and unflinching colleague in all the battles that had ensued. In the Prime Minister's mind, the decision to drop his oldest friend of thirty years demonstrated an admirable detachment: he was prepared to do his duty to put the country's needs before the claims of personal feelings. A noble Roman in this position would surely have acted likewise. Those who stuck up for the endangered Lord Chancellor did so because they liked him and believed he was the victim of a malicious injustice. But friendship was not to be confused with indispensability. Haldane did not represent any of the constituencies that Asquith needed to balance in a new Cabinet. He was not enough of an old-style Liberal for the party grassroots to demand his retention. Nor had he yet identified himself sufficiently with the any-means-necessary school of state intervention and organisation that war had made appealing to the hawkish tendency rallying to Lloyd George and to the Unionists. Politically, he was expendable. Best of all, he was enough of a gentleman to accept his fate without proceeding to snipe on the sidelines. Asquith decided to do what was necessary. He did not even attempt to save him. Indeed, according to Austen Chamberlain's memo for 17 May, it was Asquith, not Bonar Law, who volunteered Haldane's head on a silver platter.

It was a sad end made squalid by the manner of the execution. All Haldane received was a hastily scribbled note of warning on 17 May in which Asquith assured him 'we must put aside everything for which we care personally'.[60] No further word did Haldane receive from his friend and former colleague. No word of regret or explanation did Asquith write. No word of thanks for all that the partnership had meant in the many seasons it had been in flower. Perhaps shame and a sense of embarrassment caused writer's block. It was an extraordinary failure on the part of a Prime Minister who was certainly busy with the urgent tasks of statecraft but was also preoccupied by his own sense of hurt. Indeed, as he wrote to Herbert Samuel, whom he demoted to the rank of Postmaster-General, 'No one knows how much I have suffered. Very gladly would I have gone. No one has made a greater sacrifice than I have.'[61] Ever since Venetia had betrayed him for Montagu, the Prime Minister had been wrapped in this mood of self-indulgent pity. 'I miss (more than I can say) what has helped and guided me so often during these last 3 years. I can't describe to you the depth of the unbridged gulf', he wrote to Venetia's sister, Sylvia, on the day he broke up his Cabinet, adding, 'I feel almost like one half of a pair of scissors'.[62] But to Haldane, Asquith's actions had been razor-sharp. Insult to injury followed. When the list of the new coalition ministers was published, it was revealed that Haldane had not even been elbowed off the Woolsack to make way for a Unionist. It had been assumed that in Sir Edward Carson QC, the Unionists had an obvious candidate as Lord Chancellor. But Carson was only made Attorney-General. Instead, Asquith had chosen to replace Haldane with a Liberal of relatively minor importance – the former Solicitor-General, Sir Stanley Buckmaster.

Haldane, of course, went quietly. He understood why he had been axed.

He had not the temper given to public denouncements or theatrical insult-hurling. But his preference against making a scene did not mean that his sense of upset ran any less deep. His resentment at the way Asquith had handled the matter ensured that their friendship was in tatters. At the time, Asquith was too preoccupied with losing Venetia to feel the loss keenly. This was a pity. Such friendships were rare in politics. In the words of Roy Jenkins, a defender of so much of Asquith's life and work, 'It was the most uncharacteristic fault of Asquith's whole career.'[63]

What had Asquith gained? Possibly with Haldane jettisoned he imagined a better press. In this he was to be disappointed. With the scapegoat removed, Northcliffe's papers merely turned to undermining the Prime Minister directly. Where he had shown resolve in sacking a friend he showed cowardice in tackling one of the real causes of the country's woes: he opted to keep Kitchener at the War Office, for no better reason than that he was still popular with the public. As the historian Stephen Koss succinctly put it, by sacrificing Haldane 'to public ignorance and journalistic opportunism', Asquith displayed 'a lack of courage that justified the worst that had been said' about him.[64] Yet, had he but known it, he was laying the ground for his own destruction. Churchill subsequently wrote that Asquith had opted to 'end the political lives of half his colleagues, throw Haldane to the wolves . . . Not "all done by kindness"! Not all by rosewater! These were the convulsive struggles of a man of action and of ambition at death-grips with events.'[65] In his posthumously published autobiography, Haldane put it artfully, suggesting that he was no less concerned on Asquith's account: 'I saw the first signs appearing of the movement to displace him likewise, and I was not sure that he would not have done better if he had displayed more of an iron hand in maintaining his position and that of his colleagues.'[66]

And so it proved.

TWELVE

The Last Romans

The fall of Lord Haldane stirred brief rejoicing in Fleet Street's editorial floors and the dingier club rooms of Pall Mall. Yet it was not the end of the matter, for the desire to kick an ex-Lord Chancellor while he was down overwhelmed those who enjoyed the blood sport element in politics. The torment continued with the publication in Germany of a highly coloured account of the 1912 'Haldane Mission' to Berlin. This at last moved Grey, who continued as Foreign Secretary in the new coalition government, to sanction the release of information on what had actually transpired. However, the material published was so insubstantial that it begged more questions than it answered. Far from exonerating Haldane, the paucity of detail left readers to assume that he had advocated acceptance of the Kaiser's terms and that it was only his colleagues back in London who had put a stop to so craven a surrender. Nothing 'now published, or ever likely to be published, will justify that unfortunate experiment in diplomatic intercourse', *The Times* magisterially concluded.[1]

Haldane was appalled. 'I have not now many rags of character left', he pleaded with Grey, pointing out that the disclosures had encouraged the press to imply that he was ready 'to lower the flag of my country'. 'The result', he continued wearily, 'is the usual shower of abusive letters and articles.' But Grey remained deaf to the appeals from his former colleague to do more to clear his name. Having – in his mind – moved on, Asquith was no more use. Refusing to get involved, he assured Haldane, 'our previous decision against publication is still right. Publication will involve disclosure of the negotiations with regard to the Portuguese Colonies and to the Baghdad railway, and to my mind, during the war at least, this cannot be contemplated. In view of this consideration, do you not agree?'[2] But Haldane did not agree, replying that Grey's negotiations over the Portuguese colonies were already in the public domain thanks to their publication by the Germans. It was no good. Asquith and Grey were preoccupied by the war and the mounting challenges to their own claims on running it. In this difficult time when the *national* interest was a ready shield, there was no mileage for them in stooping to rescue an old friend heading towards semi-disgrace.

Instead, Haldane was left to become the scapegoat for Liberal England's supposed failures to prepare for an all-out slog to the finish with the Kaiser. The *Daily Express* marshalled a letter-writing campaign against him. On one day alone, over 2,600 letters arrived at the House of Lords denouncing Haldane for disloyalty and treason. When the sackloads of hate mail were transported over to his house at Queen Anne's Gate, Haldane inoculated himself from the contents by leaving their disposal to his kitchen maid.[3] With unsigned editorials and poison pen letters there remained sufficient remoteness to encourage extravagancies of rudeness. Only strident incivility to Haldane's face within the chamber of the House of Lords proved counter-productive. It was the Duke of Buccleuch's attempts to prevent him speaking in a Lords debate by interrupting with the slur that 'he should explain his past conduct in misleading Great Britain on the German danger, and in misleading Germany on British policy' before lecturing the House on education policy[4] that finally managed to stir for Haldane a ripple of sympathy on the Unionist benches.

The greater issue, however, was not whether his political enemies were going to be rude to his face or behind his back but rather what relationship, if any, he would now seek to conduct with Asquith and the rest of his Liberal former colleagues. On 5 July, a dinner was held in his honour at the National Liberal Club in its tiled palazzo on the Thames Embankment downstream from Westminster. The intention was that Asquith would cross the road from Downing Street to look in on the occasion and deliver a few words of gratitude for his fallen colleague. There would be nods of agreement, 'hear hears', tokens of acknowledgement and no hard feelings. With such tea-spoonfuls of honey can bitter medicine be administered. Alas, Asquith opted against making this gesture, perhaps through a sense of awkward embarrassment or just a failure to grasp any longer the human dimension in public life. Rather than show his face, the Prime Minister kept his distance, merely deputing an understudy to read out a statement on his behalf. The effect was not the same as it would have been had it come from Asquith's lips. Once again, he had shied away from a small responsibility that might have meant a lot to his old friend. Haldane thanked him all the same, albeit with the qualified sentence, 'Passing clouds do not dim the memory of years of friendship.'[5] Haldane's temperament was to harbour feelings quietly, withdrawing favour, rather than speaking out intemperately about his sense of betrayal.

Although she had never really taken to Haldane, it was Margot who made more of an effort, writing in November a friendly invitation to Violet Asquith's wedding (Violet had opted to marry her father's secretary, Maurice

Bonham-Carter). Yet, the extent of the estrangement was clear in a letter Haldane sent to his aged mother about the occasion when he added a telling exclamation mark to the statement that Margot 'and the P.M. want[ed] "their oldest friend"! to sign the register'.[6] Not everyone saw matters from so personal a perspective. There were detached observers who welcomed the liberation the relationship's demise afforded Haldane. George Bernard Shaw wrote to assure him that he was better-off out of a 'party machine' made up of those for whom 'to know them personally is to be hopelessly incapacitated from sentencing them as they will be sentenced at the bar of History; but their attempt to enlist you was an attempt to mix up the Old Bailey with the Judicial Committee, or to make an Ecclesiastical Commissioner of Martin Luther'. Instead he was now free to 'give the country a bit of your mind'.[7] At any rate, being sacked from His Majesty's Government freed Haldane from the wartime pledge of abstinence in which the King had set so sterling and inconvenient an example. Arriving for dinner with her husband Sidney, Beatrice Webb noticed without rebuke that Haldane had begun to tuck back into his champagne cellar and 'his super-excellent liqueurs'. She found that 'he wanted "intelligent criticism of the government". He seemed to be ploughing a lonely furrow. "The country is being governed by three men: Balfour, Kitchener and Lloyd George, and Balfour is the real Prime Minister." From which remark we gathered that he had broken with Asquith.'[8]

It might also be suggested that Haldane's assessment of where power was shifting demonstrated only how quickly he was isolated from what was really happening. As the new First Lord of the Admiralty, Balfour was the only Unionist given an Armed Forces portfolio in Asquith's coalition Cabinet. For, in exercising his patronage powers, the Prime Minister had skilfully diverted the Unionist front bench into the secondary offices he thought deserving of their talents. They filled nine of the twenty-three seats around the Cabinet table, but Asquith's opinion of them was scarcely concealed, as was their public-spiritedness in accepting junior status without complaint. Bonar Law settled for the Colonial Office. Meanwhile, Asquith had kept Kitchener at the War Office but had prised from his grasp control over munitions production. This was handed to a new Ministry of Munitions over which Lloyd George now presided with customary energy. Given the damage the 'shell shortage scandal' had already done politically, there was an urgent necessity not only to boost production but to be seen to be taking every measure possible in that direction. It was a role wholly suited to a man who proved the equal of his motivational platform rhetoric. Indeed, it was his sense of urgency that made him an increasingly impressive figure to the very Unionists who only five years previously had feared him as a class warrior. Yet, it was also his past radical reputation that made him acceptable to those in the Labour movement who generally suspected that patriotic appeals really involved stripping the working man of his bargaining powers. As their pre-war strike record demonstrated, the trade unions could have combined to bring the war effort to a grinding halt. With some judicious appeasement, Lloyd George succeeded in keeping them fully committed to the struggle.

Thus power was certainly shifting within the Cabinet and Asquith's problem was that – intentionally or not – Lloyd George was attracting a mini-coalition of admirers around him. Here was an essential problem besetting any leader who relies on a colleague to solve a problem only to find that the price of the colleague's success is to be talked up as a rival. Always a little suspicious of Lloyd George's busy mind and penchant for hobnobbing with press barons, Asquith was alert to the potential for competition this situation created. He opted for frankness. 'I have never believed the stories that have been going round about your intriguing against me,' he informed him in October, adding 'during all the years we have worked together you have been the most loyal of colleagues.' What was more, 'I will be quite frank with you,' he continued, 'there are only two men in this Cabinet who count at all, and we are those two. If we quarrel, it will mean disaster.'[9] The subject, at least, was out in the open.

Asquith was even increasingly dependent on Lloyd George to keep his Liberal colleagues together. Back in the first days of August 1914, Lloyd George had been the pivotal figure who persuaded Cabinet waverers of the necessity to stay and support a declaration of war. Now he found himself called upon again to justify to them dismantling the orthodoxies of individual and economic liberty they held dear as the price for fighting the conflict energetically. As A.J.P. Taylor has tartly observed, the Liberals had been won over by the cause of defending little Belgium against German militarism; because of this appeal to idealistic motives they 'wished to fight it by noble means and found it harder to abandon their principles than to endure defeat in the field'.[10] Unhappy about creeping protectionism (a tariff on the import of luxury goods was introduced in September), for these conviction Liberals the great sticking point was the introduction of military conscription.

The small professional force with which Haldane had equipped Britain was now scattered between cemeteries, nursing homes and providing instruction at training camps. In its place, Kitchener's massed volunteer 'New Army' was taking shape. By the end of 1915 it numbered thirty-eight divisions and within the following six months it would reach fifty-seven. This represented about half the number of German divisions on the Western Front. However, the aim remained to put seventy divisions in the field and the chances of voluntary recruitment providing this number looked increasingly slim. Having tried various other schemes, Asquith reluctantly bowed to the inevitable and, at a Cabinet meeting on 28 December, he conceded that conscription – in the shape of compelling unmarried men between the ages of eighteen and forty-one to serve – was inevitable. In doing so, he dismantled a particular strand of British liberalism. For some it was too much. The Foreign Secretary, Grey, the Chancellor of the Exchequer, Reginald McKenna, the President of the Board of Trade, Walter Runciman and the Home Secretary, Sir John Simon, sent in their letters of resignation from the government. In Grey's case, conscription was only part of the reason. His heart was no longer in high office and he conceded, 'I ought to have left the Cabinet when Haldane went.'[11] Margot was scornful of such self-indulgence when loyalty to her husband was what mattered most, writing to McKenna, 'Do you love yr. opinions more than you love him?'[12] In the end a fresh political crisis was largely averted when only Simon could not be dissuaded from stalking off to the back benches.

Although it was Asquith who introduced the Military Service Bill in the Commons in the new year, to the evident discomfort but half-hearted protest of much of his party, it was Lloyd George who was talked up as the man pushing for further measures. In fact, conscription was less successful than its advocates imagined, not least because many of those who had not volunteered were needed in essential production jobs on the home front. Indeed, the best argument for conscription was not that it swelled the ranks but that it provided a better means than voluntarism of separating those more profitably employing wielding a bayonet than a miner's pickaxe. At any rate, the principle of compulsion having been created, Lloyd George's response was to push for it to include married men as well. During April 1916, with the debate over conscription's extension beginning to wear the Prime Minister down, Asquith considered resignation. But the sudden news over Easter of an attempted Irish Nationalist uprising in Dublin created the sort of crisis that allowed him the leverage to act decisively. Conscription for men – married and unmarried – under the age of forty-one was thus carried through the Commons without serious difficulty. In doing so, Asquith seized an opportunity to pass a measure about which he was instinctively unenthusiastic while, at the same time, failing to grasp the last chance to honour an old Liberal pledge to grant Ireland (or at least its southern twenty-six counties) home rule before its moderate and dejected spokesmen were eclipsed by the anti-British militants of Sinn Fein.

One of the Easter Rising's immediate effects was to save Lloyd George's life. The Munitions Minister had been due to join Kitchener on a trip to confer with Britain's Russian allies. However, Asquith asked Lloyd George to stay behind to address the Irish situation. In the North Sea en route to Russia on 5 June, the ship he would have travelled on hit a mine and Kitchener and most of the crew went down to a watery grave. For the next month, Asquith assumed the additional burden of the War Office. It was a critical few weeks in which to do so for final preparations were being made for the great offensive on the Somme. This would be the New Armies' blooding. Sir John French had been replaced by Douglas Haig, who was optimistic of a breakthrough. At the very least, it would relieve the intolerable pressure on the French Army, which was being bled dry at Verdun. On 4 July, Asquith finally passed control of the War Office to Lloyd George whose petitions for the post had reached the stage of threatened resignation. His impatience was understandable, if unseemly, for he expected to be in place for the great push that could turn the tide of the war.

In this, he was to be disappointed. Three days previously, the Somme offensive had been launched into a hail of machine-gun fire. On the first day alone, there were almost 60,000 casualties, the heaviest losses ever suffered by the British Army between a single dawn and dusk. The loss equated to half the total strength of the British Expeditionary Force that had arrived in France in August 1914. That army had largely expired at the first battle of Ypres. Now the Somme did for Kitchener's New Armies: 415,000 casualties had been sustained by November when the offensive finally ground to a halt. By then, it had claimed an Asquith. The Prime Minister had tried to protect his eldest son, Raymond, with staff jobs but the Grenadier Guardsman was eager to rejoin his battalion and play his part in the great push. On 15 September, as the regiment pressed on to Lesboeufs, a bullet hit him in the chest and he fell to his knees. So as not to dishearten his men, he lit a cigarette. But before the stretcher reached the dressing station he was dead.

The news reached home two days later. His father and stepmother were entertaining weekend guests at The Wharf, the retreat they had bought in the picturesque Oxfordshire village of Sutton Courtenay south of Abingdon. It was the Sunday of a happy weekend of sunshine, good spirits and tennis on the lawn. Dinner had been served when Margot was called to the telephone. When her husband opened the door and saw her standing there, in the dining room passage, he knew instantly what had happened. Margot recorded that 'he put his hands over his face and we walked into an empty room and sat down in silence'.[13] He had allowed a certain distance to grow between him and his eldest son and – despite his epistolary fidelity to others – had been a negligent correspondent with Raymond at the front. Be that as it may: 'Whatever pride I had in the past', he brought himself to write a few days later, 'and whatever hope I had for the far future – by much the largest part of both was invested in him. Now all that is gone.'[14] He would have been touched to know that a letter sent to an old schoolmaster in south London from a private in Raymond's platoon contained a fitting tribute: 'there is not one of us who would not have changed places with him if we had thought that he would have lived, for he was one of the finest men who ever wore the King's uniform'.[15]

Asquith necessarily took time off work while he came to terms with the loss of his brilliant, unfulfilled son. He could not do so for long, though, and even after returning to his desk, the problems facing his administration were as pronounced as ever. At first his loose style of management had rather suited coalition government. On the eve of war, Leo Amery had accused the Prime Minister of holding a 'season ticket on the line of least resistance'.[16] But this had its uses. Back in November 1915, Lloyd George's secretary and lover, Frances Stevenson, had marvelled at Asquith's ability to keep his disparate colleagues together, 'by pure craft and cunning, propitiating here, or pretending to propitiate, making concessions there, or pretending to make them; giving promises which he never intended to keep, but which were just sufficient to keep the person concerned dangling … Always wait and see!'[17] But the downside of this approach had become glaring. Unionist colleagues like Curzon and Selborne despaired of poorly structured and inadequately minuted Cabinet meetings in which the Prime Minister offered little direction and ministers were allowed to depart without clear decisions being taken.[18]

In contrast, Lloyd George continued to build upon his public image as an action man. Still searching for a saviour, the national press embraced him as enthusiastically as they had previously saluted Kitchener. Years of cultivating editors and press barons paid off to the extent that by the autumn of 1916 he enjoyed the support of every major national newspaper – popular or serious – save the orthodoxly liberal *Daily News*. No less important than having Northcliffe's ear, he had also impressed Bonar Law's friend Sir Max Aitken who was in the process of gaining control of the *Daily Express* and, soon after, would be raised to the title of Lord Beaverbrook.

The downside of this press cheerleading was that it made Lloyd George's colleagues suspicious. Despite Aitken's intermediary skills, even Bonar Law wondered to what extent the War Secretary was leaking information in order to show himself in the best light. In November 1916, Lloyd George pushed for a scheme that effectively forced Bonar Law to decide where his loyalties lay. Dissatisfied by Asquith's unwieldy decision-making process, as well as

being increasingly at odds with the military 'brass hats', Lloyd George pressed
for the creation of a three-man war council consisting of himself, Sir Edward
Carson and Bonar Law. Sitting independently of the Cabinet, it would have
day-to-day executive power over the conflict's conduct. Most important of
all, it would exclude Asquith, who would remain Prime Minister but have
the war's direction wrenched from his control. In effect, Lloyd George wanted
to run a civilian junta to command the war. With Aitken's help – and the
motivating peril in which the nation found itself – Lloyd George persuaded
Bonar Law of the scheme's practicality. On Saturday 25 November, as Asquith
was preparing for a weekend at The Wharf, he was asked to approve the
change. He looked it over and immediately rejected it. He was sure that it
was not realistic. What was more it prompted him to personalise the contest,
assuring Bonar Law that Lloyd George did 'not inspire trust' and that his
proposal 'has been engineered by him with the purpose, not perhaps at the
moment, but as soon as a fitting pretext could be found, of his displacing
me'.[19] Picking up the gauntlet and tossing it high over his head, Asquith
assured the Unionist leader he was free to share these stinging accusations
with their target.

On 1 December, Lloyd George upped the stakes, making clear that he
would not back down either, although he conceded to Asquith supreme
direction and the right to refer war council decisions to the Cabinet. This
battle of wills delivered the role of kingmaker to the Unionists. On the one
hand, they preferred Lloyd George's sense of purpose to Asquith's magisterial
detachment. On the other hand, they suspected the War Secretary's personal
ambition and were distrustful of the campaign his press friends were whip-
ping up on his behalf. At Bonar Law's house on Sunday 3 December, the
senior Unionists met to assess the situation. They agreed a statement informing Asquith that 'the government cannot continue as it is' and because 'the
publicity given to the intention of Mr Lloyd George makes reconstruction
from within no longer possible', if Asquith did not tender the government's
resignation they would all withdraw from it unilaterally.[20] Did this mean
they would not serve under Asquith or under Lloyd George? Different
Unionists appear to have left the meeting with conflicting understandings as
to what was the strategic intention. At any rate, Bonar Law conveyed the
gist of the message to the Prime Minister, albeit in a manner that ensured
Asquith failed to comprehend its implied attack upon the War Secretary's
public relations efforts.

Flustered, Asquith ceded the war council's chairmanship to Lloyd George
while retaining a prime ministerial right of attendance and veto powers on
its decisions. A deal appeared to have been reached and a Downing Street

press release confirmed that the Prime Minister was to seek the King's permission later that day to reconstruct the government. It was at this moment that the fog of war finally enveloped Whitehall. When Asquith picked up his Monday morning copy of *The Times* he was aghast to read an analysis of the new arrangement written in a manner he found personally derogatory. Aware that Northcliffe had spoken to Lloyd George the previous evening, he drew the obvious conclusion (in this he was at least partly mistaken for it was Carson who had briefed *The Times*). Outraged at his colleague's supposed perfidy yet unsure whether or not he was acting in consort with the senior Unionists, Asquith scrambled to renege on the deal. His initial instinct, that the plan was unworkable and a deliberate attempt to undermine him, returned with renewed force. However, he had now to contend with the fact that Lloyd George had become coupled to Bonar Law. Raising the prospect of his own departure if Lloyd George was rebuffed, the Unionist leader pleaded with Asquith to stick to the arrangement, admitting 'there would be a certain amount of humiliation', but that 'he had gone through this sort of thing before, and in my opinion, he was a big enough man to live it down'.[21] Asquith, however, decided it was Lloyd George's turn to discover humility, regardless of the consequences.

His chairmanship of the war council duly refused, on the morning of 5 December Lloyd George tendered his resignation. Despite their differences on policy, 'as you yourself said on Sunday, we have acted together for ten years and never had a quarrel', he conceded in his letter to Asquith, before adding the rebuke 'but unity without action is nothing but futile carnage, and I cannot be responsible for that. Vigour and vision are the supreme need at this hour.'[22]

The imminent departure of his rival was no victory for the Prime Minister. The Unionists' mass resignation was still pending unless the government was wholly reconstituted, as Asquith had publicly promised to undertake. A meeting with the senior Unionists Austen Chamberlain, Lord Curzon and Lord Robert Cecil shattered any delusions he may have entertained that they would serve under him in a reconstructed administration that excluded Lloyd George and Bonar Law. To add insult to injury, Asquith did not take kindly to be being advised by Cecil 'that the finest and biggest thing that he could do would be to offer to serve under Lloyd George'.[23] His options narrowing by the hour, Asquith put on his frock coat and went to Buckingham Palace. There, at seven o'clock on the evening of 5 December, he surrendered the seals of office. He was sixty-four and had been Prime Minister for eight and a half years – a longer continuous spell than any other holder of the post since Lord Liverpool in the 1820s and a tenure that would not again be surpassed until Margaret Thatcher over seventy years later.

Asquith's decision to jump was determined by the recognition that his options were limited and the game was possibly up. Yet, such longevity in office can breed a dogged self-belief in indispensability and that even the worst of situations are retrievable. The glimmer of a chance remained. If neither Bonar Law nor Lloyd George proved able to cobble together a workable administration then Asquith would be asked back, this time on terms of his own choosing. At any rate, by refusing to serve under either of the two credible alternatives, he strengthened the likelihood that they would fail. He had no doubt that the overwhelming majority of his Liberal colleagues would fall in with his decision and without this convocation of numbers and talent, the credibility of an alternative coalition would be greatly impaired.

The King sought constitutional advice about what to do. Among those he approached privately was Haldane. Asked whether the monarch could refuse a request for a general election, Haldane replied that only a Prime Minister could seek a dissolution and, if the King was not minded to agree, he would be better dismissing the Prime Minister than acting on alternative counsel provided by those seeking the office but not yet entrusted with it.[24] Armed with this advice, the King first asked Bonar Law to try to form an administration. Far from being hungry for personal power, the Unionist leader was reluctant, believing Lloyd George was the better man. He was only persuaded to make the attempt if it meant he could sway Asquith to serve under him in a new government of national unity. When Asquith duly refused, Bonar Law even offered to stand aside in favour of Balfour if the previous Unionist leader's return to 10 Downing Street would make the prospect of joining the administration easier for Asquith. But Asquith made clear he would play second to nobody, a stance he maintained when summoned to Buckingham Palace for a conference with Bonar Law, Balfour, Lloyd George and the Labour Party's Arthur Henderson on the afternoon of Tuesday 6 December. Although he needed no persuading, in this Asquith was fortified by the views of his Liberal Cabinet colleagues who assured him he was right to remain aloof. A lone Liberal dissenter at the meeting was Edwin Montagu.

Asquith was correct in assuming Bonar Law would not manage it. But within two days it became clear that Lloyd George was capable of wooing the senior Unionists and a second eleven of Liberals to join an administration he would head. Thus, on the evening of 7 December, Lloyd George succeeded Asquith as Prime Minister. But Asquith remained leader of the Liberal Party and with the senior figures in that party sticking with him, the only one of his Liberal colleagues who still sat in the government was the man who had evicted him from 10 Downing Street and who was now at the mercy of Unionists for legitimacy. At the Foreign Office, Grey was replaced by Balfour who, in Churchill's phrase, passed from serving a supportive Prime Minister to one who had previously disparaged him like 'a powerful, graceful cat walking delicately and unsoiled across a rather muddy street'.[25] Bonar Law became Leader of the Commons and Chancellor of the Exchequer, a protectionist at last running the Treasury.

Moving in to Number 10, Lloyd George immediately converted the proposed three-man war council into a five-man War Cabinet consisting of himself, Bonar Law, Lords Curzon and Milner and the Labour representative, Arthur Henderson. All other ministers were subordinate. The effect in Whitehall, if not on the battlefields, was soon evident. The amateur spirit was dispelled. Proper minutes began to be taken. Executive power was concentrated and strengthened. A 'garden suburb' was created at the back of Downing Street to accommodate its burgeoning secretariat. The rapid fire of typewriters finally drowned out the even tick of clocks.

Having repaired to his old home in Cavendish Square, Asquith retained a mask of cool inscrutability in front of a succession of commiserating guests who railed at the injustice of his reversal of fortune. A more eloquent statement was made by Margot who sat at the dinner table in unusual silence, the occasional tear sliding mournfully into her soup. The truth, of course, was that in foreseeing how his rival intended to undermine him from within, Asquith had manoeuvred himself out of Downing Street. If he had agreed to Lloyd George's war council plan he would have remained there. But he was not prepared to accept a situation in which – like a monarchical fig-leaf – he would have represented the dignified face of government while Lloyd George ran its efficient parts.

In this, there was an irony. Such a division of labour was what Asquith, Haldane and Grey had apportioned at the Relugas fishing lodge in 1905. In order to further their own ends while keeping the Liberal Party outwardly united, they had assigned to Campbell-Bannerman the role of a figurehead Prime Minister removed to the House of Lords while real power would be exercised by Asquith in the guise of Chancellor of the Exchequer and Leader of the Commons, backed up in supporting roles by Grey and Haldane. Events transpired otherwise when the Relugas Compact came unstuck because Asquith, breaking ranks, accepted the first Cabinet offer the wily Campbell-Bannerman dangled before him. One thing that Bonar Law and Lloyd George had learnt since Asquith, Haldane and Grey had hatched their fishing lodge plot was that – when confronted by obstinacy – they should stick together.[26]

It was not just a rival's naked ambition that evicted Asquith from Downing Street. Circumstance and his inability to convey the urgency expected of a war leader had made the putsch possible. As H.C.G. Matthew has pointed out, to Asquith wartime 'was an aberration, not a fulfilment'.[27] In the midst of a war going badly, it proved his lot to be replaced by the Cabinet colleague assumed to have the energy and brute bellicosity to turn matters around. The same fate had befallen Lord Aberdeen who gave way as Prime Minister to Lord Palmerston during the Crimean War in 1855. Winston Churchill would similarly succeed Neville Chamberlain in the Second World War. In 1940, in the midst of a crisis even deadlier than that of 1916, Chamberlain found the inner character to sublimate his misgivings and personal disappointment. Retaining the leadership of the Conservative Party (as the Unionists had reverted to being called), he directed his supporters, who constituted a parliamentary majority, to put aside their doubts and back the vigorous but high-risk Churchill. Without Chamberlain's gesture, Churchill could not have carried the House.[28]

Crucially, Chamberlain in 1940 accepted Churchill's offer of a seat in his Cabinet, thereby sharing and being bound by the responsibility. In contrast, Asquith in 1916 turned down the chance to sit alongside Lloyd George. Although the truth was that he could not bear to work with the Welsh usurper, he convinced himself he had a worthwhile role to play on the outside. In this he was mistaken, for the function he proceeded to cut out for himself was a sterile one. His new vantage point in the Commons chamber was on the Opposition front bench yet he proceeded to offer no effective opposition. Too much of a patriot to be a wrecker but too indignant about his treatment to be actively positive, he adopted a posture akin to torpor. Thus he found himself the leader of a great party surrounded by many of the finest talents in Parliament but whose point or purpose was unclear, save that he was piqued at the circumstances that had got him to this impasse. While he did not contradict the government's policies, his damning verdict on its personalities was evident in the attitude he displayed towards those for whom the magnet of power exerted its irresistible pull.

Among those drawn back into the force-field was Haldane. During April 1917, he met Asquith and then Lloyd George in quick succession. The first engagement was at Asquith's request – a dinner at Cavendish Square. From Haldane's perspective it was not a success, for he found himself not, as he had hoped, alone with his ex-confederate and in a position to explore old intimacies, but merely one of many guests to whom no special consideration was attached. 'I think time has changed the outlook on life of the ex-P.M.', he sighed to his mother.[29] The episode helped convince him that with Asquith there was no way back. It was doubtless no coincidence of timing that, shortly thereafter, he made a decisive gesture by inviting Lloyd George to dinner at his home in Queen Anne's Gate. Despite the cares of office, the new Prime Minister accepted with alacrity.[30] It proved a most agreeable evening for the host. Lloyd George listened carefully and expressed enthusiasm for what Haldane had to say. It had been a long time since Asquith had shown such attention. He even hinted that he wanted Haldane back in the Cabinet in good time to deal with the problems of post-war reconstruction. This was very heartening to hear. In the meantime, Haldane accepted the offer of the chairmanship of a committee analysing the workings of government departments.

Asquith was suitably alienated by Haldane's willingness to find a new sponsor for his public work, although he should hardly have been surprised. There was more to follow. Asquith had found it in his heart to forgive Montagu for whisking off with Venetia Stanley, but he took badly the news in June 1917 that his sometime protégé had accepted Lloyd George's invitation to join the Cabinet as India Secretary. Returning to form, Margot did not hold back. 'I hear you are going in with them,' she reproached Montagu, 'Where is friendship, where is loyalty?'[31] The following month, another old Liberal colleague, Churchill, having confounded expectations by returning from the trenches, accepted Lloyd George's Cabinet offer of the Munitions Ministry. Asquith's hold over his erstwhile colleagues was weakening. The Liberal Party was being torn between two fonts of patronage – only one of which offered immediate power. As such it was an unequal contest, yet in letting successive opportunities for reconciliation pass, Asquith displayed no concern about the infection spreading across an open wound he would not allow to close up. In May, Lloyd George dispatched intermediaries to see if he could be tempted back into the government as Lord Chancellor. With his expenses greatly exceeding his resources, Asquith could have done with the money (£10,000 a year plus £5,000 pension) but he rejected the gilded olive branch. Splendid or otherwise, he preferred isolation.

Asquith may have had grounds for imagining he would live to see off his rival. Lloyd George's revolution in government did not, of itself, translate into victory on the battlefields. In April 1917, the United States entered the war but there would be a long delay before its forces were ready to cross the Atlantic. In the meantime, Haig proposed a summer offensive in the guise of another attempt to break out of the Ypres salient. Embarked upon through driving rain, the advance was soon bogged down, another failure that finally

petered out around the dismal remains of Passchendaele. The prospects of
success looked as remote as ever, leaving Lord Lansdowne, the former Unionist Foreign Secretary who had negotiated the *entente* with France, to draw the
conclusion that a compromise peace was the only way out. The government
disagreed, although when the stalemate on the Western Front was finally
broken, in March 1918, it appeared an outright German victory was a far
more likely prospect.

Calling upon troops spared from the Eastern Front by Russia's collapse,
Ludendorff launched a devastating spring offensive in the west. In the
space of days, the British and French were ejected from territory it had
taken them years and unimaginable sacrifice to inch into and hold.
Hurling numbers forward like a rugby maul pushing relentlessly towards
the try line, Ludendorff had cause to be in a hurry for he intended to
drive on to Paris before the Americans' arrival plugged the defences and
switched the arithmetic in the Allies' favour. By June, the German advance
reached the Marne, where it had not been since the last days of open
warfare in September 1914.

Suddenly, the position was as desperate as Haig's order to his First and
Second Armies made it sound. 'Every position must be held to the last man',
he had commanded as early as 12 April, 'With our backs to the wall and
believing in the justice of our cause, each one of us must fight to the end.' It
was in this environment that the accusations began to fly back in London.
On 7 May, Major-General Sir Frederick Maurice, who had until recently
been Director of Military Operations at the War Office, alleged in *The Times*
that the number of troops put at Haig's disposal had been reduced and that
Lloyd George had deceived the Commons by claiming to the contrary. While
bad judgement could be waved away as the casualty of circumstance, lying
to Parliament was a sin elevated in British politics to the highest order
of severity. Rising in the chamber, Asquith demanded a Commons select
committee to examine Maurice's allegations. The request was not unreasonable, nor was it phrased in accusatory language, but it could hardly do
other than appear a divisive attempt to unsettle the Prime Minister at a
moment of acute difficulty. In this it failed utterly. Asquith's speech fell flat
and compared badly with the fighting performance that followed it from
Lloyd George. The debate went against Asquith, who struggled to muster
100 members of his own party into the division lobby – a further 71 Liberals
joined the Unionists to give Lloyd George an overwhelming endorsement.
The issue was not, of itself, a vote of no confidence in the Prime Minister,
but it was interpreted as a verdict on Asquith's waning virility. 'There is no
real alternative to the present Government', Haldane confided to his sister

after the vote was declared, 'and I said so plainly in the House of Lords yesterday, I hear that 20 Cavendish Square has been much upset by my declaration, but the feeble way in which Asquith's motion was handled was not a good advertisement for a change.'[32]

In retrospect, the Maurice debate appeared to mark a point of no return, although this only proved so because later that month Asquith rejected another effort by Lloyd George to bring him on board. Lord Reading was dispatched to make clear that he could have any Cabinet position – save the premiership – he wanted. He spurned the offer, as he had done before when using 'perfectly plain language' to make clear 'that under no conditions wd. I serve in a Govt. of wh. Ll. G. was the head. I had learned by long & close association to mistrust him profoundly ... In my judgment he had incurable defects, both of intellect and character, wh. totally unfitted him to be at the head.'[33] The charge about character was one thing, but the assault on the Welshman's 'intellect' must have smacked hard. The Balliol scholar was pulling rank. It was a level of candour that made his attitude clear and it was repeated in September, when another of the Prime Minister's emissaries, Lord Murray, came calling.

It meant that Asquith would not be in the government when the victory bells rang out on the great enterprise to which he had committed the British Empire. The sudden collapse of the German Army took everyone – even Haig – by surprise. The early success of Ludendorff's offensive had been its undoing because it stretched his forces across an extended front lacking the natural protections of terrain. Difficult to defend, it all but invited counter-attack. Regrouping, the Allies seized the moment and over the summer the German advance was first turned and progressively rolled back. With fresh American troops pouring in, the Germans fell back into organised, but unremitting, retreat. On 11 November it was all over.

Shortly after the Armistice, Lloyd George invited Asquith to visit him in his office in the Commons. He asked him to confirm that he really did not want a place in a reconstructed government. Asquith reassured him that this was the case, although he did hope to find a role in the forthcoming peace conference in Paris. This cleared the way for Lloyd George to proceed as he intended. Three days after the war's end, the Prime Minister launched a general election campaign with his wartime coalition appealing for a fresh mandate to stick together in order to govern the post-war reconstruction. Those candidates who supported the coalition's continuance received the joint endorsement of Lloyd George and Bonar Law – a guarantee dismissed by Asquith in a food rationing jibe as a 'coupon'. Liberals endorsed in this way were spared Unionist candidates being run against them and vice versa.

The arrangement involved a degree of horse-trading over who should stand down in which constituency. The Unionist intention was to limit the 'couponed' Liberals to around 150. In the end the figure agreed was 159, with loyalty to Lloyd George in the Maurice debate providing one of the determinants to selection.

In contrast, Asquith's Liberals – often designated as Independent Liberals – fielded 258 candidates. In the vast majority of constituencies they avoided running against 'couponed' Liberals, but unlike those endorsed by Lloyd George, Asquithians faced competition from Unionists. Despite this, in a gesture of goodwill, Bonar Law decreed that no Unionist should stand against Asquith. Unfortunately, the local East Fife association thought otherwise and ran a man named Sprot as their own independent Unionist candidate against the Liberal leader. This created one small uncertainty amongst many greater ones because the effect of the wartime party truce had been to deny the country a general election for eight years. During that time change and uncertainty had been magnified by a major boundary redistribution and the granting of universal adult male suffrage and votes for all women over thirty, the effect of which increased the electorate from eight and a half million to twenty-one million. What difference the experience of war and a corresponding change on the home front – the increase of trade union membership from two million to six and a half million – would produce was equally open to speculation.

There were also matters of substance for the electorate to weigh. Of the rival Liberal leaders, only Lloyd George could claim to have been the Prime Minister who won the war. Furthermore, he presented a definite programme of action – of which the pledge to build homes 'fit for heroes' was only the most memorable. In contrast, Asquith failed utterly to find themes with which to equip his campaign. He fell back on warning against giving Lloyd George and his confederates a 'blank cheque' but made little attempt to fill in the bill his independent Liberals would be presenting the nation if called upon to serve.

On 28 December, Asquith was among the dignitaries attending a lunch at the Mansion House for the American President, Woodrow Wilson, when rumours began to circulate that the first returns were coming in. As the lunch broke up, Asquith did his best to slip away as quickly as decorum allowed. With Margot at his side, he battled through a crush of eager, whispering and anxious men. Borne along to the waiting car, they overheard enough news to give cause for alarm. Surprisingly and perhaps ominously, there was no message awaiting them when they finally arrived back at 20 Cavendish Square. Taking matters into her own hands, Margot telephoned party headquarters. Getting through, she was told the result was in from East Fife: Asquith 6,994 votes, Sprot 8,996.

In the seat he had held for thirty-two years, the leader of the Liberal Party had been heavily and humiliatingly defeated by a nonentity – and not even a nonentity with the backing of a party machine behind him. Yet, Asquith's personal calamity was of a piece in a general election that turned out disastrously for his followers. The party that had been victorious in the last three general elections on the trot, Asquith's Liberals won only 28 seats. They were overtaken by the Labour Party which claimed 57. Against this, the coalition had won 478 of which the Lloyd George Liberals numbered 133 and the real winners, the Unionists, won 335.[34] Only three of the Asquithites who survived the slaughter had any ministerial experience and all of it at junior level. None of these three were even especially Asquithian in their outlook. In contrast, those who had joined Lloyd George's camp fared rather better. In the new government, Montagu retained the India Office while Churchill became Secretary of State for War and Air.

Asquith was not only out of power but also out of Parliament. It ought to have been the cue for him to step down as leader of the Liberal Party. But the scale of the rout ensured there was nobody of sufficient standing to take his place, or at any rate, nobody who could counter Lloyd George. Rather than retire gracefully, Asquith asked Sir Donald Maclean to deputise for him in the Commons in order to hold the ring until such time as he could get re-elected at a by-election. When that opportunity would come was unclear. Ominously, the first six months of 1919 passed without Asquith receiving a single invitation to address a Liberal association anywhere in Britain. His attitude, as one of his defeated colleagues, Reginald McKenna, put it, was 'stoical to the point of indifference'.[35] It was a bad time to create a vacuum of leadership.

During 1920 relations between the rival Liberal parties got worse, with both sides building up competing organisations and abandoning the convention that had held at the 1918 election that whomever the local association adopted as their candidate would be accepted by both factions. It was not a positive statement that the Independent Liberals began to be referred to as the 'Wee Frees' after the doctrinally pure but marginalised tendency that had broken away from mainstream Scottish Presbyterianism. Perhaps appropriately, it was in Scotland that Asquith again sought salvation when he decided to stand in Paisley where a by-election was pending that would pit him against a strong local Labour candidate. The executive of the Paisley Liberal Association adopted him by twenty votes to seventeen. It was hardly a ringing endorsement.

Asquith had chosen wisely and Paisley's electors duly returned him to Parliament. However, his election campaign had been marred by a bitter controversy with a former friend. While Asquith was bestriding the public halls and sombre meeting rooms of Paisley, Haldane was opening up and speaking his mind to the press. He announced that Liberalism appeared exhausted and it was 'with Labour that the hope lies for tomorrow'. It was a general observation, not one intended as firm advice to Paisley's voters, although its timing made it look as such. Margot was so infuriated that she wrote to Haldane's mother, complaining at her son's decision to choose 'this moment to stick a knife into Henry. What odd people God makes! To think that your son and Ll. George should hunt in couples!'[36] To the same aged recipient, Haldane responded with wearying resignation, 'Margot is tiresome because she is ignorant. She has done much to make it difficult in the years gone by for Asquith to rise to the occasion.'[37] Asquith's best man might have added that his choice of Margot as his wife had also slowly but surely come between them. Haldane had time and cause to reflect on those unclouded earlier days when he had holidayed with his friend and the first Mrs Asquith, sitting up late discussing serious matters and devising strategies for making the world a better place. Reassuring his mother that he had no intention of joining the Labour Party he nonetheless admired the fact that 'they are in earnest and have great ideals'.[38] In other words, they had the attributes that had originally attracted him to the young Herbert Henry Asquith.

The separation of the two men was now all but complete. Asquith, the more worldly of the two, held on to the titles of authority – the leadership of a party over whose withered and ineffective wing he had control. Haldane, meanwhile, busied himself with committee work. His report on government departments was published in 1919. He developed other proposals involving adult education and the University of London. Although no reader of Schopenhauer himself, the King had conferred upon Haldane the Order of Merit. It was a sign that the vulgar anti-German assaults upon his character made no impression with the house of Windsor. He also had more time to reflect, writing books on the effect scientific advances were having on philosophy. He was particularly intrigued by Einstein's theories and entertained him to dinner at Queen Anne's Gate in June 1921.

'With my old friend Asquith, I had long ceased to have much opportunity to talk about politics' was how Haldane deftly alluded in his autobiography to the fact that their long partnership was no more.[39] It was not just because of the manner in which the ex-Prime Minister had dropped him. Haldane was disillusioned by Asquith's inability to inject new thinking into Liberalism. He offered nothing to suggest he had adjusted to a changed environment, but nor would he step aside for someone who might carry forward the party into the post-war world. In January 1922, Asquith invited Haldane to a major Liberal Party rally at Westminster Central Hall and this was to be the moment that they gave up pretending to be on the same side. Haldane did not care for the letter's impersonal tone. Although he replied with the assurance that it was not a question of respect, he made clear that there was 'a question of principle' separating them. The advancement and spread of educational opportunities had become his great project and he considered himself free to work with whichever party shared these goals. There was 'the almost complete lack of harmony between my strong conviction on this subject and the programme of official Liberalism ... In the official programme, and even in your own speeches, I can find no response about the thing I care for before any other at this moment.'[40]

Unsaid, but implicit in this accusation, was that Haldane too acknowledged that success in politics was about influencing those who could bring about change and that hanging around on Asquith's coat-tails proffered little opportunity of achieving that goal. Friendship might have outweighed this brazen calculation but Asquith had chosen to sever that tie in May 1915 when he put the exigencies of power before standing up for a wrongly maligned partner. To make matters worse, their exchange was subsequently printed by the press – with Haldane and Asquith blaming each other for leaking it.

In November 1922, a general election confirmed Haldane's assessment that the Liberal Party – both of them – had lost the ability to deliver. This time, it was not only Asquith's Independent Liberals that were trounced at the polls. Lloyd George's efforts at fusion to create a new centre party had been rebuffed (ironically by his Liberal supporters) and, as a result, he paid the price for dependency upon another political party to stay in power. Despite the acquiescence of most of their leaders, the Unionists had grown weary of Lloyd George's costly and needlessly aggressive foreign policy, disliked (although forced to concede to) his efforts to settle Ireland and loathed the corrupt manner in which he showered honours upon doubtful characters who paid large sums into his own fighting fund. In particular, they had tired of his restless energy ('dynamic force' was the euphemism one rising MP, Stanley Baldwin, turned into a term of disparagement). Cutting their losses, they opted to withdraw from the coalition. In doing so, they brought back party politics. Bonar Law was persuaded to put aside his ill health and return to lead them under the slogan 'tranquillity'. It appealed to the voters, and the Unionists won power in their own right.

In many constituencies, the rival Liberal factions fielded candidates against each other. The result was predictable. Labour did better than the Asquith and Lloyd George groups combined. Seeing the way momentum was shifting, eleven former Liberal MPs now sat as Labour Members. The only compensation for Asquith – who was returned at Paisley – was that while his faction had only won 60 seats, Lloyd George's wing had done marginally worse, with 53 (albeit the Asquithites had fielded double the number of candidates). It was another terrible performance but Asquith satisfied himself with the settling of small scores. 'The thing that gives me the most satisfaction is to gloat over the corpses which have been left on the battlefield,' he beamed after learning that Montagu and the other 'renegades' who had accepted office from Lloyd George had lost their seats.[41]

It seemed that his obsession with his nemesis had blinded Asquith to the destruction of the party he had led for fourteen years and to the other relationships that had existed prior to his axing of colleagues in May 1915 and his own downfall nineteen months later. Yet, just at the moment when he and Lloyd George appeared to be grappling with each other over the slippery precipice, events conspired to offer them a chance to step back from their own version of the Reichenbach Falls. In October 1923, Bonar Law died in office. His successor as Prime Minister, Stanley Baldwin, responded to mounting unemployment by declaring in favour of protectionism. To enact this, he felt he needed the mandate of a fresh general election. As had proved the case in 1906, here was the one cause that could bring even Liberals together. Asquith and Lloyd George shared a platform in defence of free trade. Absent was Haldane. No public exhibitions of a revered shibboleth could tempt him back to the fold. He was through with Liberals, disillusioned with where they had taken Liberalism. For the first time he broke ranks formally and campaigned on behalf of the Labour Party.

The general election did not go as Baldwin hoped. The Unionist Party (returning to the title 'Conservative') won 258 seats whereas Labour took 191 and the Liberals 158. This was a hung Parliament in which the Conservatives were the largest party but there was a majority for free trade. It was a predicament that made Asquith kingmaker. Some Liberals counselled him to form a minority government. But it was hard to see how the leader of the party coming third had the clearest right to become Prime Minister unless as the head of a cross-party coalition. And Asquith had no desire to put his head back in that noose. His opposition to protectionism made lending support to the Conservatives improbable, although Baldwin's decision to accept the electorate's verdict against tariffs made it technically possible. But for Asquith there was nothing to be gained by propping up a far stronger party led by Baldwin. Rather, he could exert much more authority by letting the Labour leader, Ramsay MacDonald, form an inexperienced Labour government that would be at the permanent mercy of Liberal votes in Westminster. So Asquith, the senior politician who had most failed to comprehend the impact of Labour, chose to put Labour in. After all, he concluded, if there had to be a Labour government at some stage, there could be no better controlled conditions for allowing the experiment to take place.

Ramsay MacDonald retired to the seclusion of his home at Lossiemouth in the north of Scotland to put together the historic task of forming Britain's first Labour Cabinet. While he was there, he ventured over to Cloan in order to visit Haldane, the politician who had comprehended the impact of socialism. Haldane had offered great support during the campaign and at its conclusion had been a determined advocate of MacDonald rather than Asquith becoming Prime Minister. In saying so, he asked for nothing in return. But MacDonald proffered gifts. He suggested the India Office or the job that was supposedly closest to Haldane's heart – education. But it was to the Woolsack from which he had been so summarily dismissed that Haldane wanted to return. MacDonald consented. And so it was that in January 1924 Lord Haldane of Cloan became Lord Chancellor for the second time.

The evening before he returned to the job that Asquith had first given and then removed from him, Haldane composed him a letter:

> My mind goes back to the evenings before either of us could contemplate Parliament for ourselves, evenings in which we were nonetheless concentrated on ideas. And I think of old days at Cloan and at Ambleside, or in London.
>
> Nor do I forget how you stood by me, or how you fought for me over the [Lord] Chancellorship in 1905, or how you put me there in 1912. Believe me, I am not oblivious of these things.
>
> Now it is a new period, and our adventure is both difficult and uncertain. It is not without misgiving that I face it. But I do not consider that I have [the] right to stand aside in this hour.
>
> None the less, the old sense of personal affection and of gratitude remains with me. If not for you I should not have been where I am – Whatever that may stand for.
>
> And so I shall continue to the end to describe myself as
> Yours ever affectionately,
>   H. of C.[42]

It was as if now that Haldane had walked out of the same party as Asquith – now that he was free from his patronage – he could let the hurt of more recent times pass. In truth, it was also a moment in which he could afford to be magnanimous. Not only had he broken free from Asquith's shadow, he at last had an advantage over him. He was back in government.

Apart from Arthur Henderson, Haldane was the only member of the new government who had ever sat in the Cabinet before. Consequently, he found himself relied upon by Labour ingénues for advice on matters of procedure ranging from the serious (how to handle civil servants) to the ceremonial (that the Prime Minister should be addressed as such and not by his own name). In departmental matters, his usefulness extended far beyond the immediate horizon of the Woolsack. In particular he provided an experienced voice on defence and foreign affairs. He chaired the Committee of Imperial Defence and was at ease with the military 'brass hats', a hardened group who brought out the social gaucheness of his Labour colleagues. In return, MacDonald secured the release for publication of government papers exonerating Haldane's role in the 1912 mission to Berlin. It was a favour his old Liberal colleagues, Asquith and Grey, had never delivered.

For all this, the experience of office renewed could only be brief. Without a parliamentary majority, the government's life was prolonged only by the Liberals' sufferance. At a nod from Asquith, the carpet would be pulled from under its feet. In October 1924, after the Labour experiment had entered its tenth month, Asquith decided to call a halt to it when he led calls for a select committee into the Campbell Case (which involved the handling of sedition charges against the editor of the *Daily Worker*). The ensuing Commons division went against the government and MacDonald was forced to call a general election. Thus Asquith's manoeuvre brought to an end Haldane's Indian summer in office. It proved also to be the last speech Asquith would ever give in the House of Commons.

The 1924 general election was the third in three years. Asquith's Liberal Party was in no financial position to endure these burdens and Lloyd George, looking to his own future, was careful not to let much of his fighting fund be wasted propping up the Asquithian party organisation. The election result, when it came, was a shock nonetheless. Baldwin and the Conservatives were swept triumphantly back into power. That much was not surprising. But the extent of the slaughter went beyond the worst predictions. The Liberal representation in the Commons was decimated from 158 to 40 MPs. His speeches in Paisley interrupted by agitators singing 'The Red Flag', Asquith went down to defeat, losing to the Labour candidate by over 2,000 votes. As he prepared to take his leave, Liberal activists began singing 'Will ye no' come back again?'. To this there was a clear and unavoidable answer, although one left best unspoken at the moment of departure. He was seventy-two and this time he was out for good. From Glasgow St Enoch's station, he boarded the train that would take him back to London. To pass time during the journey, he had packed four P.G. Wodehouse novels in his baggage.

There was much to take off his mind. He was still party leader, but Lloyd George would now become chairman of the parliamentary party . . . such as it was. Indeed, the 1924 general election ended the uncertainty of recent years, establishing a new two-party future dominated by the clash of Labour versus Conservative. As such it was a watershed, for henceforth the electorate appreciated that the Liberal Party was no longer in serious contention for government. Whatever its individual merits, on the question of who should govern Britain, a Liberal vote was a wasted vote. And so the great age of the Liberal Party passed. Haldane had jumped ship, Asquith had gone down with it.

In defeat, Asquith was offered a peerage. After giving it some thought, he wrote to the King, 'If it should be your Majesty's pleasure, in accordance with precedent, to confer upon me the dignity of an Earl, I should propose to take the title of Oxford, which has fine traditions in our history, and which was given by Queen Anne to her Prime Minister Robert Harley.'[43] It was a romantic thought, albeit one likely to cause a rumble in the tomb of that irreconcilable Whig, Sarah, Duchess of Marlborough. In the event, it stirred some rather high-handed representations from the remnants of the Harley family and the snobbish aside of the future Lady Salisbury who quipped, 'It is like a suburban villa calling itself Versailles.'[44] Keen to differentiate as well as honour achievement, the College of Arms ensured that Asquith ultimately had to settle for the title of 'Oxford and Asquith' which risked making him sound like a provincial outfitter. He took the qualification with good grace. It was not of course obsequies to Harley that had prompted his claim on the title but a desire to be forever associated with the ancient university that had offered him the first glimpses of worldly ambition and conferred upon him the meritocratic distinction that meant to him what ownership of ancestral properties meant to those for whom privilege was a birthright.

Oxford did not return the compliment. When in 1925 Asquith stood in the election for Chancellor of the University, its alumni – by a convincing margin of two to one – snubbed him by conferring the honour instead upon

Lord Cave. Cave was Baldwin's Lord Chancellor but his appeal was primarily that he was not Asquith. It was a pointed rebuke. Westminster offered scarcely greater reward. For a while, Asquith maintained an unconvincing double act, staying on as party leader while Lloyd George led in the Commons. But the age of Baldwin had arrived, his brand of liberal conservatism – which attracted Winston Churchill back to the Conservative Party as Chancellor of the Exchequer – ensuring that the Liberal Party could make little impression. Baldwin's laid-back manner, with his talk of fair dealing, moderation and distaste for zealots of Left or Right, successfully adopted some of old Liberalism's style. Until, of course, the late 1930s when the approach of another world war ensured that a new generation adjudged Baldwin and his successor, Neville Chamberlain, as guilty for failing to recognise the warning signals as previous critics had faulted 'wait and see' Asquith and his 'pro-German' friend on the Woolsack. For most of the period, though, aspects of Liberalism endured. It was the Liberal Party that was smashed.

In truth, it was not just Baldwin's broad voter appeal. Both Asquith and Lloyd George ran separate party funding campaigns and diverged very publicly in 1926 over the General Strike. After a mild stroke in June, Asquith finally resigned the party leadership in October 1926, retiring to The Wharf to prepare himself for the verdict of history. Margot did her best to write the first draft. By then she had already released two volumes of autobiography for publication, allowing the wider public an authentic taste of her talents for invective and colourful turns of phrase as well as a highly jaundiced analysis of the past thirty years. It sold well, as archly written gossip about the rich and famous invariably does, but it did her husband's reputation no good. This was especially unfortunate given that Lloyd George was her intended target. Towards him, the passage of time did nothing to lessen her loathing. Margot perpetuated a vendetta worthy of eighteenth-century Corsica.

There was discord and unhappiness elsewhere. All too foreseeably, clouds settled over the marriage of Edwin and Venetia Montagu. Venetia conducted numerous affairs. In 1919 she became the lover of Lord Beaverbrook, the great manipulator who had helped bring together Bonar Law and Lloyd George in order to lever Asquith out of Downing Street. She even showed him the letters Asquith had sent her. They provided useful background material for his book *Politicians And The War,* although decades would pass before the intimate sections received a public airing. Venetia became a mother, giving birth to a daughter, Judith Venetia. There was some doubt as to whether Montagu or the Earl of Dudley was the father.[45] Asquith kept his distance, disdainful of her 'rotten social gang ... who lead a futile and devastating life'.[46] In November 1924, Montagu died. Only forty-five years old – although seeming much older – he passed away a sad and depressed figure, worn down both by genuine ill health and by hypochondria and the vicissitudes of personal and political life. Beb Asquith's wife, Cynthia, was the only Asquith to make it to his funeral.

Three years later, Asquith paid a visit to the widowed Venetia. Introduced to her four-year-old daughter, he broke down in tears, murmuring 'This then is the child.'[47] On his way back to The Wharf he felt the return of pain in his leg, an infirmity that ensured the trip to Venetia proved to be his last outing. He died at The Wharf on 15 February 1928. He chose to be buried nearby, in the Sutton Courtenay parish churchyard. It was a peaceful spot, redolent of the sort of England of hedgerows and manor houses that King Charles I might have understood. It was not the England of the Rehoboth Chapel in Morley.

Declining health afflicted Haldane's last years, although he persevered with his remaining duties. He was leader of the Labour peers (not, in those hereditary-only days, an onerous shepherding commitment) and Baldwin thoughtfully asked him to stay on as a member of the Committee of Imperial Defence where he assumed the chairmanship of one of its subcommittees. His memory was finally failing him when he learned of Asquith's death but, as was expected of him, he gave an appreciation in the House of Lords. He began by admitting he thought Grey should have precedence in speaking of their departed friend and leader. After all, Grey had been closer to him in his last years. But, on reflection, it was probably best if the man who had known Asquith longest should speak first. It was a time for tributes only and in this Haldane delivered what was expected, ending with a poignant claim that rang true, 'among his intimate friends, who, like Lord Grey and myself, had been, as he always used to say, his oldest political friends, there was something that brought us still more closely to him. We had worked and lived closely together through all those years and now that he has passed away, speaking for myself, I feel that much of my interest has gone out of public life.'[48]

As fate transpired, he had only six months left before following him. His mother had finally died, aged one hundred, in 1925 and his sister, Elizabeth, who like her brother never married, transferred her caring skills to tend him at Queen Anne's Gate. A governor of the London School of Economics, Elizabeth shared more of her brother's philosophical interests than he could reasonably have expected from most political wives. But she could not provide the emotional comfort he lacked. Despite his physical deterioration, he busied himself writing his autobiography. It was a sign of how far he had moved on that the most philosophical of politicians did not bother to explain in its pages what had attracted him to the Liberal cause. He faded away while putting the finishing touches to the manuscript of his own life. He had just received notification that he had been unanimously elected Chancellor of St Andrews University – news that cheered him greatly – when the end came at Cloan on Sunday afternoon, 19 August 1928. He was buried in the family chapel at Gleneagles which had been recently restored to the memory of those of his kith and kin killed in the war. The service was accompanied by pipers from the Black Watch and there was a strong showing from both the Regular and the Territorial Army. The old faithful were roused to the Scottish version of the 121st Psalm. Later that night the grave was attacked and vandalised by a local lunatic, who appeared to be under the impression that the late Lord Chancellor was still alive underneath.

On learning of Haldane's death, Beatrice Webb wrote in her diary, 'no friend could regret it. He was not only powerless; he was wretched.' She reflected though that, 'If I had to write his epitaph, it would be "a powerful and beneficent personality, a great citizen, above all a loyal and generous friend"'.[49] He had received another tribute while still alive. Not invited to the victory march-past in London at the end of the war, he had sat up late and alone in his study in Queen Anne's Gate. It was well after dark when a distinguished-looking man in soldier's uniform knocked at the door. It was Field Marshal Douglas Haig. He explained he could not stay, but merely wanted to leave him a present. Passing a book over, he bid good evening, turned and departed. Alone again in his study, Haldane opened the gift. It was a volume of the Field Marshal's dispatches. Written on the inside in Haig's handwriting was the dedication:

> To Viscount Haldane of Cloan, the greatest Secretary of State for War England has ever had. In grateful remembrance of his successful efforts organizing the Military Forces for War on the Continent, notwithstanding much opposition from the Army Council and the half-hearted support of his Parliamentary friends. Haig F.M.

*

Margot did not take to widowhood. She lived on until 1945 in increasingly straitened circumstances. She was helped out financially by – of all people – Lord Beaverbrook. The charity of this former political foe contrasted, as she noted all too bitterly, with 'the behaviour of our Liberal friends – men who owe us not only their political reputations but their political salvation'.[50] At the last, she looked care-worn and emaciated. It was hardly surprising; she outlived not only her stepson Raymond but also his siblings Oc, a victim of Hodgkin's disease, and Elizabeth. Married to a Romanian diplomat, Elizabeth Asquith had become Princess Bibesco. Marcel Proust anointed her 'probably the most intelligent woman in the world'.[51] News of her death – while trapped in Romania at the end of the war – was the final blow for her mother. Beb followed his sister soon after in 1947, the First World War's legacy of shell-shock and its antidote, alcohol, having robbed him of the success early promise held out to him.

Of the other Asquiths, Cys prospered at the Bar, Anthony 'Puffin' struck out successfully and became a noted film director while Violet, married to her father's former secretary, Maurice Bonham Carter, maintained the family's interest in politics. Between 1956 and 1967 the Liberal Party was led by her son-in-law, Jo Grimond. Gone forever, though, were the idylls glimpsed in youth when nothing seemed more certain than the fortunes of Liberal England. Subsequent events added a nostalgic hue to memories of adolescent holidays in great houses, lawn tennis, swimming, the golf links, their father looking up from his letter-writing; Haldane's weekend bags in the hall. Archerfield was reduced to a windswept shell. Alderley was largely demolished.

Asquith had failed to save either himself or the Liberal Party, despite being prepared to sacrifice his oldest friend in the attempt. Where Haldane fell first, next Asquith and later Lloyd George followed as the Liberal Party was swallowed up and spat out by those it grimly embraced in coalition. At the outset of their journey in politics, Haldane and Asquith had championed the 'New Liberalism' in which an active state promoted social welfare legislation and widening educational opportunities. Haldane continued down this path until – his personal bonds with the Liberal leader severed – it took him into the ranks of the Labour Party. Another who believed in the state's helping hand, Lloyd George, even went into cahoots with the protectionists of the post-war Unionist Party in order to run the country like a chief signalman at a busy railway junction. In contrast, experience made Asquith more conservative. Having digested T.H. Green's tutorials at Balliol in the 1870s, he failed to maintain their progressive momentum into his own middle age. It might be said that the splintering of the Liberal Party was thus personified by the divergent ideological paths trodden by Haldane, Lloyd George and Asquith. Nonetheless, the party had a long tradition as a commune for politicians with contradictory interpretations of the creed. It was Asquith's disposal of Haldane and his subsequent war with Lloyd George that made it a broken home.

In those last years, Haldane tried to avoid showing his personal hurt in public, though he felt it deeply when left to brood, surrounded by the framed portraits of more celebrated statesmen and philosophers in his Queen Anne's Gate study. Yet, he too bore a measure of responsibility for the culture of backbiting. '"The Liberal Party is completely smashed, Mrs Webb," and he beamed defiance' was how Beatrice Webb recorded his mood at the ramifications produced by the outbreak of the Boer War in 1899.[52] The political infighting that excited the young Liberal Imperialist, and thrilled him yet more in the 1890s and early 1900s when his career was on the up, rebounded. Endemic factionalism proved the greatest enemy of the Liberal Party. Even after Asquith stepped down as leader in 1926, his supporters turned to his sword-carrier, Sir John Simon, and their own Liberal Council rather than accept the official leader, Lloyd George. They were determined to maintain a party within a party – just as the Liberal Imperialists had done. By the time of the 1931 general election, there were three separate Liberal parties appealing for votes, each with its own leader and programme. A second world war did little to convince electors that the future lay with the platoons of Liberalism. By 1951, the party was reunited, but had only six MPs and a 2.6 per cent share of the national vote. Asquith's daughter, Violet, saw the only hope of salvation in a merger with the Conservatives. Tellingly, the latter could not be bothered with the hassle. Once omnipresent, the Liberal Party had gone the way of the horse and cart. Only its trails remained, resurfaced for modern traffic.

EPILOGUE

President François Mitterrand had no difficulty coming up with a single word when asked by his adviser, Jacques Attali, what was the most important quality a leader could possess. The word was 'indifference'. There is something unnerving about this confession, shared without apparent embarrassment. It appears even more jarring when viewed from the perspective of the early twenty-first century, where evidence of 'emotional intelligence' and the projection of caring attitudes are looked for in responsive leadership. But Mitterrand's political longevity was not accidental. One of the extraordinary survivors of French politics, it must be assumed he knew what he was talking about. After all, leaders entrusted with authority are besieged by troubles. That is the nature of politics and those prepared to face the slings and arrows of outrageous fortune must accept this or duck back behind the battlements. Consequently, there has to be a mask of command. Without the ability to marshal and sublimate feelings, exposure to a continual onslaught would bend and buckle the most worthy of politicians. This is not just the case in terms of responding to – or ignoring – every provocation that comes along, but also in handling the sensitivities of colleagues forged from more brittle metals.

The problem is that indifference to people is not a basis for friendship. In this respect, it is worth asking whether friendship and leadership are compatible. There is certainly no necessary correlation. While Mitterrand was the sphinx in the Elysée, two other powerful leaders were in office in Pennsylvania Avenue and Downing Street. Yet, both Ronald Reagan and Margaret Thatcher reached their ascendancies without forming close personal friendships. They had the comfort of their convictions, the support and advocacy of the like-minded (in particular Mark Laxalt, who chaired two of Reagan's presidential campaigns and Keith Joseph, a major intellectual influence in Thatcher's decision to put herself forward) and the understanding of their respective spouses, Nancy and Denis. Otherwise alone in power, the closest friendship Reagan and Thatcher developed was a long-distance affection for each other.

In domestic politics however, Thatcher enjoyed a great advantage. She commanded the absolute loyalty (without actual friendship) of her deputy, Willie Whitelaw, a man who – even more fortuitously – hailed from the opposite wing of the Conservative Party. He was dependable, sufficiently self-confident to give honest advice and, until a stroke removed him from her side, a one-man praetorian guard for a leader who, at times, had almost as much to fear from her colleagues as from her opponents. Thatcher's revelation that 'every Prime Minister needs a Willie' was much quoted for its supposed hilarity but it should be acknowledged as a shrewd observation. No public figure can hope for more than the frank and disinterested support of a respected senior colleague who has lost the drive of personal ambition. Unfortunately, such people are even scarcer in the upper reaches of political life than the true friend whose deeper emotional entanglement may, sooner or later, become a problem.

Perhaps, the best chance for the survival of political friendships is a recognised impediment to the collision of mutual ambitions. The warm relationship – shared admiration might be the best term – between Winston Churchill and F.E. Smith provides a template in this respect. They ought not to have got on, and when in 1906 Smith entered Parliament as the Unionist MP for Liverpool Walton he had no urgent desire to make the acquaintance of Churchill, the renegade Tory turned rising star of the Liberal Party. Both were partisan fighters, reluctant to miss an opportunity to direct a quick blast of rhetoric at the other's politics. Yet, they recognised the extraordinary qualities of mind, wit and temperament of the other. 'Our friendship was perfect,' Churchill later recorded, when he wrote about a 'brilliant, loyal, lovable being' who 'had all the canine virtues in a remarkable degree – courage, fidelity, vigilance, love of the chase'.

It was membership of the Lloyd George coalition that brought them together in the same government. Becoming Cabinet colleagues introduced a potential tension that was different from the competition of being in rival parties. It created the possibility of one of them gaining ascendancy over the other in the same cause. Fortuitously, the prospect was made far less likely in 1919 when, in order to become Lord Chancellor, Smith accepted a peerage with the title Lord Birkenhead. This eased any lingering suspicions that his striving for life's glittering prizes might come into conflict with Churchill's similar goals. After all, the chances of a peer of the realm becoming Prime Minister – as Lord Curzon discovered – were much reduced in the Britain that emerged from the First World War where mastery of the democratic rather than the hereditary legislature was preferred. Burning out through hard work and brandy, Birkenhead's early death in 1930 ensured the friendship remained untarnishable. Churchill eulogised, 'Some men when they die after busy, toilsome, successful lives leave a great stock of scrip and securities, of acres or factories or the goodwill of large undertakings. F.E. banked his treasure in the hearts of his friends, and they will cherish his memory till their time is come."[1]

Most friendships in high places could not take so unthreatening a view of an active competitor. Tony Crosland and Roy Jenkins were undergraduate contemporaries at Oxford who became the bright hopes of the Labour Party in the 1950s and 1960s. They both had the means and motives to reach the top and it was the addition of mounting opportunity that converted their friendship into rivalry. Considering himself the senior partner intellectually, Crosland was jealous when Jenkins was appointed Chancellor of the Exchequer. Later, Jenkins wanted Crosland to support him in his great crusade – the cross-party campaign for British membership of the European Economic Community. Crosland, however, opted to put Labour Party unity (which he hoped yet to lead) above a matter of principle. Their failure to agree personal and political priorities had a predictable result – they stood against each other in the 1976 party leadership, helping to split the vote from their wing of the party and ensuring that James Callaghan, whom neither of them wanted, became Prime Minister instead. A year later Crosland was dead, unreconciled to Jenkins who ventured off on a course that led him out of the Labour Party. As a biographer of Asquith, Jenkins ought to have been alive to the dangers of a political partnership turning sour. In old age, he related the consequences of his falling-out with his one-time ally and collaborator to an interested listener, Tony Blair.[2]

It should not really come as a surprise that the acquisition and retention of power creates conflicts of loyalties. Queen Anne and Sarah, Duchess of Marlborough were driven apart by jealousy, personal and political inter-ference and the unavoidable problem of rank that exists between a monarch and a courtier regardless of how hard they pretend such barriers do not exist. Shared ideas about good governance brought Benjamin Franklin and Joseph Galloway together. Diverging ideas ended up driving them apart. Lord Haldane was thrown to the political wolves by his oldest friend who, as an embattled Prime Minister, was desperately trying to save himself and his party. In each of these cases, the preservation of friendship ceased to be the top priority for protagonists battling with competing considerations. E.M. Forster famously quipped that he hoped he had the guts to betray his country rather than his friends. Yet, the novelist of repressed emotions was hardly a do-or-die patriot in the first place. Whether he would have put his friends before his ideals is a more searching question.

Aristotle defined three forms of friendship: friendship of utility, friendship of pleasure and friendship based upon goodness. The first existed only so long as it remained mutually advantageous to those it involved. Similarly, the second was self-gratifying and dependent upon tastes that were fickle. The friendship of the virtuous was, needless to say, a higher level of attachment. It had a greater prospect of permanence because it involved 'those who desire the good of their friends for the friends' sake . . . because each loves the other for what he is, and not for any incidental quality. Accordingly the friendship of such men lasts so long as they remain good.' As such, this form of amity also helped spread the common good. Cicero developed this theme, stressing that the true friend should not lack candour where it was needed. Indeed, the welfare of the friend replicated that of the self, 'For every one loves himself, not for any reward which such love may bring, but because he is dear to himself independently of anything else.' Differentials of ability, fortune or rank should not cause any divergence or jealousy. 'Make up your minds to this,' Cicero advised, 'Virtue (without which friendship is impossible) is first; but next to it, and to it alone, the greatest of all things is Friendship.'³ This seems a long way from the talent Mitterrand identified for political success.

Casting off inessential ties is an uncongenial trait of the ambitious. However, for long periods all three of the friendships in this book were held together by affections that went well beyond the temporary expediencies of self-serving calculation. Theirs were partnerships fostered by shared ideals and the promotion of common causes. With faith in their own doctrines, they believed mutual advancement also promoted a more general, public good. Alas, how stealthily vanity stalks the paths of virtue.

NOTES

Full bibliographical details are given at the first citation of a work within each Part. All works cited were published in London unless otherwise stated.

Introduction: Ambition and the Limits of Loyalty

1 In Roger Lockyer's biography of George Villiers, first Duke of Buckingham, in *The Oxford Dictionary of National Biography*, vol. 56 (Oxford, 2004), p. 489.
2 Conor Cruise O'Brien, *Edmund Burke* (1997), p. 337.
3 David Gilmour, *Curzon* (1994), pp. 27, 43.
4 Gilmour, pp. 267, 380.

PART ONE: COURTIERS

Chapter 1: Girlfriends

1 In Eleanore Boswell, *The Restoration Court Stage, 1660–1702* (Cambridge Mass., 1932), p. 187.
2 Ibid., p. 130.
3 John Evelyn diary, 15 December 1675, E.S. de Beer (ed.), *The Diary of John Evelyn* (Oxford, 1959), p. 606.
4 Boswell, p. 42.
5 'Life of Dryden' by Sir Walter Scott, in Agnes Strickland, *Lives of the Queens of England*, vol. 7, Mary II (1866), p. 250.
6 Boswell, p. 177.
7 Dowager Duchess of Marlborough, *An Account of the Conduct of the Dowager Duchess of Marlborough* (1742), p. 10.
8 John Miller, *James II, A Study in Kingship* (1989 edn), p. 46.
9 Ibid., p. 71.
10 Lady Vaughan to William Russell, 23 September 1673, in Edward Gregg, *Queen Anne* (1980), p. 14.
11 Miller, p. 75.
12 Character of Sarah by Mrs Burnet, Frances Harris, *A Passion for*

Government, *The Life of Sarah, Duchess of Marlborough* (Oxford, 1991), p. 17.

13 David Green, *Sarah, Duchess of Marlborough* (1967), p. 32.

14 Princess Mary to Lady Frances Apsley, letter 12, in Lt-Col. The Hon. Benjamin Bathurst, *Letters of Two Queens* (1924), pp. 54–5.

15 Princess Mary to Lady Frances Apsley, letter 17, Bathurst, pp. 60–1.

16 Princess Mary to Lady Frances Apsley, letters 23 and 26, Bathurst, pp. 68–9 and 71.

17 Roger Lockyer, *Tudor and Stuart Britain 1471–1714* (second edn, 1985), p.318.

18 In Gregg, *Queen Anne*, p. 14.

19 J.P. Kenyon, *The Stuarts* (1958), p. 144.

20 Winston S. Churchill, *Marlborough, His Life and Times* (1934), vol. 1, p. 91.

21 John Churchill to Mrs Elizabeth Mowdie, Churchill, vol. 1, p. 122.

22 Princess Anne to Lady Frances Apsley, 22 September and 20 September 1679, Bathurst, pp. 109 and 107.

23 Princess Anne to Lady Frances Apsley, 22 September 1679, Bathurst, p. 109.

24 Churchill, vol. 1, p. 149.

25 Ibid., pp. 153–4.

26 James, Duke of York to Henry Hyde, Earl of Clarendon, 14 December 1680, in Harris, p. 30.

27 Princess Mary to Lady Bathurst (Lady Frances Apsley), 23 February 1683, Bathurst, p. 158.

28 Wm Denton to Sir Ralph Verney, 13 November 1682, Gregg, *Queen Anne*, p. 27.

Chapter 2: Mrs Morley and Mrs Freeman

1 Anne to Sarah [April 1967], in R.O. Bucholz, *The Augustan Court: Queen Anne and the Decline of Court Culture* (Stanford Ca., 1993), p. 51.

2 Duchess of Marlborough, *Conduct*, p. 10.

3 Anne to Sarah [1683], Harris, p. 35.

4 Narrative by Sarah, 1709, in Harris, p. 23.

5 Gregg, *Queen Anne*, p. 35.

6 Duchess of Marlborough, *Conduct*, p. 11.

7 Green, *Sarah*, p. 101.

8 Ibid., pp. 101–2.

9 Duchess of Marlborough, *Conduct*, p. 13.

10 Anne to Sarah [1683–4], Harris, p. 36.

11 Green, *Sarah*, p. 47.
12 John Evelyn diary, 6 February 1685, de Beer (ed.), p. 791.
13 Anthony Hamilton, *Memoirs of Count Grammont* (1906), p. 142.
14 Miller, p. 122.
15 Anne to Sarah [12 August 1686], Gregg, *Queen Anne*, p. 39.
16 Lady Russell to Dr Fitzwilliam, 18 February 1687, Gregg, *Queen Anne*, p. 47.
17 Anne to Mary, 9 May 1687, Beatrice Curtis Brown (ed.), *The Letters and Diplomatic Instructions of Queen Anne* (1935, reprinted 1968), p. 31.
18 Kenyon, p. 154.
19 Lord Churchill to William III, 17 May 1687, Gregg, *Queen Anne*, p. 49.
20 Anne to Mary, 14 March 1688, Curtis Brown, p. 34.
21 Anne to Mary, 20 March 1688, Curtis Brown, p. 35.
22 Anne to Mary, 18 June 1688, Curtis Brown, p. 37.
23 Anne to William of Orange, 18 November 1688, Curtis Brown, pp. 43–4.
24 H.C. Foxcroft (ed.), *A Supplement to Burnet's History of His Own Time* (Oxford, 1902), pp. 292, 291.
25 Duchess of Marlborough, *Conduct*, p. 16.
26 Green, *Sarah*, p. 53.
27 Gila Curtis, *The Life and Times of Queen Anne* (1972), p. 62.
28 Anne to Mary of Modena, 25 November 1688, Curtis Brown, p. 45.
29 Miller, pp. 208–9.
30 John Evelyn diary, 22 February 1689, de Beer (ed.), p. 902; Duchess of Marlborough, *Conduct*, pp. 25–6.
31 Gregg, *Queen Anne*, p. 68.
32 Notes by Sarah [1720s], Harris, p. 52.
33 J.R. Jones, *Marlborough* (Cambridge, 1993), p. 41.
34 Ibid., p. 41; Harris, p. 57.
35 Harris, p. 57.
36 Anne to Sarah [1690], Curtis Brown, p. 51.
37 Anne to Sarah [1692?], Curtis Brown, p. 60.
38 In Anne Somerset, *Ladies-in-Waiting: From the Tudors to the Present Day* (1984), p. 164.
39 Bucholz, pp. 32–3.
40 Foxcroft (ed.), p. 292.
41 Duchess of Marlborough, *Conduct*, p. 11.
42 Ophelia Field, *The Favourite: Sarah, Duchess of Marlborough* (2002), p. 71.
43 Duchess of Marlborough, *Conduct*, p. 14.
44 Ibid., p. 14.

[45] Hamilton diary, 27 December 1710, Philip Roberts (ed.), *Diary of Sir David Hamilton* (Oxford, 1975), p. 23.

[46] Anne to Sarah [1691?], Harris, p. 59.

[47] Anne to Sarah [27 April 1692], Harris, p. 63.

[48] Curtis, pp. 46–7.

[49] In Carola Oman, *Mary of Modena* (1962), p. 150.

[50] Anne to James II, 1 December 1691, Curtis Brown, p. 52.

[51] Mary to Anne, 5 February 1692, Duchess of Marlborough, *Conduct*, p. 44.

[52] Bucholz, p. 204.

[53] Mary to Anne, 5 February 1692, Gregg, *Queen Anne*, p. 86.

[54] Anne to Mary, 6 February 1692, Curtis Brown, p. 53.

[55] Anne to Sarah [5 February 1692], Harris, p. 64.

[56] Anne to Sarah [February 1692], Sarah, Duchess of Marlborough, *Conduct* in *Memoirs* (1930 edn), pp. 51, 53; Harris, pp. 64–5.

[57] Anne to Sarah [1692], Duchess of Marlborough, *Conduct* in *Memoirs*, p. 53.

[58] Anne to Sarah, May 1692, Duchess of Marlborough, *Conduct*, p. 70.

[59] Anne to Sarah, May 1692, Curtis Brown, p. 56.

[60] Anne to Sarah, 22 May 1692, Curtis Brown, p. 57; Duchess of Marlborough, *Conduct*, p. 81.

[61] Duchess of Marlborough, *Conduct*, p. 88.

[62] Marlborough to Sarah, 23 April/4 May 1703, Henry L. Snyder (ed.), *The Marlborough-Godolphin Correspondence 1701–11*, vol. 1 (Oxford, 1975), p. 176.

[63] Green, *Sarah*, p. 69.

[64] Ibid., p. 70.

[65] Bucholz, p. 204.

[66] Green, *Sarah*, p. 75.

[67] Green, *Anne*, p. 64.

[68] Green, *Sarah*, p. 75.

[69] Curtis, p. 49.

Chapter 3: Keeping the Key

[1] Curtis, p. 93.

[2] Celia Fiennes's observations in Bucholz, p. 224.

[3] Bucholz, p. 208.

[4] Ibid., pp. 210–12.

[5] Ibid., pp. 235–6.

[6] Anne to Sarah, 19 May 1702, *Marlborough-Godolphin Correspondence*, vol. 1, pp. 66–7.

7 Curtis, p. 96.

8 Sarah to Duchess of Bedford, 1 November 1733, Harris, p. 87.

9 Bucholz, p. 154.

10 Harris, p. 92.

11 Anne to Sarah [31 May 1702 ?], Harris, p. 89.

12 Anne to Sarah, 16 December 1702, Curtis Brown, p. 103.

13 Green, *Sarah*, p. 88

14 Anne to Sarah [summer 1703], Curtis Brown, p. 125.

15 Curtis, p. 121.

16 Marlborough to Sarah, 9/20 October 1704, *Marlborough-Godolphin Correspondence*, vol. 1, p. 385.

17 Curtis, p. 107.

18 Anne to Sarah, 21 November 1704, Curtis Brown, p. 100.

19 Sarah to Anne [25 November 1704], Harris, pp. 113–14.

20 Harris, p. 91.

21 Churchill, vol. 2, p. 33.

22 Duchess of Marlborough, *Conduct*, p. 122.

23 Anne to Sarah, 24 October 1702, Curtis Brown, p. 98.

24 Anne to Sarah, 18 August [1704], Harris, p. 110.

25 Godolphin to Sarah, 1 September 1704, *Marlborough-Godolphin Correspondence*, vol. 1, p. 366.

26 Curtis, p. 133.

27 Ibid., p. 133.

28 Green, *Anne*, p. 146.

29 Curtis, p. 143.

30 Sarah to Anne [27 August 1706], William Coxe, *Memoirs of the Duke of Marlborough* (1848 edn), vol. 2, p. 13.

31 Sarah to Anne, 30 August [1706], Coxe, vol. 2, p. 13.

32 Sarah to Anne [6 Sept. 1706], Harris, p. 127; Coxe, vol. 2, pp. 116–20.

33 Godolphin to Sarah, 7 September 1706, *Marlborough-Godolphin Correspondence*, vol. 2, pp. 670–1.

34 Note by Sarah, Harris, p. 127.

35 Godolphin to Sarah, 17 September 1706, *Marlborough-Godolphin Correspondence*, vol. 2, pp. 683–4.

36 Anne to Sarah [7 April 1707], Curtis Brown, p. 225.

37 Green, *Sarah*, p. 125.

38 Duchess of Marlborough, *Conduct*, p. 178.

39 Green, *Sarah.*, pp. 122–3; abridged version in Duchess of Marlborough, *Conduct*, p. 185.

40 Anne to Sarah [18 July 1707], Curtis Brown, p. 227.

41 Marlborough to Sarah, 18/29 August 1707, *Marlborough-Godolphin Correspondence*, vol. 2, p. 887.
42 Narrative by Sarah, Harris, p. 137; see also Duchess of Marlborough, *Conduct*, pp. 182–3.
43 Sarah to Anne, 29 October 1709, Harris, pp. 137–8.
44 Abigail Masham to Harley, 29 September 1707, Harris, p. 138.
45 Duchess of Marlborough, *Conduct*, p. 206.
46 Ibid.
47 Sarah to Anne, 27 December 1707, Duchess of Marlborough, *Conduct*, pp. 210–11.
48 Sir John Cropley to the Earl of Shaftesbury, February 1708, Gregg, *Queen Anne*, p. 259.
49 Marlborough to Anne, 22 July/2 August 1708, Coxe, vol. 4 (1820 edn), p. 188.
50 Sarah to Anne, 7 July [1708], Harris, p. 146.
51 Anne to Sarah, Curtis Brown, p. 229.
52 Anne to Sarah [7 July 1708], Harris, p. 146.
53 Green, *Sarah*, p. 314.
54 Maynwaring to Sarah, *Private Correspondence of Sarah, Duchess of Marlborough* (1838), vol. 1, p. 256.
55 Sarah to Anne, 26 July 1708, Green, *Sarah*, pp. 318–21; Harris, p. 147.
56 Sarah to Anne, 26 July 1708, Green, *Sarah*, pp. 318–21; Harris, p. 147.
57 Anne to Sarah [August 1708], Curtis Brown, p. 258.
58 Green, *Sarah*, p. 135.
59 Abigail Masham to Harley, 21 July 1708, Harris, p. 147.
60 Sarah to Hamilton, December 1710, Harris, p. 154.
61 Curtis, p. 165.
62 Harris, p. 160; Gregg, *Queen Anne*, p. 292.
63 Anne to Marlborough, October 1709, Curtis Brown, p. 286.
64 Sarah to Hamilton, 22 December 1710, quoting Anne's letter of 26 October 1709, Harris, p. 161.
65 Sarah to [Godolphin, 27 October 1709], Harris, p. 161; (see Brown, p. 286: Anne to Sarah [27 October 1707], for Godolphin's delivery of the letter of 26 October).
66 Gregg, *Queen Anne*, p. 295.
67 Harris, p. 164.
68 Ibid., p. 168; *Private Correspondence of Sarah*, vol. 1, pp. 295–9; Duchess of Marlborough, *Conduct*, pp. 239–44.
69 Sarah to Anne, 7 June 1710, Harris, p. 172.
70 Anne to Sarah, 12 June 1710, Harris, p. 172.

71 Anne to Godolphin, 13 June 1710, Curtis Brown, p. 303.
72 Hamilton diary, 8 July 1710, in Roberts (ed.), *Hamilton Diary*, p. 12.
73 Sarah to Anne [17 January 1711], Coxe, vol. 3 (1848 edn), pp. 175–6.
74 J.R. Jones, *Marlborough* (1993), p. 13.
75 Only a fragment of Anne's letter of dismissal to Marlborough, copied (ominously) in Oxford's handwriting survives. Gregg, *Queen Anne*, pp. 348–9.

Chapter 4: The Spoils of Ruined People
1 Bucholz, p. 228.
2 Sarah to Coningsby, 9 January [1713], Harris, p. 191.
3 Sarah to Craggs, 7 June 1713, in Green, *Sarah*, p. 185n.
4 Edward Gregg, 'Marlborough in Exile', *Historical Journal*, vol. xv (1972), pp. 607–8.
5 Gilbert Burnet, *History of his Own Time*, vol. 6 (Oxford, 1833 edn), pp. 36–7, Dartmouth's Note.
6 Geoffrey Holmes, *British Politics in the Age of Anne* (1967), p. 216.
7 Bucholz, p. 164; Gregg, *Queen Anne*, p. 388; Royal College of Surgeons, Hunter-Baillie Collection, Arbuthnot Letterbook, f. 3; Earl of Mar to John Arbuthnot, 2 August 1712.
8 Burnet, vol. 6, pp. 36–7, Dartmouth's Note.
9 Sarah to Craggs, 3–14 July 1714, Gregg, 'Marlborough in Exile', p. 611.
10 Harris, p. 201.
11 Gregg, 'Marlborough in Exile', p. 617.
12 Dr John Arbuthnot, in Curtis, p. 200.
13 In Iris Butler, *Rule of Three, Sarah Duchess of Marlborough and her Companions in Power* (1967), p. 286.
14 Diary of Mary, Countess Cowper, ibid., p. 287.
15 Wentworth Papers, in A.L. Rowse, *The Early Churchills* (1956), p. 343; Swift Correspondence, vol. 2, p. 222 (Green, p. 195).
16 *Letters of Sarah, Duchess of Marlborough . . . at Madresfield Court* (1875), p. 37, in Christopher Hibbert, *The Marlboroughs* (2001), p. 294n.
17 Sarah to Hamilton, 22 December 1710, Harris, p. 90.
18 Swift, *Journal to Stella*, pp. 658–9, in Green, *Sarah*, p. 184.
19 In 'In Defence of the Duchess' in Michael Foot, *Debts of Honour* (1980).
20 Holmes, p. 214.
21 Oxford to Abigail Masham, 14 May 1714, in Holmes, p. 216.
22 Bucholz, pp. 69, 161.
23 Somerset, pp. 275–6.
24 Green, *Sarah*, p. 17.

PART TWO: REVOLUTIONARIES

Chapter 5: The City of Brotherly Love
1 Hugh Brogan, *The Pelican History of the United States of America* (1986), p. 86.
2 Niall Ferguson, *Empire, How Britain Made the Modern World* (2003), p. 89.
3 Benjamin Franklin, 'The Interest of Great Britain Considered, With Regard to her Colonies. And the Acquisitions of Canada and Guadeloupe', *The Papers of Benjamin Franklin* (New Haven, 1959–), vol. 9, p. 90.
4 In Brogan, p. 80.
5 Benjamin Franklin, 'Observations Concerning the Increase of Mankind', *Papers of Benjamin Franklin*, vol. 4, p. 233.
6 It is possible that Deborah was Franklin's mother, but the circumstantial evidence suggests otherwise.
7 Franklin to Galloway, 11 April 1757, *Papers of Benjamin Franklin*, vol. 7, p. 178.
8 Franklin to Galloway, 10 June 1758, *Papers of Benjamin Franklin*, vol. 8, pp. 96–7.
9 Benjamin Franklin to Jane Mecom, 25 November 1762, *Papers of Benjamin Franklin*, vol. 10, pp. 154 and 155.
10 Franklin to Richard Jackson, 1 June 1764, *Papers of Benjamin Franklin*, vol. 11, pp. 214–21.
11 Benjamin Chew to Thomas Penn, 5 November 1765, in Robert Middlekauff, *Benjamin Franklin and His Enemies* (Berkeley and Los Angeles, 1996), p. 101.
12 Franklin to John Hughes, 9 August 1765, *Papers of Benjamin Franklin*, vol. 12, pp. 234–5.
13 Galloway to Franklin, [16–28?] November 1765, *Papers of Benjamin Franklin*, vol. 12, p. 376.
14 Ibid., pp. 375–9.
15 'The Examination of Doctor Benjamin Franklin, before an August Assembly, relating to the Repeal of the Stamp Act', 13 February 1766, *Papers of Benjamin Franklin*, vol. 13, p. 135.
16 Galloway to Franklin, 23 March 1766, ibid., pp. 284–6.
17 Franklin to Galloway, 13 December 1766, ibid., pp. 520–1.
18 Galloway to Franklin, 23 March 1766, ibid., p. 285.
19 Benjamin Franklin to William Franklin, 13 March 1768, *Papers of Benjamin Franklin*, vol. 15, p. 76.
20 William Franklin to the Earl of Hillsborough, 23 November 1768, Archives

of the State of New Jersey, in Willard Sterne Randall, *A Little Revenge, Benjamin Franklin and His Son* (Boston, 1984), p. 239.

21 *Pennsylvania Chronicle* 18–25 April 1768, in Benjamin H. Newcomb, *Franklin and Galloway, A Political Partnership* (New Haven, 1972), p. 187.

22 Galloway to Franklin, 9 October 1767, *Papers of Benjamin Franklin*, vol. 14, p. 277.

23 Franklin to Galloway, 9 January 1769, *Papers of Benjamin Franklin*, vol. 16, pp. 17–18.

24 Galloway to Franklin, 21 June 1770, *Papers of Benjamin Franklin*, vol. 17, pp. 177–8.

25 Galloway to Franklin, 27 September 1770 and 12 October 1772, *Papers of Benjamin Franklin*, vol. 17, pp. 228–9 and vol. 19, p. 331.

26 Franklin to Galloway, 2 December 1772, *Papers of Benjamin Franklin*, vol. 19, p. 419.

27 Franklin to Galloway, 6 January 1773, *Papers of Benjamin Franklin*, vol. 20, p. 17.

28 Franklin to Cadwalader Evans, 18 July 1771, *Papers of Benjamin Franklin*, vol. 18, p. 189.

29 Franklin to William Franklin, 30 January 1772, *Papers of Benjamin Franklin*, vol. 19, p. 51.

30 Franklin to William Franklin, 2 July 1768, *Papers of Benjamin Franklin*, vol. 15, pp. 160–1.

Chapter 6: Distant Loyalities

1 Franklin to Galloway, 18 February 1774, *Papers of Benjamin Franklin*, vol. 2, p. 109.

2 Franklin to Thomas Cushing, 2 December 1772, *Papers of Benjamin Franklin*, vol. 19, pp. 411–13.

3 Ibid., p. 411.

4 Transcript of Wedderburn's speech, 29 January 1774, *Papers of Benjamin Franklin*, vol. 21, p. 49.

5 Benjamin Franklin to William Franklin, 2 February 1774, *Papers of Benjamin Franklin*, vol. 21, p. 75.

6 Randall, p. 250.

7 In Randall, p. 456.

8 In Brogan, p. 166.

9 William Franklin to the Earl of Dartmouth, 6 September 1774, in F. W. Ricord and William Nelson (eds), *Documents Relating to the Colonial History of the State of New Jersey (1757–67)*, vol. 10 (Trenton, 1886), pp. 478–92.

[10] 'A Plan of a proposed Union between Great Britain and the Colonies . . .', copy in Thomas Balch (ed.), *The Examination of Joseph Galloway Esq., By a Committee of the House of Commons*, Philadelphia 1855 (Boston, 1972 edn), pp. 47–9.

[11] Joseph Galloway, *A Candid Examination of the Mutual Claims of Great Britain, and the Colonies: with a Plan of Accommodation, on Constitutional Principles* (New York, 1775), in Newcomb, p. 257n.

[12] Franklin to Galloway, 5 February 1775, *Papers of Benjamin Franklin*, vol. 21, pp. 469–71.

[13] Franklin to Galloway, 25 February 1775, *Papers of Benjamin Franklin*, vol. 21, p. 509.

[14] Ibid.

[15] Franklin to William Franklin, 22 March 1775, *Papers of Benjamin Franklin*, vol. 21, p. 595.

[16] Franklin to Galloway, 12 October 1774, *Papers of Benjamin Franklin*, vol. 21, p. 334.

[17] Franklin to Galloway, 25 February 1775, *Papers of Benjamin Franklin*, vol. 21, p. 509.

[18] William to Benjamin Franklin, 24 December 1774, *Papers of Benjamin Franklin*, vol. 21, p. 404.

[19] Ibid., pp. 403–4 (Randall, pp. 287–8).

[20] Benjamin to William Franklin, 6 October 1773, *Papers of Benjamin Franklin*, vol. 20, p. 437.

[21] In Ross J.S. Hoffman, *Edmund Burke, New York Agent* (Philadelphia, 1956), p. 131.

[22] James Boswell, *Letters to Temple*, in William Hunt, 'Edmund Burke', *Dictionary of National Biography*, vol. 3 (1908), p. 353.

[23] Carl B. Cone, *Burke and the Nature of Politics, The Age of the American Revolution* (Lexington, 1957) p. 285.

[24] Franklin to Burke, 19 December 1774, George H. Guttridge (ed.), *The Correspondence of Edmund Burke*, vol. 3 (Cambridge, 1961), pp. 80–1; Burke to William Baker (widower of William Penn's granddaughter, Juliana), 23 August 1775, Burke, *Correspondence*, vol. 3, p. 197.

[25] In Hoffman, p. 132.

[26] Burke, 'An Appeal from the New to the Old Whigs', 1791, in Conor Cruise O'Brien, *Edmund Burke* (1997), p. 250.

[27] Burke to Count Patrick Darcy, 5 October 1775, Burke, *Correspondence*, vol. 3, p. 228.

[28] Galloway to Samuel Verplanck, 24 June 1775, in Newcomb, p. 278.

29 Franklin to Galloway, 8 May 1775, *Papers of Benjamin Franklin*, vol. 22, p. 33.

30 Peter O. Hutchinson, *Diary and Letters of His Excellency Thomas Hutchinson*, vol. 2 (New York, 1971 edn), pp. 237–8.

31 (Joseph Galloway), *Letters from Cicero to Catiline the Second* (1781), p. 47.

32 Ibid., p. 237.

Chapter 7: A Broken Vase

1 Sheila L. Skemp, *Benjamin and William Franklin, Father and Son, Patriot and Loyalist* (Boston, 1994), p. 144.

2 William Franklin to Temple Franklin, 25 June 1776, in Randall, p. 423.

3 Elizabeth Franklin to Benjamin Franklin, 6 August 1776, *Papers of Benjamin Franklin*, vol. 22, pp. 552–3.

4 Admiral Lord Richard Howe to Franklin, 20 June 1776, *Papers of Benjamin Franklin*, vol. 22, pp. 483–4.

5 Franklin to Admiral Lord Richard Howe, 20 July 1776, *Papers of Benjamin Franklin*, vol. 22, pp. 519–21.

6 Edmund Burke to the Marquess of Rockingham, 6 January 1777, Burke, *Correspondence*, vol. 3, pp. 309–10.

7 Ibid., p. 310.

8 Richard Bache to Franklin, 20 June 1781, *Papers of Benjamin Franklin*, vol. 35, pp. 177–8.

9 Franklin to Richard Bache, 13 September 1781, *Papers of Benjamin Franklin*, vol. 35, pp. 471–2.

10 Franklin to Richard Bache, 2 June 1779, *Papers of Benjamin Franklin*, vol. 29, pp. 599–600.

11 In David McCullough, *John Adams* (New York, 2001), p. 193.

12 In Paul Johnson, *A History of the American People* (1997), p. 136.

13 Franklin to Madame Brillon, 10 March 1778, *Papers of Benjamin Franklin*, vol. 26, pp. 85–6; McCullough, p. 191.

14 Franklin to Madame Brillon, *c.* 27 July 1778, *Papers of Benjamin Franklin*, vol. 27, pp. 164–5.

15 In H. W. Brands, *The First American, The Life and Times of Benjamin Franklin* (New York, 2000), p. 549.

16 Reverend Samuel Peters, in Catherine S. Crary (ed.), *The Price of Loyalty: Tory Writings from the Revolutionary Era* (New York, 1973), p. 217.

17 William Franklin to Lord George Germain, 10 November 1778, in Randall, p. 449; William's Patriot-supporting brother-in-law, Richard Bache, was also of the view that Elizabeth had 'died broken-hearted'. Richard Bache

to Benjamin Franklin, 31 January 1778, *Papers of Benjamin Franklin*, vol. 25, p. 553.

[18] In Randall, p. 449.

[19] McCullough, p. 173.

[20] *Papers of Benjamin Franklin*, vol. 25, p. 236n.

[21] Franklin to the Marquis de Lafayette, 22 March 1779, *Papers of Benjamin Franklin*, vol. 29, p. 186.

[22] Russell F. Weigley, *Philadelphia, a 300-Year History* (New York, 1982), pp. 139–45; Willard Sterne Randall, *Benedict Arnold, Patriot and Traitor* (1991), pp. 428–9.

[23] *Freeman's Journal*, 15 March 1777, in North Callahan, *Royal Raiders, The Tories of the American Revolution* (New York, 1963), p. 98.

[24] Callahan, *Royal Raiders*, p. 162.

[25] Grace Galloway, diary entry for 20 August 1778, in Catherine S. Crary (ed.), *The Price of Loyalty: Tory Writings from the Revolutionary Era* (New York, 1973), pp. 325–6.

[26] William Franklin to Galloway, 17 November 1778, in Randall, p. 462.

[27] In Robert Harvery, *A Few Bloody Noses, The American War of Independence* (2001), p. 413.

[28] Ferguson, p. 77.

[29] Richard B. Morris, *The Peacemakers: The Great Powers and American Independence* (1965), p. 330; McCullough, p. 281.

[30] McCullough, p. 283.

[31] Comte de Vergennes to Benjamin Franklin, 15 December 1782, Albert Henry Smith (ed.), *Writings of Benjamin Franklin*, vol. 8 (New York, 1906), p. 641.

[32] Edmund Burke to Benjamin Franklin, 10 August 1782, Holden Furber (ed.), *The Correspondence of Edmund Burke*, vol. 5 (Cambridge, 1965), pp. 27–8.

[33] Joseph Galloway, *The Claim of the American Loyalists reviewed and maintained upon incontrovertible Principles of Law and Justice* (1788), pp. 86–7.

[34] In North Callahan, *Flight from the Republic, The Tories and the American Revolution* (Indianapolis, 1967), p. 124 and Lewis Einstein, *Divided Loyalties, Americans in England during the War of Independence* (1933), p. 233.

[35] Callahan, *Flight from the Republic*, p. 125.

[36] Einstein, pp. 206–29; Callahan, *Flight from the Republic*, p. 124.

[37] William Franklin to Galloway, 11 May 1782, Library of Congress, in Skemp, p. 265.

[38] Ibid., p. 266.

39 (Galloway), *Letters from Cicero*, p. 50.
40 Ibid., p. 57.
41 Ibid., pp. 61, 45.
42 Elizabeth Roberts (née Galloway) to [?], January 1811, in Balch, p. 76n.
43 John Wesley to Sarah Wesley, 17 September and 18 August 1790, John Telford (ed.), *The Letters of the Rev. John Wesley, AM*, vol. 8 (1931), pp. 238, 233, 234.
44 In Balch, p. 45n.
45 William to Benjamin Franklin, 22 July 1784, American Philosophical Society, in Skemp, p. 296.
46 Benjamin Franklin to William Franklin, 16 August 1784, Smith (ed.), *Writings of Benjamin Franklin*, vol. 9 (New York, 1906), pp. 252–4.
47 Ibid., pp. 613–14.
48 Benjamin Franklin to David Hartley, 4 December 1789, Smith (ed.), *Writings of Benjamin Franklin*, vol. 10 (New York, 1907), p. 72.
49 'Benjamin Franklin's Last Will and Testament', ibid., pp. 493–4.
50 William Franklin to Jonathan Williams, 17 May 1813, Jonathan Williams Papers, in Randall, p. 497.

PART THREE: LIBERALS

Chapter 8: Getting On

1 Alan Sykes, *The Rise and Fall of British Liberalism, 1776–1988* (1997), p. 45; see also Jonathan Parry, *The Rise and Fall of Liberal Government in Victorian Britain* (New Haven, 1993).
2 See Lucille Iremonger, *The Fiery Chariot, a Study of British Prime Ministers and the Search for Love* (1970).
3 In J.A. Spender and Cyril Asquith, *Life of Herbert Henry Asquith, Lord Oxford and Asquith*, vol. 1 (1932), p. 22.
4 Dr John Mortimer Angus in the *City of London School Magazine*, 1928, in ibid.
5 Earl of Oxford and Asquith, *Memories and Reflections 1852–1927*, vol. 1 (1928), p. 13.
6 Benjamin Jowett to Florence Nightingale, 4 December 1873, Vincent Quinn and John Prest (eds), *Dear Miss Nightingale: a selection of Benjamin Jowett's letters to Florence Nightingale 1860–1893* (Oxford, 1987), p. 249.
7 Richard Burdon Haldane, *An Autobiography* (1929), p. 83.
8 Ibid., p. 9.
9 Ibid., p. 9.
10 Ibid., p. 33.

[11] Ibid., p. 84.

[12] Violet Bonham-Carter, *The Times*, 30 July 1956.

[13] Asquith to Hilda Harrisson, 25 April 1917, *H.H.A., Letters of the Earl of Oxford and Asquith to a Friend*, vol. 1 (1933), p. 19.

[14] Haldane, *An Autobiography*, p. 8.

[15] See F.W.S. Craig, *British Electoral Facts 1832–1987* (Dartmouth, 5th edn), 1989.

[16] Haldane, *An Autobiography*, p. 104.

[17] Asquith to Haldane, 2 December [1885], Haldane Papers MS. 5902/204, National Library of Scotland.

[18] Haldane, *An Autobiography*, p. 84.

[19] Ibid., p. 92.

[20] Ibid., p. 84.

[21] *Progressive Review*, November 1896.

[22] R.B. Haldane, 'The Liberal Creed', in *The Contemporary Review*, October 1888, pp. 461–74.

[23] Haldane, *An Autobiography*, p. 117.

[24] Ibid., pp. 118–19.

[25] In William Verity, 'Haldane and Asquith', *History Today*, vol. xviii, no. 7, July 1968, p. 451.

[26] See Sophie Fuller's '"Devoted Attention": Looking for Lesbian Musicians in Fin-de-Siècle Britain', in Sophie Fuller and Lloyd Whitesell (eds), *Queer Episodes in Music and Modern Identity* (Champaign, Ill., 2002), pp. 89–90.

[27] V. [Valentine Munro Ferguson], *Betsy* (1892).

[28] Violet Bonham Carter, *The Times*, 30 July 1956.

[29] Asquith to Mrs Frances Horner, 11 September 1892, in Spender and Asquith, vol. 1, p. 73.

[30] Asquith to Mrs Frances Horner, 12 July 1892, ibid., p. 74.

[31] Asquith to Mrs Frances Horner, 1 August 1892, in Roy Jenkins, *Asquith* (1964), p. 58.

[32] Haldane, *An Autobiography*, p. 107.

[33] Ibid., p. 115.

[34] Ibid., p. 101.

[35] Ibid., pp. 208–9.

[36] Beatrice Webb diary, 16 March 1900, Norman and Jeanne MacKenzie (eds), *The Diary of Beatrice Webb*, vol. 2, 1892–1905 (1983), p. 173.

[37] Beatrice Webb diary, 12 March 1894, *Diary of Beatrice Webb*, vol. 2, p. 45.

[38] Beatrice Webb diary, 20 January 1895, *Diary of Beatrice Webb*, vol. 2, pp. 64–5.
[39] Rosebery to Asquith, in Stephen Koss, *Asquith* (1976), p. 42.

Chapter 9: All for One
[1] Margot Asquith, *The Autobiography of Margot Asquith*, vol. 1 (1920), pp. 261–2.
[2] Ibid., p. 147.
[3] Asquith to Margot Tennant, in Jenkins, vol. 1, p. 75.
[4] Margot Asquith, *Autobiography*, vol. 1, pp. 264–5.
[5] Ibid., p. 196.
[6] Colin Clifford, *The Asquiths* (2002), pp. 57–61.
[7] Spender and Asquith, vol. 1, p. 98.
[8] Koss, *Asquith*, pp. 91–2.
[9] Haldane, *An Autobiography*, pp. 103–4.
[10] Beatrice Webb diary, 28 February 1902, *Diary of Beatrice Webb*, vol. 2, p. 236.
[11] Oxford and Asquith, vol. 1, p. 105.
[12] Quoted in George Macaulay Trevelyan, *Grey of Fallodon* (1937), p. 58.
[13] Beatrice Webb diary, 3 May 1897, *Diary of Beatrice Webb*, vol. 2, pp. 113–14.
[14] Dudley Sommer, *Haldane of Cloan, His Life and Times 1856–1928* (1960), p. 141.
[15] L.S. Amery, *My Political Life*, vol. 1 (1953), p. 227.
[16] Violet Bonham Carter, *The Times*, 30 July 1956.
[17] Haldane, *An Autobiography*, pp. 165–7.
[18] Beatrice Webb diary, 19 September 1892, *Diary of Beatrice Webb*, vol. 2, p. 23.
[19] Violet Bonham Carter, *The Times*, 30 July 1956.
[20] Ibid.
[21] Raymond Asquith to Harold Baker, 24 September 1897, in John Jolliffe (ed.), *Raymond Asquith: Life and Letters* (1980), p. 26.
[22] Raymond Asquith to Harold Baker, 27 September 1898, Jolliffe (ed.), p. 48.
[23] Raymond Asquith to Harold Baker, 15 July 1900, Jolliffe (ed.), p. 70.
[24] H.C.G. Matthew, 'Richard Burdon Haldane', *Oxford Dictionary of National Biography*, vol. 24 (2004), p. 516.
[25] In Stephen E. Koss, *Lord Haldane, Scapegoat for Liberalism* (New York, 1969), p. 20.

[26] Asquith to Campbell-Bannerman, 19 December 1898, in Koss, *Asquith*, p. 44.

[27] Jenkins, *Asquith*, p. 132.

[28] Margot Asquith, *Autobiography*, vol. 2 (1922), p. 53.

[29] Haldane, *An Autobiography*, p. 157.

[30] F.W. Hirst, *In the Golden Days* (1947), p. 264, in John Wilson, *CB, A Life of Sir Henry Campbell-Bannerman* (1973), pp. 425–6.

[31] Beatrice Webb diary, 10 November 1902, *Diary of Beatrice Webb*, vol. 2, p. 260.

[32] Haldane to Asquith, 5 October 1903, Asquith Papers, MSS. 10/90-1, Bodleian Library, Oxford.

[33] Grey to Asquith, 7 October 1903, in Keith Robbins, *Sir Edward Grey* (1971), p. 109.

[34] Herbert Gladstone to Asquith, 29 October 1903, Asquith Papers, MSS. 10/98.

[35] Gosse diary, in Wilson, p. 425.

[36] Haldane, *An Autobiography*, p. 157.

[37] Ibid., p. 159.

[38] Haldane to Lord Knollys, 15 September 1905, in Sir Frederick Maurice, *Haldane 1856–1915*, vol. 1 (1937), p. 149; Haldane sent a draft of 12 September 1905 to Asquith: Asquith Papers, MSS. 10/138-140.

[39] Lord Knollys to Haldane, 16 September 1905, in Maurice, vol. 1, pp. 151–3.

[40] Haldane to Asquith, 6 October 1905, Asquith Papers, MSS. 10/151–3.

[41] Margot Asquith, *Autobiography*, vol. 2, pp. 66–8.

[42] Morley to Campbell-Bannerman, 28 November 1905, in Wilson, p. 436.

[43] Asquith to Campbell-Bannerman, 25 November 1905, in Jenkins, p. 149n.

[44] In Wilson, p. 435.

[45] Margot Asquith, *Autobiography*, vol. 2, p. 74.

[46] Sir Edward Grey to Asquith, 4 December 1905, Asquith Papers, MSS. 10/180–1.

[47] Trevelyan, p. 101.

[48] In Wilson, pp. 450–1.

[49] Asquith to Haldane, 7 December 1905, in Spender and Asquith, vol. 1, pp. 174–5.

[50] Haldane, *An Autobiography*, p. 170.

[51] Ibid., p. 180.

[52] Asquith to Haldane, 8 December 1905, in Spender and Asquith, vol. 1, p. 175.

[53] Margot Asquith, *Autobiography*, vol. 2, p. 76.

Chapter 10: Liberal England

1 Haldane, *An Autobiography*, pp. 182–3.
2 Ibid., p. 182.
3 Ibid., p. 185.
4 32.9 per cent were rejected in 1899, 28 per cent in 1900 and 29.04 per cent in 1901. G.R. Searle, *A New England: Peace and War 1886–1918* (Oxford, 2004), p. 305.
5 Violet Bonham Carter, *The Times*, 30 July 1956.
6 In Koss, *Asquith*, p. 74.
7 Dudley W.R. Bahlman, *The Diary of Sir Edward Hamilton, 1885–1906* (Hull, 1939), pp. 482–3.
8 Jenkins, p. 166.
9 Spender and Asquith, vol. 1, p. 196.
10 Margot Asquith, in Koss, *Asquith*, p. 92.
11 Harcourt's pederastic pastimes eventually caught up with him. He died in 1922 after an excess of sleeping pills nipped in the bud a pending scandal with an Eton schoolboy.
12 Asquith to the Commons, 2 December 1909 *(Hansard) 13 HC Deb. 5s.,* col. 556.
13 Asquith to Bryce, 17 January 1911, in Koss, *Asquith*, p. 126.
14 Haldane, *An Autobiography*, p. 224.
15 Ibid., p. 244.
16 Verity, p. 452.

Chapter 11: Cutting the Rope

1 Winston S. Churchill, *Great Contemporaries* (1938 edn), p. 137.
2 In Koss, *Asquith*, p. 141.
3 Violet Asquith diary, 21 and 23 January 1912, in Mark Bonham Carter and Mark Pottle (eds), *Lantern Slides, The Diaries and Letters of Violet Bonham Carter 1904–1914* (1996), pp. 297–8.
4 Asquith to Venetia Stanley, 4/5 April 1915, Michael and Eleanor Brock, *H.H. Asquith, Letters to Venetia Stanley* (Oxford, 1982), p. 532.
5 Lawrence Jones, *An Edwardian Youth*, Brock, p. 5.
6 Asquith to Venetia Stanley, 22 March 1914, Brock, p. 59.
7 Adelaide Lubbock, *People in Glass Houses*, in Clifford, p. 265.
8 Artemis Cooper (ed.), *A Durable Fire, The Letters of Duff and Diana Cooper* (1983); Naomi B. Levine, *Politics, Religion and Love* (New York, 1991), p. 233; Alistair Forbes, letter in *The Times*, 14 December 1982; Clifford, p. 207.
9 Margot Asquith to Edwin Montagu, 21 March 1914, Brock, p. 13.

[10] Asquith to Venetia Stanley, 27 January 1913, Brock, p. 27.

[11] Jenkins, p. 305.

[12] Lloyd George coyly referred to 'a neighbour of ours', although there was no doubt, in the context, that he was speaking of Germany. Lloyd George to the Commons, *65 HC Deb 5s.*, cols 727–8.

[13] Asquith to Venetia Stanley, 24 July 1914, Brock, p. 123.

[14] Haldane to his mother, 28 July 1914, Haldane Papers MS. 5991/277.

[15] Asquith to Venetia Stanley, 29 July 1914, Brock, p. 133.

[16] Arthur Ponsonby to Grey, 29 July 1914 and to Asquith, 30 July 1914, in Cameron Hazlehurst, *Politicians at War* (1971), pp. 35–8.

[17] Asquith to Venetia Stanley, 2 August 1914, Brock, p. 146.

[18] Asquith to Venetia Stanley, 1 August 1914, Brock, p. 140.

[19] J.A. Pease diary, 3 August 1914, in Hazlehurst, p. 32.

[20] David Lloyd George, *War Memoirs*, vol. 1 (1933), p. 77.

[21] Haldane, *An Autobiography*, p. 269.

[22] B.H. Liddell Hart, *History of the First World War* (1970), p. 63.

[23] J.E. Edmonds, *Military Operations, France and Belgium/British Official History*, in Liddell Hart, p. 130.

[24] Lady Cynthia Asquith, diary entry for 16 April 1915, Lady Cynthia Asquith, *Diaries 1915–1918* (1968), p. 6.

[25] Margot Asquith to Lord Rosebery, 1 September 1914, in Koss, *Asquith*, p. 165.

[26] Sommer, pp. 318–19.

[27] Haldane to his mother, 31 May 1912, Haldane Papers MS. 5987/216.

[28] Koss, *Haldane*, citing Reginald Pound and Geoffrey Harmsworth, *Northcliffe* (1959), p. 434.

[29] In Koss, *Haldane*, p. 168.

[30] Niall Ferguson, *The Pity of War* (1998), pp. 217–18.

[31] In Koss, *Haldane*, p. 69.

[32] In Koss, *Haldane*, p. 75.

[33] Winston Churchill to Haldane, 18 January 1915, Haldane Papers MS. 5911/1.

[34] Margot Asquith to Leo Maxse, 1 February 1915, in Koss, *Haldane*, p. 174.

[35] F.D. Acland to Austen Chamberlain, 1 December 1914 and 20 January 1915, in Koss, *Haldane*, p.90.

[36] Haldane, *An Autobiography*, p. 285.

[37] Arnold White to Leo Maxse, 4 February 1915, in Koss, *Haldane*, p. 136.

[38] Asquith to Venetia Stanley, 23 April 1915, Brock, p. 569.

[39] Asquith to Venetia Stanley, 21 August 1914, Brock, p. 185.

40 Asquith to Venetia Stanley, 12, 14 and 18 February 1915, Brock, pp. 428, 431 and 437.
41 Asquith to Venetia Stanley, 19 March 1915, Brock, pp. 490–2.
42 Asquith to Margot Asquith, 13 April 1915 and Margot Asquith to Edwin Montagu, 16 April 1915, Brock, pp. 547–8.
43 Asquith to Venetia Stanley, 22 April, 26 April, 2 May 1915, Brock, pp. 564, 571, 580.
44 Asquith to Venetia Stanley, 12 May 1915, Brock, p. 593.
45 Asquith to Sylvia Henley, 12 May 1915, Brock, p. 596.
46 Asquith to Venetia Montagu, 17 May, 14 May, 11 June 1915, Brock, pp. 596, 601–2.
47 Venetia Stanley to Edwin Montagu, 14 June 1915, Brock, p. 602.
48 Venetia Stanley to Edwin Montagu, 6 June 1915, Brock, p. 604.
49 Stamfordham memorandum, 19 May 1915, in Hazlehurst, p. 237.
50 Austen Chamberlain memorandum, 17 May 1915, in Hazlehurst, p. 233.
51 Bonar Law to Asquith, 17 May 1915, Sir Charles Petrie, *The Life and Letters of the Right Hon. Sir Austen Chamberlain*, vol 2 (1940), p. 22; Hazlehurst, p. 233.
52 See Hazlehurst, pp. 227–60.
53 R.J.Q. Adams, *Bonar Law* (1999), p. 186.
54 Austen Chamberlain to Bonar Law, 17 May 1915, in Sir Charles Petrie, vol. 2, pp.23–4.
55 Austen Chamberlain memorandum, 15 May 1915; Sir George Riddell's diary, 23 May 1915; Frances Stevenson's diary, 18 May 1915, in A.J.P. Taylor (ed.), *Lloyd George, A Diary by Frances Stevenson* (1971), p. 51.
56 Charles Hobhouse to Sydney Buxton, 10 June 1915, in Hazlehurst, p. 241.
57 Asquith to Churchill, 20 May 1915, in Jenkins, p. 361.
58 *Westminster Gazette*, 8 January 1915, in Hazlehurst, p. 272.
59 Sir Edward Grey to Asquith, 21 May 1915, in Oxford and Asquith, vol. 2 (1928), p. 102.
60 Asquith to Haldane, 17 May 1915, Haldane Papers MS. 5911/37.
61 Koss, *Asquith*, p. 196.
62 Asquith to Sylvia Henley, 17 May 1915, in Clifford, p. 276.
63 Jenkins, p. 362.
64 Koss, *Haldane*, pp. 182–3.
65 Churchill, *Great Contemporaries*, p. 148.
66 Haldane, *An Autobiography*, p. 286.

Chapter 12: The Last Romans
1 Koss, *Haldane*, p. 91.

[2] Asquith to Haldane, 8 August 1916, Haldane Papers MS. 5913/50.

[3] Haldane, *An Autobiography*, p. 283.

[4] *Hansard*, 12 July 1916, 22 H.L. Deb. 5s., col. 655.

[5] Haldane to Asquith, 6 July 1915, in Maurice, *Haldane* (1939), vol. 2, p. 6.

[6] Haldane to his mother, 30 November 1915, Haldane Papers MS. 5994/185.

[7] Bernard Shaw to Haldane, 3 August 1915, Haldane Papers MS. 5912/85.

[8] Beatrice Webb diary, 22 July 1915, *Diary of Beatrice Webb*, vol. 3, 1905–1924 (1984), p. 236.

[9] 5 October 1915, Frances Stevenson diary, p. 63.

[10] A.J.P. Taylor, *English History, 1914–1945* (Oxford, 1975 edn), p. 17.

[11] Koss, *Asquith*, p. 202.

[12] Margot Asquith to Reginald McKenna, in Koss, *Asquith*, p. 202.

[13] Margot Asquith diary, 17 September 1916, in Margot Asquith, *Autobiography*, vol. 2, pp. 242–4.

[14] Asquith to Lady Scott, 20 September 1916, in Oxford and Asquith, vol. 2, p. 158.

[15] John Jollife (ed.), *Raymond Asquith: Life and Letters* (1980), p. 296–7.

[16] In Hazlehurst, p. 21.

[17] 16 November 1915, Frances Stevenson diary, p. 75.

[18] David Gilmour, *Curzon* (1994), p. 454.

[19] In John Grigg, *Lloyd George, from Peace to War 1912–1916* (1997), p. 449.

[20] Bonar Law papers, in R.J.Q. Adams, *Bonar Law* (1999), p. 231.

[21] Note by Bonar Law, in Adams, p. 234.

[22] Lloyd George to Asquith, 5 December 1916, in Grigg, pp. 462–3.

[23] Sir Austen Chamberlain, *Down the Years* (1935), p. 124.

[24] Lord Stamfordham to Haldane, 5 December 1916 and Haldane's Memorandum, Haldane Papers MSS. 5913/87 and 89.

[25] Churchill, *Great Contemporaries*, p. 249.

[26] This point is well made by Grigg, p. 472.

[27] *Oxford Dictionary of National Biography*, vol. 2 (2004), p. 751.

[28] See Graham Stewart, *Burying Caesar: Churchill, Chamberlain and the Battle for the Tory Party* (1999), pp. 418–88.

[29] Haldane to his mother, 27 April 1917, Haldane Papers MS. 5997/150.

[30] Lloyd George to Haldane, 26 March 1917, Haldane Papers MS. 5913/118.

[31] In Daphne Bennett, *Margot, A Life of the Countess of Oxford and Asquith* (1985), p. 283.

[32] Haldane to Elizabeth Haldane, 9 May 1918, Maurice, vol. 2, p. 53.

[33] Asquith's memorandum of discussion with Lord Reading, 28 May 1917, Asquith Papers, MSS. 46/137–9.

[34] There remains confusion concerning the attribution accorded successful

candidates who stood without the coupon but subsequently adopted a pro-coalition attitude. Consequently, different authorities give slightly varying party totals for the results of the 1918 general election. The figures given here are those in Martin Pugh, *The Making of Modern British Politics 1867–1939* (Oxford, 1982), p. 194.

[35] Reginald McKenna to Walter Runciman, 4 January 1919, in Koss, *Asquith*, p. 241.

[36] Margot Asquith to Haldane's mother, 7 February 1920, Haldane Papers, MS. 6082/116–17.

[37] Haldane to his mother, 12 February 1920, Haldane Papers, MS. 6003/45.

[38] Haldane to his mother, 25 February 1920, Haldane Papers, MS. 6003/59.

[39] Haldane, *An Autobiography*, p. 309.

[40] Haldane to Asquith, 16 January 1922, Asquith Papers, MSS. 18/69–71.

[41] Asquith to Hilda Harrisson, 17 November 1922, in *H.H.A.: Letters to a Friend*, vol. 2 (1934), p. 37.

[42] Haldane to Asquith, 22 January 1924, Asquith Papers, MSS. 18/88.

[43] Asquith to King George V, 20 January 1925, in Jenkins, p. 506.

[44] In Koss, *Asquith*, p. 271.

[45] The evidence points to Judith Montagu being Dudley's daughter. She told her own daughter, Anna, that this was so. Furthermore Judith was buried on the Dudley estate. Levine, p. 673.

[46] Asquith to Hilda Harrisson, 20 March 1922, in Brock, p. 607.

[47] In Levine, p. 713.

[48] Haldane to the House of Lords, 16 February 1928 *(Hansard) 70 HL Deb 5s.*, cols. 160–163.

[49] Webb diary, 21 August 1928, Norman and Jeanne Mackenzie (eds), *The Diaries of Beatrice Webb* (2000), pp. 469–70.

[50] In Levine, p. 529.

[51] Koss, *Asquith*, p. 91.

[52] Beatrice Webb diary, 30 October 1899, *Diary of Beatrice Webb*, vol. 2, 1892–1905 (1983), p. 166.

Epilogue

[1] Winston S. Churchill, *Great Contemporaries* (1938 edn), pp. 174, 183.

[2] See Giles Radice, *Friends and Rivals, Crosland, Jenkins and Healey* (2002); James Naughtie, *The Rivals, The Intimate Story of a Political Marriage* (2002 edn), p. 370.

[3] Aristotle, *The Nicomachean Ethics*, trans. by J.A.K. Thomson (1976 edn), p. 263; Cicero, *Two Essays on Old Age and Friendship*, trans. by E.S. Shuckburgh (1927 edn), pp. 188, 210.

INDEX